Will Blesch has done a deep dive into topics most Christians avoid altogether and others label as "fringe." Yet, Scripture plainly points out that at the time of Jesus' return, it will be like the days of Noah. In other words, the Nephilim will be walking amongst us! Will Blesch exposes the deception of the Prince of the Power of the Air. Buckle up, put on your armor, and get ready to dive into the "deep end of the pool"!

—Dr. L. A. Marzulli,
author and filmmaker

Will Blesch covers a wide spectrum of sources discussing giants, angels, and UFOs, and gives a scholarly, thoughtful, and well-balanced overview of these perplexing topics. Highly recommended for all who are ready for exposing decades of lies, distortions, and cover-ups and embracing the challenging truth that we are not alone.

—Michael Salla, PhD

I am pleased to recommend and support the forthcoming book *In the Shadow of Goliath* by Will Blesch. He presents a detailed and compelling story, for example, about the true nature and history of what we call the Nephilim, and how the ancient Neanderthal and Denisovan may fit into this story. A compelling read, a great work of scholarship, and a wonderful addition to explaining what many would regard as a mythical and fictitious past which clearly seems to be actual historical fact.

—Brien Foerster,
author of *Elongated Skulls of Peru and Bolivia:
The Path of Viracocha*

After more than seventy-five years since Roswell, it's nearly impossible to write about UFOs with a fresh perspective—and yet, that's just what Will Blesch has done. *In the Shadow of Goliath* is easy to read, yet very informative, regardless of how familiar readers are with UFO research. His analysis is solid, biblical, and pulls back the veil on the inhuman entities responsible for those mysterious lights in the sky.

—Derek Gilbert

"What was, and is, and is to come" been here since the beginning. William Blesch, a career-long researcher and media expert shares his remarkable biblical and historical insights into the long-debated question of alien life and UFOs. Upon examining countless biblical, historical, and theological sources, his insights take you on a journey behind enemy lines and restores the theological foundation of the mythical, mysterious, and supernatural world we live in. This is a handbook for understanding the perilous times we're in and a preparation guide for the next leg of this journey.

—Rabbi Dr. Eric E. Walker

Author Will Blesch and I diverge on many counts. On this we resoundingly agree: life is a search. Will embarks on that search through the lens of independent bible and archeological study, probing the heterodox question of primeval giants and other mysterious beings once (still?) roaming earth. Most academics will hate his book. That is because they believe that you, the reader, lack discernment. Will does not believe that. That is why you should read him—and because you will fall into his vivid, adventurous, and transparently sourced narrative.

—Mitch Horowitz,
PEN Award-winning historian and host
of Discovery / HBO Max's *Alien Encounters*

IN THE SHADOW OF
GOLIATH

DEFENDER

CRANE, MO

In the Shadow of Goliath:
Angels, Giants, UFOs, and the Hidden History of the Watchers, Nephilim, and Interdimensional War

By Will Blesch

Defender Publishing
Crane, MO 65633
©2025 Defender Publishing

All Rights Reserved. Published 2025

ISBN: 978-1-948014-96-0

Printed in the United States of America.

A CIP catalog record of this book is available from the Library of Congress.

Cover designer: Brittney Jackson / SimplyBrittneyDesigns.com
Interior designer: Katherine Lloyd
Editor: Angie Peters

To YHVH, the God of Israel, and His Messiah, Yeshua of Nazareth—my God and King.

All glory belongs to Him, the giver of every good gift, who has blessed me with my three daughters—Addy, Nina, and Chloe—and who has never left me alone.

To my mother, whose steadfast encouragement pressed me to write; to my aunt Leslie, the first to read these pages; to Nina, who believed in me when no one else did; to Derek Gilbert, whose gracious correspondence helped open the door to my journey with Defender Publishing; and to my editor, Angie Peters, whose sharp eye and kind words strengthened this book—

I owe you all a debt of gratitude.

CONTENTS

Author's Note		xi
Introduction		1
Chapter One	AN INTRODUCTION	5
Chapter Two	OUR TOOLS OF INQUIRY	37
Chapter Three	ANGELS: *SHALOM ALEICHEM*	65
Chapter Four	ANGELS: PART DEUX	109
Chapter Five	ANGELS AND EXTRATERRESTRIALS	129
Chapter Six	EXTRATERRESTRIALS AND DEMONS	165
Chapter Seven	SERAPHIM AS EXTRATERRESTRIALS?	189
Chapter Eight	ISHIM AS EXTRATERRESTRIALS	229
Chapter Nine	THE HYBRID ENIGMA	267
Chapter Ten	UFOS AND THE GREYS	291
Endnotes		333

AUTHOR'S NOTE

1. All scriptural quotes, unless otherwise noted, are taken from the New American Standard Bible.
2. For the sake of clarity, I use the academic term "Hebrew Scriptures" when referencing the Tanakh or Old Testament.
3. I want to emphasize something crucial: Throughout this book, I quote many authors—scholars, theologians, researchers, and more. I respect each of them immensely.

    Some of their ideas I fully agree with; others I do not. But when I dispute a point, I never intend it as an attack on the author. Rather, it is meant to sharpen understanding, as iron sharpens iron.

    My sole intention is to add value, clarify, or gently correct where I see something incorrect. My purpose is always constructive. Respect, after all, doesn't demand agreement. It demands the courage to challenge and be challenged, all for the sake of pursuing the truth.

INTRODUCTION

Some people go looking for the unknown. Others have it forced upon them. For as long as I can remember, the unexplained has had a grip on me.

It wasn't just the vastness of the Rocky Mountains or the thrill of imagining creatures lurking in the forests of my childhood. It wasn't even the alien worlds I encountered in books, though they certainly fueled something inside me.

No, this was different. This was something that had been with me from the beginning—a gnawing certainty, a deep, unspoken knowing the world we accept as reality is a mask stretched thin over something much older, much stranger, and far more dangerous.

I was eleven years old the first time I saw it crack.

The sun was going down, and my cousins and I were playing in a field near our home in Virginia, chasing one another through the tall grass, the humid air thick with the scent of dirt and honeysuckle. Then something appeared above the trees.

A perfect black triangle glided just beneath the clouds, its three crimson lights glowing like embers in the dark. It didn't roar like a jet. It didn't hum like a drone. It moved with silence, as though the sky itself had bent to make room for it.

We stood frozen, staring as it passed overhead. Then, without warning, it shot off—vanishing with a speed that should not have been possible.

We ran to tell the adults, but they dismissed us. We were just kids letting our imaginations run wild. It must have been a plane, of course. Or a satellite. Or something explainable.

Was I sure I hadn't been watching too much *Star Trek*?

You see, the grown-ups needed it to be explainable.

But it wasn't.

That moment lodged deep inside me. It wasn't just an experience. It was a shift in my reality. A realization. The feeling I had always carried—that things were not as they seemed—had just been confirmed.

From that point on, I needed answers.

I devoured everything I could find: mythology, history, theology, archeology, philosophy. I studied ancient texts that had been passed down for millennia; I studied not just through the lens of modern academics but through the rigorous logic and tradition of the scholars who preserved them.

And the more I studied, the clearer it became.

A pattern runs through the most ancient records of human civilization: a pattern of encounters, warnings, and conflicts that have been dismissed as myth but were never intended to be. The biblical accounts, the apocryphal writings, the records of sages and scholars across generations—each one preserves traces of something far greater, something that once stood in the open but has since retreated into the shadows.

That's why I wrote *In the Shadow of Goliath*.

You see, the biblical giant wasn't just a Philistine warrior. He was a remnant—of something twisted. He was a visible pawn of a much greater, infinitely more powerful force. A symbol of something older than recorded history, something that had been struck down but not yet destroyed. A threat embodied for a single moment by a towering figure on a battlefield.

But the real danger was never Goliath.

It was what he represented.

While that ancient threat was defeated, it looms over humanity's future again.

Now, you won't find theories here about ancient astronauts handing

INTRODUCTION

fire to primitive humans. You won't hear me regurgitate the claims of Erich von Däniken or Zecharia Sitchin, twisting ancient texts to fit a pop-culture fantasy about misunderstood aliens.

That answer is too small, too comfortable.

The truth is something else entirely.

Ancient earthbound civilizations didn't misunderstand what they saw. The texts they left behind—whether biblical, apocryphal, or mythological—weren't crude attempts to explain natural phenomena with gods and monsters. They were preserving something real.

The evidence has been staring us in the face for centuries.

This book is here to take a sledgehammer to the brick walls in secular academia and religious dogma that have been hiding truth in plain sight.

A plethora of literature is available about the intersection of UFOs and religion, to be sure. Many times, these works fall into a distinct binary, often treading overly familiar paths and offering little more than full-throated speculation.

What's frequently lacking is a comprehensive exploration transcending ideological boundaries, one that invites readers to explore these mysteries with open-minded scrutiny. Rarely have I encountered a work that dares to navigate the intricate corridors of these mysteries within a comparative framework or through the stark clarity of strict, critical inquiry and a "logic-only" analysis.

I've designed *In the Shadow of Goliath* to bravely step into this void.

But I'll warn you now: Once you see the truth, you can't go back. I don't believe you should want to, because the shadow of Goliath isn't just looming, it's growing.

As you read through these pages, remember: Truth, like the colossal figures that inhabit our religious literature and myths worldwide, may dwell in the recesses of our shared past—and beyond humanity's collective amnesia.

Here's to the iron grip of obsession in the pursuit of knowledge, even amidst deliberate obfuscation and obstinate denial.

—Will Blesch

CHAPTER ONE

AN INTRODUCTION

Five hundred years before the birth of Jesus of Nazareth, Heracleitus, an ancient Greek philosopher from Ephesus, is thought to have said, "Because it is sometimes so unbelievable, the truth escapes becoming known."

We've been lied to. About history. About faith. About science. Everything we thought was true—everything we were taught to believe without question—is a shadow of reality. A mirage.

And when we finally see the truth?

It won't just change what we *know*—it will change who we *are*.

Imagine discovering the so-called myths about giants, angels, and UFOs aren't just the fever dreams of ancient civilizations, but real events recorded in texts stretching back thousands of years. For centuries, many well-known religious leaders and scientists—paragons of authority in their respective fields—have dismissed stories of giants, angels, and encounters with the unknown as fantasy.

But history doesn't care what we believe. It simply *is*.

When we confront history with fresh eyes, we find that the past doesn't always fit into the tidy boxes modern institutions, secular and religious, have constructed.

This book doesn't waste time sugarcoating reality. And although I mentioned it in the introduction, it bears repeating: This isn't some *Ancient Aliens* fanfare. If you're expecting a rehash of von Däniken's or Sitchin's pet theories, let me stop you right now. You've been sold a watered-down half-truth at best and a bald-faced lie at the worst.

While it may appear, as you read through this book, that certain arguments or elements overlap with the ancient astronaut theory, rest assured these similarities are purely surface-level. Stick with me, and you'll see just how deep this rabbit hole goes.

The reality is far older, far more unsettling, and far more intertwined with the fabric of human history than any intergalactic, extraterrestrial visitation narrative could ever explain. What this book will show is something entirely different, something foundational, and it's deliberately been obfuscated for millennia.

As you continue reading, I'll be dismantling the comforting narratives that have kept us from asking dangerous questions. As we sift through ancient texts, archeological discoveries, and forgotten testimonies together, we'll discover that a different story emerges, one that modern institutions would rather we ignore.

Bridging the gap between what we think we know and what actually might be true demands a willingness to step outside the usual boundaries of tradition. Heraclitus' words set the tone: The deepest truths are often buried under layers of disbelief.

If you're somebody brought up with Sunday-school stories but little in-depth, biblical knowledge, what follows just may be a punch to the gut. Even if you think you're well-versed, you might be in for some surprises.

The Talmud, a multi-volume record of rabbinic conversation—legal, ethical, spiritual, and sometimes bewilderingly tangential—tells us that in every generation, all people must see themselves as if they personally left Egypt (Pesachim 116b). This is a demand to understand ancient records in the Torah (the first five books of the Bible) and to experience its events as if they are unfolding before you, right now, this very moment.

They are relevant to *you*, personally.

By extension, this logically follows to the whole of the Hebrew Scriptures—also called the Tanakh by Jews and the Old Testament by most Christians. They contain living, breathing truths that you cannot, must not, ignore.

AN INTRODUCTION

This book isn't just for Christians and Jews. If you're secular, a CE-5 (close encounters of the fifth kind) experiencer, a Hindu, a Buddhist, a New Ager—or maybe something else entirely—be prepared to have your mind blown.

This chapter kicks open the door to some of the most unsettling and controversial intersections of history, faith, and the unknown—giants, angels, and, yeah, UFOs. If that makes you uncomfortable, good.

Growth never happens in comfort.

WHAT'S COMING NEXT

Laying the Groundwork

We start by defining the battlefield. What are we dealing with here? What are the sources, both ancient and modern, that force us to take a second look? We'll examine the methods serious researchers—scholars, theologians, and scientists—use to separate fact from fiction.

Peeling Back the Curtain on Ancient Mysteries

Now the gloves come off. We dig into the raw accounts of Nephilim, angels, and extraterrestrial encounters. We dissect the stories of giants—not as folklore, but as historical anomalies that demand explanation.

We examine ancient structures—megaliths, monuments, and artifacts—that defy what mainstream archeology is willing to acknowledge. We will explore why civilizations supposedly lacking advanced tools were able to accomplish feats our best scientists still can't replicate.

The Modern Battlefield

It's not just ancient history. Today, these mysteries are buried under layers of deception. Governments classify information. Institutions suppress inconvenient discoveries. The scientific community ridicules those who ask the wrong questions. But why?

We'll explore cover-ups, conspiracy theories that hold more weight than we might think, and the cutting-edge fields of genetic engineering and hybridization, topics that may have far older roots than most realize.

What Comes Next?

Finally, we bring it all together. Where is this headed? What does it mean for prophecy, eschatology, and the future of civilization? What happens when suppressed knowledge finally comes to light?

Will it shake the foundations of our religious and scientific understanding? We'll explore the implications of these discoveries on the future and why ignoring them is no longer an option.

Each chapter is designed to challenge everything you thought you knew, to force you to rethink history, theology, and even the nature of reality itself. The world is not what you've been told.

It's time to start asking the right questions.

GIANTS: COLOSSAL BEINGS THROUGH THE AGES

Before we can ask the right questions, we need to define the core mysteries this book addresses. Let's begin with giants.

Every ancient civilization worth its salt has stories about colossal beings who towered over mere mortals—sometimes as rulers, sometimes as monsters, sometimes as gods. Their fingerprints are all over human history, etched into stone, embedded in legends, and buried—literally—beneath our feet.

The *Encyclopedia of Giants and Humanoids in Myth, Legend, and Folklore* describes these beings as "tall, powerfully built individuals with near divine strength, a booming voice, and a rather terrifying, if not horrific, visage to behold."[1]

These weren't just fairy tales meant to scare children into obedience. The world's most ancient cultures took these stories as fact. For example, try looking at the monolithic structures of Baalbek in Lebanon, where 1,200-ton stones were somehow lifted and set into place with a precision that even modern cranes can't match.

Or take Tiwanaku, on the entire opposite side of the planet in western Bolivia, where massive blocks of andesite, one of the hardest stones on Earth, were shaped with laser-like precision by an unknown hand.

The book of Genesis proclaims, "The Nephilim were on the earth monster of manipulated bones meant to push a preordained narrative. Scientists, scholars, and the entire academic world fell for it.

What happened when it was exposed? Did academia suddenly become more skeptical of grand claims? More cautious of how history is orchestrated? No. They just swept it under the rug and moved on.

This tactic has been used time and again to suppress inconvenient discoveries. And I'll just go ahead and be blunt: *This is precisely what's happening with every subject in this book.*

It's not about proving or disproving the existence of giants, angelic beings, or UFOs. It's about controlling the story. The real question is: Who's written the version of history you believe?

The Misinformation Labyrinth

I know I just gave the example of the Piltdown Man, but it's important to provide a more modern, glaring example of the type of "in-your-face" misinformation that fills this space.

George Washington and the Vanishing Seven-Foot Skeletons

Let's talk about one of the most intriguing—and frustrating—stories tied to America's founding father: George Washington. It's a story that, if true, raises more questions than it answers.

According to Access Genealogy, one of the largest genealogy directories online, Washington's men unearthed a shocking discovery while building Fort Loudoun in 1755. The site, located at the northern tip of Virginia's Shenandoah Valley near Winchester, was chosen by Washington himself. During excavation, workers stumbled upon what appeared to be an ancient Native American burial ground.

So far, that's nothing too unusual. Burial sites have been uncovered all over America. But here's where things get weird. Washington reportedly noted that the skeletons dug up were *massive*—far taller than Europeans or local Native tribespeople of the time.

Several were measured to be seven feet long, when a typical European male was 5'-6" at that time. There is no known record as to what became of the skeletons and artifacts in the cemetery. In the 2½ centuries since that discovery of the 7-foot skeletons, Virginia's historians have generally scoffed at the story. You will only hear it if you visit the Fort Loudoun Museum in downtown Winchester.[9]

Access Genealogy cites Richard L. Thornton, a researcher known for his work on Native American and Mesoamerican archeological sites. When I reached out to Thornton to ask for primary sources—Washington's letters, military reports, anything—he responded, "The primary source is me walking into the Fort Loudon Museum in Downtown Winchester, VA and buying a guidebook, during the era when I lived in the Shenandoah Valley."[10]

Competing Narratives

Another version of the story pops up on BookOfMormonEvidence.org, with a few more details:

> During excavation for the fort's foundation, Washington's men dug up skeletons—skeletons which measured seven feet in length.
>
> The first written report of such large Indians dates back to 1707, when Swiss explorer Louis Michelle visited the Shenandoah Valley. Local Indians who lived or hunted in the Winchester area showed Michelle huge stones, thought to be sacrificial altars.
>
> He was also shown burial mounds of ancient warriors known to have been over seven feet tall. Michelle's diaries and maps relating to his adventures in the Shenandoah Valley are currently stored in the Royal Archives in London.[11]

So, where's the evidence?
BookOfMormonEvidence.org cites "Giants on Record" by Jim Vieira and Hugh Newman, who in turn cite author Mac Rutherford. I reached out to all of them. No response.

AN INTRODUCTION

Hoping for more clarity, I contacted the French & Indian War Foundation and Loudounmuseum.org. Finally, the former responded with this definitive statement:

> To our knowledge there is no known primary source for the claim that a skeleton or skeletons of 7-foot Indians was/were discovered during the building of Fort Loudoun in Winchester, VA.
>
> Per our historian, the only reference to this rumor is the website you reference in your email. It is also notable that, again to our knowledge, Washington himself never wrote about such a finding which would have been noteworthy.
>
> The author of the book *Fort Loudoun: Washington's Fort in Virginia*, Norman Baker, who carried out an extensive search of Washington's writings in the Library of Congress never found any mention of the discovery of any skeletons, let alone that of 7-foot Indians, at the fort site and Washington had extensive interactions with Native Americans during his life on the Frontier and later as President.
>
> It should also be noted that there could only have been a remote possibility of finding any skeletons at the fort site since it was built on limestone bedrock with only a thin layer of soil on top.
>
> Further evidence that the discovery of any skeletons had not occurred is the fact that Washington's original plans for the fort included a moat around it which could not be dug because the limestone on which the fort was built made it impractical.
>
> Lastly, rather than carrying out any excavations for building the fort, large amounts of dirt actually had to be hauled to the site to build up the bases for 3 of the 4 bastions.
>
> Unfortunately for the legend, there is no credible evidence of which we are aware supporting the claim that skeletons of 7-foot tall Native Americans were discovered at the site of Fort Loudoun in Virginia.[12]

In other words, according to official history, this discovery never happened. No skeletons. No records. Just a local legend with a wink and a nod at a small museum in Winchester, Virginia.

What do we do with this?

This is where it gets interesting. There are only two possibilities:

1. The entire story is a fabrication, one that somehow found its way into multiple accounts, spanning different sources and locations.
2. The skeletons were real but were quietly removed from history, just like countless other controversial finds that don't fit the mainstream narrative.

Now, history is full of things that were dismissed as "myths" until someone dug up physical proof. The city of Troy was just a legend until Heinrich Schliemann found its ruins.[13]

Then there are the Hittites. For centuries, they were known primarily through brief mentions in the Bible, leading many scholars to question their historical existence or significance. Then concrete archeological evidence emerged from tablets found at the Karum of Kanesh (modern Kültepe), which referenced trade with a "land of Hatti."[14, 15]

But let's get real for a second.

Washington was a man of meticulous record-keeping. He documented everything—military reports, personal letters, farm yields, even weather patterns. Yet, when it comes to something as monumental as the discovery of seven-foot-tall skeletons at the very fort he oversaw, his writings fall dead silent.

Skeptics will say that proves the story is just another tall tale. It never happened. It's nothing more than a local myth. And, to be fair, the lack of a smoking gun in Washington's letters raises valid doubts.

Right now, it's a story that can be used as a cudgel to discredit genuine accounts: "If the Fort Loudoun saga can be debunked, what else is but a fabrication and fake news?"

Now, I don't blame the websites I mentioned above, nor do I blame

AN INTRODUCTION

the sources they cite. Who can ascertain whether these narratives were deliberately seeded with falsehoods or innocently misconstrued?

But without the intent to insult anyone, I must admit that a more meticulous approach to fact-checking wouldn't go amiss. It would go a long way toward preventing hits to the overall credibility of those researching and exploring these kinds of topics.

Thank goodness, then, while the seemingly false tale of Washington and the giants is a cautionary one, verifiable stories do exist.

Abraham Lincoln Knew Something

Take, for example, President Abraham Lincoln. In an 1858 speech detailed in *The Collected Works of Abraham Lincoln, Volume 2*, he didn't just mention giants, he spoke of them as if their existence was common knowledge:

> When Columbus first sought this continent—when Christ suffered on the cross—when Moses led Israel through the Red Sea—nay, even, when Adam first came from the hand of his Maker—then as now, Niagara was roaring here. The eyes of that species of extinct giants, whose bones fill the mounds of America, have gazed on Niagara.[16]

Think about that. Lincoln wasn't a man prone to wild speculation. He was careful with his words, deliberate in his rhetoric. He tied the existence of ancient giants directly into the historical and biblical timeline.

Of course, mainstream historians argue that he was speaking figuratively about the ancient Mound Builders of North America when he talked about "extinct giants." According to them, he was speaking in metaphors.

Was he? Or was he simply mistaken? Parroting a myth?

Or could it be that he was referencing something that was widely accepted knowledge at the time, knowledge that's since been erased from mainstream discussion?

IN THE SHADOW OF GOLIATH

The idea that ancient giants once roamed the Earth isn't confined to old political speeches. It has popped up repeatedly in mainstream newspapers, including the *New York Journal,* the *New York Times,* the *Los Angeles Times,* and most recently, in a 2024 piece from the *New York Post.*

Some headlines over the years have included:

- "Is This the Ancestor of the American Race? Discovery of an Ancient Giant's Footprint in British Columbia Raises an Interesting Question"[17]
- "Giants' Skeletons Found; Cave in Mexico Gives up the Bones of an Ancient Race"[18]
- "Scientists Still Baffled from Giant Human Skeletons up to 10 Feet Tall Decades After Initial Discovery"[19]

These aren't fringe conspiracy sites, they're major, respected publications. So, why did these reports vanish from mainstream discussion? Why is it that every time discoveries like these surface, they are quickly dismissed, debunked—or worse, ignored entirely?

The Bigger Question: What Else Has Been Buried?

This pattern—discoveries made, reports written, then everything going dark—isn't unique to giants. It's happened before, and likely will again. The truth doesn't just disappear, it gets buried—sometimes literally. Sometimes through bureaucratic suppression. Sometimes through outright academic fraud.

The real question is this: If giants were a genuine part of history, if their remains *were* found in burial mounds, caves, and dig sites across the world, who benefits from keeping that knowledge hidden? And if this is just *one* suppressed truth, what else don't we know?

Unanswered Questions

The deeper we dig into this mystery, the more uncomfortable the questions become, chipping away at the comfortable, neatly packaged version of history we've been spoon-fed since childhood. Questions like:

- Were these giants a distinct species, something beyond the known branches of human evolution?
- What about a genetically distinct subspecies?
- Were they an anomaly within our own lineage? Were they an offshoot of Homo sapiens or something entirely different?
- Did they possess abilities beyond our comprehension, skills that allowed them to construct megalithic structures modern engineers still struggle to explain?
- Were they the result of something *other*? Were they perhaps an extraterrestrial—engineered biological experiment?
- Or were they, as the Hebrew Bible describes, the offspring of fallen angels and human women—in other words, hybrids?

If that last idea sounds too far-fetched, consider this: Is a hybrid between humans and angels any more unbelievable than an intelligent being bioengineered by an advanced extraterrestrial species?

We don't have hard evidence for either, do we? (Well, we might. I'll get to that later.)

The Hunt for Truth

I've said it before; I'll say it again. History is a battlefield—not just of events, but of narratives. In the middle of this war, one thing remains clear: The enigma of giants has fascinated the human mind for millennia. Maybe that's because the truth, whatever it may be, is buried deeper than we think. Maybe that's because understanding their existence (or disproving it entirely) is at least one key to unlocking a greater mystery.

That quest isn't for the weak. It requires an open mind, the courage to challenge long-accepted "truths," and a relentless hunt for real answers, no matter how unsettling they might be.

Graham Hancock, a well-known British author and journalist known to challenge mainstream archeology, put it perfectly:

> I believe we are a species with amnesia. I think we have forgotten our roots and our origins. I think we are quite lost in many ways.

And we live in a society that invests huge amounts of money and vast quantities of energy in ensuring that we all stay lost.[20]

The question is, are we willing to wake up, shake ourselves, and reach for a compass?

The recovery of lost history is more than an academic exercise. It may just be one of the greatest adventures of our time. And, once committed to the journey, it must become a primary goal.

LOGIC, INQUIRY, AND ANCIENT MYSTERIES

When setting out on this grand adventure, one of the tools I believe will serve us well is logic. Too often, books on topics deemed "fringe" are treated with slack-jawed incredulity by some authors too willing to believe every wild tale they hear.

Meanwhile, others write with so much skepticism that real evidence is tossed into the garbage out of hand—and sounds of scoffing laughter can be heard when anyone outside their academic or doctrinal echo-chamber dares to suggest "evidence" of this or that has been discovered.

Precious few works straddle a happy middle ground, taking the sort of questions raised in this book with a serious but open mind.

For me, logic is the order of the day. With it, we can separate truth from nonsense. But logic also demands that we question the "official" stories we've been handed. It requires us to doubt narratives that survive more on the power of authority than of evidence.

David D. Gilmore, in his book *Monsters: Evil Beings, Mythical Beasts, and All Manner of Imaginary Terrors*, writes, "Since earliest times, people have invented fantasy creatures on which their fears could safely settle… giants like the Algonquian Windigo and the Athabaskan Wechuge."[21]

In other words, giants have long been dismissed as the primitive people's way of explaining the unknown. That's the standard take: If a civilization recorded an encounter with a giant, it was just a myth—no different from the BogeyMan (or Boogeyman, if you've got that hip American vibe).

AN INTRODUCTION

If ancient texts mentioned supernatural beings, it was poetic symbolism. If a megalithic structure is too advanced for its time, we're told it was built with "lost" techniques that nobody today can explain.

But then comes the problem: The bones. The artifacts. The elongated skulls that show up in places where they shouldn't exist. That's when the establishment kicks into high gear.

Speaking of Elongated Skulls

Giants aren't the only anomalous beings talked about in mainstream media these days. Take, for example, a report from New Delhi Television Limited (NDTV), India's first independent, privately owned television news network, about a Peruvian discovery. This wasn't some internet hoax. It was a modern, mainstream news outlet reporting the following:

> A 16th-century Spanish conquistador documented an ancient Peruvian tale about giants who crossed the ocean on large reed rafts. He described them as being so tall that their legs from the knee down were as long as an average man's entire body.
>
> Elongated skulls, possibly 3,000 years old and much larger than normal human skulls, have also been found high in the Andes mountains. Some of these skulls are reported to have had red hair.[22]

Now, what do skeptics say?

Academic researchers are generally dismissive of elongated skulls. They see them as nothing but artificially deformed human skulls—a result of deliberate head-binding to achieve a flattened shape.

In addition to this "artificial head-modification" thesis, they sometimes also cite a medical problem called Hydrocephaly.[23]

Just like with giants, the story goes: "Nothing to see here, folks." It's either tribal head-binding or a genetic defect. Case closed.

Except it's not.

As independent researcher Mark Laplume discovered, these skulls aren't just a handful of anomalies. There are *thousands* of them.

> When I began this study in 2011, the count of skulls was known by very few people. They estimated that there were a few hundred skulls. But through web searches, I've found literally thousands of skulls!
>
> There are also about one thousand skulls in Romania, Bulgaria, Ukraine and Chile which are not yet accessible to the public.
>
> Even more skulls remain unknown, as they have not been photographed (or at least are not publicly accessible) and therefore, not available for public viewing in Chile and Peru.[24]

Thousands of skulls. Across multiple continents. With no public access.

When the Narrative Is More Important Than the Truth

Laplume cuts to the heart of the issue:

> Elongated skulls are never spoken about without terms of head-binding. It's the hole-in-the-bucket refrain from which there is no escape.
>
> But now there are also those, and I mean not only researchers but obviously people, who've woken up to the layers of lies we've been fed since the get-go.
>
> Many who look at the evidence of anomalies in the skulls are not satisfied with believing in the cranial modification dogma.
>
> People like Brien Foerster, Lloyd Pye, Graham Hancock, not to forget Michael Cremo, examine and record evidence, rather than the stories made by earlier researchers, textbooks, and other gate-keepers of conventional perspectives. The point is to keep asking questions.
>
> The verbal portrayal of "binding" is a collective projection. The reality is that 99% of those who speak about it have never examined an elongated skull first-hand.

AN INTRODUCTION

I don't know how it's so prevalent except that it's repeated all the time.[25]

Translation: People are trusting the narrative, not the evidence.

And the people who examine the skulls, those who aren't bound by institutional pressure, start seeing things they were never meant to find. Take, for example, early explorers and archeologists who encountered the Paracas mummies of Peru and who noted the presence of red hair (an important trait we'll circle back to in pages to come).

These were explorers like Peruvian archeologist Julio Tello, who first excavated the Paracas necropolis in the 1920s, and who described some of the mummies as having reddish or auburn hair in his book, *Paracas: Primera Parte*.

Another example comes from the research of Brien Foerster, as mentioned by Laplume. Foerster is a well-known figure in alternative archeology who has been involved in the study of the elongated skulls of Paracas, Peru. In his book, *The Enigma of Cranial Deformation: Elongated Skulls of the Ancients* (2013), he details how some Paracas skulls exhibit features inconsistent with normal human anatomy, such as increased cranial volume, unusual suture patterns, and single parietal plates—oh, and red hair.[26]

Importantly, like Mark Laplume, he argues that these features cannot be explained solely by intentional cranial deformation and may indicate a different species or genetic lineage. Indeed, in 2014, he collaborated with geneticists to analyze mitochondrial DNA from samples taken from the skulls. According to Foerster, the results showed genetic markers that were inconsistent with known Native American populations, suggesting an unknown origin.

For now, when it comes to red hair in Latin America, we should simply understand that the available scientific evidence consistently supports the conclusion that red hair is not a defining genetic trait of Mesoamerican peoples. In fact, scientific research indicates that red hair is present in only 2–6 percent of individuals with European ancestry.[27]

Pretty interesting, eh?

Yet, despite these remarkable findings, mainstream academia has largely dismissed or ignored them. Just the tiny bit of information above begs all kinds of questions:

- If there are indeed thousands of elongated skulls across multiple continents, why hasn't there been a large-scale, peer-reviewed study of their genetic and anatomical properties?
- Why hasn't mainstream academia actively attempted to either confirm or thoroughly debunk Brien Foerster's claims with rigorous, transparent genetic testing?
- Given that anthropology is a field designed to study human variation and migration, why is there a lack of sustained institutional interest in these skulls, despite their potential historical significance?
- Shouldn't the principle of scientific curiosity encourage research into claims that challenge mainstream paradigms rather than simply dismiss them outright?

And shouldn't we be asking:

- Why is the assumption that all elongated skulls are the result of artificial head-binding so widely accepted, even in cases where skeletal anomalies suggest otherwise?
- Have there been cases wherein scientists have been discouraged from studying these skulls due to institutional bias, funding limitations, or professional risk?
- If some skulls exhibit nonhuman or anomalous features (e.g., increased cranial volume, unusual suture patterns, single parietal plates), why is head-binding still considered the default explanation?

And there are even *more* questions we could ask:

- If Foerster's genetic analysis of the Paracas skulls indicated markers inconsistent with known Native American populations,

why has no independent, high-profile geneticist attempted to verify or challenge these findings?
- If the presence of mitochondrial DNA with unknown markers suggests an isolated, possibly extinct, human lineage, why isn't that considered a subject of serious anthropological interest?
- What percentage of red-haired individuals in pre-Columbian South America would be required to justify a reevaluation of genetic assumptions about early populations?

What's with the lack of transparency?

- If thousands of these skulls exist, why aren't they more accessible to the public and researchers for independent verification?
- Who controls access to these artifacts, and why is access restricted in some locations?
- Have any institutions or museums actively prevented DNA testing on these skulls, and if so, why?

I could go on and on with questions. Each of them deserves serious answers.

Because, while history is supposed to be a pursuit of truth, it sure seems like discoveries that challenge established paradigms often face immediate resistance—from scholars as well as from the very institutions that claim to champion knowledge.

This opposition isn't incidental. It follows a familiar pattern, one we've seen repeated time and again when evidence emerges that doesn't fit the approved narrative.

That brings us to the bigger question: Why is it so important to keep the truth buried?

The answer is simple: power and control.

If history is rewritten, people stay in the dark. If people stay in the dark, they remain easy to manipulate. If the gatekeepers of knowledge determine what is and isn't "real," they maintain their authority.

L. A. Marzulli, an author, researcher, and award-winning documentary filmmaker, has written extensively about this in *On the Trail of the Nephilim* (volumes 1 and 2), and I highly recommend those books.[28, 29] Whether we're talking about giants, elongated skulls, or lost civilizations, the reality is clear: The world is far stranger than most believe.

Which brings us to...

...ANGELS, BABY.

Are angels more than we've been told?

Mention them in a church or synagogue, and most people picture winged, glowing beings draped in robes, singing praises in a celestial choir. A comforting thought, perhaps. But what if that image is more sentimental artwork than reality?

What if angels aren't just spiritual symbols or psychological archetypes, but are as real as the chair you're sitting in?

Conversely, what if they're nothing more than projections of your mind?

What do we *really* know about these enigmatic beings?

Carl Jung, one of the most influential psychologists of the modern era, explored the idea that encounters with angels might be nothing more than manifestations of the human unconscious. In *Aion: Researches into the Archetypes of the Collective Unconscious*, he wrote:

> At least sixteen hours out of twenty-four we live exclusively in this everyday world, and the remaining eight we spend preferably in an unconscious condition.
>
> Where and when does anything take place to remind us even remotely of phenomena like angels, miraculous feedings, beatitudes, the resurrection of the dead, etc.?
>
> It was therefore something of a discovery to find that during the unconscious state of sleep intervals occur, called "dreams," which occasionally contain scenes having a not inconsiderable resemblance to the motifs of mythology.[30]

AN INTRODUCTION

In other words, Jung suggests that angelic encounters may simply be our minds projecting mythical imagery onto our dreams and subconscious thoughts. To him, these visions are part of the *collective unconscious*—psychological patterns passed down through generations.

Here's the problem with that view: People don't just dream about angels, they *encounter* them. They see them when they're wide awake, in moments of terror, crisis, and divine intervention. The Bible is filled with stories of people who had encounters with beings that were *not* part of their imagination.

This is where the discussion takes a hard turn into territory most religious institutions don't want to touch.

Is "Angels" Just Another Word for "Aliens"?

Maybe. Maybe not.

Or maybe, from a particular point of view.

Timothy Alberino, in *Birthright: The Coming Posthuman Apocalypse and the Usurpation of Adam's Dominion on Planet Earth*, challenges the traditional view of angels and suggests something that will make both theologians and scientists uncomfortable:

> An extraterrestrial is a being whose provenance is not Planet Earth. Notice that I did not say residence. Provenance is where you come from. Residence is where you reside.
>
> It is entirely possible for beings of extraterrestrial provenance to be residing on Earth (as we shall see), a concept which necessitates the defining of another associated term—alien.[31]

Alberino makes a crucial distinction. "Extraterrestrial" doesn't just mean little green men in flying saucers. It means any being whose *origin* is not from Earth. Angels, according to the Bible, are not of this world. They are ancient, powerful, and distinctly *other*.

With our terms thus defined, we may venture the question: Do extraterrestrials and/or aliens exist within the biblical paradigm?

The answer is, unequivocally, yes.

This should come as no surprise to students of the scriptures. The biblical narrative unapologetically introduces us to a race of beings that are clearly alien (in every sense of the word), indisputably extraterrestrial, and incalculably ancient.[32]

If Angels Aren't Extraterrestrial, Then What Are They?

Alberino's conclusion is blunt:

> It is plainly evident that angels are not human and not terrestrial in origin. Ergo, they must be regarded as both alien and extraterrestrial. If not, then these words have no meaning.[33]

Think about that.

If "alien" means a nonhuman being of unknown origin, and "extraterrestrial" means a being that is not from Earth—then, by definition, angels fit both categories.

Does this mean angels are simply ancient aliens, as some modern theorists in the "Ancient Aliens" crowd suggest? Not necessarily, at least, not in the way they would propose.

UFOS: MODERN FACE OF AN ANCIENT MYSTERY

UFOs: unidentified flying objects.
UAPs: unidentified anomalous phenomena, the modern renaming of UFOs.

Everyone understands the connection UFOs have with extraterrestrial, intergalactic beings because that's the understanding that's been fed to us since private pilot Kenneth Arnold reported seeing nine crescent-shaped objects flying at incredible speed near Mount Rainier, Washington, in 1947.

His description led to the press coining the term "flying saucers."[34]

Of course, that same year, the famous incident in Roswell, New Mexico, occurred. Then, science-fiction films such as *The Day the Earth*

AN INTRODUCTION

Stood Still (1951) began popping up, reinforcing the image of intergalactic travelers visiting Earth.[35]

The truth is the connection between UFOs and entities not of this Earth goes back thousands of years. In all actuality, there is no evidence to definitively state whether these craft are native to our 3D space or some other dimensional plane.

They could be one or the other. Thus, they could be craft belonging to an intergalactic or interdimensional species. There could be both.

That may sound weird, when conventional understanding by many in UFO circles is that these craft are *only* from other star systems, but the interdimensional hypothesis represents a significant alternative to the extraterrestrial (intergalactic) origin theory.

Moreover, several respected researchers have advanced the interdimensional hypothesis, including Meade Layne, John Keel, J. Allen Hynek, and Jacques Vallée, in their books:

- Vallée, *Dimensions* (1988)
- Keel, *UFOs: Operation Trojan Horse* (1970)
- Hynek, *The Hynek UFO Report* (1977)
- Layne, *The Ether Ship Mystery* (1950)

In fact, Vallée—an astronomer and computer scientist who has studied UFOs since the 1960s—noticed parallels between modern UFO close encounters and folklore of fairies, angels, and demons.[36]

As support for his view, just some of the arguments Vallée gives were published in his paper, "Five Arguments Against the Extraterrestrial Origin of Unidentified Flying Objects," in the *Journal of Scientific Exploration*, 1990.[37] Three of these are:

- Unexplained close encounters are far more numerous than required for any physical survey of the Earth.
- The extension of the phenomenon throughout recorded human history demonstrates that UFOs are not a contemporary phenomenon.

- The apparent ability of UFOs to manipulate space and time suggests radically different and richer alternatives.

He further suggests that the entities involved and the narratives they employ might simply be adapting to human cultural and technological understandings and progression, masking a deeper reality.[38, 39]

Interestingly, with a view like that, one might peg Vallée as a Christian. However, none of the four researchers mentioned above are Christians—or adherents of any Abrahamic faith, for that matter. Vallée has explored esoteric mysticism (*Forbidden Science*, 1992), while Meade Layne was inclined toward New Age and occult traditions.[40]

The other two, Keel and Hynek, were agnostic at most (e.g., *Fortean Times* interviews, 2000s, and Mark O'Connell's *The Close Encounters Man*, 2017).[41]

Regardless, whether intergalactic or interdimensional, we all know that for decades the subject has been enough to get someone laughed out of the room. It's been a topic reserved for conspiracy theorists, *Star Trek* geeks, sci-fi junkies, and wild-eyed, crazy people who claim they were abducted in the middle of the night.

The official stance? Nothing to see here.

But that's changing—fast.

People have been seeing strange things in the sky for as long as we've been recording history. The Romans documented glowing shields moving through the heavens. The medieval world had countless accounts of "fiery wheels" appearing over battlefields.

Jewish texts reference Merkavah (chariot) visions that defy earthly explanation.[42, 43]

While not peer-reviewed, Keel cites classical Roman historians such as Pliny the Elder (*Naturalis Historia*) and Julius Obsequens (*Liber Prodigiorum*), who documented celestial anomalies like "glowing shields" (*clipei ardentes*) in the sky. These accounts are analyzed in scholarly contexts as early examples of UAPs.[44, 45, 46, 47]

In modern times, we've been told it's all misinterpretation: Weather balloons, swamp gas, the planet Venus. If that didn't work, skeptics would just roll their eyes and say, "Prove it."

AN INTRODUCTION

For years, the lack of publicly verifiable physical evidence made it easy to brush off these reports. The assumption? If something was *really* there, the government would have said so.

Heck, if something was *really* there, the Bible would have said so! Right? Then came the flood of *new* testimonies.

US Military Whistleblowers Saying the Quiet Part Out Loud

In July of 2023, Retired Major David Grusch, a former Air Force intelligence officer, sat before a House Oversight subcommittee and dropped a bombshell: "The U.S. government has operated a secret 'multi-decade' reverse engineering program of recovered vessels." He also said, "The U.S. has recovered non-human 'biologics' from alleged crash sites."[48]

Let that sink in.

This isn't some random guy posting on an internet forum. This is a military intelligence officer testifying under oath before the United States Congress that the US has recovered not only craft, but also non-human "biologics."

And he isn't alone.

Retired US Navy Rear Admiral Tim Gallaudet, who led NOAA (National Oceanic and Atmospheric Administration) under President Donald Trump, and Retired Army Colonel Karl Nell have both publicly confirmed that nonhuman intelligences are not only real, but they've interacted with humanity.[49, 50, 51]

This is coming from high-ranking military officials—people who spent their careers in national security. People with everything to lose.

If they're lying, they're putting their entire legacies on the line for nothing. If they're telling the truth, the world isn't just looking at a new scientific discovery, it's looking at a total rewrite of history.

READY OR NOT: A PARADIGM SHIFT IS COMING

Thomas Kuhn, in *The Structure of Scientific Revolutions*, argued that science doesn't progress in a straight line. It shatters and rebuilds itself when evidence becomes too overwhelming to ignore.[52]

- People once thought the Earth was the center of the universe, until Copernicus and Galileo forced them to accept heliocentrism.
- People once believed in spontaneous generation, until Pasteur proved that life doesn't just pop out of nowhere.
- Today, people still assume that humanity is alone in the cosmos, even as high-ranking officials testify that we are *not*.

Giants, angels, UFOs—all are anomalies that shake the foundations of our understanding. Ignoring them doesn't make them go away.

The question is no longer *if* our worldview will change, it's *when*. And when it does, will you be ready to rethink everything you thought you knew?

A FEW HYPOTHESES

What if everything we thought we understood—about angels, UFOs, ancient civilizations, and even reality itself—was just scratching the surface? The narratives we've briefly mentioned in this chapter, from biblical accounts to modern military disclosures, crack open a Pandora's box of possibilities.

The Psychological Theory: Jedi Mind Tricks?

Some argue that UFO encounters and other supernatural experiences are just tricks of the brain, products of sleep paralysis, hallucinations, or psychological projection.[53, 54]

They point out that people experiencing sleep paralysis often report:

- Intense fear.
- The sensation of being immobilized.
- The presence of strange entities watching or interacting with them.

AN INTRODUCTION

Sound familiar? It's eerily close to reports from UFO abductees, ancient angelic visitations, and demonic encounters. But here's the problem:

- Not all UFO sightings, angelic encounters, or meetings with otherworldly beings happen while people are asleep.
- These encounters often involve *multiple witnesses seeing the same thing at the same time.* That's hard to chalk up to a shared dream.
- Physical traces: Radiation, burns, and electromagnetic interference are sometimes left behind.

While psychology might explain *some* experiences, it falls apart as a universal answer.

The Extraterrestrial Hypothesis: Are We Just One of Many?

What if UFOs are just what they appear to be: evidence that we are not alone? Statistically, it's almost impossible that Earth is the only planet in the universe teeming with life.

Consider:

- Our Milky Way alone has an estimated *100 billion stars.*
- There are at least *10 trillion galaxies*, each with its own *100 billion stars.*

That's an unfathomable number of potential solar systems that could host intelligent life.

Yet the Fermi Paradox asks: In a universe this ancient, this vast—where stars outnumber grains of sand and habitable planets may number in the billions—why haven't we seen any sign of intelligent life? Why the silence? First asked aloud by physicist Enrico Fermi in 1950, it ultimately asks: If intelligent life is common, why haven't we seen undeniable proof?[55, 56]

Could it be that some of these UFO sightings (along with encounters with various entities) *are* real evidence, but governments, institutions, and certain religious groups refuse to acknowledge it?

Globalization and Cultural Influence: Why Is the "Alien" Idea Everywhere?

Sociologist John Boli of Emory University suggests that as human civilization becomes more interconnected, the concept of "the Outside" grows stronger. The more we share information across cultures, the more the idea of *something beyond Earth* becomes mainstream.[57]

Ancient cultures described strange encounters in religious and mythical terms. Today, those same encounters are described in technological, scientific language: UFOs, aliens, interdimensional beings.

But what if, in some or all cases, they were *always* the same thing? What if we're just now beginning to interpret them through a different lens?

The Interdimensional Hypothesis

A growing body of modern physics and speculative theology suggests angels may not be confined to the three dimensions we all know and love but may inhabit spaces and dimensions we're only beginning to suspect exist—spaces that sometimes intersect with ours—or spaces in which their inhabitants have the ability to cross over into ours.

In this view:

- The angels described in the Bible aren't just supernatural, glowing hippies spouting messages of love and light; they're beings that operate outside of our normal perception of reality.
- They could be mistaken for extraterrestrials because they don't originate from *here*. Additionally, what makes anyone think some might not lie about their place of origin? (The Pleiadians anyone? Just a thought.)
- Encounters with them might look different depending on the observer's cultural framework: one person sees an angel;

another sees a sci-fi-inspired alien; yet another sees a glowing, amorphous "light being"; a Nordic; a Tall White; a dead relative; or even (dare I say it?) an "ascended master."

Consider that the Bible and other religious texts talk about angels in terms of powerful entities with an otherworldly presence defying normal physics—some of whom are benevolent and act for humanity's benefit on orders from *HaShem* (Yahweh/*YHVH*/the Tetragrammaton)—the God of Israel. At the same time, others actively worked to corrupt and destroy the nascent human race. At no time do any of these accounts suggest we're dealing with spiritual metaphors. They describe real beings—highly advanced, nonhuman intelligences that today's world would almost certainly classify as "extraterrestrial" if met face-to-face.

The Ancient Advanced Civilization Hypothesis

Maybe the question isn't "Who's out there?" Maybe it's "Who was here before us?" And no, in this hypothesis, angels (interdimensional beings) don't figure in. This is the notion proponents of the ancient astronaut theory typically put forth.

This argument—championed by authors like Erich von Däniken, best known for his ancient astronaut theory and the book *Chariots of the Gods?*, and Zechariah Sitchin, author of the *Earth Chronicles* series—suggests ancient aliens from distant star systems played the role of Prometheus, gifting humanity with knowledge and technology.[58, 59] These extraterrestrials also played our gods—and, even cooler, they inspired the *Stargate* film franchise.

In this view, they're totally just beings from other star systems who are restricted to the same space-time continuum as we are.

Some researchers argue:

> ▶ Ancient structures, like Göbekli Tepe, Baalbek, and the Great Pyramid of Giza were built using technology that doesn't fit with the capabilities of their supposed creators.

- Legends of giants, angels, and gods ruling the Earth might not be myths, but distorted memories of past extraterrestrial civilizations that were wiped out.
- There may have been nonhuman intelligences (or even a prehuman civilization) that once lived here, leaving behind advanced knowledge and artifacts.

If true, then what we call "supernatural" might just be forgotten technology. (Never mind the logical question as to whether angelic, interdimensional beings might not have some type of technology of their own.)

All of this sounds intriguing.

I personally think there are elements of truth here. But the ancient aliens hypotheses described by von Däniken and Sitchin and popularized on the History Channel are missing some *huge* pieces of the overall puzzle—and the elements of truth I mentioned here can just as easily fit the interdimensional hypothesis.

More importantly, the preponderance of evidence weighs heavily on the interdimensional side of the scale—with some significant caveats. But we'll get to that.

Quantum Consciousness: Reality Is Stranger Than We Think

Recent discoveries in quantum physics suggest reality itself might be way more layered than we ever imagined. Some physicists and researchers propose that:

- Consciousness itself might not be generated by the brain; it might exist outside of the body, more like a field we "tap into."
- Nonlocality means information can travel faster than light, bypassing normal space-time limitations.
- What we call "supernatural" experiences—visions, UFO sightings, and angelic encounters—could be the result of brief interactions with this larger reality.

AN INTRODUCTION

What if angels, UFOs, and other spiritual encounters are glimpses into a deeper level of existence—one where time, space, and consciousness all merge?

These hypotheses don't give us neat, easy answers...but that's the point. They represent just a sampling of the many approaches emerging in recent decades as scholars, scientists, and theologians work to bridge the gap between ancient mysteries and contemporary scientific inquiry.

THE QUEST FOR TRUTH

As we sift through conflicting theories, legends that refuse to die, government disclosures that seem like controlled leaks, ancient texts that speak of things we barely understand—one thing becomes painfully clear: We are chasing a truth that has been buried, distorted, and ridiculed for generations. From the debunked Fort Loudoun tale to the undeniable testimonies of military officials, from ancient accounts of giants and angels to modern disclosures of nonhuman intelligences (and "biologics"), a single truth remains:

People have always known there is more.

The deeper we dig, the clearer it becomes: Our history isn't what we were taught in grade school. Heck, it's not what we've been taught in universities, either.

But, the fragments of forgotten knowledge, buried truths, and suppressed discoveries are waiting for those willing to seek them. That's vitally important because history leads to identity—yours and mine. This is a conflict about reality itself.

If we are to reclaim the true story of humanity's past and our future, we must be relentless. As George Orwell warned: "Who controls the past controls the future. Who controls the present controls the past."[60]

The ones pulling the strings today were never meant to have that power. Most will never recognize it. Most will never question it.

Indeed, speaking to the dark power behind the scenes, the Christian rock group Petra wrote an apt description of the situation:

IN THE SHADOW OF GOLIATH

> Pied Piper playing the tune they want to hear
> Putting a tickle in their ear
> Pied Piper wanting them all to follow you
> No knowing where you lead them to
> But all the time you're leading them astray.
> The sheep just sit there grinning as they listen to your lies
> Never knowing when you pull the wool over their eyes.[61]

Heraclitus was right: The truth is unbelievable. That's exactly why it's so easy to bury.

But you're still here because you want the truth.

What happens when we finally dig it up? What happens when we stop playing their game and by their rules?

Turn the page. Let's find out.

CHAPTER TWO

OUR TOOLS OF INQUIRY

History is a set of lies agreed upon.
                    NAPOLEON BONAPARTE (ATTRIBUTED)

In a world where tradition fights to preserve its version of history and skepticism demands cold, hard evidence, one question looms over everything: What if the real story—the one that explains giants, angels, and UFOs—has been deliberately buried?

What if, as Graham Hancock suggests, we're a *species with amnesia*, clinging to a *sanitized* version of our past because it's safer, because it keeps the institutions in power, because it prevents us from asking the "wrong" questions?

If we want answers, we need to rethink our tools of inquiry. We need a *multidisciplinary approach*, one that doesn't blindly accept the status quo but challenges it at every turn.

That starts with archeology.

THE SCIENCE OF DIGGING UP INCONVENIENT TRUTHS

Archeology is supposed to be about *uncovering the past, one layer at a time*. It's ideally about piecing together history from what's been left behind. In theory, it's an unbiased discipline, an unflinching look at who we were and where we came from.

But in practice? Not so much.

Every time a new discovery emerges, something that doesn't fit into the clean-cut timeline of human history, it gets ignored, reinterpreted to fit the mainstream narrative, or conveniently "disappears."

Take the Dead Sea Scrolls, for example.

Discovered in 1947 by a Bedouin shepherd, these scrolls rewrote everything we thought we knew about early Judaism and Christianity. They revealed alternative biblical texts, hidden prophecies, and a completely different understanding of the Essenes, an apocalyptic Jewish sect that may have influenced early Christianity.[62]

Yet, for decades, access to these scrolls was *controlled* by a small group of academic elite who dragged their feet on publication, keeping the public in the dark about what the texts contained.

Vermes, a leading Scrolls scholar, critiqued the "small, closed team" of editors who monopolized access for decades, delaying publication. He describes how the editorial committee, led by Roland de Vaux, excluded outsiders and failed to publish critical texts for more than forty years.[63]

Further, the *Los Angeles Times* quoted him saying, "Forty years since the beginning, and we still haven't gotten a list of the documents.... Nobody knows what's there. Such a scandal is difficult to quantify."[64]

If something as monumental as the Dead Sea Scrolls was kept under wraps for years, what else might be sitting in secret vaults?

The Giants No One Wants to Talk About

We've heard the stories about the Greek Titans, the Norse Jotuns, and the biblical Anakim. Cultures all over the world describe giant humanoid beings *towering over mankind*, ruling ancient civilizations, and waging wars against the gods.

Mainstream archeology dismisses this as mere mythology—because, of course, if *actual* giant skeletons were being dug up, that would be world-changing. But here's the problem: People *have* claimed to find giant skeletons. Every time they do, something strange happens:

- The bones "disappear."
- The discoverers are discredited.
- The findings get dismissed as hoaxes.

Reports of giant human remains being collected and never seen again have circulated for years, with some saying institutions like the Smithsonian may have dismissed or "lost" anomalous findings. But, while mainstream academia rejects these claims, the lack of transparency in certain cases raises valid questions about what has or has not been disclosed.

Why should we accept academia's rejection of these assertions anyway? Haven't there been some prominent examples of suppression by academia and those in positions of intellectual power?

Indeed, there have!

Consider what happens when "primitive" knowledge embarrasses modern science.

Gather round, sit right down, and lend me thine ears.

In the blistering heat of Mali, where the Sahara meets the Niger River, sits a problem science doesn't want to talk about. A problem that shouldn't exist. A problem that asks: How did an "isolated" African tribe know more about a distant star system than Western astronomers before telescopes could even confirm its existence?[65]

Way back in the 1930s, French ethnographer Marcel Griaule embedded himself within the Dogon, a tribe nestled in Mali's Bandiagara Escarpment. For over two decades, he and his colleague Germaine Dieterlen studied their culture, rituals, and mythology.

Then things got weird.

The Dogon described Sirius, the brightest star in the night sky, with eerie accuracy. They claimed it had a dense, invisible companion star—Sirius B—so tiny yet so heavy that it defied belief. They even detailed its fifty-year elliptical orbit around Sirius A, complete with hand-drawn trajectories in the sand.

Of course, the "experts" in the West began to squirm because Sirius B is a white dwarf star too faint to see with the naked eye. Western astronomers only confirmed its existence in 1862. And its orbital period? That wasn't precisely calculated until the 1920s.

Yet, somehow, the Dogon—who had no telescopes, no written records, and no "proper education"—knew all this centuries earlier.

The Nommo

Ask the Dogon how they got this knowledge, and they'll tell you they got it from the Nommo—amphibious, fishlike beings that allegedly descended from the Sirius system in a "spinning ark" that arrived amid fire and thunder. According to Dogon tradition, the Nommo taught them astronomy, agriculture, and the fundamentals of the cosmos. (Sounds a lot like the Sumerian Apkallu to me!)[66]

Science calls the Dogon legend "nonsense." Yet the Dogons' description of Sirius B being "heavier than all iron"? That's white dwarf physics, something science didn't figure out until much later.

Their mythology even references a third star in the Sirius system, one astronomers only began speculating about in 1995…which brings us to the cover-up.

"Experts" Scramble for Explanations

Academia hates unsolved mysteries. So, when Griaule and Dieterlen published their findings in 1950 (*Un Système Soudanais de Sirius*), the backlash was swift. Mainstream scholars threw out two knee-jerk explanations:

1. Cultural contamination: The idea that the Dogon heard about Sirius B from European missionaries or travelers. (Small problem: Those Westerners didn't even have the correct data at the time.)
2. Misinterpretation: That Griaule imposed astronomical meaning onto vague tribal stories. (Because, you know, African tribes can't possibly have advanced knowledge of space—right?)

There's one major flaw in these excuses: The Dogon had this knowledge embedded in their culture long before Europeans ever arrived.

Their rituals, calendars, and ancient artifacts—all tied to Sirius—existed long before Westerners could have "contaminated" them.

Some Serious Questions

If the Dogon simply regurgitated European astronomy, why did they also describe a third Sirius star, one that wasn't even proposed until the mid-nineties?

Why do their Nommo legends mirror the Sumerian Apkallu and the Babylonian Oannes, both cultures with eerily similar fishlike "gods" bringing civilization?

The Dogon case presents a problem no one wants to deal with because if their knowledge didn't come from contamination or guesswork, we're left with two possibilities:

1. An advanced, premodern civilization once had astronomical knowledge rivaling modern science.
2. Extraterrestrial contact of one type or another isn't just a sci-fi fantasy, it's been recorded for centuries in oral traditions.

Both scenarios make the gatekeepers of academia very uncomfortable, which is why they ignore it. Dismiss it. Pretend it's been "debunked."

But here's the reality: The Dogon mystery has never been solved. Nobody's even trying. Their ancient knowledge of Sirius B still defies explanation, and their artifacts, like four-hundred-year-old ceremonial masks based on Sirius, still sit in the Musée de l'Homme in Paris gathering dust.

So, yeah, *if giants were real*, if the Dogon people's Nommo were real, then history as we understand it would have to be rewritten.

Who Decides What's Allowed to Be Discovered?

If you think archeology is just about digging up pottery shards and translating ancient texts, you're missing the bigger picture.

History is power.

And if you control history, you control people.

IN THE SHADOW OF GOLIATH

There are plenty of cases in which archeological discoveries have been used for political and ideological purposes, sometimes justifiably so—and other times, well…

- Archeology can be used to justify territorial claims.
- Artifacts have been used to support nationalistic agendas, cultural pride, and maintain official historical narratives.
- In America, certain discoveries about pre-Columbian civilizations are downplayed to maintain existing narratives.

Imagine if a discovery threatened to rewrite human history itself.

- What if a buried civilization was found that predated the accepted timeline of human development?
- What if ancient technology was discovered that couldn't be explained by known historical advancements?
- What if artifacts pointed to direct contact between ancient humans and nonhuman intelligences?

As previously mentioned, there are more than enough stories (called "conspiracy theories" by some) wherein governments, religious organizations, even scientific institutions have conspired to hijack archeological digs and spirit away their findings. That's saying nothing of all the online tales regarding private collectors, cults, secret societies, "black-budget" special-access programs, and more that have been accused of doing the same thing.

Let's be clear: A conspiracy theory is only a theory until it's proven true. People used to mock the ideas that:

- The US government spied on its citizens (then Edward Snowden leaked the National Security Agency files).[67, 68]
- Elements of the Catholic Church covered up child-abuse scandals (until the evidence came out).[69, 70]
- The CIA secretly experimented on human beings with mind control (until MKUltra documents were declassified).[71, 72]

OUR TOOLS OF INQUIRY

So, when people call us crazy for questioning the *official history of humanity*, remember this: They said the same thing about whistleblowers *before* they were proven right.

After all, what might be the impact of substantial changes in the established historical narrative if hoaxes ended up being the real deal?

What if an alternative explanation suggests that a certain archeological find belongs to a different cultural group or civilization than previously thought? Couldn't it have significant implications for national or ethnic identities, and couldn't it lead to disputes over land rights, cultural heritage, or political legitimacy?

Of course it could.

What about cultural and nationalistic narratives?

We've already noted how archeology is frequently used to bolster both. But isn't it possible that some discoveries might contradict these narratives?

If they did, wouldn't it provoke controversy and debate, particularly if they question deeply held beliefs or myths about a nation's origins or historical achievements?

Of course they would.

And, needless to say, historical narratives often reflect and reinforce existing power structures. Might alternative findings challenge these narratives and therefore threaten the legitimacy of those in power? Wouldn't that lead to resistance or efforts to suppress the new interpretations?

For example, if an archeological find suggests a particular group did not conquer or dominate as previously believed, it could undermine claims to authority, superiority, victimhood, or oppression. Likewise, the finding of giant humanoid bones might legitimize biblical stories as well as the myths of countless indigenous cultures worldwide. At the same time, it could threaten perceptions of the theory of evolution—even though some scientists might readily rejoice at the discovery of one or more new hominin species and the thought of adding them to the theory's already growing mix.[73, 74]

There's a reason history is written by the winners. It's not just about controlling the past; it's about controlling the *present*. Nothing disrupts power more than the sudden realization that everything we've been taught is, at best, incomplete and, at worst, a fabricated lie.

So, let's be blunt: If a discovery validated aspects of biblical history, Jewish and Christian theology, or even ancient pagan myths, while at the same time forcing an overhaul of evolutionary theory, who do you think would fight it the hardest?

Both secular academia *and* religious institutions have spent centuries keeping their narratives separate. One side preaches atheistic materialism, the other clings to denominational dogma. Both fear a world where the two realities start to merge because if science and faith suddenly align in very particular ways, a *new reality* emerges—a reality neither group can control.

This is exactly why Graham Hancock's warning is more relevant than ever: "We live in a society that invests huge amounts of money and vast quantities of energy in ensuring that we all stay lost."[75]

When the *truth is dangerous*, history isn't just ignored, it's actively suppressed.

Most Powerful Barrier to Discovery

Hancock, along with others who challenge the establishment, has exposed how *academia, government,* and *elite institutions* work together to suppress inconvenient truths. If something contradicts their preapproved narrative, it is:

- Sealed away in museum basements.
- Misclassified and buried under bureaucratic nonsense.
- Debunked before the evidence is even examined.

Sometimes this isn't even something intentional or consciously carried out. Occasionally these institutions are just slow to accept radical discoveries—not always due to conspiracy, but because of deeply ingrained biases.

Regardless of the underlying reasons—to pierce the veil of obfuscation, archeologists (and really, scientists and researchers in all disciplines) must become torchbearers of truth, lighting the way through an encroaching fog of conformity.

They must also be tenacious, ready for attacks from peers and the media for those brave enough to step out of line. Careers are destroyed. Funding disappears. Tenure is revoked.

This isn't wild conspiracy. It's historical fact.

The only way truth prevails is through fearless, unrelenting transparency.

- Excavation sites must be free from government control.
- Independent minds, not institutional gatekeepers, must scrutinize findings.
- Raw data must be open-sourced and published without the censorship of biased peer-review systems.
- Artificial barriers to publishing groundbreaking discoveries must be obliterated.

Let the methodology be laid bare for all to see, the findings trumpeted from the rooftops, and the path to publication be freed of unnecessary obstacles (the overall corruption of the "gold standard" of the peer-review system itself comes to mind). We must bulldoze the walls that have been built around knowledge because it's not that the evidence doesn't exist, it's that we *refuse to acknowledge what's right in front of us.*

Take the Antikythera mechanism. It's a piece of precision clockwork pulled from a Greek shipwreck that shouldn't exist in the timeline of human technological development: a two-thousand-year-old computer that challenges everything we thought we knew about ancient engineering.[76, 77]

Or consider the Baghdad Battery, an artifact suggesting that ancient civilizations may have understood electricity long before Benjamin Franklin flew his kite.[78]

Honestly, while some might argue that these are just examples of isolated technological innovations that did not develop further, I've got to ask: Why haven't we found evidence of precursor devices? Technological progress doesn't happen in a vacuum. Complex machines don't just appear and disappear without a developmental lineage... do they?

These aren't fringe discoveries. They are *mainstream anomalies*—evidence that our ancestors knew more than we're comfortable admitting.

And these are just the cracks in the dam.

We must dig deeper because the time for timid inquiry is over.

Textual Analysis

Archeology is vital. Digging through the ruins of past civilizations, unearthing artifacts that don't fit the accepted narrative, and exposing truths that have been buried (sometimes quite literally) are essential to understanding who we are.

But now let's turn our gaze to the power of textual analysis.

The ancients weren't stupid. They left us records written in stone, carved into clay, and inked onto scrolls. These were the testimonies of civilizations, legends, and events that modern academia either refuses to acknowledge or lazily dismisses as "myth."

Yet when we *read* these texts with an open mind, the pattern is undeniable. The same themes appear again and again across cultures that, according to mainstream historians, *had no contact with each other:*

- Giant beings—sometimes divine, sometimes monstrous—ruling the Earth.
- Celestial visitors descending from the heavens, interacting with humanity.
- A war between godlike beings, resulting in the destruction of an ancient, advanced civilization.

These aren't random fairy tales. They are *historical fingerprints* scattered across time and geography. The deeper we dig into them, the clearer the picture becomes.

Textual analysis is a powerful tool for cracking the code of these ancient texts. Through this lens, we can set out on a thrilling voyage of rediscovery, unearthing truths that challenge the orthodox narrative.

OUR TOOLS OF INQUIRY

From the fearsome Nephilim of the Hebrew Bible to the Olympian Titans who warred with Zeus himself, these towering figures fill the pages of antiquity and have woven themselves into the fabric of our collective consciousness.

Textual analysis can allow us to weave seemingly disparate narratives into a more complete, interconnected whole. As Dr. Andrew Collins, a tireless iconoclast, wrote in his groundbreaking work, *From the Ashes of Angels*:

> Should we see accounts like Lamech's torment at the miraculous birth of his son Noah, and untold others like it, as tantalizing evidence for the idea that fallen angels were something far more than simply incorporeal beings cast out of heaven by the archangel Michael, as the theologians and propagators of the Christian, Islamic and Jewish faiths have taught during the last two thousand years?
>
> Could their very existence be confirmed by making an in depth study of Hebrew myths and legends and then comparing these with other Near Eastern and Middle Eastern religions and traditions?
>
> Most important of all, might evidence of their physical existence on earth be incidentally preserved in the records of modern-day archaeology and anthropology?[79]

One of the earliest stories ever written—*The Epic of Gilgamesh*—introduces us to Humbaba, a giant whose mere presence shakes the earth.[80] This wasn't some metaphorical monster. Humbaba was described as a real, living force of nature, a being so powerful only a demigod like Gilgamesh could stand against him.

Move eastward, and the Vedic texts of India relate tales of the Danavas, an ancient race of giants who went to war with the gods themselves. These weren't minor myths. These stories are deeply woven into the foundation of Hindu cosmology, just as the Nephilim are in the biblical tradition.

Even in North America, indigenous tribes like the Lakota and Cheyenne pass down stories of the Tall Ones, giants who once roamed the Black Hills.

Pause for a second.

How is it that every major culture—from Mesopotamia to Mesoamerica, from India to Israel, from Greece to the Great Plains—tells similar stories? The idea of celestial beings and/or their progeny interacting with humans is a consistent theme throughout the ancient world.

How is that possible?

Skeptics argue that shared myths result from common psychological archetypes rather than real history. In other words, our myths arise from the collective human psyche instead of a communal experience.

But this perspective fails to account for cases in which mythology preserves accurate historical events, like the Great Flood narratives in Mesopotamia, the Bible, and Hindu texts, which even mainstream science is acknowledging may be linked to real, post-Ice Age flooding events.[81, 82, 83]

This debate over mythology versus history and academia's suppression of evidence that conflicts with "The Narrative!" extends beyond flood accounts. It challenges the entire foundation of how academia has framed human origins.

And the role of catastrophism is rewriting much.

For centuries, humanity's origin story has been framed as a slow, linear march from primitive hunter-gatherers to modern civilization. Everything before that just consisted of cavemen grunting in caves. Mainstream academia clings to this "gradualist" dogma, dismissing ancient myths of lost worlds and cosmic disasters as mere allegory.

But what if everything we have today was passed down to us by survivors of a cataclysm?

If you're a Bible believer, that shouldn't be too hard to accept. Every human alive today is a descendant of Noah, his three sons, and their wives. Their story fits perfectly within what's known as catastrophism—the idea that Earth's history hasn't been a slow, steady march of progress, but a brutal cycle of sudden, civilization-ending disasters.

The Great Reset No One Talks About

In 2007, physicist Richard Firestone and his team dropped a bombshell. They found nanodiamonds, platinum spikes, and shock-fused glass in sediment layers dating back 12,900 years—direct proof of an extraterrestrial impact.[84]

Translation? Something hit Earth. Hard.

This event triggered the Younger Dryas, a 1,300-year, "mini" Ice Age that wiped out mammoths, saber-toothed tigers, and—oh yeah—possibly an advanced human civilization.

Firestone's paper in the *Proceedings of the National Academy of Sciences* (*PNAS*) got the usual response from academia: ridicule. "Pseudoscience!" they cried.

Except follow-up studies confirmed the evidence:

- A comet fragmented over North America, igniting continent-wide wildfires.
- Ice sheets melted instantly, unleashing apocalyptic floods.
- Temperatures plummeted, and ecosystems collapsed overnight.

Graham Hancock, in *Magicians of the Gods*, asks the question academia won't touch: What if survivors of this disaster seeded the civilizations we now call "ancient"?[85]

Of course, as noted above, the Bible already has an answer to that question.

Megafloods

Geologist Randall Carlson has spent decades pointing out what mainstream science ignores: the evidence of planet-wide, civilization-ending floods. Take the Channeled Scablands in Washington State—a desolate wasteland not carved by slow erosion, but by a single, catastrophic flood dumping five hundred cubic miles of water in days.[86, 87]

Carlson argues that this wasn't just a local event. It was global. And what do we see in nearly every ancient culture?

- The Sumerians: The Flood of Ziusudra
- The Bible: Noah's Flood
- The Hindus: The Manu Flood
- The Mayans: Flood of Huracan

Coincidence? Please.

Then there's the Saginaw Bay impact crater in Michigan. Some researchers believe an asteroid slammed into the North American ice sheet, triggering floods so massive they make Hollywood disaster movies look tame.

Hancock lays it out: "If a comet struck here, the resulting meltwater would have been like a nuclear bomb detonating every second—for weeks."[88]

But sure, let's keep pretending these stories are just primitive people telling bedtime tales.

Pole Shifts

In 1958, geologist Charles Hapgood proposed something radical: The Earth's crust shifts violently every few thousand years, displacing entire continents in a matter of centuries, or even faster.[89]

Sound crazy?

Albert Einstein didn't think so. He wrote the foreword to Hapgood's book, *Earth's Shifting Crust*, saying, "His idea is original, of great simplicity, and—if it continues to prove itself—of great importance."[90]

Einstein knew something most scientists today won't admit: The Earth doesn't play by slow, predictable rules. But world-shaking events don't happen by chance, either.

What was it Einstein also said? "God does not play dice with the universe."[91]

Hapgood's theory explains a lot—like, for example, why Antarctica is buried under miles of ice but was once warm and inhabited. Ancient maps like the Piri Reis map (drawn in 1513, based on much older sources) show Antarctica's coastline without ice.[92]

How did medieval mapmakers know what Antarctica looked like

before modern radar could confirm it? Someone long before them mapped it when it was ice-free.

The Real Reason Academia Hates This

If ancient texts aren't just myths...

If they're historical records, not fiction...

If Plato, the Vedas, the Bible, and Sumerian tablets are all pointing to the same forgotten reality...

...then the academic establishment is dead wrong.

It means the past wasn't a slow, steady evolution of civilization. It was a cycle of rise and catastrophic fall—with knowledge lost and rediscovered over millennia.

Instead of seriously engaging with these texts, mainstream scholars dismiss them as allegory, metaphor, or superstition, because the moment they admit these records might be real history, they lose control over the narrative.

That's what this is really about.

Not "interpretation," not "scholarship."

Control.

By now you get the idea. But just to kick a dead horse, let me point out that there are even *more* cases where the skeptics got it wrong.

For example:

- The medical community long believed ulcers were caused by stress or diet. Researchers Barry J. Marshall and J. Robin Warren faced intense skepticism for proposing a bacterial cause (*H. pylori*).[93]
- Alfred Wegener's theory of continental drift was ridiculed as pseudoscience until the 1960s, when seafloor spreading and plate tectonics provided evidence. (In fact, major critics stated his theory was "a fairy tale...unworthy of serious discussion.")[94]
- Stanley B. Prusiner's claim that proteins (prions) could transmit disease without DNA/RNA was met with derision.

Critics called it "heresy." But eventually, experimental proof silenced skeptics.[95]

In light of these and many other instances I could list, isn't it possible that the ancients were telling stories based on real truths, real events, and real entities when they talked about giant humanoids walking the Earth?

A man with one of the great minds of our time, the late Dr. Michael S. Heiser, dedicated his life to digging into these ancient accounts—not as myths, but as records of real episodes in Earth's (and Heaven's) past. If you're serious about understanding what the Bible actually says about angels, the Nephilim, and the "higher intelligences" that interacted with humanity, his books are required reading:

- *Angels: What the Bible Really Says About God's Heavenly Host*
- *The Unseen Realm: Recovering the Supernatural Worldview of the Bible*
- *Supernatural: What the Bible Teaches About the Unseen World—And Why It Matters*

Unlike watered-down, mainstream theology that pretends these stories are just metaphors, Heiser faced them head-on. If you follow that trail long enough, it leads to some deeply unsettling conclusions.

Moving on, if the giants of old were real, what about the *other* stories, the ones that describe beings descending from the sky?

Because, again, every major civilization records these events, too.

- The Vedic texts of India describe Vimanas, flying machines that could traverse the skies with ease.[96, 97, 98]
- The Popol Vuh, the sacred book of the Maya, speaks of beings who arrived from the stars and taught civilization to their ancestors.[99]
- The Hebrews, Egyptians, Sumerians, Greeks, and Native Americans all left behind stories of flying chariots, celestial beings, and gods who descended from the heavens. While

some dismiss these as mythological metaphors, it's worth noting that modern governments take similar reports seriously.

- ▶ The *2021 U.S. Office of the Director of National Intelligence Report (ODNI)* examined 144 unexplained aerial phenomena, concluding that "some exhibit flight characteristics beyond known technological capabilities."[100]
- ▶ In a 2019 *New York Times* interview, former Senate Majority Leader Harry Reid confirmed that "we are dealing with something not from Earth's technology."[101]
- ▶ The Pentagon's 2023 UAP hearings revealed that high-ranking officials had documented aerial encounters that defy known physics.[102]

If modern governments acknowledge unknown aerial entities, shouldn't we reconsider ancient accounts of sky beings? Were they merely symbolic, or were they early attempts to describe actual encounters with advanced nonhuman intelligences?

Moreover, while the accounts of the ancients at one time have been dismissed as legend, modern research into UAPs is forcing us to reconsider their potential historical basis.

Christopher Mellon, former US Deputy Assistant Secretary of Defense for Intelligence, has stated: "We know that UFOs exist. This is no longer an issue," and, "We have observed craft capable of hypersonic speeds with no visible propulsion systems and that defy our current understanding of physics."[103]

Luis Elizondo, former head of the Pentagon's AATIP (Advanced Aerospace Threat Identification Program), confirmed, "We are dealing with an intelligence that is beyond next-generation technology."[104] He added, "We should be transparent about the fact that there are things in our airspace that we don't fully understand."[105]

If cutting-edge defense analysts are admitting these craft operate outside of known aviation capabilities, then ancient descriptions of aerial beings in "chariots of fire" may not be mere mythology, but an attempt to describe real encounters using the vocabulary of the time.

The claims of the ancients weren't just poetic embellishments. These were accounts of real events—and modern UFO sightings may simply be a continuation of the same phenomenon. They are pieces of a puzzle, and textual analysis offers us a chance to put them together, to separate fact from fiction, and to uncover the truths that have eluded us far too long.

The War Between Myth and Reality

The quest to understand the collective consciousness of humanity is a labyrinthine journey. While archeology unveils the physical remnants of the past, another potent tool exists in our arsenal: comparative mythology.

The late Joseph Campbell famously said, "Myths are public dreams."[106] They aren't *random* fairy tales. They're humanity's subconscious trying to process something bigger than itself.

As Heiser reminds us, "The biblical writers had a supernatural worldview.... Their writings reflect a belief in an unseen spiritual realm inhabited by divine beings."[107]

If you think that's just religious talk, think again. This wasn't just the Hebrew perspective. Every major civilization—Egyptians, Greeks, Babylonians, Native Americans, and on it goes—shared this belief... because they had *seen* things. They had a shared awareness of realities beyond the material world.

Helen Morales, in *Classical Mythology*, notes how psychoanalysis connects mythology to deeper, repressed truths.[108] So, here's the uncomfortable question: Are these stories truly symbolic? Or are they distorted memories of something real, or at least a truth our ancestors were aware of, but that we presently are not?

Here's what we *do* know:

- They were real enough for every major civilization to document them.
- They interacted with humanity—sometimes as guides, sometimes as oppressors.
- They left behind technology, wisdom, and chaos.

OUR TOOLS OF INQUIRY

Perhaps these "gods" represent encounters with advanced intelligences from beyond our world, or maybe they were ancient aliens from star systems unknown. Or it could be that they were interdimensional beings (truly ancient, alien, and extraterrestrial).

Let me ask: If the ancients saw celestial beings arriving in flying machines, how is that any different from modern UFO reports? What's the difference between a UFO and a "fiery chariot" from ancient texts?

Only the language. The encounters are the same.

In the end, comparative mythology empowers us to set out on a voyage of rediscovery, piecing together fragments of a forgotten past through the lens of shared narratives.

STRENGTHS AND WEAKNESSES

We've explored how archeology, textual analysis, and comparative mythology have each played a role in exposing the hidden realities of our past—giants, angels, extraterrestrial beings, and advanced ancient civilizations.

But if we're being honest, these tools, as powerful as they are, aren't perfect. Every method has its blind spots, its weaknesses, and if we don't acknowledge them, we risk replacing one dogma with another. That's why we need more than just one lens; we need to combine disciplines.

Let's break it down.

Archeology

As we've seen in this chapter, archeology is one of the most powerful weapons we have in proving that ancient texts aren't just myths, but records of real events.

A single artifact can shatter the official version of history in an instant. But there's a problem: The past doesn't speak.

A buried civilization won't rise up and explain itself. An excavated site won't grab the archeologist's arm and say, "Hey, by the way, we were ruled by these incredibly large individuals and...."

Instead, *we must interpret* the evidence. That's where things get tricky, because interpretation is subjective.

The truth, at the end of the day, is that the silence of the past is often deafening. Material remains rarely provide definitive answers. Interpretation is key, and without supporting evidence, conclusions can remain speculative.

Textual Analysis

Textual analysis helps us decode messages from the past, but let's not kid ourselves: Ancient texts come with baggage.

- Ancient writers used metaphors, allegories, and coded language. Not every mention of a "serpent" refers to an actual reptile, and not every "chariot of fire" was a poetic flourish. Some descriptions may have been attempts to describe technology the writers didn't fully understand. Distinguishing between what's symbolic and what's literal is the eternal struggle.
- Who wrote the texts? What was their goal? Kings, priests, and rulers shaped history as much as they recorded it. Texts were sometimes written to control populations, not to enlighten them. When reading ancient documents, we have to separate truth from propaganda, which is easier said than done.
- Modern scholars often force their own worldview onto the texts they analyze. A secular historian will insist that biblical accounts of giants and angels are mythology, while a theologian may contend that they are purely spiritual metaphors.
- Claims about giants, angels, or UFOs based solely on textual analysis may be dismissed as speculative or pseudoscientific without corroborating physical evidence.

Yet...

- If every culture describes giants, are they really just symbols?
- If every civilization speaks of celestial beings coming to Earth, can we really say it's all coincidence?

- If ancient texts describe technology and structures beyond what we believe ancient cultures were capable of, are we willing to admit we might not be the pinnacle of civilization?

Textual analysis is necessary, but it cannot stand alone.

Comparative Mythology

What happens when we compare the ancient myths of multiple civilizations? We find the same themes, the same beings, and the same events told in different languages and with different names, but often describing the same or similar events.

"Coincidence" is the lazy answer. The smarter one is that these myths share a common source, a historical event so massive, so impossible to ignore, it was burned into the collective consciousness of the human race.

But here's where comparative mythology fails:

- Not every similarity means a shared origin. Sometimes cultures borrow ideas from one another. Other times, humans gravitate toward certain symbols—war, creation, destruction, gods, and giants.
- Skeptics use this against us. The mainstream approach is to claim everything is a cultural archetype instead of admitting it might be a cultural memory of something real.

That's why comparative mythology alone won't get us to the truth.

- It needs archeology to provide physical evidence.
- It needs textual analysis to preserve historical accuracy.
- It needs modern science to bridge the gaps.

To address these limitations and gain a more comprehensive understanding of the subjects at hand, it is crucial to integrate the methods we've talked about so far with additional methods and interdisciplinary approaches.

IN THE SHADOW OF GOLIATH

ADDITIONAL DISCIPLINES

As we've seen, archeology, textual analysis, and comparative mythology all have weaknesses, which pushes us to look for additional tools to use in our quest for knowledge. Here, disciplines like astronomy, genetics, and astrophysics offer additional, powerful lenses to examine these enduring mysteries.

Astronomy

Astronomy is the oldest science in the world. Before men (allegedly) built pyramids, before they carved laws into stone, before they even figured out how to write, they were looking up—tracking the heavens, mapping the stars, watching celestial events unfold with a mixture of awe and terror.

Deep down, they understood something we've spent centuries trying to ignore: The heavens are not empty.

The ancients weren't just watching for seasons or marking time. They were observing something. Something moving. Something alive.

Astronomy has taken us from crude rock carvings to space telescopes that can peer billions of light-years into the void. We've charted planets, measured the life cycles of stars, and mapped entire galaxies—but even with all our technology, we've barely scratched the surface.

The universe isn't just big, it's terrifyingly massive.

As American astrophysicist Neil deGrasse Tyson bluntly put it, "We are part of a cosmos that is very much alive. There are more stars in the universe than grains of sand on all the beaches on Earth."[109]

Try to wrap your head around that for a second.

If even fractions of those stars have planets, and even fractions of those planets are habitable, then the idea that we're the only intelligent life in the cosmos is beyond arrogance. It's absurd.

As modern science advances, we're beginning to find strange anomalies, evidence that suggests someone, somewhere, is harnessing power on a scale beyond anything we can imagine. One of the most fascinating possibilities? Dyson spheres.

A Dyson sphere is a massive, engineered megastructure that surrounds a star, capturing its energy to sustain an advanced civilization. In theory, an extraterrestrial race far beyond our level of development could dismantle entire planets to construct one, giving them access to nearly limitless power.[110]

Does it sound like science fiction? Maybe. But according to two recent studies published in the *Monthly Notices of the Royal Astronomical Society and Cornell University*, scientists have actually identified multiple Dyson sphere candidates:[111, 112]

- The first study found potential Dyson spheres in seven different solar systems.
- The second study expanded that number to fifty-three.

We're not talking about conspiracy theories. We're talking about peer-reviewed research, published by mainstream astronomers, suggesting that something—or someone—out there is building on a scale we can barely comprehend.

Astronomy continues to profoundly impact our comprehension of the cosmos. It will certainly open new avenues for exploring the possibility of extraterrestrial life and phenomena often associated with it.

Ancient texts. Modern astronomy. They're both pointing in the same direction.

We've never been alone in the cosmos.

Genetics

Genetics isn't just about eye color or ancestry tests. It's the language of life itself. It's the blueprint that dictates who we are, where we came from, and maybe even where we're going.

And if you think DNA is just about modern biology, think again.

Genetics is a scientific wrecking ball capable of exposing truths we've been told never existed. If you think that's hyperbole, keep reading. I've got some truth bombs to drop later on.

For the moment, consider this: Every living thing carries genetic fingerprints, traces of its history woven into its DNA. Scientists use this information to reconstruct evolutionary lineages, identifying who is related to whom, how species changed over time, and even how different groups of humans migrated across the planet.

Here's where it gets fascinating. The Human Genome Project, completed in 2003, mapped the entire human genetic code. It was one of the greatest scientific achievements in history, giving us the instruction manual for the human body.[113][114,][115]

It also raised questions mainstream science is still struggling to answer. For example:

- Why are there sections of DNA that don't seem to come from any known ancestor?
- Why do human intelligence, consciousness, and language seem to have "switched on" suddenly—in a way that doesn't match normal evolutionary patterns?
- Most importantly, what happens when we start testing the DNA of ancient remains that don't fit the standard human timeline?
- What happens when the genetic tests start showing evidence of something beyond known hominid history? (Here's a hint: they are. Round results are simply being shoved and boxed into predefined square cubbyholes. But again, more on that later.)

Genetics isn't only about solving medical mysteries anymore.

It might just be the tool that exposes the truth about who we are, where we came from, and whether humanity has been alone on this planet after all.

The evidence is there. The only question is: Are we ready to face what it tells us?

Astrophysics and Astrobiology

Astrophysics—the science of stars, galaxies, and the very fabric of the cosmos—isn't just about mapping distant planets or measuring radiation levels in deep space. From the moment humans first gazed at the night sky, we've been obsessed with the idea that we are not alone—for good reason.

We now know the universe is teeming with exoplanets—worlds beyond our solar system that could, theoretically, support life. Thanks to cutting-edge technology, astrophysicists can now analyze the atmospheres of these planets, searching for chemical markers—biosignatures—that might indicate life.[116, 117]

Here, the argument becomes especially difficult to defend for the mainstream scientific community. What if life isn't just biological? (You may have heard terms like "nonhuman biologics," "clones," "cybernetic," et cetera. These will come into our discussion later as well.)

What if some interdimensional, "angelic" species creates a race of "nonhuman biologics" that act like "biological robots" with a "hive mind" to serve as their eyes, ears, and means of physical interaction with humanity—when they've been personally barred, banned, restricted (for the time being), and restrained from doing so?

Just some questions. In any case, for decades, science has focused on finding life that looks like us—carbon-based organisms requiring water, oxygen, and sunlight. But what if that's a primitive assumption?

Astrobiology, the field that studies the possibility of life beyond Earth, is already considering the idea that life might not be bound by our physical laws. Some researchers even suggest beings could exist in higher dimensions—realities beyond what we can see or touch.

If interdimensional life exists, then what we call angels, demons, or supernatural entities might not be "supernatural" at all. They might just be a different form of "natural."

Remember, the God of the Bible didn't create the Earth as part of a separate universe from Heaven. What does Genesis say?

> In the beginning God created the heavens and the earth. (Genesis 1:1)

בְּרֵאשִׁית בָּרָא אֱלֹהִים אֵת הַשָּׁמַיִם וְאֵת הָאָרֶץ:

This verse presents the creation of Heaven and Earth as a unified act, suggesting they are part of the same created order. The use of the Hebrew word *et* (אֵת) before both "heaven" and "earth" in the original text emphasizes their connection as direct objects of God's creative action.

Now, there might be multiple universes—who can say? But the Bible records Heaven and Earth being created as part of His kingdom—and while kingdoms have different geographic areas (and every geographic area has properties unique to it), every region is part of the same kingdom.

Think of it like this: Texas and California are both part of the United States, but they are distinct locations, each with its own defining characteristics. In other words, interdimensional aliens (angels) would therefore be part of the same universe and reality you and I inhabit. They would merely be from an entirely different locale within that universe, just as Texans and Californians both inhabit the United States but live in separate locations.

The concept of God's kingdom (singular) encompassing both Heaven and Earth is also reflected in the New Testament, such as in the Lord's Prayer, which states, "Thy kingdom come, Thy will be done, on earth as it is in heaven" (Matthew 6:10). This reinforces the idea of a unified divine realm with different aspects rather than separate universes.

Author Timothy Alberino agrees, stating, "The biblical paradigm does not portray two distinct creations, one for the natural world and one for the supernatural, but a singular universe in which all things abide and are bound together by synergistic forces."[118]

Now, understanding Alberino's comment, it's reasonable to hypothesize that a lifeform beyond our three-dimensional reality wouldn't necessarily obey our rules. For example, it might appear or disappear at will or manipulate space and time. It could exist in a way our physics simply isn't yet equipped to understand.

If these beings have interacted with humanity in the past, as ancient texts from the Bible, the Vedas, and Sumerian records claim, then modern science is centuries behind in catching up to what our ancestors already knew.

Door to Another Dimension

If you think the idea of interdimensional beings sounds like sci-fi, think again.

One of the world's top physicists, Sergio Bertolucci, director for research and scientific computing at the *Conseil Européen pour la Recherche Nucléaire* (CERN), (French for "European Council for Nuclear Research"), made a shocking statement most people have never heard. At a press conference covered by the British technology site The Register, Bertolucci spoke about the Large Hadron Collider (LHC), the world's most powerful particle accelerator.

His exact words: "Out of this door might come something, or we might send something through it."[119]

Let that sink in.

The director of research at CERN openly admitted their work could briefly open a doorway to another dimension. Even though this doorway would only be open for a fraction of a second, Bertolucci hinted at the possibility of something coming through.

What, exactly, did he mean by "something"? Did he mean particles? Energy? Or is there a reason CERN's work has fueled speculation that they're playing with forces they don't fully understand?

Could it be that modern physics, rather than *disproving* "the supernatural," is instead on the verge of *proving* it?

Here's the uncomfortable reality: The deeper we go into astrophysics, quantum mechanics, and theoretical physics, the more it starts to sound like ancient religious texts.

- The Bible describes angelic beings who can appear and disappear at will, just as a higher-dimensional being might do.
- The Book of Enoch speaks of "Watchers" descending from the heavens.
- Ezekiel's vision of a spinning, metallic, glowing, fiery object sounds disturbingly close to modern UFO reports.
- Even Jesus' (Yeshua's) post-Resurrection body, which could walk through walls yet still be touched (John 20:26–29),

behaves like something operating on a higher-dimensional level.[120]

So, if science and Scripture are pointing in the same direction, why is the world so desperate to keep them separate?

The tools of inquiry we have discussed—archeology, textual analysis, comparative mythology, and the additional disciplines of astronomy, genetics, and astrophysics—are weapons. Each can tear down the lies we've been sold about our past, our origins, and our place in the cosmos, a piece at a time.

And now?

Now we're going to start bringing down the house.

CHAPTER THREE

ANGELS: *SHALOM ALEICHEM*

*Peace be upon you, ministering angels, angels of the Most High,
Of the King, the King of kings, the Holy One, blessed be He.
Come in peace, angels of peace, angels of the Most High
Of the King, the King of kings, the Holy One, blessed be He.
Bless me in peace, angels of peace, angels of the Most High,
Of the King, the King of kings, the Holy One, blessed be He.
Depart in peace, angels of peace, angels of the Most High,
Of the Kings of Kings, the Holy One, blessed be He.*

—Traditional Hebrew song[121]

Here's the sad truth: Within the Judeo-Christian tradition, unless the description of an angel is based on firsthand experience or observations of that experience, anything said about these enigmatic beings is little more than overly pious assumption.

Those assumptions have become doctrine. For thousands of years, rabbis, priests, and pastors have all been guilty (and are still guilty) of perpetuating various narratives that cannot be backed by the Scriptures of either Judaism or Christianity.

They can, therefore, safely and summarily be dumped into the garbage.

Let me give you a hint of what I mean.

For far too long, angels have been boxed into the realm of mythology and religious faith—dismissed by scientists as superstition and by theologians as purely spiritual beings with no physical presence.

No angels are dancing to Madonna's "Material Girl" here!

Okay, sure. But which theologians make that claim? We'll get to that.

But also...wait a minute! Doesn't the Bible talk about angels walking around, appearing as humans, eating human food, and even breaking people out of jail on occasion—you know, doing distinctly material things in a material world?

Well, yes.

Check out Genesis 18, where we read that three men visit Abraham by the oaks of Mamre. Abraham initially perceives them as travelers and offers hospitality, only later realizing they were divine in nature. Then there's the very next chapter, in which two angels visit Lot in Sodom.

Appearing as ordinary men, the visitors accept Lot's hospitality but have come to warn him about the city's impending destruction. Lot prepares a feast for these angelic dudes, and they eat it.

Then, in Acts 12, we read that an angel breaks the apostle Peter out of jail! This isn't some floaty spiritual apparition. The angel smacks Peter in the side to wake him up, then verbally orders him to get up and follow him.

But despite evidence from both the Hebrew Scriptures and the New Testament, the belief that angels are purely spiritual, nonphysical entities is a well-established view within Jewish and Christian theological traditions.

Consider the following figures:

- **Moses Maimonides**, also known as Rambam, an acronym for Rabbi Moshe ben Maimon, was a towering Jewish philosopher, physician, and legal scholar during the twelfth century. He argued in *The Guide for the Perplexed* that angels should be understood as metaphors for divine causality, rather than as beings with physical presence.[122]

- **St. Augustine of Hippo**, one of the most influential Christian theologians and philosophers in Western history (354–430 CE), described angels as incorporeal intellectual beings, stating in *The Literal Meaning of Genesis*, "The angel, a spiritual light, is an 'intellectual life in itself.'"[123]
- **St. Thomas Aquinas** (1225–1274 CE), is best known for integrating Aristotelian philosophy with Christian theology, creating a system of thought that became the foundation of Scholasticism—the dominant intellectual tradition of medieval Europe. In his *Summa Theologiae*, Aquinas categorized angels as "separate substances"—pure intellect and will, without material form.[124]
- **John Calvin** (1509–1564 CE), a French theologian, pastor, and reformer who became one of the most important figures of the Protestant Reformation, and later Karl Barth (1886–1968 CE), a Swiss Reformed theologian best known for challenging liberal theology), emphasized that angels exist outside of physical human experience, *serving as divine messengers rather than embodied beings.*[125]

These and many others have articulated the perspective that angels are "only" spiritual beings with no physical presence in ways that have deeply influenced Jewish, Catholic, and Protestant thought. Today, these views are taught as doctrine in many synagogues and churches around the world.

The Doctrine of Angels Across Religious Traditions

Thus, across millennia and denominations, angels have continued to be universally understood as entirely incorporeal beings—in clear contradiction of the scriptural narrative. In fact, almost all official interpretations appear to be blatant refusals to accept a plain reading of the text.

Jewish and Christian theologians alike have had a distinct inability to take Scripture at face value—even when the language clearly isn't metaphorical or poetic. For example, the ultra-Orthodox Hassidic organization Chabad holds the following as doctrine:

Notwithstanding the great spiritual level of the angels, the holiness of the Jewish soul supersedes that of the angel. Only the Jewish soul has the ability to descend to this physical and corporeal world and refine and elevate it.[126]

Note that Chabad differentiates between this physical world, which is corporeal, and angels, which it believes are not.

Mainstream Orthodox Judaism today holds largely the same views put forth by Maimonides as expressed in his *Guide for the Perplexed*, again asserting that both God and angels are incorporeal—purely spiritual, with no physical form.[127]

Meanwhile, in Reform and Reconstructionist Judaism, angels don't even exist. These movements see angels as symbolic, not literal. They represent divine messages, qualities, or human virtues like justice and mercy. For instance, in the Torah commentary, *Angel Spotting*, on ReformJudaism.org, angels are described as "metaphors of healing, blessing, promise, justice, mercy, compassion, and enlightenment."[128]

The Catholic Church's Nonnegotiable Doctrine

On the Christian front, the Catholic Church maintains a clear doctrinal stance on the noncorporeal nature of angels. This is explicitly stated in the Catechism of the Catholic Church, the official compendium of Catholic doctrine worldwide:

> As purely spiritual creatures, angels have intelligence and will: they are personal and immortal creatures, surpassing in perfection all visible creatures, as the splendor of their glory bears witness.[129]

This teaching isn't merely theological speculation but represents the formal position of the Catholic Church taught throughout its global institutions. The Catechism further emphasizes this point by stating:

> The existence of the spiritual, non-corporeal beings that Sacred Scripture usually calls "angels" is a truth of faith.[130]

Vatican theologian Father Serge-Thomas Bonino continues reinforcing this teaching today.[131]

Orthodox Churches: Angels Are Incorporeal and Immaterial

Then there are the Orthodox Churches, which essentially teach the same thing: Angels are purely spiritual beings without physical bodies. They're created by God as active, incorporeal spirits endowed with reason, will, and knowledge, serving and fulfilling His will. Although they can manifest in forms perceivable to humans, these appearances are not reflective of their true, immaterial essence.[132]

Saint John of Damascus, a prominent Orthodox theologian, emphasized that angels, by nature and definition, have no bodies or material properties of any sort; they are strictly spiritual beings.[133] Likewise, the Russian, Greek, Serbian, Romanian, Bulgarian, Georgian, Cypriot, Polish, and Orthodox Church in America (OCA) all hold this as doctrine.[134]

The Oriental Orthodox Churches (Coptic, Syriac, Armenian, Ethiopian, and Malankara [Indian] Orthodox Churches) all teach the same: Angels are bodiless entities, invisible to our physical eyes and do not possess bodily needs, desires, or passions.[135]

Protestant Churches Agree

Protestants—from Presbyterians to Pentecostals—hold to the incorporeality of angels.

- **Presbyterian Church:** "Doctrine: Angels do not have bodies. That is, they are immaterial and incorporeal."[136]
- **Lutheran Church:** Urbanus Rhegius, an influential German Lutheran pastor, explicitly taught in a sermon preached in 1537 (later translated into English) that angels "cannot eyther bee felt, handled, or holden with handes, or seene with carnall eyes."[137] This early Lutheran position established a foundation for later doctrinal development within Lutheran denominations.

- **Reformed Theology:** John Calvin stressed that angels "do not deal with us in a way which makes us familiar with their nearness and reveals it to our senses." Calvin's position on angels as incorporeal beings has been foundational for Reformed denominations. His teachings were "closely echoed" by other Reformed writers who maintained that angels operate "silently and imperceptibly behind the scenes."[138]

From Anglicans to Baptists, Methodists, and Pentecostals, the theme is the same. Even Charismatic churches, though avoiding the term "incorporeal," teach that angels are spirits (Hebrews 1:14) whose physical appearances are temporary and miraculous, not essential to their nature.[139] The National Association of Christian Ministers sums it up well: Angels "are generally portrayed as incorporeal and immortal, although they can manifest in physical forms when necessary."[140, 141, 142, 143, 144]

The Bottom Line

Across Judaism and Christianity and its many denominations, one thing is clear: The overwhelming consensus is that angels are incorporeal, spiritual beings. The details and emphasis vary, but the doctrine is near-universal: Angels are real, but they have no bodies.

But let me ask: What if the idea that angels are purely spiritual beings is a false dichotomy? What if angels exist within the spiritual realm—which we could equate with a separate dimensional space from our own—*and* in ways that intersect with our physical reality?

Further, understanding what's been pushed on the masses for thousands of years, let me ask: Are you ready to journey through texts that might challenge what you've thought of as truth?

I hope so, because a correct understanding of what humanity has been dealing with is far more interesting—indeed, mind-blowing—than anything taught in most synagogues or churches these days.

So let me begin with what we *actually know*.

Angels appear in the Hebrew Scriptures, apocryphal texts, the New Testament, the Talmud, and Jewish mystical traditions—not as sweet, harp-playing Renaissance cherubs, but as formidable, terrifying, and often incomprehensible beings.

Let's be clear: The Bible does not describe angels as cute, chubby babies with wings. That's a Hallmark card, not Scripture. The angels of the Bible are messengers, warriors, and divine enforcers. Some stand before the throne of God radiating indescribable power. Others descend to Earth on missions that shake the course of human history. Some execute divine judgment with brutal finality.

These beings are not human and never were. The same is true vice versa: Humans are not angels, and they never will be, despite popular depictions in Hollywood films like *It's a Wonderful Life* (1946), starring James Stewart as George Bailey.[145] Humans don't become angels or "get our wings" when we die.

No, angels are entirely different beings.

The Biblical Record

From Genesis to Revelation, angels appear again and again, interacting with humans in ways that are awe-inspiring.

- **Cherubim** (Genesis 3:24): The first time an angel appears in the Bible, it doesn't bring good news, it blocks the way to the Garden of Eden with a flaming sword. The message? "You aren't getting back in here."[146]
- **The divine council** (Psalm 82, 1 Kings 22:19–22, Job 1:6–7): The Hebrew Bible describes a heavenly assembly, a council of divine beings who advise and execute the will of God.[147, 148, 149]
- **Gabriel and Michael** (Daniel 10, Revelation 12:7–9, Luke 1:19–26): Gabriel delivers prophetic messages while Michael leads God's armies in battle.[150, 151, 152]

Some of the most striking angelic encounters are found in the Bible's apocalyptic books like Daniel, Ezekiel, and Revelation, where angels reveal mind-bending visions of the future and the culmination of God's plan for humanity, the angels, and indeed for all of Heaven.

The Dead Sea Scrolls Expansion

Books within the Dead Sea Scrolls take the biblical framework and expand on it in sensational ways.

- The angel Metatron is described as the scribe of Heaven who records divine decrees.
- The Book of Enoch describes Watchers—angels who descended to Earth and corrupted humanity, fathering the Nephilim (Genesis 6:1–4). These weren't cute little helpers; they were divine rebels whose actions led to God wiping out the world with Noah's Flood.[153]

From wheels within wheels, to angels with multiple faces, to gems blazing like fire—these bizarre accounts push the boundaries of human comprehension. Could they be mere symbols and metaphors recorded by ancient seers? Or do they reflect actual encounters with higher intelligences, interdimensional entities, or ultra-terrestrial beings almost incomprehensible to our limited senses?

Let's ask some questions most theologians won't touch.

What *are* angels? Are they:

1. Spiritual beings created by God? (This is the traditional religious view.)
2. Interdimensional intelligences? (This is a possibility modern physics might support.)
3. Intergalactic extraterrestrials interacting with humanity under divine command? (Or possibly, for some, are they under satanic command?)
4. Something even stranger?

The Hebrew word for angel, *mal'akh* (מַלְאָךְ), means "messenger." That doesn't tell us what they are, only what they do. Throughout the Bible, angels:

- Appear and disappear at will.
- Shift between forms (sometimes looking human, sometimes looking terrifying).
- Communicate messages across dimensions.
- Engage in battle with other angels.
- Interact with physical reality in ways that break the known laws of physics.

Now think about this: Modern theoretical physics already speculates about higher dimensions, parallel universes, and beings that might exist beyond our sensory perception. Is it really a stretch to say the angels of the Bible fit this profile perfectly?

If angels are real and aren't metaphorical, what does that mean for us? The Bible makes it clear:

- There was a war in Heaven (Revelation 12:7–9).[154]
- Some angels fell from their original position and turned against God.
- These fallen beings interacted with humanity, leading to chaos, corruption, and destruction.
- An ongoing spiritual battle directly impacts the physical world.

If the Bible, the Dead Sea Scrolls, and countless ancient texts are right—if these beings are still active today—then:

1. The war isn't over.
2. Humanity is caught in the middle of that war.
3. The truth about these beings has been deliberately suppressed.

That leads us to the next inevitable question: If angels are real and have interacted with humans throughout history, what about their enemies? If you think this world is only being influenced by the good guys, you haven't been paying attention.

But let's not get ahead of ourselves. Let's focus for the moment, again, on what we absolutely know.

The *B'nei Elohim*

There is a Hebrew term that appears only four times in the entire Hebrew Bible. It's used exclusively for angels, never for humans: *b'nei Elohim* (בְּנֵי־הָאֱלֹהִים), which means "sons of God." This term is used in the following passages, presented here in Hebrew following the English translation:

Genesis 6:1–2:

> Now it came about, when mankind began to multiply on the face of the land, and daughters were born to them, that the sons of God saw that the daughters of mankind were beautiful; and they took wives for them.

> וַיְהִי כִּי־הֵחֵל הָאָדָם לָרֹב עַל־פְּנֵי הָאֲדָמָה וּבָנוֹת יֻלְּדוּ לָהֶם:

> וַיִּרְאוּ בְנֵי־הָאֱלֹהִים אֶת־בְּנוֹת הָאָדָם, כִּי טֹבֹת הֵנָּה; וַיִּקְחוּ לָהֶם נָשִׁים, מִכֹּל אֲשֶׁר בָּחָרוּ.

Genesis 6:4:

> The Nephilim were on the earth in those days, and also afterward, when the sons of God came in to the daughters of mankind, and they bore children to them. Those were the mighty men who were of old, men of renown.

> הַנְּפִלִים הָיוּ בָאָרֶץ בַּיָּמִים הָהֵם וְגַם אַחֲרֵי־כֵן אֲשֶׁר יָבֹאוּ בְּנֵי הָאֱלֹהִים אֶל־בְּנוֹת הָאָדָם וְיָלְדוּ לָהֶם הֵמָּה הַגִּבֹּרִים אֲשֶׁר מֵעוֹלָם אַנְשֵׁי הַשֵּׁם:

Job 1:6:

> Now there was a day when the sons of God came to present themselves before the Lord, and Satan also came among them.

> וַיְהִי הַיּוֹם וַיָּבֹאוּ בְּנֵי הָאֱלֹהִים לְהִתְיַצֵּב עַל־יְהוָה וַיָּבוֹא גַם־הַשָּׂטָן בְּתוֹכָם:

ANGELS: *SHALOM ALEICHEM*

Job 2:1:

Again, there was a day when the sons of God came to present themselves before the Lord, and Satan also came among them to present himself before the Lord.

וַיְהִי הַיּוֹם--וַיָּבֹאוּ בְּנֵי הָאֱלֹהִים, לְהִתְיַצֵּב עַל־יְהוָה; וַיָּבוֹא גַם־הַשָּׂטָן בְּתֹכָם, לְהִתְיַצֵּב עַל־יְהוָה.

In each of these passages, *b'nei Elohim* is used to describe supernatural beings—divine entities that exist above and beyond human reality. They stand before God in Job. They descend to Earth in Genesis. They are not mortal men.

Why, then, do so many modern translations, particularly within Judaism, try to twist this term into something else? Instead of translating *b'nei Elohim* literally—"sons of God," "divine beings"—certain Jewish and Christian translators have bent over backwards to redefine the term into something more theologically comfortable.

Look at some of these linguistic contortions:

- The Koren Jerusalem Bible: "distinguished men."
- Metsudah Publications (2009): "sons of the rulers."
- Jewish Publication Society (JPS) (1917): "sons of the nobles."
- The Living Bible (TLB): "evil beings from the spirit world."
- Charles Kahane (1963): "sons of Seth."[155, 156, 157, 158, 159]

Excuse me—"sons of Seth"?

Where in Genesis do we find anything about Seth in these passages? Nowhere. These aren't translations; they're doctrinal manipulations.

One might argue that these translations find their justification in the musings of select Talmudic sages, the writings of Josephus, or the commentaries of certain later scholars, but these aren't mere differences in linguistic nuance.

The earliest Jewish sources never had this problem. The Septuagint (LXX)—the Greek translation of the Hebrew Bible from the third century BCE—renders *b'nei Elohim* as ἄγγελοι τοῦ Θεοῦ ("angels of God").[160]

Why?

Because the ancient Jewish translators understood exactly what the term meant.

The tragedy lies in the fact that Scripture itself doesn't support these modern translations. They're a departure not only from the literal meaning, but from the ancient Jewish interpretations found in the Septuagint, the vast corpus of Talmudic lore, and the medieval commentaries.

It is telling that only two Jewish English translations keep to the plain meaning of the Hebrew and align with the Septuagint,[161] the bulk of Talmudic commentary,[162] medieval commentary,[163] Jewish mystical texts,[164] modern Jewish commentary,[165] and Christian translations. Those courageous two are the Jewish English Torah from opensiddur.org and the Modernized Tanakh—based on JPS 1917 and edited by Adam Cohn.[166, 167] These stand out as brilliant flares of honesty—indeed, of bravery—in a sea of unmerited theological conformity. By aligning themselves with the ancient wisdom that speaks of interactions between the divine and the earthly, and of knowledge passed down from celestial realms, they put doctrinal targets on their backs in some circles for daring to adhere to a (currently) unpopular narrative and interpretation. They asserted that the *b'nei Elohim* weren't figments of poetic imagination, mere metaphors, or exalted men, but were highly advanced, nonhuman intelligences from beyond—some of which, both righteous and fallen, walked among humankind during all but forgotten epochs of human history.

Moreover, if *b'nei Elohim* were indeed divine, nonhuman intelligences, we're left with some terrifying questions:

- What exactly are these beings?
- If they interacted with humanity in past epochs, do they still do so today?
- If some fell into rebellion, what became of them?

ANGELS: *SHALOM ALEICHEM*

Either way, their existence is undeniable if we hold the Bible as the Word of God—unless, of course, we prefer a sanitized, neutered, politically correct version of the Bible that avoids the uncomfortable truth.

That's exactly why we need to take a hard look at what the world doesn't want us to know: The sons of God were real. And if they were real way back when, the next question is: Where are they now (the good guys AND the bad guys)?

Did they ever actually leave?

More importantly, if they did leave, what happens when they return?

MORNING STARS AND CELESTIAL TITLES

Imagine, for a moment, a time so ancient, so primordial, the world itself is just taking shape. The ground beneath our feet doesn't exist yet. The air we breathe hasn't yet been formed. The very concept of time itself is still being written into the structure of reality.

Yet before all of it—before Adam, before Eden, before the first human breath was drawn—there were beings who already existed.

The Hebrew Bible calls them *kochavei boker* (כּוֹכְבֵי בֹקֶר), the "morning stars." Rabbi Ibn Ezra, a prominent rabbi and scholar who lived in the eleventh and twelfth centuries, best known for his biblical commentaries, dared to declare the morning stars, those radiant heralds of dawn mentioned in Job's cosmic account, are none other than the enigmatic *b'nei Elohim*, the sons of God.[168]

These ancient, powerful entities were watching as the foundations of the Earth were being laid.

Timothy Alberino puts it bluntly: "These beings are indisputably extraterrestrial, and incalculably ancient."[169]

The phrase "morning star" (or "morning stars") appears only five times in Scripture (one time more than *b'nei Elohim*), but every instance carries cosmic weight. Alberino's insightful analysis suggests these morning stars share certain attributes with none other than Jesus of Nazareth, who is also bestowed with this celestial title.[170]

But what could a carpenter's son from Nazareth, a human, possibly have in common with these primeval entities?

Well, first we must consider that it's pretty likely that if Jesus, as Christians argue, is God (an aspect of God, an Avatar of the Father-God part of YHVH, the God of Israel), then isn't it likely He would share certain qualities with beings described as "sons of God?"

I've heard some Christians completely freak out and vehemently argue that this simply isn't possible because, hey, Jesus didn't die for the angels—right?

But that's not the argument here.

The claim is that Jesus possesses certain qualities in common with angels that He does *not* share with humans. Likewise, He embodies traits of humanity that are not found in angels. For example, one characteristic Jesus has in common with angels is exceptional agedness, since it is assumed in the biblical narrative. These morning stars were present at the genesis of our planet and were party to the creation of Adam, the progenitor of humanity.

Can you grasp the implications? We're not merely dealing with beings of great age, but with entities who have watched the birth of worlds and the rise and fall of civilizations lost to conventional history.

Consider Job 38:4–7:

Where were you when I laid the foundations of the earth? Tell me, if you have understanding. Who determined its measurements? Surely you know! Or who stretched the line upon it? To what were its foundations fastened? Or who laid its cornerstone, when the morning stars sang together, and all the sons of God shouted for joy?

אֵיפֹה הָיִיתָ, בְּיָסְדִי־אָרֶץ, הַגֵּד, אִם־יָדַעְתָּ בִינָה:

מִי־שָׂם מְמַדֶּיהָ כִּי תֵדָע אוֹ מִי־נָטָה עָלֶיהָ קָּו:

עַל־מָה, אֲדָנֶיהָ הָטְבָּעוּ אוֹ מִי־יָרָה, אֶבֶן פִּנָּתָהּ:

בְּרָן־יַחַד, כּוֹכְבֵי בֹקֶר וַיָּרִיעוּ, כָּל־בְּנֵי אֱלֹהִים:

The Messiah, likewise, is described in literature written by Jews as existing before the formation of Earth and participating in its creation, and He is called a "morning star":

> From the beginning of the creation of the world, King Messiah was born; for He arose in the thought [of G-d], at a time when the world was not even created. Indeed he [Isaiah] says: ויצא חוטר מגזע ישי —"And a rod came forth from the root of Jesse" (Isa. 11:1); he does not say here "and he will come forth," but rather "and he came forth." (Pesiqta Rabbati 152a)
>
> Rabbi Shim'on ben Laqish explained: ורוח אלהים מרחפת על-פני המים—"And the spirit of God hovered over the face of the water" (Gen. 1:2)—this is the spirit of King Messiah, as it is written, "ונחה עליו רוח ה" "And the spirit of the L-rd will rest upon him" (Isa. 11:2). (Bereshit Rabbati, Parashat Bereshit 2)

2 Peter 1:19:

> And so we have the prophetic word made more sure, to which you do well to pay attention as to a lamp shining in a dark place, until the day dawns and the morning star arises in your hearts.

The *Jamieson-Fausset-Brown Bible Commentary* specifically links the "morning star" here with Jesus, as do the *Cambridge Bible for Schools and Colleges* (97), *Bengel's Gnomen*, and the *Pulpit Commentary*.[171]

Revelation 2:28 further confirms this association: "and I will give him the morning star." In this verse, Jesus is speaking to the church in Thyatira, promising to give the one who is victorious the "morning star." The interpretation of this phrase varies among theologians, but it's often understood to symbolize Jesus Himself or some aspect of His glory or authority.

Again, here, the *Jamieson-Fausset-Brown Bible Commentary* says:

> The morning star—that is, "I will give unto him Myself, who am 'the morning star' (Re 22:16); so that reflecting My perfect

brightness, he shall shine like Me, the morning star, and share My kingly glory (of which a star is the symbol, Nu 21:17; Mt 2:2)."[172]

Note, too, that this commentary links "morning star" with royalty.

Gill's Exposition of the Entire Bible likewise refers to the "morning star" as a title for Jesus, and the *Expositor's Greek Testament* suggests that its judicial authority over the nations was symbolically understood by the prophets.[173]

The *Pulpit Commentary* further elaborates on this symbol of brightness, beauty, and regal authority.[174]

Finally, Revelation 22:16 states:

I, Jesus, have sent My angel to testify to you of these things... I am the root and the descendant of David, the bright morning star.

Gill's Exposition notes:

Aijeleth Shahar, in the title of Psalm 22:1, which is a psalm that belongs to the Messiah, is, by some Jewish writers...interpreted, "the morning star", the title of Christ here.[175]

Pause to think about all of this for a second. According to Scripture and the writings of the sages, who was present when the Earth was created?

- God the Father,
- The morning stars (*kochavei boker*), and
- The Messiah.

Who is given the title "morning star(s)"?

- The *b'nei Elohim,* and
- The Messiah.

What are the qualities this title encompasses?

- ▸ Royalty
- ▸ Judicial authority, and
- ▸ Extreme agedness.

Also interesting: Rebellious angels didn't lose their titles when they fell, "for the gifts and the calling of God are irrevocable" (Romans 11:29). You see, Satan is also specifically named within the Hebrew Scriptures as one of the morning stars.
Isaiah 14:12:

How you have fallen from heaven, You star of the morning, son of the dawn! You have been cut down to the earth, You who defeated the nations!

אֵיךְ נָפַלְתָּ מִשָּׁמַיִם הֵילֵל בֶּן־שָׁחַר; נִגְדַּעְתָּ לָאָרֶץ חוֹלֵשׁ עַל־גּוֹיִם׃

It is therefore no strange thing to say that "morning star(s)" in reference to angelic beings and the Messiah in literature written by Jews is a title and descriptor meant to convey preexistence and preeminence—royalty and judicial authority. Nor is it strange to say that, within that literature, both Jesus and the angels share this epithet and these characteristics.

It's clear they do. Both preexisted the creation of the Earth and humanity. Both are royalty in the family of God the Father. As sons of God, they're preeminent over all of creation.

Timothy Alberino argues that although Adam was created to be a son of God, he gave up that birthright, and it took Jesus to restore us to the position and title of "sons of God," which we will attain in the resurrection.[176]

Until then, we are indeed "a little lower than the angels":

What is man, that thou art mindful of him? or the son of man, that thou visitest him? Thou madest him a little less than angels, thou hast crowned him with glory and honour. (Psalm 8: 4–5, LXX)[177, 178]

The biggest difference between angels and Jesus is, as Paul said in Colossians 1:15–17:

> He is the image of the invisible God, the firstborn of all creation:
> for by Him all things were created, both in the heavens and on earth, visible and invisible, whether thrones, or dominions, or rulers, or authorities—all things have been created through Him and for Him.
> He is before all things, and in Him all things hold together.

So now, let's bring this full circle. Again:

- The morning stars are present at creation.
- The *b'nei Elohim* ("sons of God") are described in the same breath.
- The Messiah is also called the "morning star."

What does this tell us?

1. The *b'nei Elohim* are not random sentient beings. They are part of a divine royal family.
2. Jesus is the ultimate, preeminent Son of God, the true Morning Star.
3. The fallen morning star (Satan or Lucifer, the fallen cherub) tried to claim a throne that was never his.
4. Although not a morning star, Adam was created to be a son of God like the morning stars before the Fall.

Psalm 8:4–5 drives this home:

> What is man, that thou art mindful of him? Or the son of man, that thou visitest him? Thou madest him a little less than angels, thou hast crowned him with glory and honor. (LXX)

In other words:

- Jesus is the rightful heir, the true "Bright Morning Star."
- Lucifer was a pretender, cast down from his high place.
- The morning stars (sons of God) were meant to rule under divine authority.
- Humanity, through the Messiah, is restored to that same royal, rulership status.

Through Christ, we are destined to be coheirs in the divine family (Romans 8:17). But the war is still raging. Factions of angels and most of humanity are still in rebellion.

The only question is: Which side are you on?

Before moving on to the next section, I want to pause because some Jewish readers, especially, may argue that a preexistent Messiah is an idea subscribed to only by Jews of the Second-Temple era, Jews who believed Jesus of Nazareth was the Messiah, later Talmudic sages, and Christians today.

However, it should be noted that some modern Orthodox Jewish sects also believe in the concept—even in the twenty-first century. For example, messianists within the Chabad Lubavitch Hasidic movement believe their last Rebbe, Menachem Mendel Schneerson (1902–1994), didn't actually die, but rather continues to live in a spiritual sense as the Messiah. Some even believe he will "rise again" and/or "come again" in a fashion similar to what Christians believe about Jesus' Second Coming. They refer to him as the *Melech HaMoshiach* ("King Messiah").

"Rabbi Ariel Sokolovsky is a Moldova-born Chabad rabbi in Portland, Oregon...[who] maintains a blog he entitled "Rebbegod" and [he] refers to Schneerson as "Rebbe-Almighty."

Others have stated, "The Rebbe was not created; the Rebbe has always been around and always will be."[179, 180, 181]

In other words, there is plenty of backing for the concept of a preexistent/always- existent Messiah. The Messiah was present in God's plan before the world began. This is exactly what Jesus says in John 8:58: "Before Abraham was, I Am."

Watchers

The primary term for "Watchers" is *'erin* (עִירִין). This word is Aramaic rather than Hebrew and is a plural form of the *'ir* (עִיר), which means "watcher" or "one who is awake." It's another biblical term for angelic beings, but it's also a title. These are angelic beings who were part of God's divine council.

That's right, I said "divine council." I know some might be thinking, "Wait a minute! Why does God need a council? Isn't that polytheistic? Doesn't that mirror Canaanite religion with El and his divine council?" Is the "God of Israel" a copycat or something?

Far from promoting polytheism, the divine council concept affirms monotheism. In Jewish tradition, God is utterly unique—*Ein Sof*, the Infinite. But He often works through intermediaries—angelic beings and humans, too.

Maimonides discusses various classes and hierarchies of angels in his Mishneh Torah. And Psalm 82 doesn't weaken monotheism; it rebukes divine beings for failing in their roles. They're not rivals; they are accountable functionaries.

As the late biblical scholar Dr. Michael Heiser explained in his book, *The Unseen Realm*, biblical writers weren't polytheists, but they did believe in a multiplicity of spiritual beings under God's authority.[182] The divine council model is not borrowed from Canaanite religion, it's inherited from a shared ancient-Semitic worldview, then theologically reframed.

Dr. John H. Walton, a prominent scholar of the Hebrew Scriptures and expert in ancient Near Eastern (ANE) backgrounds, expounded on this idea, noting the Bible speaks in the cultural language of the ancient Near East, but reveals a radically different theology. The concepts may feel similar on the surface—divine councils, temples, cosmic battles—but the theological core is uniquely and unmistakably biblical.[183]

Now, going back to the Watchers—they're first mentioned in the book of Daniel, where they are portrayed as divine messengers executing God's decrees. Rabbi Aryeh Kaplan, a respected Orthodox Jewish scholar, explains in his commentary on Ezekiel:

> The angels are arranged in a hierarchy, with some having authority over others. This is alluded to in Daniel's vision, where he sees "Watchers" and "Holy Ones" decreeing judgment (Daniel 4:14).[184]

But they didn't just have authority over other angels. They also had power over nations or perhaps ethnicities of humanity. As Dr. Heiser has pointed out, "the number of nations disinherited by Yahweh at the judgment of Babel was seventy."[185]

He continued:

> That number is telling. Israel's nearest religious competition, the worship of El, Baal, and Asherah at Ugarit and in Canaan, held that their divine council had seventy sons. When Yahweh disinherited the nations and allotted them to the sons of God, a theological gauntlet was thrown down:
>
> > Yahweh *alone* commands the nations and their gods.
> > Other gods serve *Him*.
>
> The Exodus account follows that theological punch in the nose with another: Not only is Israel Yahweh's son and portion on Earth, but it is to be governed by a special group of *seventy* under Moses and, later, the Israelite king who is Yahweh's enthroned son.[186]

Shortly after crossing through the sea, Moses and Israel encountered Jethro. The account is recorded in Exodus 18. Seeing the throngs, Jethro advises Moses to select men to help him govern the people. No number is given in that passage, but later, in Exodus 24, we read:

> Then He said to Moses, "Come up to the LORD, you and Aaron, Nadab and Abihu, and seventy of the elders of Israel, and you shall worship at a distance.
>
> Moses alone, however, shall approach the LORD, but they shall not approach, nor shall the people come up with him. (Exodus 24:1–2)

וְאֶל־מֹשֶׁה אָמַר עֲלֵה אֶל־יְהוָה אַתָּה וְאַהֲרֹן נָדָב וַאֲבִיהוּא וְשִׁבְעִים מִזִּקְנֵי יִשְׂרָאֵל; וְהִשְׁתַּחֲוִיתֶם מֵרָחֹק:

ANGELS: *SHALOM ALEICHEM*

וְנִגַּשׁ מֹשֶׁה לְבַדּוֹ אֶל־יְהוָה וְהֵם לֹא יִגָּשׁוּ; וְהָעָם לֹא יַעֲלוּ עִמּוֹ:

Also consider the following:

Then Moses went up with Aaron, Nadab and Abihu, and seventy of the elders of Israel, and they saw the God of Israel; and under His feet there appeared to be a pavement of sapphire, as clear as the sky itself. (Exodus 24:9–10)

וַיַּעַל מֹשֶׁה וְאַהֲרֹן נָדָב וַאֲבִיהוּא וְשִׁבְעִים מִזִּקְנֵי יִשְׂרָאֵל:

וַיִּרְאוּ אֵת אֱלֹהֵי יִשְׂרָאֵל וְתַחַת רַגְלָיו כְּמַעֲשֵׂה לִבְנַת הַסַּפִּיר וּכְעֶצֶם הַשָּׁמַיִם לָטֹהַר:

The wording suggests these seventy elders were drawn from a larger group—as were the *elohim* of Yahweh's council, who were given different ranks and tasks. Not every member of the divine council has equal rank. The sons of God with authority over the nations were assigned that role, but at least some became corrupt and are the object of the sentencing of Psalm 82.[187]

Psalm 82:1–7, A psalm of Asaph:

God takes His position in His assembly;
He judges in the midst of the gods.

How long will you judge unjustly
And show partiality to the wicked? Selah
Vindicate the weak and fatherless;
Do justice to the afflicted and destitute.
Rescue the weak and needy;
Save them from the hand of the wicked.
They do not know nor do they understand;
They walk around in darkness;
All the foundations of the earth are shaken.

I said, "You are gods,
And all of you are sons of the Most High.

Nevertheless you will die like men,
And fall like one of the princes.

מִזְמוֹר לְאָסָף אֱלֹהִים נִצָּב בַּעֲדַת־אֵל בְּקֶרֶב אֱלֹהִים יִשְׁפֹּט׃

עַד־מָתַי תִּשְׁפְּטוּ־עָוֶל וּפְנֵי רְשָׁעִים תִּשְׂאוּ־סֶלָה׃

שִׁפְטוּ־דַל וְיָתוֹם עָנִי וָרָשׁ הַצְדִּיקוּ׃

פַּלְּטוּ־דַל וְאֶבְיוֹן מִיַּד רְשָׁעִים הַצִּילוּ׃

לֹא יָדְעוּ וְלֹא יָבִינוּ בַּחֲשֵׁכָה יִתְהַלָּכוּ יִמּוֹטוּ כָּל־מוֹסְדֵי אָרֶץ׃

אֲנִי־אָמַרְתִּי אֱלֹהִים אַתֶּם וּבְנֵי עֶלְיוֹן כֻּלְּכֶם"

אָכֵן כְּאָדָם תְּמוּתוּן וּכְאַחַד הַשָּׂרִים תִּפֹּלוּ׃

Lest anyone doubt the psalm is speaking of angels who are being castigated, rebuked, and sentenced by the Most High (the God of Israel), the Jewish sage Ibn Ezra states the following, setting the context from verse 1:

> In the midst of the gods—these are the angels, who are called "gods" and the heavenly host, the sons of God, for it is through the angels that all the judgments of God are executed on earth.
>
> בקרב אלהים - הם המלאכים שהם האלהים וצבא השמים בני האלהים, כי על ידי המלאכים הם כל משפט להים בארץ.

Additionally, he wrote:

> And some say that "in the midst of gods" is like [the verse,] "You shall not curse a judge (elohim)" (Exodus 22:27). The meaning is: because He (God) is among them, they must be careful not to judge unjustly.[188]

ויש אומרים: כי בקרב אלהים—כמו: אלהים לא תקלל. והטעם: כי הוא בקרבם ויש להם לישמר שלא ישפטו עול.

Note that we're not to curse the angels (or one another); indeed, even holy angels don't curse each other—or even the fallen!
Jude 1:9:

But Michael the archangel, when he disputed with the devil and argued about the body of Moses, did not dare pronounce against him a railing judgment, but said, "The Lord rebuke you!"

Dr. Heiser continued:

The correspondences are deliberate. The seventy nations were placed under the dominion of lesser gods in the wake of Yahweh's judgment of the nations at the Tower of Babel.

Yahweh's own kingdom is structured with a single leader (Moses for now), with whom he speaks directly, and a council of seventy. Historically, this leadership structure would continue into Jesus' day, as the Jewish Sanhedrin, led by the high priest, numbered seventy.[189]

The Watchers were high-ranking members of God's divine council—seventy who were given the special responsibility of guiding and guarding the seventy nations of humanity that dispersed from the Tower of Babel fiasco.

They were supposed to "watch over" humanity. And then some—perhaps all except Michael—snapped. (Recall that Michael is referred to as "your prince," referring to Israel's "watcher," or guardian prince, in Daniel 10:21.)

Daniel's Snippet

In the canonical book of Daniel, the Watchers appear briefly, almost innocuously. Nebuchadnezzar's dream features a "holy one" descending from Heaven to pronounce divine judgment.

Daniel 4:13–23:

I was looking in the visions in my mind as I lay on my bed, and behold, an angelic watcher, a holy one, descended from heaven.

> He shouted out and spoke as follows:
> "Chop down the tree and cut off its branches,
> Shake off its foliage and scatter its fruit;
> Let the animals flee from under it
> And the birds from its branches.
> Yet leave the stump with its roots in the ground,
> But with a band of iron and bronze around it
> In the new grass of the field;
> And let him be drenched with the dew of heaven,
> And let]him share with the animals in the grass of the earth.
> Let his mind change from that of a human
> And let an animal's mind be given to him,
> And let seven periods of time pass over him.
> This sentence is by the decree of the angelic watchers,
> And the decision is a command of the holy ones,
> In order that the living may know
> That the Most High is ruler over the realm of mankind,
> And He grants it to whomever He wishes
> And sets over it the lowliest of people."

This is the dream that I, King Nebuchadnezzar, have seen. Now you, Belteshazzar, tell me its interpretation, since none of the wise men of my kingdom is able to make known to me the interpretation; but you are able, because a spirit of the holy gods is in you.

חָזֵה הֲוֵית בְּחֶזְוֵי רֵאשִׁי עַל־מִשְׁכְּבִי וַאֲלוּ עִיר וְקַדִּישׁ מִן־שְׁמַיָּא נָחִת:

קָרֵא בְחַיִל וְכֵן אָמַר גֹּדּוּ אִילָנָא וְקַצִּצוּ עַנְפוֹהִי אַתַּרוּ עָפְיֵהּ וּבַדַּרוּ אִנְבֵּהּ תְּנֻד חֵיוְתָא מִן־תַּחְתּוֹהִי וְצִפְּרַיָּא מִן־עַנְפוֹהִי:

בְּרַם עִקַּר שָׁרְשׁוֹהִי בְּאַרְעָא שְׁבֻקוּ וּבֶאֱסוּר דִּי־פַרְזֶל וּנְחָשׁ בְּדִתְאָא דִּי בָרָא וּבְטַל שְׁמַיָּא יִצְטַבַּע וְעִם־חֵיוְתָא חֲלָקֵהּ בַּעֲשַׂב אַרְעָא:

לִבְבֵהּ מִן־[אֲנָשָׁא] (אנושא) יְשַׁנּוֹן וּלְבַב חֵיוָה יִתְיְהִב לֵהּ וְשִׁבְעָה עִדָּנִין יַחְלְפוּן עֲלוֹהִי:

בִּגְזֵרַת עִירִין פִּתְגָמָא וּמֵאמַר קַדִּישִׁין שְׁאֵלְתָא עַד־דִּבְרַת דִּי יִנְדְּעוּן חַיַּיָּא דִּי־שַׁלִּיט (עליא) [עִלָּאָה] בְּמַלְכוּת (אנושא) [אֲנָשָׁא] וּלְמַן־דִּי יִצְבֵּא יִתְּנִנַּהּ וּשְׁפַל אֲנָשִׁים יְקִים (עליה) [עֲלַהּ]:

דְּנָה חֶלְמָא חֲזֵית אֲנָה מַלְכָּא נְבוּכַדְנֶצַּר (ואנתה) [וְאַנְתְּ] בֵּלְטְשַׁאצַּר פִּשְׁרֵא אֱמַר כָּל־קֳבֵל דִּי | כָּל־חַכִּימֵי מַלְכוּתִי לָא־יָכְלִין פִּשְׁרָא לְהוֹדָעֻתַנִי (ואנתה) [וְאַנְתְּ] כָּהֵל דִּי רוּחַ־אֱלָהִין קַדִּישִׁין בָּךְ:

אֱדַיִן דָּנִיֵּאל דִּי־שְׁמֵהּ בֵּלְטְשַׁאצַּר אֶשְׁתּוֹמַם כְּשָׁעָה חֲדָה וְרַעְיֹנֹהִי יְבַהֲלֻנֵּהּ עָנֵה מַלְכָּא וְאָמַר בֵּלְטְשַׁאצַּר חֶלְמָא וּפִשְׁרֵא אַל־יְבַהֲלָךְ עָנֵה בֵלְטְשַׁאצַּר וְאָמַר מָרִאי חֶלְמָא (לשנאיד) [לְשָׂנְאָךְ] וּפִשְׁרֵהּ (לעריד) [לְעָרָךְ]:

אִילָנָא דִּי חֲזַיְתָ דִּי רְבָה וּתְקִף וְרוּמֵהּ יִמְטֵא לִשְׁמַיָּא וַחֲזוֹתֵהּ לְכָל־אַרְעָא:

וְעָפְיֵהּ שַׁפִּיר וְאִנְבֵּהּ שַׂגִּיא וּמָזוֹן לְכֹלָּא־בֵהּ תְּחֹתוֹהִי תְּדוּר חֵיוַת בָּרָא וּבְעַנְפוֹהִי יִשְׁכְּנָן צִפֲּרֵי שְׁמַיָּא:

(אנתה) [אַנְתְּ־]הוּא מַלְכָּא דִּי (רבית) [רְבַת] וּתְקֵפְתְּ וּרְבוּתָךְ רְבָת וּמְטָת לִשְׁמַיָּא וְשָׁלְטָנָךְ לְסוֹף אַרְעָא:

וְדִי חֲזָה מַלְכָּא עִיר וְקַדִּישׁ נָחִת | מִן־שְׁמַיָּא וְאָמַר גֹּדּוּ אִילָנָא וְחַבְּלוּהִי בְּרַם עִקַּר שָׁרְשׁוֹהִי בְּאַרְעָא שְׁבֻקוּ וּבֶאֱסוּר דִּי־פַרְזֶל וּנְחָשׁ בְּדִתְאָא דִּי בָרָא וּבְטַל שְׁמַיָּא יִצְטַבַּע וְעִם־חֵיוַת בָּרָא חֲלָקֵהּ עַד דִּי־שִׁבְעָה עִדָּנִין יַחְלְפוּן עֲלוֹהִי:

Daniel Interprets the Vision

Then Daniel, whose name is Belteshazzar, was appalled for a while as his thoughts alarmed him. The king responded and said, "Belteshazzar, do not let the dream or its interpretation alarm you." Belteshazzar replied, "My lord, if only the dream applied to those who hate you, and its interpretation to your adversaries!

The tree that you saw, which became large and grew strong, whose height reached to the sky and was visible to all the earth, and whose foliage was beautiful and its fruit abundant, and in which was food for all, under which the animals of the field lived and in whose branches the birds of the sky settled—

it is you, O king; for you have become great and grown strong, and your majesty has become great and reached to the sky, and your dominion to the end of the earth.

And in that the king saw an angelic watcher, a holy one, descending from heaven and saying, "Chop down the tree and destroy it; yet leave the stump with its roots in the ground, but with a band of iron and bronze around it in the new grass of the field, let him be drenched with the dew of heaven, and let him share with the animals of the field until seven periods of time pass over him."

Some might argue that because the Watchers are only mentioned once in canonical Scripture—and in symbolic, dreamlike language—anything that follows from here on out is only speculative.

While it's true that Daniel mentions the Watchers only briefly, we must remember a critical hermeneutical principle: Frequency doesn't determine importance.

Consider Melchizedek, who appears only twice in the Hebrew Scriptures (Genesis 14 and Psalm 110), yet becomes central in the book of Hebrews as a Christological archetype.[190,191]

As the late Chuck Missler, an American Christian Bible teacher, engineer, and founder of the Koinonia House ministry, often said in his Bible studies and lectures, "When you come across something weird in the Bible, it's probably important—and worth digging into."[192]

That principle certainly applies here. The mention of a "Watcher, a holy one," descending from Heaven (Daniel 4) isn't poetic fluff—it's a breadcrumb. And like all breadcrumbs in Scripture, it leads to something deeper.

Dr. Heiser stated:

Here we see that the ultimate authority behind the decree is God, the Most High, and yet the watcher who delivered the decree in verse 17, said, "the sentence is by decree of the watchers." Both God and his divine agents were involved in the decision.[193]

Heiser goes on to explain that "the Most High is sovereign." Period. No committees. No votes. No "Team Heaven" collaboration. It's a singular declaration of who's running the show. But then things get a little more interesting.

The phrase "heaven is sovereign" shows up. That might sound poetic to modern ears, but there's more going on than meets the eye. In the Aramaic, "heaven" is plural—*shemayim*—and it comes with a plural verb.

That's not a typo. It's intentional. It points to what scholars call the *divine council,* as I mentioned before—a heavenly assembly of angelic beings who work under God's authority.

Think of it this way: God isn't micromanaging every pixel of the universe by Himself. He has representatives doing His work both in Heaven and on Earth. He gives the commands; they carry them out. That part's clear as crystal.

But here's the twist most people miss: God doesn't script every step. He sets the destination—the *end*—but often leaves the *means* to His representatives. In other words, free will isn't just a human thing. It's built into the structure of how God governs.

His "imagers," as Heiser called them, divine or human, can make real decisions within the boundaries of His plan. And it's the key to understanding Eden.

Wait! I can almost hear some readers screaming right now: "Angels don't have free will. Full stop. We're taught that in seminary, we hear it from the pulpit! *Only* humans, made in the image of God, have free will!"

If that's you, I understand where you're coming from. But what you're asserting is not biblical in the slightest. Scripture itself attests that not all angels remained obedient. The serpent in Eden (Genesis 3), the "sons of God" in Genesis 6, and the dragon sweeping stars from Heaven in Revelation 12 all suggest celestial rebellion.

Unless you think God ordered Satan to become Satan and drag a third of Heaven to Hell, well, free will is the only viable explanation.

God's representatives, both heavenly and earthly, are not puppets. They are partners. And we can see that here on Earth—as it was in Heaven—some, tragically, defect.

Genesis 3 wasn't a setup. The serpent didn't *have* to rebel. Adam and Eve weren't *forced* to disobey. God didn't need that rebellion to pull off some master plan. He foresaw the risk of giving His imagers agency, and He allowed it.

Why?

Because a real image-bearer, a real representative, isn't a Pinocchio dancing on strings. Angels aren't out there wishing they were real boys. They are real beings with real agency. Without agency, there's no moral accountability. The Watchers sinned precisely *because* they had the freedom to reject God's command. For that, they're judged (2 Peter 2:4, Jude 1:6).[194, 195]

God rules, no question. But He delegates. He empowers. And He takes the risk of letting His representatives choose how to carry out His will.

That's not weakness. That's God having overall confidence in His creations. That's sovereignty with teeth. And when His creations mess up, God's got confidence in Himself.

He is the ultimate authority, and the ultimate in responsibility. The buck stops with Him, which is precisely why He came up with a plan to redeem all of creation by becoming that redemption Himself.

In any case, the references to Watchers in the book of Daniel are only the tip of the iceberg.

The Apocrypha

The Book of Enoch (really Enoch 1)—conveniently booted from your Bible by both Jewish and Christian theologians (but not all of them)—gives us a more detailed report.

Two hundred angels, led by Samyaza (also spelled "Semjaza," "Shemyaza," or "Samyaza"), go AWOL. They don't just break rank, they set up shop on Mount Hermon, hook up with human women, and father the Nephilim. They were freaks of nature who tore the world apart.

But the real crime wasn't just unsanctioned interspecies dating. It was the data dump.

These angels handed over forbidden knowledge—what was likely everyday stuff in their own realm, maybe even trivial or toy-like by their standards. Think of it like American soldiers trading cheap trinkets to Native Americans in exchange for land—items that meant little to the giver but seemed like treasures to those receiving them.

In the same way, these celestial beings gave a bit of basic technological knowledge and philosophical concepts foreign to humanity—which was still young, innocent by comparison, and new to the cosmic stage. These Watchers did it knowing full well this knowledge would be corrupted and misused and would ultimately lead to the destruction of the very people they gave it to.

Interestingly, while Enoch 1 says "only" two hundred angels descended on Mount Hermon, Enoch 2 clarifies the number. It was two hundred *myriads*—or two million. If true, that's not a small incursion into humanity's domain. It's not even a vanguard.

It's a full-on invasion.

While I get it that some think the Book of Enoch is noncanonical and therefore uninspired and irrelevant, I don't entirely agree. At least, I don't agree as to Enoch 1. As we move on, you'll come to see why. For the moment, let me say that even if one rejects the Book of Enoch (especially Enoch 1) as having been inspired, it is historically indispensable. Why? Because the New Testament authors were familiar with it. In fact, they quoted from it word-for-word.

Jude 1:14–15:

> It was also about these people that Enoch, in the seventh generation from Adam, prophesied, saying, "Behold, the Lord has come with many thousands of His holy ones, to execute judgment upon all, and to convict all the ungodly of all their ungodly deeds which they have done in an ungodly way, and of all the harsh things which ungodly sinners have spoken against Him."

Enoch 1:9:

> And behold! He cometh with ten thousands of His holy ones to execute judgement upon all, and to destroy all the ungodly: And to convict all flesh of all the works of their ungodliness which they have ungodly committed, and of all the hard things which ungodly sinners have spoken against Him.[196]

Even if you argue that no serious theologian would build doctrine solely on Enoch, the truth is it echoes and amplifies what's already hinted at in Genesis, Daniel, and Psalms. Because of that, it's also a powerful interpretive lens—one the ancients understood, even if we have forgotten.

Moreover, early Church Fathers like Tertullian, Irenaeus, and Justin Martyr affirmed its value. And at Qumran, fragments of Enoch were discovered alongside canonical scrolls, suggesting its respected status in Second-Temple Judaism.

In other words, if it's just religious fan fiction, no different than Marvel's *Avengers*, then why was it treated as sacred literature by some of the earliest Jewish communities, quoted directly in the New Testament, respected by early Church Fathers, is still considered canon by the Ethiopian Church, and preserved among the Dead Sea Scrolls alongside Isaiah and the Torah?

I don't believe you can just wave off the Book of Enoch as being irrelevant without also indicting the apostolic witness. If Jude saw fit to cite Enoch (verbatim) as prophetic, then either Jude was wrong (which undermines Scripture itself) or Enoch had a place in the theological imagination of the Early Church that deserves to be understood and reckoned with.

Not just that, but Jesus calls Himself "the Son of Man"—a title He uses twenty-eight times in the Gospel of Matthew. This count is based on the most widely accepted critical Greek texts (such as the Nestle-Aland edition), which exclude Matthew 18:11 due to its absence in early manuscripts.

Jesus also uses this title fourteen times in Mark, twenty-five times in Luke, and eleven times in the Gospel of John.

In contrast, the Hebrew Scriptures never use the term "the Son of Man" as a title—especially a messianic one—although Daniel 7:13–14 provides the symbolic seed for its later development into that.

Indeed, the phrase "Son of Man" (*bar enash*) in Daniel 7 is deliberately symbolic. It describes a humanlike, exalted figure who approaches the Ancient of Days and receives eternal dominion. This is the seed of the Messianic title Jesus later claims for Himself. But during the Second-Temple period, that image wasn't locked in. It was developing—and Enoch's authors explored it through apocalyptic imagination, not unlike how modern theologians speculate about end-times scenarios today.

Daniel 7:13–14:

I kept looking in the night visions, And behold, with the clouds of heaven One like a son of man was coming, And He came up to the Ancient of Days And was presented before Him.

And to Him was given dominion, honor, and a kingdom, So that all the peoples, nations, and populations of all languages Might serve Him.

His dominion is an everlasting dominion Which will not pass away; And His kingdom is one Which will not be destroyed.

חָזֵה הֲוֵית בְּחֶזְוֵי לֵילְיָא וַאֲרוּ עִם־עֲנָנֵי שְׁמַיָּא כְּבַר אֱנָשׁ אָתֵה הֲוָא וְעַד־עַתִּיק יוֹמַיָּא מְטָה וּקְדָמוֹהִי הַקְרְבוּהִי:

וְלֵהּ יְהִב שָׁלְטָן וִיקָר וּמַלְכוּ וְכֹל עַמְמַיָּא אֻמַּיָּא וְלִשָּׁנַיָּא לֵהּ יִפְלְחוּן שָׁלְטָנֵהּ שָׁלְטָן עָלַם דִּי־לָא יֶעְדֵּה וּמַלְכוּתֵהּ דִּי־לָא תִתְחַבַּל:

Meanwhile, the Book of Enoch reinterpreted Daniel's vision messianically, which Jesus understood and applied to Himself (which means Jesus was familiar with the Book of Enoch, too).

Consider the following: The Similitudes of Enoch present the Son of Man as a preexistent, divine figure who executes judgment and rules eternally.

1 Enoch 48:2–7:

> At that hour, that Son of Man was named in the presence of the Lord of Spirits, and his name before the Head of Days.
>
> Even before the sun and the constellations were created, before the stars of heaven were made, his name was named before the Lord of Spirits.
>
> He will be a staff to the righteous, that they may lean on him and not fall; he will be the light of the nations, and the hope of those who grieve in their hearts.
>
> All who dwell on earth will fall down and worship before him, and they will glorify and bless and sing hymns to the name of the Lord of Spirits.
>
> For this purpose he was chosen and hidden before Him before the world was created, and forever.

One final objection Christians especially may have is the fact that the Book of Enoch eventually names the Son of Man as Enoch himself. On the surface, that may sound like a theological land mine, particularly to Christians who see that title as belonging uniquely to Jesus. But the solution isn't to throw Enoch in the heresy bin. The solution is to look at what that development reveals about the Second-Temple Jewish worldview that shaped the New Testament.

Here, Enoch's identification with the Son of Man is theological poetry, not dogmatic fact. The text isn't saying "Enoch is the Messiah"; rather, it dramatizes the idea that the human mediator—who stands between Heaven and Earth—reveals the Son of Man, embodies His message, and is caught up into His glory.

Jesus didn't inherit a messianic title from Enoch like a borrowed costume. He claimed the fulfillment of what that title pointed toward in Daniel and what it evolved into during Second-Temple expectation. He took a title that had been filled with apocalyptic anticipation, in part shaped by the Book of Enoch, then applied it to Himself in real-time, in flesh and blood.

In doing so, He wasn't affirming every speculative thread woven around the title. He was seizing its true meaning and declaring: "I am the One Daniel saw. I am the One Enoch's visions longed for. I am not a symbolic stand-in; I'm the real thing."

There's more to that story—but we'll get there shortly.

Other Apocryphal Texts

The Book of Jubilees also references the Watchers (Jubilees 4:15, 5:1), as does the Book of Giants, which further elaborates on the story of the Watchers and their offspring.[197]

The Dead Sea Scrolls

When the Dead Sea Scrolls were discovered in 1947, they included texts like the Damascus Document, which framed the Watchers as the "first sinners," their rebellion mirroring humanity's struggle with temptation. The Qumran community saw themselves as spiritual warriors battling the same corrupting forces.

Yet, as scholar Géza Vermes noted, access to these scrolls was monopolized for decades by a small academic cadre. Key fragments detailing the Watchers—and their theological implications—remained hidden from public view.

The parallels are striking: Just as ancient authorities scrubbed the Watchers from official texts, modern institutions delayed their rediscovery.[198]

Coded Clues in the New Testament

I already mentioned that Jude quotes the book of Enoch verbatim, but the New Testament never names the Watchers outright. Still, traces linger.

Let's talk about Paul's infamous curve ball in 1 Corinthians 11:10—the one where he says a woman should have "authority on her head… *because of the angels.*"[199] Most modern scholars read that and feel like they're going to break out in hives. They scratch their heads, write long, vague commentaries, and pretend it's just symbolic or cultural fluff.

That's Paul and Christians getting all patriarchal and misogynistic!

But when you know what Paul knew—specifically, the Watcher narrative from 1 Enoch—it's not cryptic, patriarchal, or misogynistic at all. It's tactical, and it's protective.

You see, Tertullian, one of the early Church Fathers, had zero confusion about this. He flat-out said the reason women should be veiled is because of the angels' lust.[200] That's just like back in Genesis 6, where we read that the "sons of God" (aka angels) couldn't keep their hands to themselves and went after human women.

That's not poetry, it's history. And Paul is warning about it. He's speaking to an audience that already knew what he was talking about. He's literally trying to prevent women from getting taken—perhaps against their will—by lustful angels who might think Earth girls are easy.

Jude 1:6 speaks of angels who "did not keep their own domain, but abandoned their proper dwelling."[201] This *exactly* matches the transgression of the 1 Enoch Watchers who left their native realm and descended to Earth. Jude doesn't cite the Hebrew Scriptures, and while he could have referenced Genesis 6, he didn't.

Surely you must wonder why, since both cover the same events. If Jude saw Genesis, but not Enoch 1, as canon, shouldn't he have just quoted Genesis and be done with it? Instead, he drew directly from an accepted Second-Temple-era narrative, one that greatly expands upon the Genesis 6 account. This tells us something important: The story of the Watchers wasn't fringe, heretical, or seen as fan fiction. It was part of the spiritual worldview of devout Jews, including the New Testament authors, during that period.

In Jude 1:9, we see another striking example: "Michael the archangel...disputed with the devil over the body of Moses." This isn't found in any canonical Scripture but comes from another extrabiblical Jewish text—The Assumption (or Testament) of Moses.[202, 203]

Again, Jude considers the story authoritative enough to incorporate it into Scripture without any qualification or apology. Why? Because it was part of the shared theological tradition of the Jewish world in which he lived and taught.

This brings us to an essential point: None of these references comes from the Hebrew Scriptures. They originate from Second-Temple Jewish literature and oral traditions—texts like 1 Enoch, Testament of Moses, and other writings from the intertestamental period that were widely known, read, and respected among devout Jews of that time.

Okay, sure. But what about Paul quoting Greek poets? Are we going to say the writings of pagan philosophers ought to have a place in canon, too—or at least a wee bit of respect from a biblical point of view? Isn't there little difference between quoting Enoch, the Assumption of Moses, and Epimenides?

Nice try. Let's kill that argument now.

Yes, Paul quoted Greek poets in Acts 17.[204] You know what else he was doing at the time? Evangelizing pagans. He used their cultural currency as a bridge—a rhetorical hook, not a theological foundation.

He wasn't saying Zeus was real. He was baiting the hook for the gospel.

But when Jude or Peter referenced Second-Temple literature, they weren't talking to Gentile philosophers. They were writing to people who were already steeped in Jewish tradition. They weren't quoting these texts for style points. They were pulling from well-established spiritual frameworks—not to prove a point to outsiders, but to explain supernatural truths their audience already recognized.

That's a massive difference.

So, no, Jude wasn't quoting Enoch like Paul quoted Epimenides and others. He was quoting it because it was part of the theological foundation his readers stood on.

The apostles weren't making this stuff up.

They weren't borrowing from pagan myth.

That tells us something vital: If inspired authors of Scripture saw fit to employ these ancient traditions to explain angelic rebellion, spiritual warfare, and divine justice…maybe we should, too.

Mysticism and Reinvention

Later Jewish mystics resurrected the Watchers in cryptic form. The Zohar, a cornerstone of Kabbalah, describes Shamsiel, a Watcher.

Now, before any critic tries to wave that away by saying, "But the

Zohar is a thirteenth-century text, and it's all mystical mumbo-jumbo!" let's address the elephant in the room.

Yes, it's late. No, it's not a fraud. The Zohar is a written crystallization of much earlier oral traditions and Midrashic motifs that circulated for centuries before being compiled. Many of its ideas mirror, and in some cases directly preserve, cosmic frameworks found in earlier texts like 1 Enoch, 2 Baruch, and the Dead Sea Scrolls.

Even if we don't grant the Zohar infallible status (I certainly don't), its descriptions line up shockingly well with older apocalyptic sources. In that sense, it's less "innovation" and more "continuity"—just with a medieval, mystical voice.

Dismissing it outright is like tossing out the Talmud because it wasn't written down until centuries after the Temple fell. Use it with discernment? Yes. Discard it entirely? That's lazy exegesis.

Now, according to the narrative, Shamsiel wasn't just another wing-flapping choirboy. He was the guardian of Eden—posted at the gates after Adam and Eve got booted. Eyes like fire. Cloaked in glory. One of the heavy hitters.

But, like so many before him, he got too close to humanity's mess. And he fell—hard.

The thing is, this angel didn't just fall into darkness. He became one of the princes that descended on Mount Hermon, the same rebel angels we meet in 1 Enoch. However, Shamsiel isn't only a villain in the Zohar. He's conflicted. (This is actually something I've wondered: If a third of the angels in Heaven fell, did some waver before ultimately making their choice?)

According to *Sha'ar HaGilgulim* ("Gate of Reincarnations"), his spark is still entangled in the souls of men. He isn't watching from the sidelines; he's embedded in us.[205]

Think that's weird? Welcome to Jewish mysticism, where the boundaries between angel and demon, teacher and traitor, are razor-thin.

Now enter the Book of Raziel—a medieval manual of angelic secrets. This thing doesn't play safe, either. It portrays some of the "fallen" Watchers—like Azael—as more than just corruptors. They're reluctant guides. Dangerous mentors. They give humanity forbidden knowledge not out of pure malice, but because in some twisted way they believe we might be able to handle it.

Sometimes they're right; most times they're not.

The Book of Raziel also features Raziel himself, an angel who delivers the secrets of creation to Adam after the Fall. He teaches astrology, divine language, and cosmic order.[206] And guess what? That kind of knowledge is exactly what the Watchers were condemned for sharing in 1 Enoch.

What's going on here?

The line between "fallen" and "faithful" isn't as clean as most people think. In Kabbalistic thought, there are no cardboard angels. Every being in Heaven's bureaucracy is layered, conflicted, and playing a high-stakes game with humanity's future. We don't get clean categories like "good angel" or "bad angel" standing on each shoulder.

However, an important caveat must be included when discussing the Watchers in the context of Jewish mystical texts. These depictions—as compelling as some may think they are—don't carry the same theological weight in Judaism as canonical Scripture (Tanakh) or even major apocryphal works like Enoch 1. The Zohar, *Sha'ar HaGilgulim*, and *Sefer Raziel HaMalakh* represent the mystic and esoteric fringes of Jewish tradition. They don't speak for the whole.

Yet they *do* reflect something vital: the ongoing evolution of angelology within Jewish thought. They show us how later sages wrestled with these celestial rebels, reinterpreting them as much more than cautionary tales—as complex, multidimensional figures whose legacies echo through hidden knowledge and cosmic tension.

As scholar Peter Schäfer details in *The Origins of Jewish Mysticism*, the enduring presence of these narratives involving angels who transgress or pose challenges suggests a continued engagement with themes of celestial influence and potential for negative actions within the divine and human spheres.[207]

And Gershom Scholem, the father of modern Kabbalah scholarship, argued that mystics often used these narratives not to challenge the canon but to explore its shadow.

So, take it seriously—but hold it loosely.

That said, let's not mince words. The "angelology" taught from polished pulpits and synagogue lecterns today is a neutered mythology. It's a hushed echo of the raw, terrifying truth pulsing through the pages of Scripture and ancient Jewish thought. We've been fed a spiritual nursery rhyme, one in which angels are fluttering spirits, polite emissaries, noncorporeal chess pieces moved by the divine hand. One in which rebellion in Heaven is a poetic metaphor, not a mutiny. One in which the sons of God are conveniently rebranded as "noble men" or "sons of Seth" to avoid confronting what the Hebrew actually says.

But the real narrative, the one preserved in the oldest canonical manuscripts, the Targums, the Midrash, the Pseudepigrapha, and the Dead Sea Scrolls—is far less tame. The *b'nei Elohim* were not human. They weren't metaphors. They were celestial princes—superintelligences with jurisdiction, agency, and authority. They sat in council. They executed judgment. Some descended to Earth. Some fathered hybrids. Some were punished.

And some will return (we'll get to that).

But don't take my word for it. I ask: What kind of incorporeal metaphor smacks Peter awake and drags him out of a Roman prison (Acts 12:7)? What kind of allegory eats Abraham's food (Genesis 18:8)? Are we really calling steak and bread "metaphors" now?[208, 209]

These aren't fringe views. They're ancient and rabbinically anchored. They're just *inconvenient* for certain theologians back in the day—and for many now—who wanted—and want—a sanitized, symbolic faith.

But the evidence isn't hiding. It's screaming.

From the book of Job—where the *b'nei Elohim* present themselves before God and Satan joins them (Job 1:6)—to Psalm 82—where God rebukes these divine beings, declaring: "You are gods…but you shall die like men"—the Hebrew Bible is relentless in its portrayal of a celestial hierarchy that is entirely fallible.

These beings have rank. They have roles. And some of them rebel.

The fallen Watchers weren't just wayward angels. They were a specialized strike force—a faction of a much larger rebellion. Not the whole war, but an opening gambit.

Their descent wasn't random. It was strategic. A boots-on-the-ground incursion into the human realm, designed to corrupt, infiltrate, and derail God's plan from the inside. These were operatives—rogue members of the divine council and their angelic underlings—sent to exploit a critical vulnerability within the nascent human race.

But they weren't alone.

Scripture and tradition point to other fallen angels—a vastly greater host—those who didn't follow their compatriots or "leave their former estate," beings like the princes of Greece and Persia (Daniel 10:13, 20) and beings like Satan—who held back, and who fought in the heavens:[210] "The stars fought from heaven" (Judges 5:20).[211]

The dragon of Revelation swept a third of the stars from Heaven (Revelation 12:4). That's not poetic flair, it's a cosmic statistic, a chilling indication that the fallen Watchers were just one division of a far more expansive insurrection.[212]

Two hundred myriads. That's what the Book of Enoch says landed on Mount Hermon. Do the math; as noted previously, that's two million angels. It's not metaphorical or symbolic. It's an invasion force.

But here's the real question: How many rebelled altogether?

We're told a third of the angels in Heaven fell (Revelation 12:4). But a third of *what number*? Thousands? Millions? Trillions? Heaven's army isn't a parish choir. It's not called the heavenly "host" for nothing. (And who says all angels are in the army? Humans aren't. Maybe there are countless angelic beings with all kinds of other vocations. We simply don't know.)

So, if two million Watchers hit Earth, what happened to the rest?

Seems like someone, somewhere—some high-ranking defector—wasn't going to blow the whole army on the first strike. No, he kept most of his forces in reserve. Smart move. Strategic.

You don't burn your A-team on the opening play unless you're planning to end the war in one move. Clearly, the angelic prince calling the shots didn't think he could do that. He knew this war wasn't ending at Mount Hermon.

Or maybe there's another angle.

Maybe the rest of the rebels didn't have the same weakness for human women. Maybe they weren't the seducers, they were the strategists.

Watching. Waiting. Using their brothers' weakness as a tactical tool to execute a portion of their strategy.

Or maybe a great many of the "angels" are so mind-bendingly different from humans that no physical attraction is possible. Maybe only one angelic species was chosen to make this specific incursion *because* of their similarity to humanity in appearance.

(We'll talk more about this later. Hang on ...)

Either way?

This wasn't a one-off rebellion. It was a campaign.

I once saw a sermon by Chuck Missler in which he made a bold claim: Satan was the first anti-Semite.

If you follow Missler's teaching, that checks out. He frequently pointed out that Haman's plot to wipe out the Jews in the book of Esther wasn't mere politics, it was Satan's ancient hatred bubbling up again.[213]

Missler didn't stop there. He connected the dots through history, tracing the anti-Semitism of Pharaoh, Hitler, and the other usual suspects back to a single source: Satan's obsession with derailing God's promises to Israel. Especially the promise of a coming Messiah—One who wouldn't just save Israel, but who would redeem all of humanity.

Honestly, Missler nailed it.

Here's the part most people miss: Satan wasn't just the first anti-Semite. He was also either the first among the angelic beings to be filled with rage at the thought that God was going to make a new being bearing His image or he was the first to take that rage and channel it into fuel for an interspecies genocidal plot—a celestial Hitler, if you will.

Either way, the whole of Hebrew literature makes it clear that destroying the human race became one of his primary objectives.

To the theistic Satanists and Luciferians out there who like to paint Satan as the groovy, misunderstood rebel and God as the tyrant, here's something you need to hear. In the immortal words of Commander Adama to President Adar, right before the Cylon genocide in the original *Battlestar Galactica*: "Forgive me, Mr. President, but they hate us with every fiber of their existence."[214]

These angels hate *you and me* with every fiber of their existence, and they're willing to say and do anything to get us to believe otherwise—as long as our destruction in the end is the outcome of belief in their benevolence.

And if Daniel, Revelation, the Dead Sea Scrolls, and more are right, then we're not dealing with myth; we're dealing with real nonhuman intelligences—ancient, conscious, and highly organized—whose infiltration into our dimensional space has had catastrophic consequences.

This is no ancient bedtime story.

This is war.

It's still unfolding.

And, to this day, we're living in the fallout.

CHAPTER FOUR

ANGELS: PART DEUX

The Bible must be interpreted in context, and that context isn't your own or that of your theological tradition; it is the context that produced it (ancient Near East / Mediterranean). Put another way, if you're letting your theological tradition filter the Bible to you, you aren't doing Bible study or exegesis.[215]

Dr. Michael Heiser
Heiser's Laws for Bible Study

The ancients didn't talk about the heavens like they're a symbolic art museum. They talked about it like the heavens are a populated empire.

The modern concept of angels is a reduction. A safe, neutered image—streamlined, commodified, and embalmed in metaphor—that it fits nicely into children's books, sermons, and, as already noted, sanitized theology.

But that image is a carcass. The real thing is stranger. Older. More terrifying. And far more diverse.

The ancient sources—Hebrew Scripture, Apocalyptic texts, the Dead Sea Scrolls, the New Testament, the Talmud, and the Zohar—testify with violent clarity: The heavens are populated, not uniform.

Of course, this raises some dangerous questions: How many kinds of "angels" are there? Do they all come in one model? (Humans don't.)

Are they mere variants on a theme? Are they the same type of creature that sometimes just happens to wear different appearances the way we wear different clothes?

Are their origins all the same? Do they have different languages, different nationalities? Do all angels have the same purpose? And what species did a third of them belong to when they fell?

Listen, most of what we've seen or heard was clipped from a single branch of the tree. The rest has been pruned. Censored. Flattened into symbol or metaphor by systems that couldn't tolerate the metaphysical sprawl of the divine realm. That's not conspiracy, it's coping, because once we let these beings off the leash, we can no longer control the narrative.

This chapter isn't about poetic symbolism; it's about taxonomy.

You've seen them named—Cherubim, Seraphim, Archangels, Malakhim, Hashmallim, Ishim, Chayot. But you've likely been told they're interchangeable—just different ranks for the same type of being, varying in function or poetic flair.

Wrong.

The ancient texts—from the Tanakh to the New Testament, from the Dead Sea Scrolls to the Talmud, from the Midrashim to the Zohar—paint a very different picture: a hierarchically structured, biologically diverse, and potentially interdimensional ecology of sentient celestial life.

Different forms. Different functions. Different species.

The real "angelology" isn't a lineup of soft-faced spirits lounging on clouds. It's a structured, perhaps not altogether militarized, species-rich ecosystem—more like a map of an interdimensional empire than anything we'd find in a Renaissance painting or a kitschy New Age crystal shop.

And you're about to see it laid bare: The Chayot HaKodesh, who carry the throne of God. The Hashmallim, beings of electric fire. The Erelim, the "valiant ones" referenced by Isaiah.

The job of the Seraphim—blazing serpentine, reptilian entities—is explicitly described in Isaiah 6, where we read that they purify Isaiah's lips with a burning coal from the altar. They serve as temple attendants, operating in direct proximity to the divine throne, mediating purification and glory.

The Cherubim, on the other hand, are colossal composite guardians—flashing between dimensions in Ezekiel 1 and 10, famously stationed at the gate of Eden in Genesis 3 to *prevent access to the tree of life*. They're not purifiers, they're *bodyguards, protectors,* and *warriors*. Functionally and narratively, the Cherubim's purposes are entirely different from those of the Seraphim. These two terms aren't literary metaphors of the same thing. They're distinct entities with nonoverlapping roles, appearances, and functions.

Then there are the Ishim, humanoid entities to whom we may have a distinct resemblance.

And, of course, the last species on the list: Adam, the composite, digital, Earth-made.

Each of these is distinct. Together, they form a seven-species roster of intelligent life described or hinted at in the Hebrew Scriptures.

Of these seven, only one was made in Eden. Only one has a body, an avatar, made from the same materials as this Earth.

The others came first.

So, we must ask: If a third of the angels in Heaven fell, who exactly went with them? What kind of beings defected? What ranks? What species?

If you're ready for an answer, keep reading.

This is where the Sunday school stories flatline and the real story begins.

Celestial Species and the Misnomer "Angels"

The orthodox narrative we've been fed about angels is but a tiny slice of a much vaster and more mind-bending reality. The religious texts and traditions speak of distinct categories of angelic beings—Cherubim, Seraphim, Archangels, and others—each playing specific heavenly roles.

Yet a more accurate term for these entities might be "celestial" rather than "angelic," as some (e.g., Cherubim and Seraphim) are never once called "angels" (מַלְאָכִים, *mal'akhim*) in the Hebrew Scriptures. This insight alone could be a glimpse of something profound. But for the sake of common usage, we'll continue to use the term "angels" in reference to these otherworldly entities.

Now, what if some of these "angels" represent not just ranks and classifications, anthropomorphic images, or symbolic creatures, but different lifeforms altogether—separate species of conscious, highly-advanced interdimensional entities?

The mind reels at such possibilities.

Before we dive headfirst into these so-called heretical rabbit holes, let's slam the brakes and set the stage. Without a clear-eyed look at who—and *what*—we're dealing with, the rest is just theological cosplay.

Crack open the ancient scrolls and here's what we'll find: a bizarre, blazing lineup of beings that make modern angel memes look like kindergarten scribbles.

But let's not get ahead of ourselves.

Back to God and the Divine Council

To briefly recap: In the Hebrew Bible, a captivating portrait emerges—a divine hierarchy presided over by God Himself, encompassing a celestial assembly known as the divine council. Within this assembly, lesser spiritual beings referred to as the "sons of God," "holy ones," "gods with a little *g*," and collectively as the "heavenly host," partake in the deliberations and directives of the Almighty.

As Dr. Michael Heiser wrote:

> Most discussions of what's around before creation omit the members of the heavenly host. That's unfortunate, because God and the sons of God, the divine family, are the first pieces of the mosaic.[216]

These celestial entities, though created by God and subservient to His supreme authority, evidently play a discernible role in divine governance, contributing to decisions and executing divine mandates.

References to this celestial congress abound in the Hebrew Scriptures. For example, Psalm 82:1 portrays God as seated "in the divine council; in the midst of the gods he holds judgment," while 1 Kings 22:19–23 recounts the vision of the prophet Micaiah, who beheld God amidst "the whole host of heaven."

Contrary to polytheistic interpretations prevalent in neighboring cultures, biblical tradition maintains that these beings, despite their exalted status, are fundamentally creatures under the dominion of the singular Almighty.

Timothy Alberino extends this discourse into provocative realms, envisioning these beings as a singular "Elder Race," a concept positing a remarkable shared likeness between these beings and humanity itself.[217]

Citing Genesis 1:26 as a foundational verse, he discerns a shared likeness between humankind and these celestial beings.

> Then God said, "Let Us make mankind in Our image, according to Our likeness; and let them rule over the fish of the sea and over the birds of the sky and over the livestock and over all the earth, and over every crawling thing that crawls on the earth."

וַיֹּאמֶר אֱלֹהִים נַעֲשֶׂה אָדָם בְּצַלְמֵנוּ כִּדְמוּתֵנוּ וְיִרְדּוּ בִדְגַת הַיָּם וּבְעוֹף הַשָּׁמַיִם וּבַבְּהֵמָה וּבְכָל־הָאָרֶץ וּבְכָל־הָרֶמֶשׂ הָרֹמֵשׂ עַל־הָאָרֶץ׃

Dr. Heiser stated:

> Many Bible readers note the plural pronouns (us; our) with curiosity. They might suggest that the plurals refer to the Trinity, but technical research in Hebrew grammar and exegesis has shown that the Trinity is not a coherent explanation.
>
> The solution is much more straightforward, one that an ancient Israelite would have readily discerned. What we have is a single person (God) addressing a group—the members of his divine council.[218]

Alberino expounds further, noting:

The decision to give life to mankind and appoint him regent of Planet Earth was the consensus of the divine council, but the act of creating him was the sole prerogative and power of the King who presided over it.

He goes on:

So manifold are the similarities between men and morning stars that, if not for the testimony of scripture, one might be tempted to conclude that we are in fact the same race.

It is clear, however, that the divine council resolved to create a new kind of creature to govern the earth, one that did not previously exist in the cosmos: mankind. Whereas mankind was fashioned from terrestrial clay, the physiology of the morning stars is of a different nature—a higher nature some might say.

Perhaps, in the same way that we were created from the substance of a planet, they were created from the substance of a star.[219]

Psalm 104:4:

Who makes His angels spirits, His ministers a flame of fire.

עֹשֶׂה מַלְאָכָיו רוּחוֹת מְשָׁרְתָיו אֵשׁ לֹהֵט:

Indeed, both Scripture and Jewish tradition vividly describe angels as being made of fire, light, or radiant energy. But who can say with certainty whether that's a description of fact or not?

Timothy Alberino doesn't tiptoe around the cosmic family tree. He drops a hammer: We're not the same *race* as the sons of God, but we're in the same *family*. Meaning? We carry the same imprint. The same divine DNA. We're cut from the same cloth—in other words, our species looks like each other—because, like them, we bear the image of the same Father.

Now, I don't agree with him in terms of appearance, but as far as the overall concept, I think he's right. He backs it with Scripture most people skim over without blinking—Luke's genealogy of Jesus. Track it backward and what do you get? Adam, "the son of God." Not metaphorically. Not poetically. *Literally*.[220]

Adam was a direct creation of YHVH (Yahweh) in the same way most believe angels are: He was a *son* of God. "Sons of God" doesn't just mean a direct creation; God has directly created lots of things and lots of creatures. He directly created the birds in the sky and the fish in the oceans in the beginning, for example. But they aren't His "sons."

While "sons of God" are direct creations in Scripture, the term is also a *title*. A legal, familial designation.

Alberino breaks it down plainly and simply: It's about *paternity* and *estate*. In other words, it's about who your Father is and what you're entitled to because of that relationship.

This title doesn't get downgraded in the New Testament; it gets expanded. Now, through Christ, sons of *Adam* can be upgraded into sons of *God*. Not by warm feelings. Not by church attendance. But by divine right, sealed by blood…and the promise delivered at the Resurrection.

Alberino then drops John 1:12–13 to drive his point home, just in case anyone's still daydreaming in the pews:

> But as many as received Him, to them He gave the right to become children of God, to those who believe in His name, who were born, not of blood, nor of the will of the flesh, nor of the will of a man, but of God.

Most pastors twist that passage into spiritual mush. They slap it on coffee mugs and preach it like we're already walking around as fully realized sons of God just because we believe.

Wrong.

Alberino calls this out for what it is: a butchered interpretation that ignores the original context. The verse is *crystal clear* if we don't let modern theology gut it: Being a "son of God" isn't automatic. It's not about going to church or saying a prayer. It's not about bloodlines, genetics, or human will.

John's not saying believers *are* sons of God. He's saying they're given *power*—the *right*—to *become* sons of God.

That transformation doesn't happen at conversion. It happens at the resurrection. That's the gospel's real hope: not floating off to Heaven with wings but stepping into a glorified estate that Adam lost and Yeshua (Jesus) of Nazareth reclaimed.

Most people can't handle that because it doesn't fit their soft, domesticated theology. But it's there, plain as day—for those with eyes to see and the spine to accept it.

Look, I'm with Timothy Alberino on nearly everything he lays out in *Birthright: The Coming Posthuman Apocalypse and the Usurpation of Adam's Dominion on Planet Earth*. The guy's done his homework, connecting dots many theologians are too scared or too domesticated to even touch, and his insights are sharp.

However, there are two areas where I part ways with his views, and I'll lay them out up front before unpacking them in more detail later.

First, I don't agree with the idea that the "Elder Race" is a *single* race. Or that the "image of God" means we physically *look* like God or the angels (as I mentioned previously). Yes, I agree angels share in the image of God, but boiling that down to physical form is too narrow. It clips the wings off something far more profound.

Second, I'm not on board with the idea that the biblical descriptions of Cherubim and Seraphim are just metaphor or symbolic iconography, which is something he argues for—and which we'll get to in a moment.

Of course, I'll be the first to admit I could be wrong.

None of us are cracking Heaven's master files just yet. Until we get the chance to ask God face-to-face or see the full scope of reality without the training wheels of human perception, we're all, to some degree, speculating.

That said, while Alberino's take is absolutely *on the table*—and worth serious consideration—I don't think it's the only game in town. Frankly, I don't think (regarding the two points I mentioned above) it's the *best* one either, especially not when we stack it up against the ever-growing pile of UFO sightings and the laundry list of "intergalactic species"

ANGELS: PART DEUX

people keep encountering. There's a deeper pattern here, and it doesn't fit neatly inside a single narrative about an "Elder Race."

Here's why.

Jewish and Christian Angelic Hierarchies

In Judaism, various hierarchies and rankings of angels are proposed by different theologians and scholars. The most well-known hierarchy is described by Maimonides in his work, *Mishneh Torah*, wherein he counts ten ranks of angels from highest to lowest:

1. Chayot Ha Kodesh
2. Ophanim
3. Erelim
4. Hashmallim
5. Seraphim
6. Malakhim (messengers or angels)
7. Elohim ("godly beings")
8. B'nei Elohim ("sons of God")
9. Cherubim
10. Ishim ("manlike beings")[221, 222]

Other Jewish texts propose slightly different hierarchies. The Zohar lists the ten ranks in a different order, with Malakim as the highest. Jacob Nazir's *Maseket Atzilut* has Seraphim at the top, followed by Ophanim, Cherubim, and seven other ranks in descending order.

Across some Christian traditions, a parallel list of celestial hierarchy emerged in which angels were organized into groups based on their roles and proximity to God. The most influential model was proposed by the fifth–sixth-century writer Pseudo-Dionysius the Areopagite, who described nine levels of angels grouped into three orders:

Highest orders:

1. Seraphim
2. Cherubim
3. Thrones

Middle orders:

1. Dominions
2. Virtues
3. Powers

Lowest orders:

1. Principalities
2. Archangels
3. Angels

In this hierarchy, Seraphim are the highest-ranking angels, who directly attend to God, while Angels and Archangels are the lowest; they interact most with humans.[223]

However, neither the Hebrew Bible nor the New Testament expounds upon a structured hierarchy of angels, diverging notably from the elaborate classifications upheld by later traditions. This is significant because instead of telling humans about ranks and classifications, they describe different individuals and species. These species are:

1. Chayot Ha Kodesh
2. Erelim
3. Hashmallim
4. Seraphim
5. Cherubim
6. Ishim ("manlike beings")

Notice I don't list the Ophanim as a rank or species like Rambam and the rest of the Jewish angelology charts do. Why? Because I don't think they were beings in the traditional sense.

This is because the Ophanim are Ezekiel's wheel intersecting a wheel (Ezekiel 1:16). If you read the *text* instead of overly pious, filtered *commentaries*, you'll see they might not be creatures at all. They look a whole lot more like interdimensional, angelic tech,[224] or possibly even a kind of divine transport—the same kind the living creatures and Cherubim were associated with. UFOs? UAPs? Call it what you want. Ezekiel just called it like he saw it.

Now, before anyone starts screaming "ancient aliens!"—slow down. Walk with me here.

Notable Christian researchers have made solid arguments against this view. They trace the "Ophanim = spaceship" idea back to Josef F. Blumrich's *The Spaceships of Ezekiel* (1974), which was part of that whole von Däniken wave.

Fair enough. The ancient aliens crowd absolutely hijacked Ezekiel's vision and tried to make it fit their ET narrative.

But here's where I break ranks. Based on their research, they conclude that Ezekiel's wheels within wheels were "a royal throne and its divine guardians"—"a common image a Mesopotamian living 2,600 years ago" would recognize.

They're not wrong. That symbolism was all over the ancient Near East. Ezekiel's audience would've known it cold. However, I think the ancient aliens crowd is right about one thing: Ezekiel did see a craft. They're just dead wrong about who built and operated it.

I don't believe you'd ever find some hip, pot-smoking, atheist alien—like Simon Pegg's 2011 film, *Paul*[25]—necessarily flying the thing. And it sure wasn't some bug-eyed Roswell gray joyriding through Jerusalem in a Zeta Reticulan party cruiser.

Look—if it looks like tech, moves like tech, and scares the living daylights out of prophets way back when *and* trained military pilots today like tech, maybe that's because it *is* tech.

The ancients didn't have a vocabulary for "gravitic propulsion" or "interdimensional vehicles." So, they described what they saw the only way they could—using the language of their day: wheels within wheels, fire, lightning, and radiant beings riding these things like divine chariots.

The lack of modern vocabulary doesn't make the account symbolic; it makes it even more literal.

Now let me ask this: Where, exactly, does Scripture say angels *don't* use technology?

I'll wait.

I mean, some think they're riding around in literal, fiery chariots! Isn't that technology?

Another question: Why would anyone assume that angels would travel around in the heavenly equivalent of a Bronze-Age—uber primitive—military vehicle? That's not theology, it's nostalgia dressed as orthodoxy.

Seriously, how is that any more theologically acceptable than what seems much more likely? An angelic, interdimensional group of incalculably ancient beings who existed before the Earth was created, using wildly advanced technology that seems pretty much like magic to humans even today.

Some might still argue, "Sure, the Bible doesn't *deny* angelic tech—but that doesn't mean we should imagine it, either. You're adding ideas to Scripture!"

But I'm not.

I'm *reading it plainly*, without the filters of post-Enlightenment theology. Ezekiel describes mobility, propulsion, structure, symmetry, lightning, sound, and coordinated movement. That's *specifically described function*. If that's not tech, what is?

The overwhelming evidence points to someone flying some kind of unidentified craft that can do things no human-made, advanced military air or spacecraft can do. So, we can choose one of three options:

1. Humans possess sci-fi levels of technology and nobody knows about it.
2. Intergalactic extraterrestrials are visiting Earth using sci-fi levels of technology.
3. Interdimensional beings are utilizing craft that have been interpreted as intergalactic spaceships.

Only one of these options doesn't collapse under its own weight.

If it's secret, black-budget, human tech, then we've had physics-breaking power for decades and no one's leaked it or provided verifiable,

ANGELS: PART DEUX

physical evidence of it. If it's intergalactic aliens, then we're inviting a theological framework upon which Scripture is (almost entirely) silent.

But if it's angelic, interdimensional beings using advanced divine tech, suddenly Ezekiel's vision isn't weird, it's *clear*...which brings us back to the actual structure of the unseen realm—and yes, the lists and charts.

Where Rambam, the Zohar, and Jacob Nazir get it wrong is the suggestion that *b'nei elohim*, *elohim*, and *malakhim* are separate classifications or ranks. They are not.

As detailed in the previous chapter, *b'nei elohim*, *elohim*, *malakhim*, and *kochavei boker* are not distinct species or fixed ranks. They're contextual titles—terms that reflect function, authority, or origin. The truth is that:

- Some or all are *b'nei elohim* (sons of God).
- Some or all are *elohim* (gods or divine beings).
- Some or all are *kochavei boker* (morning stars).
- Some may be *malakhim* (messengers).

These are titles. They are neither ranks nor species.

Interestingly, when we take the Ophanim away from the list of species, we're left with the realization that the Hebrew Scriptures describe seven sentient species—some or all of whom originally shared the "sons of God" moniker.

They are the following:

1. Chayot Ha Kodesh
2. Erelim
3. Hashmallim
4. Seraphim
5. Cherubim
6. Ishim ("manlike beings")
7. Adam (or *b'nei Adam*, sons of Adam)

Of these seven sentient species, *b'nei Adam* is the youngest—the baby of the bunch, the new kid on the block, the last to the party.

Now, I tend to think that, in terms of looks, Alberino may be partially right about humans bearing a physical resemblance to an Elder Race—and in this case, it would be to the Ishim.

Jewish tradition isn't alone in getting it wrong. Christian tradition drops the ball, too—especially with all that talk of "dominions, powers, and principalities" being angelic ranks.

They're not.

Alberino nails it here, explaining what these actually are. He begins by quoting Colossians 1:16: "for by Him all things were created, both in the heavens and on earth, visible and invisible, whether thrones, or dominions, or rulers, or authorities—all things have been created through Him and for Him."

Many evangelicals (especially) have butchered the phrase "principalities and powers." They hear it and instantly think "high-ranking demon." Sorry, no. That's theology on autopilot.

A principality isn't a *being*, it's a *realm*. It's a territory ruled by a prince. Could a being be tied to that realm? Sure, just like a throne can refer to both a seat and the one who sits on it. But the word itself isn't a synonym for "angel" or "demon."

It's political language.

That's Political Science 101 in the heavenly court. It's not about spooky beings with horns hiding in the shadows; it's about jurisdictions, cosmic boundaries, and seats of power that were *created* through Christ and for Christ.

Where I feel Alberino gets it wrong is in stating that:

> The chimeric depictions of cherubim (and seraphim) found throughout the scriptures are not meant to be taken as literal diagrams of their anatomy but iconographic portraits of their attributes.
>
> For example, Ezekiel's description of cherubim having four faces (human, lion, ox, eagle) and four wings and full of eyes all around conveys the attribute of vigilance.[226]

ANGELS: PART DEUX

It's possible that Alberino states this because some of the prominent rabbis, such as Saadia Gaon (892–942 CE), who came about four hundred years after the Talmud was compiled and redacted, discussed angels and heavenly beings in a nonliteral manner.

For instance, in his *Emunot ve-Deot*, Saadia Gaon discusses angels and heavenly beings. He posits that these descriptions should not be understood literally as physical beings with wings and humanlike forms, but rather as symbolic representations of spiritual entities or divine forces.[227] But Gaon was talking about *all* angels, not just Cherubim and Seraphim.

Likewise, but with vastly greater influence, Maimonides taught that biblical descriptions of all angels were not meant to be taken literally. In his view, any story in the Bible depicting angels with physical characteristics like wings or humanlike forms was a prophetic vision, dream, or metaphor—not a literal account.

One of the core tenets of Maimonides' philosophy, as expounded in his seminal work *The Guide for the Perplexed* (מורה נבוכים), was the rejection of anthropomorphic descriptions of God and angels, as well as his view that prophecy was a natural phenomenon, a product of the perfection of the human intellect rather than a divine gift bestowed upon select individuals.[228]

His departure from traditional Jewish thought didn't end there. His philosophical leanings also led him to reject many well-established Jewish traditions and beliefs, such as the notion of a physical resurrection of the dead, which he interpreted metaphorically. In fact, to get a sense of just how much Maimonides (Rambam) viewed anything not rooted in the physicality of this world with disdain, consider the following. Rabbi Gavin Michal notes:

> Rambam paints a dim picture of those who continue to believe in "Angels" in the usual or traditional sense. Notice his typically harsh language when he refers to those who harbour what he considers to be such common beliefs.

Rambam makes mention of the belief, upon which a whole rabbinic literature developed, that verses like Genesis (1:26), "Let us make man in our image," allude to G-d consulting with the heavenly hierarchy of 'angelic beings' before He created the universe."

ואין הכונה באלו המאמרים כולם מה שיחשבוהו הפתאיים שיש לו ית' דברים, או מחשבה או התבוננות אל שאלת עצה והעזר בדעת אחרים—ואיך יעזר הבורא במה שברא

These verses are not meant to be taken in the way ignorant people interpret them as G-d discussing with, or seeking the opinion of, the very (angelic) beings He is said to have created.

Here Rambam has no issues with referring to many important rabbinic dictums—that do insinuate such discussions with the "Angels" having taken place—as words of the foolish (*petaim*).[229]

With the above in mind, we can confidently speculate that if confronted with compelling firsthand accounts of UFO sightings and abductions, Rambam would likely have dismissed it all with a derisive snort, a disdainful scoff, and a sweeping gesture of dismissal.

To him, such phenomena would have been relegated to the realm of dreams, metaphors, or symbolic representations reflecting deeper aspects of the human psyche—stuff for the common, dirty, unwashed, ignorant masses.

However, it's worth acknowledging that while Rambam ascended to towering prominence in medieval Jewish intellectual circles and remains venerated in certain quarters even now—"From Moses our teacher (Moses of the Torah) to Moses our teacher (Maimonides), none arose like Moses!"—his doctrines bear the unmistakable imprint of Greek rationalism and Aristotelian philosophy.[230]

In other words, many of his ideas that became part of "normative Judaism" and remain ingrained in Orthodox Jewish thought today originated in non-Jewish, pagan views and philosophy. These ideas gained

ANGELS: PART DEUX

widespread acceptance by virtue of being articulated in Hebrew and dressed in the vestments of Jewish religious tradition—that, and because they offered a compelling synthesis for those seeking to reconcile traditional Judaism with the prevailing philosophical currents of the time, which were largely non-Jewish in origin.

Of course, this led to substantial deviations from Scripture and tradition, which in turn led to intense criticism from many of his rabbinic contemporaries like Rabbi Abraham ben David of Posquières (Ravad), Rabbi Yitzchak of Akko, and Rabbi Moses ben Nahman (Nachmanides, or Ramban).[231] They accused Maimonides of heresy and of distorting the fundamental principles of Judaism—and they were right to do so.

Ramban directly criticized Maimonides' assertion that all biblical stories with angels are nonliteral prophetic visions. He argued that the Torah clearly depicts angels like the three men who visited Abraham as having temporarily taken on physical bodies to interact with people in the real world. In fact, he considered Maimonides' figurative reading of these passages to be "forbidden to believe."[232]

The Kabbalists and other Jewish mystics also sharply differed with Maimonides. The mystical tradition embraced a complex hierarchy of angels who could take on corporeal form. The Zohar depicts angels not merely as abstract intelligences, but as real spiritual beings with will and personality.

Later critics, like R. Yaakov Emden in the eighteenth century, were so bothered by Maimonides' statements in the *Guide for the Perplexed* that they couldn't believe he actually wrote them. Emden called anyone who attributed these ideas to Maimonides a liar![233]

Christian views that interpret descriptions of Seraphim, Cherubim, and other angelic beings in a nonliteral, symbolic, or iconographic sense were influenced by the earlier philosophical and exegetical traditions that developed (mostly) after Rambam.

But here's the problem for the allegorical crowd: The actual biblical texts don't play along.

Take Isaiah 6. The Seraphim aren't described like dream figures or artistic metaphors. They *speak*, *fly*, and *act*. One takes a live coal from the altar and physically touches Isaiah's lips. That's not poetic symbolism. That's interaction.

Isaiah doesn't say, "I imagined a presence." He says he saw the Lord and was so overwhelmed that he cried out, "Woe is me, for I am undone!" That's not the reaction of a guy parsing metaphor; it's the panic of someone encountering an overpowering being face-to-face.

Also look at Ezekiel 1 and 10. The Cherubim appear with wheels full of eyes, multiple faces, and synchronized movement. These aren't abstract icons. They move, they lift, they transport the throne of God.

Ezekiel spends half the chapter trying to describe what he saw because it's so alien, not because it was so symbolic. And again, his response? Flat on his face.

Fear is a clue. Prophets don't faint when they encounter metaphors. They faint when they meet something *real*.

In any case, during the medieval period, Christian thinkers like Thomas Aquinas were deeply impacted by Maimonides philosophical works like *The Guide for the Perplexed*. Aquinas adopted a similar stance of interpreting biblical descriptions of God and angels in a nonliteral and metaphorical sense.

This interpretive approach of reading angelic accounts as icons or symbols representing spiritual truths, rather than as depictions of physical realities, became widely accepted in Christian theology and biblical hermeneutics going forward.[234, 235] However, from the evidence we have in the Hebrew Scriptures themselves, Second-Temple-era writings, the Dead Sea Scrolls, and the opinions recorded in the Talmud, the consensus before the medieval period leaned toward a literal interpretation of the physical descriptions of cherubim, seraphim, and other angelic beings.[236, 237, 238]

Additionally, just before Rambam, Rabbi Shlomo Yitzchaki (Rashi)—best known for his comprehensive commentaries on the Torah, Talmud, and other Jewish scriptures and writings (as mentioned earlier in this book) saw descriptions of Seraphim and Cherubim in a literal sense.[239] Plainly put, to the ancient Hebrews, these beings weren't literal entities but were entirely distinct from one another.

ANGELS: PART DEUX

Dr. Mika Ahuvia, an Israeli researcher, professor, and expert in classical Judaism, says it straight: "No Israelite would confuse the fierce winged-lion cherub in the temple with the snake-like seraph."[240]

This distinctions between celestial beings in early Jewish thought raise important questions about interpretive consistency—especially among modern researchers and theorists who reference ancient rabbinic traditions. For instance, Timothy Alberino argues that Meroz, mentioned in Judges 5:23, was understood by ancient rabbis to be a *planet*—an interpretation we'll explore in detail later. But if that's the case, and Alberino wants to ground his claims in rabbinic cosmology, then shouldn't he also interpret Seraphim and Cherubim in line with those same ancient sources, who saw them as literal, distinct beings?

And, let's be real: Reading them as actual, differentiated species doesn't just line up with ancient texts. It syncs disturbingly well with how certain extraterrestrial entities have been described for decades.

Coincidence? Maybe.

But it fits a little too well to ignore.

CHAPTER FIVE

ANGELS AND EXTRATERRESTRIALS

If we find ourselves to be but one among a million races, scattered through a million spheres, how can we, without absurd arrogance, believe ourselves to have been uniquely favored?[241]

C. S. Lewis, *Religion and Rocketry*, 1958

Humanity has always claimed encounters with "supernatural" beings. Call them "angels" if you're from a Judeo-Christian background. Add in the "jinn" if you lean toward Islam. The point is these beings aren't new.

In this chapter, we're going to dive deeper into some questions we touched on earlier, then discuss some truly thought-provoking issues.

As we've seen, angels show up in the oldest records we have—watching as humanity was created, delivering cryptic visions, fathering half-human hybrids, and ferrying prophets across different realms.

Then, something changed. In 1947, another kind of "otherworldly" presence took center stage: the "alien." Now, instead of prophets claiming to have had visitations from celestial beings, abductees are describing eerily similar encounters. Instead of fiery chariots and divine messengers, we get flying saucers and "visitors" of varying types conducting bizarre genetic experiments.

Just like angels, some of these entities claim they've been guiding humanity since the beginning, and according to many ufologists, sometimes we see them as benevolent teachers, other times as manipulative overlords.

That raises an uncomfortable question: What if angels and aliens are the same entity?

Think about it. Angels have always been described as nonhuman intelligences with powers beyond human understanding. They appear, they vanish, they manipulate matter, they defy time and space. Sounds an awful lot like what modern experiencers report when talking about certain extraterrestrials, doesn't it?

But before jumping to conclusions, let's break this down.

1. Are all so-called aliens actually angels?
2. I've already argued that angels are not all in the same species. Interestingly, this is extremely similar to modern reports describing multiple extraterrestrial, intergalactic alien types.
3. If some angels are masquerading as intergalactic (as opposed to interdimensional) extraterrestrials, what's their endgame?

ANGELS AND ALIENS: ONE AND THE SAME?

Short answer? Not necessarily.

It is critical to avoid assuming that angels and extraterrestrials must be either the exact same entity or completely unrelated beings.

Instead, it is more accurate to consider the possibility of a spectrum of entities ranging from purely physical, biological beings to purely spiritual or interdimensional ones, with various hybrids and intermediary forms existing in between.

For clarity:

▶ On one end of the spectrum, we may find physical extraterrestrials—biological lifeforms originating from other planets or star systems within our own material universe.

- Somewhere along the spectrum are hybrid beings or non-human biologics, which could include artificially created entities (e.g., physical clones) or genetic amalgamations resulting from interspecies interactions. This includes potential Nephilim-like beings or biological robots (e.g., androids or replicants) engineered by other species.
- Closer to the spiritual end, we encounter interdimensional entities, which include angels as traditionally understood within Judeo-Christian theology—beings that originate outside our dimensional space, but that can enter and manifest within it.

  Some so-called aliens could be angelic beings disguising themselves to push a particular narrative—one that conveniently strips the interdimensionality or supernatural nature out of the equation.

  Some angels may have once been physical beings who ruled over planets before transitioning into an interdimensional existence. Or maybe they always existed beyond our physical plane but still interacted with the "material" world.
- Finally, at the farthest end, there may be purely interdimensional, spiritual entities that exist entirely outside our dimensional space and that cannot manifest within it under any circumstances.

SMASHING THE "NO EVIDENCE" ARGUMENT TO BITS

Before diving into the deep end, let's address an underlying tension. The favorite go-to criticism against any discussion about extraterrestrials or interdimensional beings is the "lack of empirical evidence." Critics love to throw that argument out like it's a conversation-ender. If you can't slap it under a microscope or put it in a glass case, it must be fantasy, right?

Wrong.

The absence of physical proof doesn't disqualify the hypothesis, it just means we need a smarter approach, one that's willing to go beyond the narrow confines of hard science and include scriptural analysis, historical accounts, personal testimonies, and modern research. Real insight doesn't always fit neatly into a lab report.

1. Scriptural analysis as evidence: Sure, science likes to deal with hard evidence. But theology and religious studies? They deal in textual, anecdotal, and experiential evidence.

2. Historical accounts and testimonies: Let's not kid ourselves. Cultures around the world have been recording encounters with non-human entities for centuries. While these accounts are mostly anecdotal, the sheer consistency and recurrence across time and geography are staggering.

3. Modern testimonies and research: This isn't just ancient history. Researchers like Jacques Vallée, Timothy Alberino, and Karla Turner have emphasized the importance of examining testimonies and historical accounts as pieces of a much larger puzzle.

4. A cumulative case: It's not about relying on any one type of evidence. It's about building a cumulative case that blends scriptural analysis, historical accounts, modern testimonies, and interdisciplinary research. Physical proof would be nice, but it's not a dealbreaker. Just like a judge or jury doesn't always need physical evidence to reach a verdict, a strong case for extraterrestrials or interdimensional beings can be built through the convergence of multiple lines of evidence.

Let's be honest: This isn't about trying to force a square peg into a round hole. No one is claiming to have bulletproof, lab-verified proof of extraterrestrials or interdimensional beings. But here's the rub: The sheer weight of theological, historical, and testimonial evidence is more than enough to warrant serious attention.

The lack of physical proof is a limitation, no doubt. But it's not a reason to dismiss everything else out of hand. It's just a sign that the conversation isn't over.

As for me, when we stack all the evidence together—Scripture, history, testimonies, and modern research—it points to one undeniable truth: There's a whole ecosystem of beings out there—spiritual, physical, interdimensional, you name it—and, whatever you want to call it, they're either operating under divine authority or flat-out rebelling against it. There's no middle ground. It's all part of the cosmic chessboard, whether people want to see it or not.

If some angelic species are posing as intergalactic aliens, we have to ask why. Is it because modern humans are more willing to believe in advanced extraterrestrial, higher intelligences rather than in biblical beings? Is it because they're guiding civilization toward a particular future, one wherein they play the role of saviors rather than servants of a higher power?

> Hey, Earthlings—don't freak out. But, the God of the Bible isn't a thing. Okay? Sure, a higher Creator might be out there somewhere. Even some of us believe that. Why not? But, we showed up on Earth way back when, took some of the local animals, and spliced OUR genes into yours and created humanity.
>
> *Voila!* Zechariah Sitchin was right on, especially in that last "fictional" (wink, wink) book of his before he kicked the bucket and joined the Galactic Federation of Light. (High Five!)
>
> Pretty groovy, right? Well, we're back now because you've completed a few steps in your spiritual evolution and we're ready to help you ascend to an even HIGHER physical level! Now you'll REALLY be like us. And we're already like gods.
>
> So, yeah…how does THAT sound?

Here's something to consider: The moment we start seeing angels as just another species from another star system, we strip them of their theological weight. Many stop seeing them as beings with moral and spiritual consequences. Instead, they turn them into scientific curiosities rather than forces shaping human destiny.

Alternatively, for some reason, there are also some who think that because an alien from another star system is technologically advanced enough to visit Earth and is therefore superior to humanity in technological understanding, it must also be more *spiritually advanced.*

All kinds of spiritual assumptions are made. Take the following, for example: Padre Pio, a revered twentieth-century Catholic saint known for mystical experiences, reportedly suggested there might be unfallen races in the universe, saying, "there were other races out there that were not Fallen as we are."[242]

Well, that's a possibility. After all, according to Scripture and myriad supporting texts, there are angels who never fell. But who says an alien species from another star system was created with the same purpose or status as humanity? What if there was no need for fallen angels to tempt these other intergalactic aliens into rebellion against the Creator of the universe?

What if they were not created to be "sons of God" in the same way angels and humans were?

Here's another example:

Pope St. John Paul II, when asked about aliens, reportedly said, "Always remember: They are children of God as we are."[243]

Again, really?

How does the pope know that they are "children of God as we are"? Isn't that a huge presupposition? Did he sit down with one of these entities and quiz it on its origins and theology? Even if he did do that, what makes anyone think this representative of an alien species is the mouthpiece of every type, ethnicity, or belief system its species may possess?

Consider that historical attempts to classify human populations have resulted in widely differing numbers of proposed races or ethnicities, ranging from three to more than sixty.[244] And, "according to the Pew Research Center, more than eight in ten people, or about 85% of the world's population, identify with a religious group." When it comes to the number of religious belief systems humans hold, some estimate that "the number exceeds 4,000."[245]

If humans are this diverse, why should anyone assume intergalactic extraterrestrials from a single planet are not? Heck, throw angelic species into that mix, too. Why should anyone assume there are no variations within their number?

There is the possibility that they're also not as diverse as we are. But multiply all of this by the number of supposed contacts with a dizzying array of intergalactic (and angelic) species. Are we to assume they *all*

ANGELS AND EXTRATERRESTRIALS

hold the same beliefs? (We know angels don't all agree with one another!)

The point is that religious leaders making these kinds of blanket statements are assuming a lot and really have no idea what they're talking about. Unfortunately, these same kinds of assumptions are made about angels, as we will see. But for the moment, let's consider the possibility that there are alien species in the cosmos that are native to the same time-space continuum we're in. Let's say for the sake of argument that *they are not* angelic beings.

If alien beings exist, they could fall into one of four categories:

1. Unfallen beings, loyal to divine order.
2. Rebellious beings, like fallen angels, beyond redemption.
3. Beings in need of salvation—just like humanity.
4. Beings existing in a state of ignorance, never having been introduced to YHVH (Yahweh) or divine law.

What happens if God created aliens before He created humanity? God created angels before us, didn't He? What happens if, like us, some joined the angelic rebellion? Does it automatically follow that God would choose to redeem their fallen? Would God have to incarnate within their species as He did with ours? (Of course, I am speaking as a believer in Jesus/Yeshua of Nazareth, the Messiah.)

Some Christians would emphatically argue, "Yes! Of course! He wouldn't be a loving God if He didn't!" Examples of this mentality can be found throughout Christian literature and music. For example, C. S. Lewis wrote that "redemption, starting with us, is to work from us and through us [to the extraterrestrial beings]," and "Those who are, or can become His sons, are our real brothers even if they have shells or tusks. It is spiritual, not biological, kinship that counts."[246] In other words, humans could theoretically evangelize a fallen alien race, and they could also be redeemed through Jesus Christ.

Another example comes from the lyrics to a song titled "UFO" by one of the first Christian rockers, Larry Norman, in 1976, included in his *In Another Land* album.[247]

And if there's life on other planets

Then I'm sure that he must know
And he's been there once already

And has died to save their souls.

But why would anyone assume Jesus would show up in an alien world as one of their species to redeem them, when YHVH, the God of Israel, did not do this for the angels that rebelled?

Aren't the angels special to Him? Or is there something about sin and salvation in connection with the universe as opposed to humanity alone that we don't understand?

I would argue it is much the latter.

We don't know how long angels have existed. We don't know their languages, cultures, mentality, or the specifics of the relationship they have with the Father as sons of God. All we have are brief flashes of insight provided by the Hebrew Scriptures, the Dead Sea Scrolls, the New Testament, and a few supporting texts. Then we have religious organizations and figures who deny that any kind of intergalactic extraterrestrial life is even a possibility. There's no need for salvation for beings that don't even exist, right?

Some claim that because God gave the Torah and the New Testament to humans, the possibility of alien life is automatically off the table. Take Rav Yaakov Kaminetsky, a highly respected rabbi and leader of modern Orthodox Jewry who served on significant rabbinic councils like the Moetzet Gedolei HaTorah of Agudath Israel following World War II, for example. It's reported that he said there may or may not be living creatures in outer space, but there cannot be humanlike beings with free will.

Why? Because the Torah was given specifically to the Jewish people on Earth. He reasoned that God wouldn't create free-willed beings without a Torah to guide them.[248]

Answers in Genesis, a Christian apologetics organization that "focus[es] particularly on providing answers to questions surrounding the book of Genesis, as it is a foundational book of Christianity and the most-attacked book of the Bible,"[249] has this to say about the existence of sentient extraterrestrial life:

> In a biblical worldview, we don't expect alien life to exist. The Bible tells us Earth was formed to be inhabited and the other celestial bodies were created for signs, seasons, days, and years.[250]

With all due respect, the answer provided by Answers in Genesis regarding the existence of extraterrestrial sentient life is completely unbiblical. It is an example of an argument-from-silence fallacy. The truth is that just because something isn't mentioned in Scripture does not mean it doesn't exist.

Moreover, are they and others so sure He didn't provide this information within inspired Scripture?

Isaiah 45:18 says:

> For this is what the LORD says, He who created the heavens (He is the God who formed the earth and made it, He established it and did not create it as a waste place, but formed it to be inhabited).

> כִּי כֹה אָמַר־יְהוָה בּוֹרֵא הַשָּׁמַיִם הוּא הָאֱלֹהִים יֹצֵר הָאָרֶץ וְעֹשָׂהּ הוּא כוֹנְנָהּ לֹא־תֹהוּ בְרָאָהּ לָשֶׁבֶת יְצָרָהּ אֲנִי יְהוָה וְאֵין עוֹד׃

Nowhere does this verse (or any other) state that other worlds cannot *also* be inhabited.

As Rabbi Aryeh Kaplan, a prominent mid-twentieth-century rabbi, has said:

> The Midrash teaches us that there are seven earths.
>
> Although Ibn Ezra tries to argue that these refer to the seven continents, the Zohar clearly states that the seven are separated by a firmament and are inhabited. Although they are not inhabited by man, they are the domain of intelligent creatures.[251]

Then there's Sinai and Synapses, a Jewish organization dedicated to bridging the gap between science and faith. Their website features the following story:

> The late Dr. Velvl Greene was a bacteriologist with a secular, Zionist upbringing. In the 60's, he became an Orthodox Chabad Jew. He is the perfect person to bring to our discussion today, as he was a religious person who sought to harmonize science and religion.
>
> In the 1970s, Dr. Greene worked with NASA's Planetary Quarantine Division, looking for life on Mars, particularly microbes that could hitch a ride back to Earth. Some Orthodox Jews told him to stop, saying that what he was doing was against the Torah.
>
> Concerned, Dr. Greene asked the famous Lubavitcher Rebbe of blessed memory, Rabbi Menachem Mendel Schneerson [the rabbi many Chabadniks think is the Messiah] if his work was appropriate for a religious Jew or if he should quit.
>
> The Rebbe answered: "You should look for life on Mars, and you should keep looking for life on Mars. If you don't find it, then keep looking elsewhere, and do not stop looking, because to sit here in this world and say there is no life elsewhere is to put a limit around what G-d can do. And nobody can do that!"

The sentiment is summed up in the statement, "the universe belongs to God and God can do what God wishes to do with the universe."[252]

The statement by Answers in Genesis is also lacking because its argument states celestial bodies exist only to provide signs, seasons, days, and years (Genesis 1:14). Isn't that overly restrictive?

Genesis 1:14:

> Then God said, "Let there be lights in the expanse of the heavens to separate the day from the night, and they shall serve as signs and for seasons, and for days and years."

ANGELS AND EXTRATERRESTRIALS

וַיֹּאמֶר אֱלֹהִים יְהִי מְאֹרֹת בִּרְקִיעַ הַשָּׁמַיִם לְהַבְדִּיל בֵּין הַיּוֹם וּבֵין הַלָּיְלָה וְהָיוּ לְאֹתֹת וּלְמוֹעֲדִים וּלְיָמִים וְשָׁנִים׃

While this passage states one function of celestial bodies, it doesn't limit their purpose to timekeeping. The truth is that the Answers in Genesis argument is also an example of a hasty generalization fallacy—assuming one stated function excludes all others.

Still, I get it.

The idea that God's plan might extend beyond humanity is unsettling to many. It disrupts traditional theological boundaries, especially within some circles in Christianity, and forces us to confront the hidden layers within Scripture itself.

Throughout the Hebrew Bible and New Testament, there are recurring patterns of concealment, encoded revelations, and divine mysteries that must be unraveled rather than passively accepted or ignored outright. This is evident in the nature of God Himself. The Hebrew Scriptures declare:

Isaiah 55:8–9:

"For My thoughts are not your thoughts, Nor are your ways My ways," declares the Lord.

For as the heavens are higher than the earth, So are My ways higher than your ways And My thoughts than your thoughts.

כִּי לֹא מַחְשְׁבוֹתַי מַחְשְׁבוֹתֵיכֶם וְלֹא דַרְכֵיכֶם דְּרָכָי נְאֻם יְהוָה׃

כִּי־גָבְהוּ שָׁמַיִם מֵאָרֶץ כֵּן גָּבְהוּ דְרָכַי מִדַּרְכֵיכֶם וּמַחְשְׁבֹתַי מִמַּחְשְׁבֹתֵיכֶם׃

If God has deliberately withheld key aspects of theology—such as the full nature of the angelic realm(s), the structure of the cosmos, and more—why should we assume He has revealed everything about extraterrestrial life?

Consider the following theological mysteries that remain ambiguous in Scripture.

The nature of angels:

- ▸ The Bible describes angels as messengers and warriors, but their purpose is only partially revealed. We know nothing outside of observations based on interactions with humanity described in the Scriptures.
- ▸ The Book of Enoch (quoted in Jude 1:14–15) expands upon the Watchers' fall, yet these details are not fully explained in the Torah or New Testament. If they occurred, we know zero facts about their relationship to the overall angelic rebellion mentioned elsewhere.

The destiny of angels:

- ▸ Unlike humanity, fallen angels receive no explicit offer of redemption that we're aware of.
- ▸ Some Jewish traditions suggest degrees of rebellion—wherein some angels fell beyond saving while others remained in an uncertain state.
- ▸ A Talmudic tradition relates that the angel Gabriel disobeyed an order because he took compassion on humans, and he wasn't punished harshly for it.

The afterlife and the unseen realms:

- ▸ The Hebrew Bible is cryptic about life after death, and concepts like Heaven and Hell evolve throughout biblical history.
- ▸ Paul writes in 1 Corinthians 2:9: "No eye has seen, no ear has heard, and no mind has imagined what God has prepared for those who love Him."
- ▸ If even the afterlife remains hidden, what else has been left for humanity to discover?

The absence of an explicit mention of the Trinity in the Old Testament:

- ▸ The doctrine of the Trinity had to be pieced together through theological reasoning. (The word "trinity" isn't even

used one time in the entire New Testament! Does that mean there's no such thing?)
- The origins of Satan are cryptic, scattered across Isaiah 14, Ezekiel 28, and Revelation 12.

In other words, most Christians would acknowledge that progressive revelation plays a significant role in how knowledge is dispensed throughout history. Case in point: The whole concept of the Messiah didn't just drop out of the sky fully formed. It unfolded gradually—from the Hebrew Bible to the New Testament. Same goes for heavy-hitter doctrines like the Trinity, mentioned above, or the resurrection of the dead.

We don't see those laid out in clear detail in the Torah. They only came into focus later, piece by piece, through additional revelation and interpretation. Likewise, the Bible was written for a specific audience within a specific cultural and historical context. It wasn't designed to address every possible reality or phenomenon within the vast cosmos.

The Bible Was Given to Humans, Not Angels!

To this, I've just gotta say: So what?

While some argue that the Bible's focus on humanity implies exclusivity of divine revelation, I understand that this perspective is rooted in a genuine concern for preserving the integrity of Scripture.

It's a solid theological stance, especially for those who champion the Bible's sufficiency for laying out God's plan for humanity. Plenty of respected scholars cling to this view for good reason. They see Scripture as a streamlined, coherent narrative about God's relationship with *us*. And, yeah, I get it—tossing aliens or other sentient beings into the mix feels like it could muddy the waters and throw a wrench into the theological machinery. But the Torah itself states it was given to the Hebrews and the "mixed multitude" (which, by extension, includes all of humanity) at Sinai.

Yet, angels exist. We know this. We also know they're not human. And they are as intelligent as we are—maybe even moreso than us.

According to Jewish texts ranging from the Hebrew Scriptures to the Dead Sea Scrolls to the Talmud, the Zohar, and various commentaries, angels have free will.[253]

If angels exist with intelligence and free will, but the Torah (and, by extension, the whole Bible) wasn't given to them, why does that automatically exclude the possibility of other beings with free will who were *also* not given the Torah?

It doesn't. Both arguments above are built on assumptions with no real foundation.

The Bible Never Says Earth Is the Only Inhabited World

As just stated, nowhere does the Bible say God's creation of intelligent life is limited to Earth. In fact, it repeatedly emphasizes the sheer vastness of the cosmos: "In the beginning God created the heavens and the earth" (Genesis 1:1). The Hebrew word for "heavens" here is *shamayim* (שמים), which has a broader cosmic connotation beyond just Earth's atmosphere.

Additionally, Psalm 8:3–4 proclaims:

When I consider Your heavens, the work of Your fingers, The moon and the stars, which You have set in place;
What is man that You think of him, And a son of man that You are concerned about him?

כִּי־אֶרְאֶה שָׁמֶיךָ מַעֲשֵׂה אֶצְבְּעֹתֶיךָ יָרֵחַ וְכוֹכָבִים אֲשֶׁר כּוֹנָנְתָּה׃

מָה־אֱנוֹשׁ כִּי־תִזְכְּרֶנּוּ וּבֶן־אָדָם כִּי תִפְקְדֶנּוּ׃

These verses marvel at the expanse of the heavenly bodies, suggesting a creation far grander than just our planet and the life on it.

Now, we've already asked whether Jesus would really have to die for aliens that sinned. We've asked whether He would have to incarnate for them if He did not do the same for the angels. But again, I ask: If they exist, why do we assume their relationship with God would mirror ours?

And if they did need salvation, why do we assume it would look exactly like the salvation plan given to humanity? Or could it be that God's plan of salvation for all of creation is part and parcel of the Messiah Yeshua's mission on Earth (which would fit in with C. S. Lewis' comment provided earlier)?

The truth is that, according to some interpretations of Christian theology, due to the sacrifice Jesus made on the cross, all of creation that comes into repentance and then becomes loyal to, or renews loyalty to, the Son of Man/the Son of God will be redeemed and renewed.

Colossians 1:19–20:

> For it was the Father's good pleasure for all the fullness to dwell in Him, and through Him to reconcile all things to Himself, whether things on earth or things in heaven, having made peace through the blood of His cross.

Notice Paul states that through Jesus, it was the Father's good pleasure to reconcile all things to Himself—not just on Earth, but in Heaven (some translations say "the heavens") as well. The apostle reiterates this universal theme in Ephesians 1:9–10:

> He made known to us the mystery of His will, according to His good pleasure which He set forth in Him, regarding His plan of the fullness of the times, to bring all things together in Christ, things in the heavens and things on the earth.

These verses (and others in Pauline literature) suggest God used the situation of humanity's fall to bring about a universal redemption—not only to bring the children of Adam and Eve back into the position of being "sons of God" as the unfallen angels are, but to reconcile other beings in the heavenly spheres to Himself as well.

This brings us to the controversial interpretation by Chuck Missler and others regarding what Jesus was doing during those three days in the grave. First Peter 3:18–20 describes Jesus making a proclamation to "spirits in prison."²⁵⁴ In this verse, Jesus "also went and made proclamation to the spirits in prison, who once were disobedient when the patience of God kept waiting in the days of Noah."

According to Missler, Jesus wasn't sharing the gospel and showing Himself as the Messiah to the spirits of evil humans who may or may not have been corrupted by the genes of the Watchers. Instead, according to this theory, Jesus was showing the fallen Watchers, bound in chains in eternal gloom until the judgment, that He had won—and no one was coming to spring them out of jail or get them off death row, as it were.

In his commentary on 1 Peter, Missler argues that the "spirits in prison" refers to the fallen angels who sinned by interbreeding with humans in Genesis 6, producing the Nephilim. Missler taught that after His crucifixion, Jesus proclaimed His triumph over these evil spirits who were bound in Tartarus awaiting final judgment.²⁵⁵

This interpretation can also be found in the notes of some popular study Bibles like the Scofield Reference Bible and the Spirit-Filled Life Bible published by Thomas Nelson. The idea traces back to some early Church Fathers like Justin Martyr and Tertullian.²⁵⁶

I don't buy this argument. I don't see why Yeshua would need to gloat or make proclamations to fallen angels about how they "could just forget about getting sprung out of jail." I see it as, "He won. The end." There's no need to tell those locked in Tartarus, "Hey—guys—you, uh, you lost. Just thought you should know."

In contrast, Missler argues that 1 Peter 3:19–20 can't be talking about Jesus sharing the gospel and showing Himself as the Messiah to the spirits of evil humans who may or may not have been corrupted by the genes of the Watchers because the Bible never talks about "conversion after death." However, just because the Bible doesn't explicitly mention the concept of conversion or a second chance after death doesn't mean it is precluded or impossible—especially as these were humans who would never have had the opportunity to put their faith in Jesus prior to His incarnation.

In addition, Missler's assertion contradicts passages like Colossians 1:19–20 that speak of Christ reconciling "all things" to God through

His work on the cross. If this reconciliation is truly universal in scope, it implies the possibility of redemption extending beyond just the living—at least during three-day period between Jesus' death and resurrection.

It should also be considered that while Jesus was dead for three days, time may have no meaning outside the dimensions in which we currently exist. Thus, Jesus could have preached to all spirits who were in prison from the dawn of time, as it were, until its end.

However, Missler's interpretation (obviously based on others' views) suggests that people who have never heard the gospel of Yeshua the Messiah from prior to the Flood to today—or who may have heard it amiss—are essentially "out of luck."

But, to entirely rule out post-mortem repentance limits God's sovereign freedom to offer grace and salvation as He wills, based on an argument from silence.

What did Jesus Himself say? "Now go and learn what this means: 'I desire compassion, rather than sacrifice,' for I did not come to call the righteous, but sinners" (Matthew 9:13).

And, of course, "mercy triumphs over judgment," we read in James 2:13.

The bottom line is that just because the Bible doesn't elaborate on the notion of post-mortem repentance (especially during the window between Jesus' death and resurrection), it isn't ruled out as a possibility. That's especially true when other Scriptures point to the Messiah's cosmic and comprehensive redemptive work.

Moreover, there are other Christian scholars who see that three-day span when Jesus preached or made proclamations to the spirits in prison as potentially extending the offer of salvation also to the fallen angels, or Watchers, referred to in passages within 1 Enoch and Genesis 6. The reasoning is that if Christ's death and resurrection had cosmic implications to "reconcile all things" in Heaven and on Earth, as stated in Colossians 1:20 and Ephesians 1:9–10, this reconciliation would logically apply not just to humans, but to angelic beings who were in rebellion against God as well. (Perhaps that would extend to sinful intergalactic alien races as well.)

Early Church Fathers like Clement, Origen, and Gregory show there was some patristic support for the notion that Christ's descent offering "second chances" could theoretically extend beyond just human souls to angelic beings, based on their interpretation of passages like 1 Peter 3.[257]

As Thomas Talbott, in *The Inescapable Love of God*, writes:

> I see no biblical requirement...for the idea that the angels were created instantaneously as fully rational and morally mature agents. For all we are told in the primary sources of the Christian faith, they may have experienced eons of evolution and moral development before they appear on the human scene.[258]

This implies that, if true, the angelic rebellion and sin may have occurred at a point when some may still have had moral/spiritual "growth" ahead of them rather than being perpetually "locked" into an evil state. Further, it could mean that, like humans, angels were not created with their eternal destiny unalterably fixed from the outset. This notion may be supported further by research linking some angelic species to planets elsewhere in the physical universe. (We'll get to that in a moment.)

With all of the above said, it's also possible that Chuck Missler and others were correct when they taught that there is no reconciliation for any angels that fell. The truth, however, is that we simply don't know for certain.

While it is entirely possible that Yeshua (Jesus) may have offered the fallen angels in Tartarus a second chance, the Bible states that Satan—the dragon and his angels (those, at least, that remained loyal to him)—did not accept any offers of mercy from the throne of God, if indeed any offers were made.

The book of Revelation makes clear their destiny.[259]

Well! That's a great discussion, you might say. But, what's with the thought exercises here? Isn't most of this hypothetical anyway?

Again, let's shout about how the Bible is silent on the existence of intergalactic extraterrestrials. Because of that, we can safely say we are alone in the universe.

ANGELS AND EXTRATERRESTRIALS

Let's throw up our hands and scream that if God had wanted to create other intelligent species, He would have let us know about them! Right?

Not necessarily. Remember what God told Job from the whirlwind?

> Where were you when I laid the foundation of the earth?
> Tell Me, if you have understanding. (Job 38:4)

What if I told you God did reveal the existence of other "people," "creatures," or "sentient beings" in our universe within the Hebrew Scriptures?

While I disagree with Chuck Missler on his interpretation of what happened when Jesus died and spent three days in the belly of the Earth before the resurrection, I respect him tremendously and agree with him on a lot.

Remember what I quoted him on in one of the previous chapters? "When you come across something weird in the Bible, it's probably important—and worth digging into." It's a principle that seemingly incongruous or peculiar passages often contain profound theological significance.

Missler frequently argued that anomalies in Scripture—passages that appear disconnected from their immediate context or that contain unusual details—are intentional-design features rather than editorial oversights. He posited that these "Easter eggs" in the text often conceal advanced cryptographic layers, prophetic patterns, or theological truths requiring deeper investigation.

This approach aligned with his broader view of the Bible as a multidimensional "hypertext" engineered by divine authorship, where surface-level readings insufficiently capture its complexity.

Understanding the way Missler thought about Scripture, let's consider one of the more obscure, weird, and seemingly out-of-place verses ever. In fact, it's an earth-shattering example about a place called Meroz, which I mentioned briefly in the previous chapter (Judges 5:23).[260]

Let me build on that by saying there are books you read once and forget. Then, there are those like Dr. Michael S. Heiser's works and Timothy Alberino's *Birthright: The Coming Posthuman Apocalypse and the*

Usurpation of Adam's Dominion on Planet Earth that don't just inform, but force readers to rewire how they see reality.

Alberino doesn't tiptoe around the uncomfortable. He dives into the idea that ancient Scripture may be telling us loud and clear that we're not alone in this universe, and that beings from other realms, dimensions, and even planets have been interfering in human history from the start.

Isaiah 63 presents a chilling picture: The King is furious with the nations—not because they fought against Him, but because *they refused to help.*

> I have trodden the wine trough alone,
>
> And from the peoples there was no one with Me.
> I also trod them in My anger
> And trampled them in My wrath;
> And their lifeblood is sprinkled on My garments,
>
> And I stained all My clothes. (Isaiah 63:3)

> פּוּרָה ׀ דָּרַכְתִּי לְבַדִּי וּמֵעַמִּים אֵין־אִישׁ אִתִּי וְאֶדְרְכֵם בְּאַפִּי וְאֶרְמְסֵם בַּחֲמָתִי וְיֵז נִצְחָם עַל־בְּגָדַי וְכָל־מַלְבּוּשַׁי אֶגְאָלְתִּי׃

Then, the text drives it home again:

> I looked, but there was no one to help,
>
> And I was astonished and there was no one to uphold;
> So My own arm brought salvation to Me,
> And My wrath upheld Me.
> I trampled down the peoples in My anger
> And made them drunk with My wrath,
>
> And I poured out their lifeblood on the earth. (Isaiah 63:5–6)

וְאַבִּיט וְאֵין עֹזֵר וְאֶשְׁתּוֹמֵם וְאֵין סוֹמֵךְ וַתּוֹשַֽׁע־לִי זְרֹעִי וַחֲמָתִי הִיא סְמָכָֽתְנִי׃

וְאָב֥וּס עַמִּים֙ בְּאַפִּ֔י וַאֲשַׁכְּרֵ֖ם בַּחֲמָתִ֑י וְאוֹרִ֥יד לָאָ֖רֶץ נִצְחָֽם׃

The King went to war. Those who should have fought at His side *stood back and did nothing.*

And then we get the bombshell in Judges 5:23, where the Song of Deborah condemns a specific group that refused to stand with God's forces:

> "Curse Meroz," said the angel of the Lord,
>
> "Utterly curse its inhabitants,
> Because they did not come to the help of the Lord,
> To the help of the Lord against the warriors." (Judges 5:23)

אוֹרוּ מֵרוֹז אָמַר מַלְאַךְ יְהוָה אֹרוּ אָרוֹר יֹשְׁבֶיהָ
כִּי לֹא־בָאוּ לְעֶזְרַת יְהוָה   לְעֶזְרַת יְהוָה בַּגִּבּוֹרִים׃

Alberino states the following:

> Two questions necessarily arise from this scenario: who are the mighty against whom the Lord requested support? And who or what is Meroz? The answer to the first question is apparent: the forces of the dragon's confederacy.
>
> And, according to ancient rabbinic tradition, the answer to the second question is a planet.[261]

Before anyone gets all bent out of shape, let's be clear: I've been bringing extrabiblical texts and commentary into the conversation from the beginning of this book. So, just as a reminder, the following discussion isn't about replacing or overriding the canonical Bible.

Not at all.

It's about supplementing our understanding—filling in gaps and shedding light on concepts that weren't fully unpacked within the canon. Think of it like adding color to a sketch, not redrawing the whole picture.

THE RABBINIC CASE FOR OTHER WORLDS

Let's be clear: Not all Jewish sources agree on who or what Meroz is.

Many traditional commentators have seen it as a town, a people, or even an angelic prince. However, not a shred of archeological evidence pins Meroz down. Zero. Zilch. Nada.

Unlike Meroë in Sudan—loaded with pyramids, temples, inscriptions, and all the trimmings—Meroz is a ghost, a no-show in the Near Eastern archeological record. We'd have better luck finding Atlantis.

Meanwhile, the Talmudic tradition and later Jewish scholars repeatedly connect Meroz to a celestial body inhabited by beings who failed to stand with God in battle.

As the Talmud notes:

> The reference is to a star and not a human being, and that it did not aid the Jewish people in their battle, as it is stated: "The stars fought from heaven; in their courses they fought against Sisera," (Judges 5:20). [But], this star, which did not help the Jewish people, was cursed. (Moed Katan 16a:8)

The Jewish organization Chabad, discussed earlier in the section about morning stars due to its former Rebbe being considered a "preexistent messiah" by messianists within the institution, supports Alberino's statement.

In an article titled "Is There Life on Other Planets?" Rabbi Tvi Freeman writes:

> Where is Meroz, and who are its inhabitants? The Talmud gives two explanations, one of them being that Meroz is a star or

planet.... as Deborah stated just one verse earlier, "From the heavens they fought, the stars from their orbits."[262, 263]

Rabbi Aryeh Kaplan, also mentioned earlier, wrote:

The Talmudic teaching (Avoda Zara 3b) is that "God flies through 18,000 worlds." Since they require His providence, we may assume that they are inhabited.

In the song of Deborah, we find the verse, "Cursed is Meroz... cursed are its inhabitants" (Judges 5:23). In the Talmud, we find the opinion that Meroz is the name of a star. According to this opinion, the fact that Scripture states, "Cursed is Meroz...cursed are its inhabitants" is clear proof from the words of our Sages for extraterrestrial life.[264]

He wasn't alone. In an article on Aish.com, Rabbi Benjamin Blech writes on the same topic of Meroz:

In his book Sefer HaBrit ("Book of the Covenant"), Rabbi Pinchas Eliyahu Horowitz, (18th century) quotes as his authority a clear Talmud reference—the statement that contends that Meroz is an inhabited planet somewhere in outer space.

Furthermore, he affirms emphatically that God created an infinite number of worlds, of physical, spiritual and inter-dimensional nature.[265]

Then there's Hasdai Crescas (1340–1411), one of Judaism's greatest philosophers. In Ohr Hashem, he points to Psalm 19:2:

The heavens declare the glory of God.

הַשָּׁמַיִם מְסַפְּרִים כְּבוֹד־אֵל וּמַעֲשֵׂה יָדָיו מַגִּיד הָרָקִיעַ׃

Why? Because the vast cosmic expanse isn't empty. It speaks of a God who rules over countless inhabited worlds.[266]

Psalm 145:13 reinforces this:

Your kingdom is a kingdom spanning all olamim (worlds).

מַלְכוּתְךָ מַלְכוּת כָּל־עֹלָמִים וּמֶמְשַׁלְתְּךָ בְּכָל־דּוֹר וָדֹר׃

If these worlds were empty, what kind of kingdom would that be? Turning to the New Testament, Timothy Alberino writes:

Paul references thrones, dominions, principalities, and powers when referring to things created in heaven and on the earth. These terms are indicative of a vast kingdom with many realms. There is a plurality of thrones, a plurality of dominions, and a plurality of principalities.

There exists a persistent mythology among Evangelicals concerning the word *principality*, which is widely regarded by these to be the title of a high-ranking demonic being. However, a principality does not denote an entity but rather a realm governed by a prince....

It is perfectly logical to infer that nonhuman intelligent beings were inhabiting other worlds in the cosmos before Adam was created on Earth.

Indeed, the inference is made by the writer of Hebrews:
Hebrews 11:3:

By faith we understand that the worlds were prepared by the word of God [Son of God], so that what is seen was not made out of things which are visible.

In concert with Paul's letter to the Colossians identifying Christ as the creator of thrones, dominions, principalities, and powers, the writer of Hebrews (perhaps Paul himself) reaffirms a plurality of realms, which were both made through and relegated by the Son of God, the Prince and heir of the kingdom.

Like the morning stars themselves, these primordial worlds preexisted the age of man.[267]

ANGELS AND EXTRATERRESTRIALS

The reader should spend some time within Alberino's book as he goes into far more detail than the scope of this work allows. His insights, however, are salient and concern biblical passages that serve a dual purpose—to recount historical human events and prophecies as well as reveal in detail an esoteric, yet very real, cosmic war (and more). Because this isn't just a thought experiment!

The Talmud, Kabbalistic writings, and medieval Jewish commentaries contain hints that some celestial beings have the ability to choose, just as humans do. If that's true, then Meroz' inhabitants' refusal to fight may not have been passive disobedience. It was an active choice, one that put them on the wrong side of universal, cosmic history.

If Meroz represents a celestial body inhabited by intelligent beings, then its curse for failing to aid in a war in which the Lord went to battle is not an isolated incident, it's a precedent. A glimpse into a war much larger than the human conflicts recorded in history.

Why would Meroz' inhabitants refuse to fight? There are only a few possibilities:

1. **They were afraid.** If these beings saw the power of the opposing force and hesitated, it suggests that the enemies of God are not weak. Of course, why would they be? Remember all the descriptions of angels elsewhere in the Hebrew Scriptures?

    One hundred eighty-five thousand Syrian soldiers dead by the hand of a single angel in one night? Fallen angels didn't stop being angels and turn into devils. They didn't become another creature when they fell.

    And if the enemy the King was fighting in this description wasn't angelic, who's to say this enemy wasn't just as powerful? (I'd probably be scared, too. Remember the spies who went into Canaan? They'd seen all God's wonders, but still brought back a report that said there was no *way* Israel could defeat the giants they'd seen there.)

2. **They were loyal to the opposition.** If they intentionally refused to aid God, it suggests an alliance—a connection

between these intergalactic celestial inhabitants and the forces of darkness described in Scripture.
3. **They chose neutrality.** However, as history has repeatedly shown, neutrality in war is an illusion. Inaction itself is a choice. In this case, it was a choice that led to a curse.

If Meroz really was an inhabited planet, and its inhabitants refused to help the King (a preincarnate Yeshua?), what does that mean for the modern world?

- Are there cosmic forces—other intergalactic civilizations—that have taken sides in a war most of humanity doesn't even realize is happening?
- Could some of these entities be actively interfering in human affairs?
- Are modern UFO phenomena part of the same story—beings from "elsewhere" refusing to take God's side—or worse, siding against Him?
- Is it possible that there are intergalactic civilizations that stayed true to YHVH?
- Is it possible that, like humans, there may be some intergalactic civilizations that have no knowledge of YHVH one way or the other?

Those are some interesting and thought-provoking questions.

If Meroz represents an inhabited celestial body that refused to stand with divine order, then the curse upon it is not just a moment in history, it's a warning. If you don't fight *with* and *for* the Lord, you're fighting *against* Him. Even if you stand and do nothing, as Yeshua said: "The one who is not with Me is against Me; and the one who does not gather with Me scatters," (Matthew 12:30).

If this interpretation regarding Meroz is true, we must ask whether there were other galactic civilizations in other star systems that were similarly tested and faced the decision to stand with or against the divine.

Now, while determining the precise location of Meroz within the heavens is a heavy-duty task and far beyond what I'm trying to accomplish in this book, allow me to say it's a topic that vastly interests me; I'd love to spend significant time on it.

For now, let me throw out some interesting candidates with the understanding that I'm only hypothesizing.

As we've seen, some ancient sources suggest Meroz could be a star or celestial body that was "cursed" for not aiding in battle. This interpretation opens the possibility of identifying Meroz with a specific star known in ancient times—or with a general astronomical position. With that in mind, a number of possible locations immediately come to mind.

The first is based on Rashi's commentary wherein he elaborated that Meroz represented Sisera's zodiacal sign, which failed to protect him despite astrological expectations.[268] Rashi's identification of Meroz with Sisera's zodiac rests on nuanced wordplay. The Hebrew for Meroz (מֵרוֹז) shares consonantal roots with *mazzal* (מַזָּל), a term later associated with signs of the zodiac.

What was Sisera's sign?

Identifying it requires caution, given the anachronism of the Greco-Roman zodiac in Iron-Age Canaan. However, Mesopotamian zodiacal traditions, which influenced Canaanite astrology, associated certain constellations with months and deities.

If Sisera's campaign occurred in spring (consistent with the Kishon's flooding), his birth sign might correlate with Nisan/Aries, a month linked to military campaigns in Babylonian texts. Has modern astronomy mapped any star systems associated with the Aries zodiac sign? If so, are any star systems within it that have recognized exoplanets?

The answer to both questions is yes.

Several stars in the Aries constellation are known to host exoplanets. Some notable ones include:

- ▶ HIP 14810—A sun-like star with multiple exoplanets, including HIP 14810 b, c, and d.
- ▶ HD 12661—Hosts two confirmed gas giants.

- HD 20367—A star with an exoplanet detected using radial velocity measurements.
- Teegarden's Star (sometimes considered part of Aries)—Hosts potentially habitable exoplanets Teegarden b and c.

So, there are at least six exoplanets, with three known to be potentially habitable, within the Aries constellation.

Further, historical reports have mentioned the detection of unusual radio signals originating from the direction of Aries and Pegasus, leading to speculation about extraterrestrial communications.[269]

Other possible locations are listed below based on historical interpretations, mythological mentions, UFO research, testimonies of alleged "whistleblowers," and connections to "aliens" channeling messages to humans.

Note: I do not believe channeled messages can be trusted in any sense. I personally believe they are designed to deceive humanity. In other words, they are disinformation disseminated from a nefarious interdimensional entity rather than an intergalactic source. Later chapters will expound on the logic and reasoning behind this assertion.

I also believe there are elements of truth in every lie. Additionally, the "channeled" messages are only one data point among many. With that in mind, I list the following.

1. Aldebaran (α Tauri):
- Why? Aldebaran is one of the brightest stars in the sky and has been associated with war and judgment in many ancient cultures.
- Some scholars associate Taurus with divine battles.
- Could it be Meroz? If Meroz was a star "cursed" for refusing to fight, Aldebaran (in a constellation linked to battle) could be a candidate.

Further:

- Aldebaran, the brightest star in the constellation Taurus, is often associated with the "fiery eye" of the bull. In various cultures, it has been linked to themes of war and vigilance.

  In Persian mythology, Aldebaran is one of the four "royal stars" known as the "Watcher of the East," symbolizing a guardian of the heavens.

  In ancient Greek, it was known as ςαίδαπμαΛ Lampadias, literally "torch-like" or "torch-bearer."[270]

- There could be an exoplanet orbiting Aldebaran: In 1993, initial radial velocity measurements suggested the presence of a giant exoplanet, named Aldebaran b, orbiting this orange giant star. Subsequent studies in 2015 provided further evidence supporting its existence.[271]

- Maria Orsic, a medium and leader of the Vril Society, claimed to have received telepathic messages from extraterrestrials in the Aldebaran system. These messages allegedly contained technical data and instructions for building advanced flying machines.

  Authors Norbert Jürgen-Ratthofer and Ralf Ettl, in their 1992 publication, *The Vril Project*, discuss how the Vril Society, influenced by these alleged communications, pursued the development of flying saucers, leading to stories about Nazi UFOs.[272]

- The German conspiracy theorist Axel Stoll, considered the star the home of the Aryan race and the target of expeditions by the Wehrmacht.[273]

2. Sirius (α Canis Majoris):

- Why? Sirius is the brightest star in the night sky and has been linked to supernatural events and divine warnings throughout history.
- Egyptians associated Sirius with the goddess Isis and the flooding of the Nile, marking the start of a significant season.

If Meroz was a star, its "curse" might refer to its association with judgment or an important cosmic event.

- Could it be Meroz? Some believe biblical curses on celestial objects could correspond to fallen angelic beings or events in the heavens. Sirius, as a major focal point of ancient astronomy, fits that profile.

Further:

- The Dogon people of Mali, West Africa have an ancient tradition describing beings called the Nommo, whom they claim came from a planet orbiting Sirius B. The Nommo are often depicted as amphibian, fishlike beings that brought knowledge and civilization to Earth.

    Some researchers, such as Robert Temple in *The Sirius Mystery* (1976), argue that the Dogon had knowledge of Sirius B (a white dwarf companion to Sirius A) before Western astronomers discovered it in 1862.
- Various ufologists and New Age sources describe the Sirians as tall, humanoid, highly advanced spiritual beings. Some claim they played a role in genetically engineering early humans or helping ancient civilizations (e.g., Atlantis, Egypt).

    Many channelers, such as Patricia Cori in *The Sirian Revelations*, claim to receive messages from "benevolent" Sirian entities that guide humanity's spiritual evolution.[274]
- Some early UFO contactees, like Billy Meier, claimed that the Sirians were peaceful extraterrestrials who warned humans about nuclear war. The Sirians are often depicted as more technologically and spiritually advanced than Pleiadians but not as directly involved in Earth affairs.[275]
- In theosophy and Freemasonry, Sirius is known as the "Great Central Sun" and a major spiritual influence. Helena Blavatsky described Sirius as the source of hidden wisdom and believed that it influenced spiritual development on Earth.[276]

- Ancient Egyptians associated Sirius with the goddess Isis, as it played a role in their calendar and the annual flooding of the Nile. Some theorists believe that the pyramids and temples were aligned with Sirius for spiritual or extraterrestrial reasons.[277]

3. Regulus (Leo):
- Why? Regulus (meaning "Little King") is one of the four "royal stars" of ancient Persia and has long been associated with kingship and divine authority.
- Leo (the lion) has strong biblical significance, often representing the tribe of Judah. But if Meroz was a rebellious or fallen entity, its curse could represent a royal star that was rejected.
- Could it be Meroz? If Meroz was a celestial entity expected to take part in divine warfare but failed, Regulus (a star often linked to rulers and war) could be relevant.

4. Betelgeuse (Orion):
- Why? Betelgeuse is part of the Orion constellation, which has strong biblical and mythological associations with warriors, giants, and cosmic battles.
- Some interpretations of Nephilim (the fallen beings in Genesis 6) connect them with Orion.
- Could it be Meroz? Orion is often linked to warfare, so a celestial object cursed for not fighting could be part of this constellation.

Further:

- Within the Orion constellation, an exoplanet designated HD 290327 b was discovered in 2009. This gas giant has a minimum mass of approximately 2.5 times that of Jupiter and orbits its host star, HD 290327, at a distance of 3.35

AU (astronomical units) with an orbital period of about 6.7 years. The Orion constellation encompasses numerous stars, and ongoing astronomical surveys continue to search for exoplanets within this region. While HD 290327 b is a confirmed exoplanet, other potential discoveries await further verification.
- Some theorists claim that malevolent reptilian, interdimensional humanoids originate from the Orion constellation. The British author David Icke "stated on multiple occasions that many world leaders were, or are possessed by, so-called reptilians."[278]
- The Orion correlation theory suggests a link between the positions of the three main pyramids of the Giza pyramid complex and the three stars of Orion's Belt. Proponents argue that ancient civilizations had connections with extraterrestrial beings from Orion.[279]

5. HD 20794 (82 Eridani):
- Why? HD 20794 is in the constellation Eridanus, which represents a celestial river in Greek mythology.
- This river is often associated with the myth of Phaëton, the son of the sun god Helios, who lost control of his father's chariot, causing devastation before being struck down by Zeus. The river Eridanus was said to be where Phaëton fell to Earth.
  This mythological backdrop ties the star to themes of divine retribution and cosmic order.
- This system contains HD 20794 d, an exoplanet super-Earth in the habitable zone, meaning it has the potential for Earthlike conditions.

6. TOI-700:
- This system is relevant because TOI-700 hosts at least two Earth-sized exoplanets (TOI-700 d and TOI-700 e) within

the habitable zone. This system is located approximately one hundred light-years away in the constellation Dorado.
- NASA's Transiting Exoplanet Survey Satellite (TESS) identified multiple planets orbiting TOI-700. Notably, TOI-700 d and TOI-700 e are Earth-sized planets situated within the star's habitable zone, where conditions might allow for liquid water. These findings have been confirmed through additional observations and studies.[280]

7. Trappist -1:

- The TRAPPIST-1 system is famous for having multiple planets in the habitable zone, making it a top target in the search for alien, extraterrestrial life.
- TRAPPIST-1 is an ultra-cool red dwarf star located approximately 40.7 light-years away in the constellation Aquarius. It hosts seven Earth-sized exoplanets, some of which reside within the star's habitable zone, where conditions might allow for liquid water.[281]
- Recent disclosures from self-proclaimed whistleblower Charles McNeal have reignited interest in the purported interstellar exchange program known as Project Serpo, which allegedly involved collaboration between the US government and an extraterrestrial civilization. Central to McNeal's claims is the planet Serpo, described as the home world of an alien species referred to as the Ebens (extraterrestrial biological entities).[282]
- McNeal emerged in 2024 with claims of having served in a "top-secret U.S. Air Force intelligence unit" tasked with maintaining a seventy-year truce between Earth and an extraterrestrial civilization. McNeal's claims circulate on platforms like X (formerly Twitter) and podcasts (Total Disclosure Podcast), where hosts amplify his stories without rigorous vetting.[283]
- McNeal alleges that the James Webb Space Telescope (JWST) will soon detect a "space fleet" or extraterrestrial vessels traveling from TRAPPIST-1 to our solar system.[284]

- McNeal has appeared as a guest on podcasts with Richard Doty, a former Air Force Office of Special Investigations (AFOSI) agent known for propagating UFO-related narratives. Doty has suggested that there is some credibility to McNeal's claims of being part of a secret Air Force program before being removed due to being compromised. (His personal behavior led to incarceration, which McNeal readily and honestly admits.)[285]
- However, to date, research shows that due to their proximity to the star, most TRAPPIST-1 planets are likely tidally locked, with permanent day and night sides. This could create extreme climatic conditions, challenging the notion of Earthlike habitability.[286]

Here's the brutal truth: No one has done the in-depth research needed to make a final determination, if indeed one can be made. This isn't a quick Google search or a feel-good theory; it's a puzzle that demands rigorous biblical, historical, and scientific analysis.

If Meroz is an exoplanet, then we need to:

1. Cross-reference historical accounts of celestial anomalies.
2. Analyze the biblical text in-depth to identify linguistic patterns.
3. Examine exoplanetary data to see if any of these star systems match the description.
4. Consider UFO research, ancient myths, and cosmic warfare narratives in both the Bible and other traditions.

Let's cut to the chase: If we accept the idea that angelic or even extraterrestrial beings might be hanging out on or ruling over certain celestial bodies in the same material universe we inhabit, then spiritual warfare isn't just an Earthbound affair.

Remember that we humans engage in "spiritual warfare":

ANGELS AND EXTRATERRESTRIALS

For our struggle is not against flesh and blood, but against the rulers, against the powers, against the world forces of this darkness, against the spiritual forces of wickedness in the heavenly places. (Ephesians 6:12)

The "heavens" aren't just the dimensional space we flit off to after we die.

The heavens tell of the glory of God; And their expanse declares the work of His hands. (Psalm 19:1)

הַשָּׁמַיִם מְסַפְּרִים כְּבוֹד־אֵל וּמַעֲשֵׂה יָדָיו מַגִּיד הָרָקִיעַ:

This is cosmic.

When we start identifying specific stars or planets as home bases for rebellious entities or loyal divine agents, it's not just some geeky exercise in speculative astronomy. It's about proving a core theological truth: God's sovereignty stretches across every realm imaginable. Physical, spiritual, interdimensional—you name it, He owns it.

And when we take modern UFO testimonies and slot them into this framework, suddenly they make a whole lot more sense. They're not just random weirdness; they're pieces of a much bigger cosmic drama in which divine authority is either accepted or spit on.

This isn't just about proving the phenomenon is real. It's about showing it fits perfectly within the broader Judeo-Christian paradigm. Listen, if Meroz was a real celestial body—and we could pinpoint it—the implications are staggering. But right now, we aren't even scratching the surface.

With all the above in mind, it's crucial to hammer home the point that the Judeo-Christian Scriptures make it abundantly clear that we are not alone in the universe. The Bible, the Talmud, and centuries of Jewish scholarship suggest we're dealing with something far bigger than just human history.

And the idea that extraterrestrial life and interdimensional entities are part of the picture?

That's not science fiction.

It's theology.

It's prophecy.

If the biblical and rabbinic tradition is correct, it's a reality Christians, Jews—indeed, all of humanity—will have to face...sooner or later.

CHAPTER SIX

EXTRATERRESTRIALS AND DEMONS

The devil does not have a body. Then how does he manage to have intercourse with men and women?

JACQUES F. VALLÉE
Dimensions: A Casebook of Alien Contact[287]

The previous chapter left us grappling with a staggering possibility: The universe is far more populated than most theologians or scientists dare to admit.

God's rule doesn't hover over Earth like it's a fragile snowglobe. His sovereignty blankets every dimension, realm, and plane of existence imaginable. Ancient Jewish texts, modern UFO sightings—all of it points to a sprawling cosmic drama wherein divine authority is either embraced or rejected.

Here's the real question: What happens when we start connecting the dots between all these "alien" encounters and the cookie-cutter theology most people cling to like a security blanket?

For many Christians, the default answer is painfully predictable: Anything resembling an alien? Must be demonic. Case closed, nice and tidy...except it's not. It's a convenient categorization—one that wraps the phenomenon in a familiar moral narrative. Yet, this oversimplification may be more than just a theological mistake; it might be a deliberate misunderstanding by some.

If the universe is as teeming with life as the Scriptures, rabbinic tradition, and modern accounts suggest, then cramming every nonhuman entity into the "demon" box is like trying to paint a galaxy with a crayon. It's a two-dimensional map for a multidimensional battlefield.

Let's be real—the knee-jerk "aliens = demons" mantra has become a crutch, a theological fast-food combo meal for people too lazy or too scared to wrestle with the implications of a populated universe. It's convenient, it's comforting, and it's wrong.

It's time to challenge that assumption head-on. It's time to examine what the Scriptures, rabbinic tradition, and even modern scholarship truly say about the distinction between fallen angels, demons, and potential extraterrestrial beings. Most importantly, it's time to question whether associating all nonhuman entities with demonic forces holds up under scrutiny.

What if the truth has been staring us down all along, but we've been too shackled by our own assumptions to see it?

WORDS MATTER

Let's get this straight: What Christians often refer to as "demonic in nature" ought to more rightly be referred to as "satanic in nature" or simply "fallen in nature."

Consider the following:

- ▸ "Satanic" does not equal "demonic." The two are not one and the same.
- ▸ Christianity largely teaches that Satan is the leader of an angelic rebellion.[288]
- ▸ Fallen angels are not demons.[289]

In other words, the claim that fallen angels are not demons finds support in:

1. The Hebrew Scriptures (they never equate any kind of angel with demons).
2. Apocryphal Jewish texts (e.g., 1 Enoch, Jubilees).
3. The New Testament (it never equates Satan or any other angelic being with demons).
4. The Babylonian Talmud (e.g., Berakhot 6a).
5. Early Christian writers (e.g., Justin Martyr).
6. The works of the Acharonim (Jewish sages from 1600 onward—e.g., The Vilna Gaon on Sifra DeTzniuta).
7. Modern scholarship (e.g., Dr. Michael Heiser).

Before continuing, it's important to acknowledge that the distinctions between demons, fallen angels, and extraterrestrials may be foreign to mainstream Christian thought today. Despite the sources I just mentioned, many will likely grimace and say, "Well, that's not how I was taught!" or, "Your argument leans too heavily on noncanonical texts like 1 Enoch or later theological constructs!"

Settle down, Sparky.

First, people are raised being taught all kinds of unbiblical gobbledygook. Second, I already noted that the canonical Hebrew Scriptures and New Testament support what I'm arguing here. Third, the heavyweights of early Christianity weren't all sipping the same theological Kool-Aid as many are today. What I'm discussing here has been firmly established in ancient Jewish texts, early Christian apocrypha, and Christian, patristic writings. Those bodies of work reflected a far more complex and varied understanding of angelology and demonology than the sanitized, streamlined doctrines most people cling to today. Recognizing this historical and theological diversity doesn't weaken my case; it supercharges it. It proves that the distinction between demons and fallen angels isn't some modern, scholarly invention. It's a return to a deeper, richer, original understanding—one the gatekeepers have been trying to bury for centuries.

Firstly, demons: They are evil, yes. They belong in the camp of rebel angels, yes. But they're small fry—and humanity existed before them! (That is, if we're paying attention to Hebraic sources.)

Fallen angels, in contrast, existed before humanity and, according to both scriptural and apocryphal texts, are the real, corrupted, rebellious power on the interdimensional, spiritual battlefield.

Secondly, there is no evidence that demons are extraterrestrial or alien in nature. In fact, evidence suggests quite the opposite. Meanwhile, as we already discussed, angels—whether righteous or fallen—*can* be described as both extraterrestrial and alien.

Thirdly, demons never manifest visually or physically in any way, shape, or form within the narratives provided by the Hebrew Scriptures or the New Testament.

I think it's necessary here to pause and clarify that my argument is based on *consistency* rather than *absence*. The Hebrew Scriptures and the New Testament consistently depict demons affecting people psychologically, spiritually, or through possession—never through direct, physical manifestation one can touch, see, or bump into on the street.

Their presence is always inferred through changes in behavior, speech, or psychological torment, not through material appearance or tangible contact. Therefore, any claim that demons appear physically must establish evidence beyond mere assertion.

The consistent pattern throughout Scripture paints a clear picture: Nonphysical interaction is the rule, not the exception. Anything outside of that is stepping outside the boundaries of the biblical framework.

EXTRATERRESTRIALS AND DEMONS

Some critics might cite extrabiblical sources such as the Book of Tobit (which is canon in Catholicism and Eastern Orthodox Churches) to show that demons can, in fact, appear physically.

They might also cite medieval grimoires, which often claim physical manifestations of demons.

There are two crucial points here.

1. In texts outside the Book of Tobit, such as the Testament of Solomon, the demon Asmodeus claims to have been born of a human mother and an angel father. This would, in fact, make him a demonic spirit if he is one of the dead Nephilim.

Still, in the Book of Tobit, Asmodeus does not manifest physically in a tangible form. His presence and actions—such as killing Sarah's seven husbands—are described, but there is no indication that he appears in a visible or physical manner to the characters.

2. There should be a clear distinction, especially for a follower of Yeshua (Jesus of Nazareth), between genuine biblical accounts and magical texts that often involve occult practices outside the framework of Jewish or Christian orthodoxy.

Does it make the occultic testimony untrue? Maybe, maybe not.

But when compared to scriptural evidence, the scriptural evidence must supersede all others.

BIBLICAL AND EXTRABIBLICAL EVIDENCE

You might ask, "Okay, well, what about the spirit that tormented King Saul? Wasn't he psychologically tormented?"

While the Hebrew Scriptures mention the evil spirit tormenting King Saul (1 Samuel 16:14–23) and the lying spirit influencing King Ahab (1 Kings 22:19–23), these spirits operated differently from later New Testament depictions of demons.

First, the text does *not* describe the visual appearance of the spirit that visited Saul. Its presence is inferred through Saul's psychological and behavioral deterioration (e.g., his repeated attempts to kill David).

Second, unlike demonic entities in the New Testament, this evil spirit is explicitly said to have come "from the Lord":

> Now the Spirit of the LORD left Saul, and an evil spirit from the LORD terrified him. (1 Samuel 16:14)

וְרוּחַ יְהֹוָה סָרָה מֵעִם שָׁאוּל וּבִעֲתַתּוּ רוּחַ־רָעָה מֵאֵת יְהֹוָה:

The Jewish sage Radak interpreted this verse as God sending a spirit of madness upon King Saul, as did Rabbi Steinsaltz, a world-renowned Israeli scholar, educator, philosopher, and prolific author.[290] This could have been an angelic being sent to cause madness in King Saul in the same way an angel caused madness in the Babylonian King Nebuchadnezzar (Daniel 4:13–16).

Still, even if it is argued that this was indeed a demon, it doesn't manifest in a visual or physical manner.

The same holds true for the lying spirit sent to King Ahab in 1 Kings 22:19–23. In fact, the spirit in these verses stands in front of God while He is holding court!

> And Micaiah said, "Therefore, hear the word of the LORD. I saw the LORD sitting on His throne, and all the angels of heaven standing by Him on His right and on His left."

And the Lord said, "Who will entice Ahab to go up and fall at Ramoth-gilead?" And one spirit said this, while another said that.

Then a spirit came forward and stood before the Lord, and said, "I will entice him."

And the Lord said to him, "How?" And he said, "I will go out and be a deceiving spirit in the mouths of all his prophets." Then He said, "You shall entice him, and you will also prevail. Go and do so."

"Now then, behold, the Lord has put a deceiving spirit in the mouth of all these prophets of yours; and the Lord has declared disaster against you."

וַיֹּאמֶר יְהֹוָה מִי יְפַתֶּה אֶת־אַחְאָב וְיַעַל וְיִפֹּל בְּרָמֹת
גִּלְעָד וַיֹּאמֶר זֶה בְּכֹה וְזֶה אֹמֵר בְּכֹה:
וַיֵּצֵא הָרוּחַ וַיַּעֲמֹד לִפְנֵי יְהֹוָה וַיֹּאמֶר אֲנִי אֲפַתֶּנּוּ וַיֹּאמֶר יְהֹוָה אֵלָיו בַּמָּה:
וַיֹּאמֶר אֵצֵא וְהָיִיתִי רוּחַ שֶׁקֶר בְּפִי כָּל־נְבִיאָיו
וַיֹּאמֶר תְּפַתֶּה וְגַם־תּוּכָל צֵא וַעֲשֵׂה־כֵן:
וְעַתָּה הִנֵּה נָתַן יְהֹוָה רוּחַ שֶׁקֶר בְּפִי כָּל־נְבִיאֶיךָ אֵלֶּה וַיהֹוָה דִּבֶּר עָלֶיךָ רָעָה:

Clearly, this isn't a demon, unless you believe demons can somehow get into Heaven (if that's the case, I'd be delighted to see your evidence). Either way, this lying spirit never manifests visually or physically to Ahab or anyone else.

Third, what about the spirit of Samuel when King Saul visited the witch of Endor? Haven't you heard pastors preach that surely this was a demon? It was a demon pretending to be Samuel; therefore, this is evidence that demons can manifest visually when called upon, right?

Not so fast, my friend.

This event is recorded in 1 Samuel 28, where we read that a witch summons the spirit of the prophet Samuel.

What does the text say she saw?

But the king said to her, "Do not be afraid; but what do you see?" And the woman said to Saul, "I see a divine being coming up from the earth."

וַיֹּאמֶר לָהּ הַמֶּלֶךְ אַל־תִּירְאִי כִּי מָה רָאִית וַתֹּאמֶר הָאִשָּׁה
אֶל־שָׁאוּל אֱלֹהִים רָאִיתִי עֹלִים מִן־הָאָרֶץ:

"A divine being"? The word translated as "divine being" here is *Elohim*.
She and King Saul saw a god?
Who else are called "gods" in the Hebrew Scriptures?
Angels, that's who.
Psalm 82:6 has God in His divine council speaking to angelic beings:

I said, "You are gods, And all of you are sons of the Most High."

אֲנִי־אָמַרְתִּי אֱלֹהִים אַתֶּם וּבְנֵי עֶלְיוֹן כֻּלְּכֶם:

Lest my Jewish readers think I'm crazy, just let me say that Rashi, one of the most influential Jewish scholars and commentators of all time, agrees with me on Psalm 82:6.

Now, while most Jewish commentators, such as Rashi and Rabbi Steinsaltz, interpret this divine entity that both the witch and King Saul saw as being the prophet Samuel in a glorified state rather than an angel pretending to be Samuel, the Targum (Aramaic translation) interprets *Elohim* as referring to angels of God.

Targum Jonathan on 1 Samuel 28:13:

And the king said to her, "Do not be afraid. But what do you see?" And the woman said to Saul, "I see a divine being/godlike figure/angel of God rising from the earth."

וַאֲמַר לַהּ מַלְכָּא לָא תִדְחֲלִין אֲרֵי מָה חָזֵית וַאֲמַרַת אִתְּתָא לְשָׁאוּל מַלְאֲכָא
דַּיְיָ חֲזֵיתִי דְּסָלֵיק מִן אַרְעָא:

Interestingly, however, the view held by most Jewish commentators is supported by the Septuagint (LXX), which renders 1 Chronicles 10:13b, "And Samuel the prophet made answer to him" (King Saul), and by Sirach 46:20.

Of course, many Christian commentators have held the same view as Rabbi Steinsaltz,[291] including Augustine, Origen, and Justin Martyr. In addition, John Wesley (eighteenth century) cautiously allowed for this possibility, noting: "The words are express. The woman saw Samuel, instead of the spirit whom she expected to see."[292]

Other Christian commentators have argued that this was an angelic impersonator (aligning with what's written in the Hebrew and the Targum), which is tied to the idea that angels could act as divine messengers even in unconventional ways—albeit this is a decidedly minority view.

Others have seen this "divine being" as a fallen angelic entity—also acting as an impersonator. For example:

▸ Church Father Tertullian stated, "In the extravagant pretensions of their art, the ancient ventriloquistic spirits even claimed to represent the soul of Samuel, when Saul consulted the dead after losing the living God."[293]
▸ British Bible expositor Matthew Henry (eighteenth century), meanwhile, saw the divine being as an angelic figure, but as a fallen one, Satan putting on a disguise. ("God permitted the devil, to answer the design, to put on Samuel's shape.")[294]
▸ John Calvin, theologian, pastor, and key figure in the Reformation, held to the same view as Matthew Henry.[295]

The main point is that whether we agree that the "divine being" seen by the witch and King Saul was an angel (good or bad) or the prophet Samuel in a glorified state, no biblical commentator, Jewish or Christian, sees this spirit as a demon.

In the New Testament, demons only manifest as entities that possess the bodies and/or minds of human individuals, as in Mark 5:1–20 and Matthew 17:14–18. Again, their presence is inferred through speech or actions, never through visual descriptions.

Fourth, it is important to note that most testimonies from individuals who claim to have encountered extraterrestrial aliens—particularly in abduction scenarios—involve direct, physical interaction with these beings. Unlike vague or purely psychological experiences, these accounts often include seeing, touching, and even conversing with the entities involved.

MODERN SCHOLARSHIP AND ENCOUNTERS

Dr. John E. Mack, a Harvard-educated psychiatrist, extensively documented such encounters in his seminal work, *Abduction: Human Encounters with Aliens* (1994).[296] Through his clinical interviews, Mack collected numerous accounts in which experiencers reported not only visual and tactile contact with these beings, but also communication, often through telepathy. Additionally, many subjects described undergoing physical procedures, such as surgical operations, conducted by these entities.

It's crucial to highlight Mack's methodology here: He relied on non-hypnosis interviews and approached these accounts as authentic trauma narratives rather than dismissing them as mere hallucinations or delusions. His approach was groundbreaking precisely because he treated these testimonies with the same seriousness and rigor he would apply to any trauma victim recounting a genuinely distressing experience.

Dr. David M. Jacobs, in his later work, *Walking Among Us: The Alien Plan to Control Humanity* (2015), presents a particularly unsettling dimension of the abduction phenomenon—what he describes as encounters with "hubrids," or human-alien hybrids.[297] Unlike earlier reports confined to isolated, nocturnal experiences, Jacobs details cases in which abductees encounter these beings in everyday, public settings such as workplaces, homes, and even casual social environments.

Significantly, many of these interactions were recalled without the use of hypnosis, suggesting a conscious, waking reality rather than a dream state or purely psychological experience. According to Jacobs, these encounters frequently involved face-to-face interactions, often accompanied by telepathic communication or even physical touch, such as being grabbed or led by these entities.

He underscores the strangeness of these encounters with the following observation: "Many abductees have conscious memories of seeing hybrids in public places, often mistaking them for odd-looking humans."

Jacobs' work suggests a troubling overlap between the mundane and the extraordinary, wherein alleged hybrids operate in plain sight, their presence largely undetected by the general population.

Some of you may be saying that just because neither set of Scriptures explicitly declares that demons can manifest visually or physically, it doesn't logically follow that they can't.

That's true. But the evidence we do have doesn't suggest they can, either. In the absence of supporting evidence, we should not assume a phenomenon exists. Otherwise, we could justify any claim using this logic.

Some might also argue that historical or modern demonology accounts outside the Bible (e.g., medieval grimoires, exorcism accounts) describe demons appearing visually. But, honestly, the standard of evidence for believers should be based on Scripture, not folklore or anecdotal experiences.

The point is that the claims by some that aliens/extraterrestrials are demons aren't supported by evidence from the Hebrew Scriptures or the New Testament. The fact that people who have claimed to have had interactions with extraterrestrial aliens see, touch, and speak with these beings (and are not possessed by them) is a huge indication—based on everything listed above—that these beings are not, in fact, demons. These descriptions are inconsistent with how Scripture describes demons as operating. Thus, both Jewish and Christian believers (as well as everyone else) should reject these ideas out of hand.

Well, you might argue, this is all just semantics, right? Tons of Christians use the terms "demons" and "fallen angels" interchangeably, but I think I've shown that they're not at all the same, and this isn't just about word choice, but about accuracy. If we label everything evil as "demonic," we dilute theological clarity. (To be sure, being abducted by anyone—a human, an alien, a fallen angel, a clone, a "nonhuman biologic"—sure seems like a nefarious act to me.)

I am absolutely not arguing that alien encounters are good—only that they do not align with biblical demonology. Rejecting the idea that what people think of as aliens are in fact demons doesn't mean endorsing alien encounters as good or reliable.

Listen, as an aside, if you're a Christian, I urge you to cut out the "churchese" lingo. When unbelievers see Christians seemingly labeling as "demonic" everything bad or even everything satanic, the term loses its import and impact—particularly when it is factually inaccurate.

I can tell you, coming from a perspective that's a bit outside the Bible Belt, the constant references to demons and/or the demonic this, that, and the other makes Christians in general look like wild-eyed caricatures. It brings to mind the character of Mama Boucher, played by Kathy Bates in Adam Sandler's 1998 film, *The Water Boy*, whose mantra was that everything bad (according, naturally, to her judgment) is "the Debil."[298]

Of course, that's not how it should be. There really are demonic entities that torment people. But why should unbelievers have any kind of correct concept about these issues if believers can't even get them right?

But wait!

I can almost hear the howls of outrage and accusations of heresy despite the evidence presented above. (Listen, if you insist extraterrestrials and aliens are demons despite everything you just read, well, the burden of proof is yours to bear.) I know some will press on and demand to know—if what I have said vis-à-vis aliens and extraterrestrials *not* being demons above is true—how does the claim that "fallen angels are extraterrestrials" or "fallen angels are aliens" hold up?

Are they or are they not?

EXTRATERRESTRIAL FALLEN ANGELS?

It's obvious I don't believe extraterrestrials, aliens, or the experiences people have, by and large, with these entities are demons or demonic. (I can think of a few specific exceptions within UFO religions. In these cases, the founder or writer of a particular book "slept" while a being possessed him and did the actual writing. But these devotees expressly admit to the possession aspect. Thus, in these exceptions, I *would* say that's demonic.)

In any case, and this is critical to understand, I *am not arguing* that all beings labeled "extraterrestrial" are necessarily true interstellar travelers from distant star systems. To suggest otherwise would be to uncritically accept the assumptions of New Age practitioners, channelers, and even certain researchers who eagerly promote such interpretations, as well as those who adhere to the theories put forth by Erich von Däniken and Zechariah Sitchin.

The truth is likely far more complicated.

It's necessary to acknowledge the possibility that some—perhaps even most—of these beings are not interstellar in origin at all. I've already established that:

- "Angels" can be defined as both extraterrestrial and alien (again, see Alberino's work).
- Fallen angels are not demons.
- Demons are not extraterrestrials.

What's left?

- Some aliens and extraterrestrials may be interstellar in origin.
- Some aliens and extraterrestrials are not interstellar at all—but may be pretending to be.

The theory I am putting forth is this: Some of the entities labeled by New Age practitioners, channelers, and (some) abductees as "extraterrestrials" may be interdimensional beings—specifically, fallen angels who have rebelled against divine authority. This isn't some high-minded theological claim pulled out of thin air. It's a logical conclusion based on cold, hard evidence—patterns of deception, manipulation, and straight-up false teachings these beings keep dishing out like candy. It's all there, plain as day, if we're willing to look past the smoke and mirrors and connect the dots.

Again, to be clear, I'm *also* not saying real, flesh-and-blood, interstellar aliens aren't out there. The universe is massive, teeming with life of all shapes and sizes. It'd be pure arrogance, as C. S. Lewis noted, to think Earth is the only rock with intelligent beings on it.[299]

But here's the thing: Many of the entities humans have bumped into throughout history act a heck of a lot more like interdimensional tricksters than straightforward biological aliens cruising over from Alpha Centauri. The shady, unpredictable nature of their motives practically screams "deception." It's entirely possible—no, it's probable—that some of these interdimensional beings are fallen Seraphim and Ishim (fallen angels from a variety of species, rebels in a cosmic war) and are simply playing dress-up. They're masquerading as intergalactic visitors, or whatever suits their agenda, while hiding their true intentions behind a shiny, benevolent façade, with some acting as teachers, guides, and, yes, "ascended masters."

THE DECEPTION CONNECTION

Jacques Vallée, a pioneer in UFO research and author of *Messengers of Deception* (2024), whom I mentioned way back in chapter 1, emphasizes the manipulative nature of these encounters. "UFOs and 'extraterrestrials,'" he writes, are phenomena that "create a distortion of the witness's reality, that does so for a purpose, which is to project images or fabricated scenes designed to change our belief systems."[300]

Graham Hancock, whose work explores altered states of consciousness and their connections to ancient mythologies, notes a similar theme of deception. During his ayahuasca (a powerful, psychoactive plant-based brew traditionally used by Indigenous peoples of the Amazon for spiritual, medicinal, and shamanic purposes) experiences, he reported having had encounters with intelligent, often serpentine entities who claimed to be spiritual guides but whose motives were unclear. He wrote in his book, *Supernatural: Meetings with the Ancient Teachers of Mankind* the following:

> One very plausible, and for me very persuasive, explanation, in the school of thought of Huxley, James, and Hoffman, is that

there do indeed exist "separate, freestanding realities"—or "parallel dimensions" of the kind quantum physics predicts—that vibrate at a different frequency to our own and thus are invisible to us except when we approach them in altered states of consciousness.

These other realities seem to be inhabited by intelligent beings who are non-physical in our dimension—although they would apparently like to acquire permanent physical forms—and who have had a long-term interest in us, interfering in and manipulating human affairs in the guise of spirit guides, supernatural teachers, fairies, and recently aliens.[301]

As in the television series *V*, these beings could appear claiming to be advanced humans or advanced beings from another star system, the "original" progenitors of the human race on planet Earth.[302] They might offer knowledge, technology, and medical breakthroughs to secure humanity's "buy-in" before their true intentions are ultimately revealed. Or perhaps their true intentions would never even need to be revealed at all, as long as humanity follows the path they've chosen for us.

Today, innumerable YouTube, X (formerly Twitter), and Instagram channels feature human "contactees" interacting with "channeled" beings claiming to be from various star systems such as the Pleiades star cluster. One example is titled *Channeling the 9th Dimensional Pleiadian Collective—Interview with Extra-Dimensionals*.[303]

Another example, presenting an interesting deviation from the common "channeled-message" scenario, is the "Lacerta Files." Back in 1999, an anonymous Swedish researcher dropped a bombshell that's still making waves today. He claimed to have sat down—physically, like two pals yacking—and interviewed a being named Lacerta, a reptilian entity supposedly living among us, hiding in plain sight.

The researcher recorded the interview, then had it transcribed. Where are the tapes today? Who was this researcher? Don't know. Nothing has ever been verified. But the transcriptions are long and detailed.

Various YouTube channels and podcasts have picked it up and run with it, though. One channel that takes a neutral stance without pushing the narrative as truth is Area52.[304] Interestingly, according to Lacerta—who, by the way, claims to be female—this isn't about some underground civilization or dusty ancient history. She dives headfirst into the whole UFO crash phenomenon, and states that those "accidents" were not accidents at all. They're the nasty byproduct, she says, of a dirty deal between human authorities and nonhuman entities. We're talking about a secret agreement, wherein advanced technology was dangled in front of greedy, power-hungry officials like bait.

The real price? Something far more personal and disturbing: access to humanity itself.

WHAT'S WITH THE RELIGIOUS AND SPIRITUAL OVERTONES, ET?

In any case, claims of contact with extraterrestrial beings, often associated with channeling, span a wide array of purported star systems and alien species.

For instance:

- **Sirius:** Associated with beings known as the Sirians or Sirian beings. These entities are often described as advanced spiritual guides or beings of higher consciousness.[305]
- **Arcturus:** Linked with beings referred to as the Arcturians. They are often portrayed as highly evolved entities with a focus on spiritual growth and healing.[306]
- **Orion:** Beings from Orion are sometimes called Orionites or Orionians. They are portrayed differently in various accounts, ranging from benevolent to malevolent entities.[307]
- **Zeta Reticuli:** Associated with the Zeta Reticulans or Greys. These beings are commonly depicted in popular culture and UFO lore as short, grey-skinned humanoids with large heads and black eyes.[308]

- **Pleiades:** In addition to the Pleiadians, some channelers claim contact with other beings from the Pleiades cluster, often referred to as Plejarens or Plejadians.

The exploration of claims surrounding extraterrestrial contact, particularly through the lens of channeling, offers a fascinating glimpse into the intersection of spirituality, belief systems, and the human fascination with the unknown.

This phenomenon, often associated with the New Age movement, involves individuals who claim to communicate with beings from distant star systems beyond our own. Note that in the examples above, some of the channeled entities claim to be *both* interdimensional and intergalactic in nature.

Channeling, the central practice in these encounters, involves a person acting as a conduit or medium through which extraterrestrial beings purportedly communicate messages or information. This process is often described as a form of telepathic or intuitive communication, with the channeler entering a trancelike state to facilitate the exchange of information. Channelers may claim to receive guidance, wisdom, or prophecies from these beings, which they then share with others.

One common thread among these descriptions is the emphasis on spiritual themes and higher consciousness. Many channeling experiences focus on topics such as enlightenment, personal transformation, and the evolution of consciousness.

These encounters often present teachings on how to live more harmoniously with oneself, others, and the universe at large. The messages purportedly conveyed by these extraterrestrial beings often resonate with New Age beliefs in interconnectedness, love, and the power of intention. The experiences are not restricted to channelers or mediums, per se.

Reiki: The Universal Energy Often Connected to ET

Reiki practitioners and well-known YouTube channels that offer Reiki ASMR act in the same capacity as gateway drugs to the occult, introducing people who are often unfamiliar with New Age or neopagan spirituality to a "universal life force energy" that flows through all living things.

The discovery of "Reiki energy" is attributed to Mikao Usui, a Japanese Buddhist monk who lived in the late-nineteenth and early-twentieth centuries. Usui is said to have developed the system of Reiki healing after undergoing a spiritual experience during a meditation retreat on Mount Kurama in Japan.[309, 310, 311]

According to tradition, Usui received the knowledge and ability to heal through touch after a period of fasting, meditation, and spiritual revelation. This energy purportedly enhances healing and restores balance on physical, emotional, mental, and spiritual levels. However, it also teaches concepts that are innately contradictory, such as:

- "The energy is not guided by the practitioner, but the energy has its own innate wisdom to guide itself."
- "Reiki energy is not based on belief, faith or suggestion."[312]

If Reiki energy indeed possesses innate guiding wisdom, as the first statement suggests, that implies a form of intelligence or consciousness inherent within the energy, or that a higher intelligence or consciousness other than the practitioner is "guiding" it.

However, if Reiki energy isn't based on belief, faith, or suggestion, as the second statement claims, that raises the question of how the energy's guidance is determined or manifested independently of these factors. Of course, this leads back to the de facto conclusion that a higher intelligence or consciousness other than the practitioner is "guiding" it.

Reiki.org gets even more explicit and excited about a "new development" called "Holy Fire Reiki," which absolutely smacks of religious belief. The organization has also conveniently trademarked the term: "Holy Fire® energy is noticeably more refined and comes from a higher level of consciousness."[313] This begs the question as to whose higher level of consciousness this form of Reiki originates from—that of the practitioner or that of a "higher intelligence?"

Practitioners assert that Reiki can address a wide range of health issues, alleviate pain, reduce stress, and enhance overall well-being. Their language is couched in affirmations and, often, in female empowerment. It's described as a spiritual practice, but it's super low-key. As a viewer, one can participate in the "energy exchange" by simply thinking or saying out loud, "I accept." It purportedly never violates the participant's free will.

Somehow, this supposed respect for the participant's free will seems reminiscent of the vampire in myth. It is an evil monster, but it stands at the door in the guise of, perhaps, a beautiful person. Interestingly, it cannot touch someone in their own house unless they actively "invite it in."

In any case, the majority of these Reiki Master practitioners in their YouTube video channel not only "universal life-force energy," but entities as well. They call upon angels (often the archangel Michael, Raphael, Uriel, or Metatron), intergalactic aliens, ancient pagan gods, or ascended masters.[314, 315, 316, 317, 318]

MORE "SERIOUS-MINDED" CHANNELING

Then there are more (supposedly) science-minded individuals, like Dr. Steven M. Greer, an American ufologist and retired physician who founded the Center for the Study of Extraterrestrial Intelligence (CSETI) and the Disclosure Project.

While putting out serious work through the Disclosure Project and coproducing films such as *Sirius*, a documentary detailing his work and hypotheses regarding extraterrestrial life and government cover-ups, he also can now "summon" extraterrestrial entities using his "CE-5 protocol" (close encounters of the fifth kind). The CE-5 protocols are based on the idea that humans can make conscious contact with extraterrestrial civilizations through meditation, remote viewing, and other techniques. The protocols involve groups of people gathering in a specific location, usually at night, and attempting to contact extraterrestrial beings through thought and consciousness.[319]

With all the above in mind, those who channel entities claiming to be aliens from another star system, angels, ascended masters, et cetera, would do well to ask some clarifying questions:

- What empirical evidence supports the assertion that these entities are indeed aliens from a different star system?
- Are there any scientific observations, data, or documentation corroborating their extraterrestrial origin?
- If they are as advanced as they say, why can't they "downgrade" their communications from telepathy and verify themselves as physical beings using technology they "know" we possess?
- If they are beings of "higher vibrational frequencies" and are spiritually more advanced, with mental abilities we're only now beginning to develop (or that we can develop once we've also raised our vibrational frequencies to the point of ascension), why can't they telepathically speak to crowds of people "who are on the path toward ascension"—all at the same time, so hundreds or thousands of people receive the same message simultaneously?
- Why do so many contactees/channelers seem to contact a mishmash of entities (e.g., they're in contact with aliens, angels, *and* ascended spiritual masters)?
- Are we to believe that *all* these various species (Reptilians, Nordics, Tall Whites, et cetera) are telepathic *and* can communicate with humanity via mind power alone across hundreds, thousands, even hundreds of thousands of light-years?
- How do we determine whether an angel is *actually* the angel called upon, such as the archangel Michael?
- How do we determine the true intentions of any entity called upon?
- What evidence exists to support the claim that they are genuinely benevolent or have humanity's best interests at heart?
- Are there any inconsistencies or contradictions in their actions or messages that might indicate ulterior motives?
- What objective criteria are being used to distinguish between different types of beings, such as aliens, angels, or the old pagan gods?

- Are there any potential biases, psychological factors, or external influences that could affect the accuracy or authenticity of the messages received?
- Can the claims of channelers be independently verified? If not, why not?
- Why should anyone "let go and trust the process" when the practitioner doesn't even know where the "universal life-force" of Reiki energy comes from, or who or what intelligence is guiding it?

The ET channelers, New Age spiritualists, Reiki Masters, and even some within the UFO community have the following in common:

- They engage in very little science and a whole lot of religious practice.
- They rehash old, spiritual, pagan practices that put them in contact with, or open them up to contact with, entities they know nothing about—and they are gullibly taking these beings at their word.

Why would any educated, modern person do that? Let's let Timothy Alberino once again elucidate:

Human history bears witness to the fact that men are oft inclined to worship what they cannot comprehend.

Hence, the veneration of heavenly bodies—the sun, moon, and stars—and of the elemental forces of nature—water, wind, and fire—is an ever-present characteristic of primitive cultures.

Considering this proclivity to prostrate before the unexplained, it is not profitable for men of antiquated knowledge to be acquainted with beings of superior intelligence....

Man is at a disadvantage in such an encounter, susceptible to deception and manipulation.[320]

IN THE SHADOW OF GOLIATH

Humanity tends to not only worship what it doesn't understand, but also to listen to and obey what it considers a higher authority. It often does so unquestioningly, regardless of the folly doing so might entail. A great example of this lies within the classic film, *Star Trek V: The Final Frontier*.

Near the end of the movie, the characters of Captain Kirk, Mr. Spock, and Dr. McCoy find themselves on an alien world where an incredibly powerful entity claiming to be God is trying to hitch a ride off the planet. It resorts to displays of power, demonstrates hidden knowledge, and employs emotional and mental manipulation to accomplish its ends.

Then, it slips up and makes a mistake. It demands a ride out on Kirk's starship.

The following dialogue demonstrates Kirk's critical thinking and McCoy's tendency to believe the alien being really is "God," based on its demonstrations of power alone. (And he's supposed to be a man of medical science!)

> Kirk: What does God need with a starship?
> McCoy: Jim, what are you doing?
> Kirk: I'm asking a question.
> God: Who is this creature?
> Kirk: Who am I? Don't you know? Aren't you God?
> Sybok: He has his doubts.
> God: You doubt me?
> Kirk: I seek proof.
> McCoy: Jim, you don't ask the Almighty for His I.D.[321,322]

Like Dr. McCoy, channelers, Reiki Masters, New Agers, and so-called alien contactees are all intelligent people, some highly educated, who are essentially entertaining beings of "higher intelligence"—or their teachings—and are too awed by demonstrations of power, miracles, esoteric knowledge, and promises of ascension to demand verifiable credentials.

One other thing must be said. While most Christians invariably call these practices "demonic" and say these ET channelers, New Age spiritualists, Reiki Masters, and even some within the UFO community are actually "worshiping the devil," the vast majority of these individuals would deny such an accusation. They would do so vehemently and would undoubtedly be insulted at the very notion.

So, let's rearrange the furniture in the collective consciousness' mental space and use different language. Let's admit that 99.999 percent of these people are not falling on their knees and praying to entities they believe are demons. They are not (knowingly) calling upon Satan. They are not drinking blood, engaging in animal or human sacrifices to fallen angels, and engaging in "black magic" to summon devils.

However, if you're an ET channeler, New Age spiritualist, or Reiki Master practitioner who likes to get "a little witchy" and who calls upon interdimensional beings of any kind (aliens, angels, or ascended masters), you're engaging with beings about whom you are wildly ignorant. Maybe you will "manifest abundance" or a romantic relationship, or perhaps you'll gain a deep knowledge of "esoteric healing modalities."

Maybe you will receive visions, maybe you'll get glimpses of the future (yours or someone else's), or maybe these entities will converse with you and relate hidden mysteries.

There's power there. It's real.

But you are undoubtedly engaging with the teachings and doctrines of beings described long ago in texts predating the oldest grimoires, older than the teachings of Mikao Usui and his masters, and certainly older than the CE-5 protocols. You're acting as a conduit to entities who claim to have your "highest good" at heart, but who may belong to malevolent, rebel, cosmic factions—entities who have no problem lying to you, getting you on their side, and then using you to deceive others.

Listening to them and engaging in these practices, then, is perhaps an incredibly foolish decision. It's one based upon what author John Daniel Davidson states is "a radically subjective worldview that rejects both objective reason and objective morality, and posits the individual self as the final arbiter of truth."[323]

The evidence presented above dismantles the simplistic assumption that all extraterrestrial encounters are inherently demonic. While the term "demonic" is often used indiscriminately to categorize nonhuman entities perceived as malevolent, the reality is far more complex. If we dig into Scripture, rabbinic tradition, and even modern encounters, a clear pattern emerges. Demons, as described in the Hebrew Scriptures, the Dead Sea Scrolls, the New Testament, and more are a whole different breed from fallen angels or interdimensional beings.

Here's a main takeaway: Demons don't show up physically. They don't abduct people, leave scorch marks on the ground, or play games with government radar systems. But the entities modern-day abductees and channelers keep running into? They sometimes do those things.

They act more like interdimensional hustlers—twisting perceptions, presenting themselves as enlightened beings, and pushing agendas that smell a lot like occultism in disguise. It's manipulation, plain and simple, dressed up in a slick, futuristic wrapper. A likely, logical, and ultimately disturbing possibility is that some of these entities are fallen angels dressing themselves up as interstellar visitors to hide their true nature.

But it doesn't stop there. It goes way deeper.

Think about this: What if the fiery, serpentine beings known as Seraphim—some of the same creatures described in biblical and rabbinic sources as worshiping God (Isaiah 6:2–3)—are themselves implicated in the modern narratives surrounding reptilian overlords?

From Graham Hancock's vivid encounters with intelligent, serpentine beings during ayahuasca ceremonies, Rick Strassman's documented reports of reptilian entities encountered by volunteers in *DMT: The Spirit Molecule* and Dr. Karla Turner's chilling accounts of abductees confronting reptilian beings—alongside ancient texts describing heavenly beings with reptilian traits—the parallels are too glaring to ignore.

The next chapter is where it all comes together.

We're diving headfirst into the possibility that the terrifyingly powerful Seraphim of Scripture and the serpentine entities described in modern UFO lore are, in fact, one and the same.

CHAPTER SEVEN

SERAPHIM AS EXTRATERRESTRIALS?

The serpent is not a hallucination but a constant. From Eden's *nachash* to Dulce's Dracos, these beings defy time and culture. As Winkelman—a renowned anthropologist and researcher best known for his work on shamanism, altered states of consciousness, and cross-cultural studies of religious experience—warns, their ubiquity points to a "liminal space" where biology and cosmology collide. One species. One high-ranking class of celestial power: the Seraphim. And not the loyal ones, the rebels.

> Seraphim were standing above Him, each having six wings: with two each covered his face, and with two each covered his feet, and with two each flew. (Isaiah 6:2)

> שְׂרָפִים עֹמְדִים ׀ מִמַּעַל לוֹ שֵׁשׁ כְּנָפַיִם שֵׁשׁ כְּנָפַיִם לְאֶחָד
> בִּשְׁתַּיִם ׀ יְכַסֶּה פָנָיו וּבִשְׁתַּיִם יְכַסֶּה רַגְלָיו וּבִשְׁתַּיִם יְעוֹפֵף׃

A handful of celestial species—on paper—look a whole lot like the so-called aliens people claim to encounter in close-contact situations. The primary objective of this chapter is to explore whether the fiery, serpentine beings known as Seraphim from biblical and rabbinic sources are, in fact, the same entities as the reptilian overlords described in modern UFO lore.

This chapter weaves together theological analysis, various theories, historical accounts, and eyewitness testimony to determine whether the repeated descriptions of these beings point toward a common origin.

Let's start by naming names.

The Seraphim and the Ishim (the manlike beings) map eerily well onto the typical lineup: Reptilians, Nordics, and (perhaps) Tall Whites.

We'll kick things off with the Seraphim—the ancient, snakelike beings that show up in old texts as fiery, winged, humanoid serpents. In theology, they're high-ranking. Elite. Sitting front-row, nearest to the throne of God.

While the Seraphim, the *nachash* of Genesis, and the so-called Dracos and native Terran Reptoids of UFO lore appear distinct in origin and narrative, the possibility that these are culturally fragmented recollections of a common entity type—serpentine, radiant, wise, and rebellious—isn't just plausible, it's increasingly likely, given the pattern repetition across time, culture, and textual traditions.

What I'm about to discuss isn't a case of careless conflation, it's deliberate synthesis. The goal here is not to erase the lines between species or traditions, but to consider whether these lines were drawn later, after the core archetype had already fractured and was scattered across the mythologies and theologies of human history.

Remember to keep in mind that Pseudo-Dionysius and the rest of the Christian thinkers gave Seraphim top-tier status in their manufactured hierarchies. But here's the uncomfortable question: What if those same revered Seraphs match the reptilian entities that show up in extraterrestrial accounts?

Think about it. The overlap is almost too clean:

- ▶ Both are described as powerful, interdimensional entities.
- ▶ Both are tied to occult knowledge and supernatural encounters.
- ▶ Both have status—either in the divine council or the alien pecking order.
- ▶ And, yeah, both are reptilian.

SERAPHIM AS EXTRATERRESTRIALS?

As I asked before, coincidence? Maybe.

But once you see the pattern, you can't unsee it.

SERAPHIM AND INTERDIMENSIONAL REPTILIANS

As we covered earlier, Seraphim sit at the top of the food chain in Christian angelology. And, wouldn't you know it? The reptilian entities in modern UFO lore hold a similar spot. They're advanced, powerful, and reportedly in charge of other alien races.

Interestingly, this includes Reptilians being somehow "the overlords in the background" to the infamous Greys, the creepy little guys whose interactions with humanity are often directly linked to UFO abduction cases.[324, 325]

Now, the UFO crowd loves to yap about the so-called Dracos or Draconians—big, bad reptilian overlords that are supposedly pulling strings from the shadows. And guess what? These lizard folks aren't just making cameo appearances in some random abduction story. No indeed. They're allegedly top brass in the extraterrestrial hierarchy, often described as running the show from deep underground, other planets, or even other dimensions. (Big clue right there.)

According to the lore, these Draconians claim Earth as their "original home." They say they were booted out ages ago after some colossal war with human ancestors.

Where did they go after getting the boot? The answer according to that same lore is deep down in subterranean lairs, off-world bases, or dimensions most people don't believe exist.

Then there are the somewhat-closer-to-home Terran Reptoids—alien, humanoid reptilians that evolved on Earth during the time of the dinosaurs.

Whether we're talking Dracos or Reptoids—regardless of supposed origin—these guys have qualities that scream "power."

Sounds crazy, right? But if we dig through the reports, it's like a broken record. Same story, different sources...and we'll get to all that in a bit.

Descriptions of the leadership caste of these reptilian aliens suggest the Seraphim, or maybe the Seraphim that got kicked out of the Divine Clubhouse.

I'm not saying that just looking the part makes them Seraphim. But bear in mind that while physical similarity alone doesn't prove identity, when these similarities are paired with overlapping traits—intelligence, status, wings, fire, interdimensionality, and an obsession with deception—the case becomes more than coincidental.

DAVID ICKE'S CLAIMS AND ANALYSIS

In logic, when patterns pile up, you've got evidence. The overlap isn't being used to prove identity outright, but to build a cumulative case based on converging descriptions found in religious texts, myth, and modern testimony.

Is it proof? No. But it's not a gentle suggestion, either. It's a cosmic elbow in the ribs saying, "Hey, pay attention."

As the controversial author David Icke states:

> Summarising all the research I have read, the people I have met, and the accounts of those who claim to have experienced these reptile humanoids or reptilians, the following appears to be the case. There are many sub and crossbreed races of the reptilians.
>
> Their elite [are] known by UFO researchers as the Draco. These are the "big boys" in every sense and they are usually between seven and twelve feet tall. They have wings which are flaps of skin supported by long ribs.
>
> The wings can be folded back against the body and they are the origin of the term "winged serpent." They are also the origin of the term "fallen angels."[326]

According to Icke, these reptilian entities hail from the Draco constellation, but they're not just space tourists, they're interdimensional, shape-shifting, and capable of masquerading as humans. He goes on to state that "one of their other planets of influence long ago is reckoned to have been Mars." It's important to recognize the dual material/spiritual nature of these reptilian aliens as described by Icke (and many others).

Indeed, Icke's theory combines elements of the ancient astronaut hypothesis, New Age religion, and conspiracy theories. If he was alone in his views, some might write them off as just the odd ideas of a "crackpot" theorist.

Let me just say that, yeah, David Icke says a lot of wild stuff. Some of it's earned every bit of the backlash—especially when it veers into anti-Semitic tropes or pure, uncut tinfoil. But tossing *everything* he's ever said into the garbage because of that?

That's intellectual laziness. It's like bulldozing an entire archeological site because one bone turned out to be a goat, not a god.

In the infamous words of Barack Obama: "Let me be clear."

Or as George H. W. Bush said: "Read my lips."

I'm not here to wave Icke's flag. I'm here to point out something most people miss. Even broken compasses sometimes point north. The fringe has a funny way of warping old truths. Sometimes, buried beneath the crazy, you catch the outline of something ancient—and real.

Case in point: Icke's reptilian overlords.

Strip away the New Age and conspiracy-theory frosting, and what you're left with looks a *heck* of a lot like the Seraphim of Scripture and the dragon archetypes that show up in the myths of nearly every ancient culture.

Icke's ideas didn't arise in a vacuum. At least in some ways, he's picked up on some things that may be entirely real, at least to a degree.

While there is no doubt his descriptions of these winged, serpentine overlords have been widely ridiculed—partly because of how far he takes the theory, and partly because of who he is—his core claims aren't as isolated as critics might assume. In fact, Icke's picture of these interdimensional beings finds strange resonance in the works of researchers who come from radically different backgrounds—psychonauts, theologians, scholars of mythology, and abductees themselves.

IN THE SHADOW OF GOLIATH

GRAHAM HANCOCK'S EXPERIENCES

Best-selling author and journalist Graham Hancock has described vivid encounters with intelligent serpentine beings while under the influence of ayahuasca in the Amazon. In his book *Supernatural*, Hancock shares a journal entry written after one of his experiences:

> January 29: Strange and terrifying (briefly), although it didn't start that way. I drink at 8.05 p.m. For the first half-hour, as usual, nothing much happens, just queasy and formless luminescences. Then I begin to see snakes, not a lot and not spectacular. By 9:05 I'm feeling more intoxicated, dizzy and nauseous.
>
> But still just snakes. Not many. Mid-size. They're coiling and writhing around a bit more. I begin to wonder (foolish bravado) if this is all I'm going to get. The nausea increases and the whole visionary experience ratchets up a notch and becomes more sinister.
>
> My eyes are closed throughout, but when I "look" up, the visions are "up" and when I "look" down they're "down." I have the sense of gazing through a tunnel—a tunnel with serpents coiled at the side of it, close to my eyes, threatening to fall on me.
>
> I throw up over the back of the bench I'm sitting on.
>
> As I shift position the serpents shift with me. The visions stay strong while I'm vomiting. As I stop and return to the seated position, everything ratchets up another notch. The serpents morph into Chinese dragons with beards and long serpentine bodies.
>
> Serpents and serpentine dragons with beards and rows of teeth. It's as though a Chinese painting has come to life. And again—where did the ancient Chinese originally mine this imagery from, if not from the visionary world?
>
> I'm convinced it's not a matter of my vision being inspired by Chinese paintings—which I hardly ever think of. I'm getting a glimpse into the same visionary realm that inspired the Chinese artists—and countless other mythologies in which dragons feature.[327]

These serpentine visions aren't limited to Hancock's experiences. Giorgio Samorini, a reputable ethnobotanist, has documented strikingly similar encounters across various cultures in his work *Animals and Psychedelics: The Natural World and the Instinct to Alter Consciousness* (2002).[328]

Samorini's research highlights how archetypal experiences, including interactions with serpentlike beings, emerge repeatedly across cultures and time periods. Such consistency suggests these encounters may be indicative of deeper, underlying realities rather than mere hallucinations or cultural artifacts.

Similarly, Michael Winkelman's *Shamanism: A Biopsychosocial Paradigm of Consciousness and Healing* (2010) provides further evidence that encounters with reptilian or serpentine beings are common cross-culturally.[329] Through his biopsychosocial approach, Winkelman demonstrates that mystical experiences involving serpentine entities are not only recurrent but are often central to shamanic traditions worldwide.

This supports the idea that these beings exist within a shared visionary realm accessible through altered states of consciousness.

Anthropologist R. J. Castillo also examined these phenomena in his peer-reviewed article, "Culture, Trance, and the Mind-Brain Relationship" (1995), noting the consistency of such visions, particularly those involving serpentine entities, across various cultures and historical periods.[330]

Castillo's findings reinforce the notion that these visions aren't isolated to modern psychonauts like Hancock, but are part of a broader, historically rooted phenomenon.

Going back to Hancock's journal entry, at this point, he isn't just seeing things; he's feeling them. And the vibe turns dark. Fast. No more harmless light shows or trippy visuals. The whole atmosphere shifts—like flipping a switch from curiosity to cosmic threat.

Suddenly, he's face-to-face with a classic Grey alien again—one he saw in a previous trip—but this time, it's different. Harsher. Colder. It's not just observing, it's commanding. Looming.

He starts seeing what looks like flying saucers—pulsing with light, spinning upward through some kind of dimensional funnel. Not sci-fi. Not metaphor. Present.

And here's the part that should make you sit up: He feels like if he doesn't stop the vision, he's going to be taken. This is the classic abduction scenario. It isn't a dream. It's not sleep paralysis. It's a full-on spiritual hijacking, with ships and all. So, he forces his eyes open to break the sequence.

But the weirdness doesn't end there. Even back in the "real world," he can feel them—serpentine beings, dragons, insectile aliens, ships—whirling just out of sight. They're not gone, just veiled.

Then it gets more specific: The main entity morphs. Sometimes it's a serpent. Sometimes it's a dragon. But other times, it's something worse, like a giant insect with humanoid traits.

And it's not alone. There's a whole team of them—smaller insectoid creatures, like worker ants. About three feet tall. Moving with purpose. Doing something.

Then two planetary visions burn into his memory. One's a massive world surrounded by rings—think Saturn on steroids. The other's a transparent, iridescent Earth, delicate like a soap bubble, floating between two cupped hands. You can see straight through the continents—like the planet is being held, examined, maybe even owned.

Hancock later admits these beings—like the ancient, feathered serpents of Mesoamerican lore—weren't just showing him stuff for fun. They were *teaching*. Think of that—a malevolent teacher, and *manipulative*.

Makes me think of a reptilian, cackling Emperor Palpatine from *Star Wars*: "Yes, my young apprentice, yes—something, something, something—your journey to the dark side—(cackle, cackle)—will be complete!"

Only this isn't pretend, and it's not a joke.

Hancock is left wondering—and so should we—if these entities exist in a dimension that only opens when consciousness is altered.

If Hancock had approached the biblical texts with the same seriousness he gives other ancient traditions, he might have realized something profound: Altered states of consciousness don't fabricate illusion, and they're not the only way to access another side of reality. They do, however, *reveal* a layer of reality that's usually sealed off from human perception.

SERAPHIM AS EXTRATERRESTRIALS?

There's a reason for that.

According to the biblical worldview, this veil exists as a safeguard—a divine firewall, if you will—separating us from an ancient coalition of powerful, malevolent intelligences. Beings who exist just beyond the threshold of ordinary awareness.

Beings we, in our current form, are wholly unprepared to face, let alone overcome, on our own.

This is why the biblical God lays down such fierce prohibitions against sorcery and ritualistic drug use. It's not out of fear of knowledge; it's to keep the door *shut* to hostile entities who disguise themselves as teachers, guides, and cosmic benefactors.

It's why, in the harshest language possible, "witches" and sorcerers were condemned. Not for challenging orthodoxy—but for aligning themselves, knowingly or unknowingly, with forces bent on subverting and enslaving the human race.[331]

These figures were more than mystics. They were conduits—*collaborators*—helping enemy intelligences infiltrate human civilization. Spiritual kapos. Traitors to their own kind. Some were deceived. Others knew exactly what they were doing.

While the rituals have changed, the recruitment hasn't stopped.

So, to circle back, Graham Hancock's spent years diving into altered states of consciousness—especially through ayahuasca trips. Guess what keeps showing up? These serpent-like beings. Over and over.

Personally, I wonder why such a smart guy (and, as with most of the authors I mention in this book, I respect Hancock and his research) doesn't seem to put two and two together and come up with what seems obvious: He was experiencing something a heck of a lot darker than just "wise mentors" putting on a friendly face.

SUPPORTING CLINICAL STUDIES

Rick Strassman's work in *DMT: The Spirit Molecule* further corroborates these reports. During his clinical studies, volunteers frequently encountered entities, including reptilian figures, during their DMT (dimethyltryptamine) sessions. These beings often conveyed messages or engaged in complex interactions, suggesting the existence of intelligences in other dimensions.

One set of Strassman's notes reads:

> When reviewing my bedside notes, I continually feel surprised to see how many of our volunteers "made contact" with "them," or other beings. At least half did so in one form or another. Research subjects used expressions like "entities," "beings," "aliens," "guides," and "helpers" to describe them. The "life-forms" looked like clowns, reptiles, mantises, bees, spiders, cacti, and stick figures.
>
> It is still startling to see my written records of comments like, "There were these beings," "I was being led," and "They were on me fast." It's as if my mind refuses to accept what's there in black and white.[332]

Strassman's research is particularly striking when considered alongside Hancock's reports involving reptilian or serpentine beings.

Also, it's crucial to recall that Strassman's investigations and analysis are not simply anecdotal; they're rooted in clinical studies involving DMT, conducted under rigorous scientific conditions.

Dr. Karla Turner, a dedicated UFO researcher and abductee herself, also reported cases where individuals encountered reptilian beings during abduction experiences. These things weren't just physically imposing; they had the power to mess with human perception itself—total control over we see, hear, and feel.

More importantly, Turner's findings blow a hole in the convenient, "it's all psychedelics and mystical visions" argument. These meetings aren't just occurring to people tripping on ayahuasca or meditating themselves into another dimension. They're happening *in the flesh*, during full-on physical abductions.

Turner pulled no punches. She knew the difference between hallucination and hostile intent. What she found sure wasn't friendly.

Describing one abductee's experience, she wrote:

SERAPHIM AS EXTRATERRESTRIALS?

Around this same time, in September 1989, Polly's family also had an experience with a different sort of creature. They perceived it as "sloshing" through solid matter, moving "through physical objects as if they were water."

In spite of no clear confrontation with this being, Polly felt that it was, "reptilian, huge and loud," making "crashing sounds in the woods like some very large two-legged creature lumbering through the woods in a very wet area."[333]

Stack up the testimony of David Icke, Graham Hancock, Rick Strassman, and Karla Turner, and we've got a pattern too blatant to ignore.

From trippy ayahuasca visions and ritualistic encounters to *full-on* physical abductions, one thing keeps showing up like a bad penny: reptilian or serpentine entities. Same types. Same tactics. Different methods of contact.

Icke's depiction of Draco overlords may seem extreme, but when placed alongside Hancock's reports of serpentine teachers in ayahuasca visions, Strassman's accounts of reptilian beings encountered during DMT studies, and Turner's chilling accounts of abductions involving perception-altering reptilians, the convergence is undeniable. These experiences suggest a shared thread: intelligences capable of interfacing with humanity through altered states, abduction scenarios, and even direct physical encounters.

With all the above in mind, none of this is easy to shrug off. No matter what we think these beings might be, the parallels to Seraphim, dragon-like beings, and serpent deities from ancient history are too consistent to be coincidence.

This isn't just a modern phenomenon: The same figures have been lurking in the myths and religions of nearly every ancient culture. And that's exactly where we're heading next.

CROSS-CULTURAL SERPENTINE ARCHETYPES

Serpentine gods and dragon-type beings show up in just about every major culture across the planet and feature prominently in mythologies across numerous cultures worldwide.

In ancient Egypt, the cobra goddess Wadjet was revered as a protector of kings and childbirth. Mesoamerican cultures worshiped serpent gods like Quetzalcoatl, the feathered-serpent deity of the Aztecs, associated with wisdom and creation. Hindu mythology features powerful Naga serpent deities such as Shesha, who supports the world.

Chinese mythology reveres dragons as symbols of imperial power and divine blessings. Norse legends tell of Jörmungandr, the World Serpent encircling the earth. African traditions include serpent spirits like Mami Wata, associated with fertility and healing.

The Rainbow Serpent is a prominent deity in Aboriginal Australian mythology, often depicted as a creator god imparting knowledge and establishing laws and customs for the people.

In Native American mythology, particularly among tribes such as the Hopi, Navajo, Apache, and Cherokee, the Thunder Lizard is a powerful serpent or dragon-like creature associated with thunder, lightning, and storms. It is often depicted as a primordial being that shaped the land and waters, creating mountains, rivers, and lakes. The Thunder Lizard is also believed to possess the ability to shape-shift.

These widespread serpentine myths often attribute qualities of wisdom, power, and cosmic significance to immensely powerful, often-winged, snakelike or reptilian beings that frequently also have the power to change shape.

Sure, some of these myths may have popped up on their own. But let's not kid ourselves—when radiant, winged, serpentine brainiacs keep showing up across disconnected civilizations, we're not dealing with random storytelling; we're seeing a pattern, a shared typology. Maybe even the same players wearing different masks.

C. S. Lewis argued that myth works like memory—it warps, stretches, and dramatizes.[334] But it doesn't just make stuff up out of thin air. When the *same* freaky motifs keep repeating from one culture to the next, it raises the question of whether humanity is remembering different faces of the same ancient reality—filtered through the symbols and worldviews of their time.

SERAPHIM AS EXTRATERRESTRIALS?

IN THE OCCULT

These serpent-like beings are also described in theosophical ideas of the "lost worlds" of Atlantis and Lemuria, particularly Helena Blavatsky's *The Secret Doctrine* written in 1888, with its reference to "'dragon-men' who once had a mighty civilization on a Lemurian continent."[335]

In the 1940s, American occultist Maurice Doreal (also known as Claude Doggins) wrote a pamphlet entitled "Mysteries of the Gobi" that described a "serpent race" with "bodies like man but…heads…like a great snake" and an ability to take human form. These creatures also appeared in Doreal's poem, "The Emerald Tablets," in which he referred to Emerald Tablets written by "Thoth, an Atlantean Priest king."

Across the board, these snakelike beings weren't seen as pests or metaphors. They were cosmic powerhouses—wise, winged, shape-shifting, and divine. Reptilian? Absolutely.

Imaginary? You sure about that?

It's easy for religious Jews and Christians to dismiss all this as occult nonsense or pagan fairytales. But let's not forget: The best lies are dressed in just enough truth to pass inspection.

Satan quoted Scripture in the wilderness.[336] Fallen angels twist biblical language into counterfeit gospels.[337] And, as uncomfortable as it may be, some of what shows up in esoteric religions and mystery cults has *roots* in Scripture.

Just because the occult hijacked the imagery doesn't mean they made it up.

IN GENESIS

Let's get back to Genesis. There are hints that the "serpent" in the Garden of Eden described in the Bible's first book wasn't a mere snake, but rather a Seraph—or some type of reptilian humanoid, a sentient being some believe may have existed as a member of a pre-Adamic race.[338]

To reiterate: The thing in Eden wasn't a cartoonish snake slithering around like a talking zoo animal. It was radiant. It was serpentine. It was divine. Most likely, it was a rogue Seraph—one of the high-ranking, celestial-throne-room dudes who decided to go off script.

And guess what?

That same type of being keeps popping up across the board. Ancient myth? Check. Esoteric occult trash? Check. Modern UFO abduction reports? Check. Winged serpent, dragon-god, Draco overlord—different names, same blueprint.

Let me say it again lest it gets lost in translation: This chapter doesn't argue that these are *similar* beings. It argues that they're the *same* type of being, filtered through the stories and symbols of different cultures.

One species, one high-ranking class of celestial power: the Seraphim. And not the loyal ones, the rebels.

Check it out. Dr. Karl Shuker—legit British zoologist, Scientific Fellow of the Zoological Society of London, and not your average armchair theorist—points out something most Bible teachers wouldn't touch with a ten-foot pole. According to the Zohar, the backbone of Jewish Kabbalistic thought, the serpent in Eden wasn't a scaly garden pest. Before the curse, it *walked upright*—on two legs. Humanlike.

It wasn't small, either. We're talking *camel height*. The average camel stands about 6 to 7 feet (1.8 to 2.1 meters) tall at the shoulder. Factoring in the height of the hump, camels' height can reach 7 to 8 feet (2.1 to 2.4 meters) overall.

Yeah. Let that sink in.

This is an intelligent, humanoid, reptilian being standing much taller than most humans.[339]

Some critics will say I'm taking metaphors too literally. But take into account that I've said the same thing repeatedly. It's just as likely—perhaps more so—that literal beings were later allegorized by theologians who were uncomfortable with their physicality.

Ancient writers didn't flinch at hybrid creatures, radiant entities, or full-blown encounters with divine beings. That was their *normal*. It's modern theology—post-Enlightenment, sterilized, and scared of the so-called supernatural—that turned fiery Seraphim into harmless metaphors and flattened the supernatural into abstract poetry.

I'd ask you to keep that in mind going forward.

In Genesis 3, the serpent is described as being "more crafty than any of the wild animals the Lord God had made," and engages in a conversation with Eve, leading to the Fall of Man. The text doesn't explicitly identify the serpent as Satan or any other supernatural being, but later interpretations and texts have made this connection because of the language used.

וְהַנָּחָשׁ הָיָה עָרוּם מִכֹּל חַיַּת הַשָּׂדֶה אֲשֶׁר עָשָׂה יְהוָה אֱלֹהִים וַיֹּאמֶר אֶל־הָאִשָּׁה אַף כִּי־אָמַר אֱלֹהִים לֹא תֹאכְלוּ מִכֹּל עֵץ הַגָּן׃ (Genesis 3:1)

Interestingly, the phrase "more crafty than any of the wild animals" is also translated as "the shrewdest of all the wild beasts." In Genesis 3:1, the Hebrew word used for "animal" or "beast" in the phrase "more crafty than any of the wild animals" is *chayyat* (חַיַּת). This word is derived from the root *chai*, (חַי), which means "life" or "living." The full phrase in Hebrew is:

וְהַנָּחָשׁ הָיָה עָרוּם מִכֹּל חַיַּת הַשָּׂדֶה אֲשֶׁר עָשָׂה יְהוָה אֱלֹהִים

Here, *chayyat ha-sadeh* (חַיַּת הַשָּׂדֶה) translates to "beast of the field." The term *chayyat* (חַיַּת) is a general term for living creatures.

The Hebrew word used for "creature" when speaking of the celestial "living creatures" seen in visions, such as those described in the book of Ezekiel, is *chayyot* (חַיּוֹת). This term is the plural form of *chayyah* (חַיָּה), which was used to describe the serpent in Genesis.

Now, the *chayyot* (חַיּוֹת) are described in Ezekiel's vision of the heavenly chariot (Merkabah) in Ezekiel 1 and 10. These beings are depicted as having four faces (that of a man, a lion, an ox, and an eagle) and are identified as cherubim in Ezekiel 10.

As we've already seen, the term "Seraphim" is often associated with fiery, burning ones, and they are depicted as serpentine, celestial beings. Yet, as mentioned earlier, and despite later traditions, they're never referred to as "angels" in the Hebrew Scriptures. Not once do we see serpentine, celestial beings sent as messengers to humankind—just as we never see Cherubim described as angels or sent as messengers.

The Seraphim are also never referred to explicitly as "living creatures" as are the Cherubim. However, it is doubtful anyone would argue that the Cherubim are "living animals" or "living beasts." "Living creatures," though, is an excellent description for the Cherubim. Logically, the Seraphim also fit this description, as they're undoubtedly depicted as "living" and as "creatures."

Thus, a more fitting translation of the serpent's description in the Garden of Eden might be: "The shrewdest of all living creatures God had made."

As Dr. Michael Heiser wrote:

> The pivotal character of Genesis 3 is the serpent. The Hebrew word translated serpent is *nachash*. The word is both plain and elastic.
>
> The most straightforward meaning is the one virtually all translators and interpreters opt for: serpent. When the Hebrew root letters n-ch-sh are a noun, that's the meaning.
>
> But n-ch-sh are also the consonants of a verb. If we changed the vowels to a verbal form (recall that Hebrew originally had no vowels), we would have *nochesh*, which means "the diviner." Divination refers to communication with the supernatural world.
>
> A diviner in the ancient world was one who foretold omens or gave out divine information (oracles). We can see that element in the story. Eve is getting information from this being.[340]

Then Dr. Heiser goes on to talk about this Hebrew root *n-ch-sh* again. And, yes, it usually gets translated as "serpent." But here's where it gets interesting. Turns out, *nachash* can also work as a descriptive noun (like an adjective), and when we start digging, we find it in some weird places.

Take 1 Chronicles 4:12, for example, which mentions a guy named Tehinnah—some random, otherwise unknown dude—who's called the

SERAPHIM AS EXTRATERRESTRIALS?

"father of Ir-Nachash." Now, what in the world is Ir-Nachash? According to Heiser, it translates to "city of copper/bronze (smiths)."

If you've been paying attention, that should set off alarm bells.

Why? Because *nechosheth*—another word from the same root—means "bronze" or "copper." It isn't just some trivial metal tools. Back in the day, copper and bronze were shiny, polished, and significant. They were symbols of craftsmanship and power.

Here's where Heiser cranks up the heat:

> In the Hebrew Scriptures, *nechosheth* is actually used to describe divine beings. Check out *Daniel 10:6*—that's where the divine being's arms and legs are described like polished bronze. Shiny. Gleaming. Otherworldly.[341]

See where this is heading? *Nachash* have layers—metal, brilliance, supernatural connections. This isn't just a "serpent," it's something with radiance.

"We have words with such elasticity in English," says Heiser, "where meaning depends on the part of speech." He lists, for example:

> (Noun): Running is a good form of exercise.
> (Verb): The engine is running on diesel.
> (Adjective): Running paint is an eyesore.

Sometimes writers, when they use a term, want their readers to think about all possible meanings and nuances. If I ask, "How has your reading been?" the reader is forced to think about all three.

> Do I mean the latest assignment (noun)? Am I wondering if you got the right glasses (adjective)? Or am I referencing the process (verb)? What I'm suggesting is that, since there are immediate clues in the story that the serpent is more than a mere snake, that he may be a divine adversary, the term *nachash* is a triple entendre.[342]

Heiser isn't dropping random Hebrew trivia here. He's making us look at the *nachash* from every possible angle, because each one packs serious theological weight.

Rather than being a convenient word for "snake," in the ancient world, the term *nachash* was an image tied to divine guardians. We're talking Seraphim—entities with status. Given Eden's backdrop, that tells us right away: This *nachash* villain isn't any old animal handing out temptation like it's Halloween candy. It's giving Eve an oracle. An omen. What sounds like kingdom-level, classified info is really straight-up, three-letter-agency-style disinformation.

> And the serpent said to the woman, "You won't really die. God knows when you eat, you'll be like the elohim, knowing good and evil."
>
> וַיֹּאמֶר הַנָּחָשׁ אֶל־הָאִשָּׁה לֹא־מוֹת תְּמֻתוּן׃
>
> כִּי יֹדֵעַ אֱלֹהִים כִּי בְּיוֹם אֲכָלְכֶם מִמֶּנּוּ וְנִפְקְחוּ עֵינֵיכֶם וִהְיִיתֶם כֵּאלֹהִים יֹדְעֵי טוֹב וָרָע׃

Dr. Heiser noted that the way these words are used is "also consistent with the imagery from Isaiah 14 and Ezekiel 28."[343] He's right on the money. His insight makes much more sense than the infantile, straightforward interpretations generally given to the identity of the serpent.

Indeed, I believe Genesis uses allegory and what amounts to a certain level of steganography (e.g., hiding critical information within something else that looks innocent or harmless) to conceal earth-shattering truths about humanity's past and origin.

While Timothy Alberino doesn't consider the fallen power behind the serpent in the Garden of Eden to be a serpentine angelic species, he writes of the word *nachash*: "In adjective form it means 'bright, burnished, and shining." While that is certainly true, Alberino connects this being with "Ezekiel's shining son of the morning, the signet of perfection, full of wisdom and perfect in beauty, who was in Eden, the garden of God."[344]

In other words, he sees it as a member of the "Elder Race" of whom we bear a physical resemblance. But some dispute the interpretation of

SERAPHIM AS EXTRATERRESTRIALS?

"the Garden of Eden" as being the same as "Eden the Garden of God" in Ezekiel.

Moreover, all angelic species—whether Cherub, Seraph, Ishim, or another—are almost always described as "bright, burnished, shining, light lightning, or fiery" despite other differences.

Returning to Dr. Heiser:

> God's judgment of Eve is in some sense entwined with the curse of the *nachash*. Eve would suffer intensified pain in childbirth (Genesis 3:16: "I will multiply your pain.").
>
> There is no indication that, had she borne children before the fall, Eve would have felt no pain at all. She was human. And it was important that she bear children, since her childbearing would have some relationship to the destiny of the *nachash* and his deed.
>
> I will put enmity between you and the woman,
> and between your offspring and her offspring;
> he shall bruise your head,
> and you shall bruise his heel (Genesis 3:15, ESV).
>
> The wording of Genesis 3:15 is veiled.... I believe prophecies like this that ultimately move in a messianic direction were deliberately cryptic. At the very least the verse tells us that God was not done with humanity yet. The goal of his rule on earth through humanity would not be abandoned.
>
> A descendant of Eve would come forth who would someday undo the damage caused by the divine rebel, the nachash. That this descendant is linked to Eve implies that the score will be settled through her bloodline.
>
> ...the judgment on Eve also tells us that the nachash would have offspring as well. The rest of the biblical story doesn't consist of humans battling snake people. That's no surprise, since the enemy of humanity wasn't a mere snake.
>
> The Bible does, however, describe an ongoing conflict between followers of Yahweh and human and divine beings who follow the spiritual path of the *nachash*.[345]

THE "BEAST OF THE FIELD" PROBLEM

Dr. Heiser makes a few more salient points.

As we've stated, many folks still cling to the idea that the *nachash* in Eden was simply a talking snake. They think the curse laid on it—that it would thereafter crawl on its belly—proves that. But Dr. Heiser's point is this: Taking that literally is like trying to read Shakespeare with Google Translate. We'd miss all the rich context and meaning.

According to Heiser, we've got to read Genesis 3 with our heads wrapped around the theological messaging and the ancient worldview. The take-away isn't that the snake gets "downgraded" to a worm's-eye view. It's about being cast down, humiliated, and dethroned.

Look at the judgment language in Ezekiel 28 and Isaiah 14. Both passages talk about cosmic villains brought low, hurled down to the dirt—or, in some cases, the underworld (*erets*, a word that can mean literal earth or the realm of the dead). Ezekiel 28:8, 17 and Isaiah 14:11–12, 15 are all about high-and-mighty beings getting knocked off their pedestals.

So, when the *nachash* is cursed by having to crawl on its belly, it's a status downgrade, an exile from the divine council to the dust of the Earth—a metaphorical free fall from power to disgrace. It's about losing access to the heavenly realm and being sentenced to the dirt—or worse, to the underworld.

Specifically, Heiser wrote:

> The curse also had him "eating dirt," clearly a metaphorical reference, since snakes don't really eat dirt as food for nutrition. It isn't part of the "natural snake diet."
>
> The point being made by the curse is that the *nachash*, who wanted to be "most high," will be "most low" instead—cast away from God and the council to earth, and even under the earth.
>
> In the underworld, the *nachash* is even lower than the beasts of the field. He is hidden from view and from life in God's world. His domain is death.[346]

Dr. Heiser's words find traction in the opinions of modern rabbis and within some Rabbinic literature and later Jewish commentaries that explored the idea that the serpent in Eden was a more complex being than merely a snake.

As Rabbi Dovid Rosenfeld wrote in an article for Aish.com:

What was the original Serpent?
It was really more than just a smart snake with legs. It was an intelligent, human-like creature (Talmud Sanhedrin 59b) whose mission was to tempt Adam and Eve to sin. Before Adam and Eve ate from the Tree of Knowledge, they had no inherent desire to sin. Evil was not yet a part of the human psyche.[347]

A significant source from antiquity is the Targum Pseudo-Jonathan, an Aramaic translation and interpretation of the Hebrew Bible. This text explicitly identifies the serpent with Samael, an angelic being often equated with Christianity's Satan/Lucifer. (He's essentially the leader of the rebellious angels in Talmudic/Midrashic thought.)

In Genesis 3:6, the Targum Pseudo-Jonathan states:

And the Woman beheld Samael, the angel of death, and was afraid; yet she knew that the tree was good to eat, and that it was medicine for the enlightenment of the eyes, and desirable tree by means of which to understand. And she took of its fruit, and did eat; and she gave to her husband with her, and he did eat.

Further, *In Pirkei de-Rabbi Eliezer*, Samael is depicted as riding the serpent. This text suggests Samael conspired with the serpent to deceive Eve. The narrative portrays Samael as a rebellious angel who descends to Earth out of jealousy and animosity towards Adam.[348]

This association between Samael and the serpent creates a composite figure that embodies both the angelic and serpentine characteristics, thus linking the serpent to a fallen angelic being.

The Zohar further elaborates on the connection between Samael and the serpent. It describes Samael as the force behind the serpent, thus reinforcing the idea that the serpent was not just a snake but a manifestation of a fallen angelic being.[349]

Likewise, the Talmud (Shabbat 146a) suggests the serpent had a more intimate and corrupting influence on Eve—which some later texts interpret as a metaphor for a deeper, more sinister interaction involving a fallen angel (i.e., this being lusted after her sexually and, in fact, fathered Cain—which may bring the reader to remember another group of angels who carried out their desires to completion in Enoch 1 and Genesis 6.)

Indeed, this story is "a response to the enigmatic verse in which Eve says, I have gotten a man with the aid of Yahweh" (Gen. 4:1). Targum Pseudo-Yonathan translates this verse as "I have acquired a man, the angel of the Lord."

One reading of this verse in the Talmud (B. Shab. 146a), as mentioned above, suggests Eve had intercourse with the serpent: "When the serpent consorted with Eve, he cast impurity into her." This interpretation is echoed in the Zohar: "From the impurity with which the serpent infected Eve emerged Cain."

Pirkei de-Rabbi Eliezer builds on the Talmudic interpretation, but changes it in an essential way. Here the true father of Cain is the angel Samael, who came to Eve riding on the serpent.

The angel and serpent are closely linked in this passage, creating a satanic figure and suggesting Eve had intercourse with the serpent. In *Pirkei de-Rabbi Eliezer*, the Torah upbraids Samael as he rides upon the serpent like a camel:

> The Torah began to cry aloud, saying, "Why, O Samael, now that the world is created, is it time to rebel against God? Is this the time to lift yourself on high? God will laugh at the horse and its rider."

This establishes the role of the Torah as the defender of the human race against the evil intentions of Samael.

SERAPHIM AS EXTRATERRESTRIALS?

—•—•—

There are significant problems with the story found in Perkei de Eliezer and Shabbat 146a.

While they rightly suggest that the serpent in Eden was influenced by a fallen angelic presence, the story of Samael or the serpent having relations with Eve and fathering Cain introduces the concept of human-angel hybrids from the dawn of human history.

If Cain were indeed the offspring of a union between Eve and a fallen angel, this would imply that human-angel hybrids existed from the earliest generations, potentially negating the need for the later narrative of the Watchers (*b'nei Elohim*) descending in Enoch 1 and Genesis 6 to corrupt humanity.

—•—•—

Of course, Timothy Alberino has argued that human women wouldn't likely have been amenable to marriage and intercourse with serpentine beings, and he's probably correct. Moreover, it isn't likely that Eve had intercourse with any angelic entity of any species, as both she and Adam were still within the protected space of Eden.

Another case in point is that Satan is identified as a Cherub (Ezekiel 28:12–17), not a Seraph. However, some Christian readers may well object, pointing to Scriptures like Revelation 12:7–9:

> And there was war in heaven, Michael and his angels waging war with the dragon. The dragon and his angels waged war, and they were not strong enough, and there was no longer a place found for them in heaven.
>
> And the great dragon was thrown down, the serpent of old who is called the devil and Satan, who deceives the whole world; he was thrown down to the earth, and his angels were thrown down with him.

However, these descriptors of Satan as a dragon aren't literal, nor are they descriptive of the physical characteristics of the specific cherub identified as "THE" Satan.

As Alberino states:

> Because Satan is associated with a serpent, many have assumed that he is serpentine in appearance. According to this logic, one ought to draw the same conclusion concerning Christ, who is often portrayed as a lamb, and yet the proposition that Jesus had the physical features of a sheep would certainly be considered ridiculous by all.[350]

This now begs the question: If Satan is a Cherub, and there was a fallen angelic presence in the Garden of Eden, does it necessarily follow that this angel was "the Satan"—the fallen Cherub? And, although Samael is identified as a "satan" character and is specifically identified with the serpent, does it mean he is THAT Cherub?

The answer to both questions is: Not really.

As Derek P. Gilbert writes in *The Great Inception: Satan's Psyops from Eden to Armageddon*:

> Who was the serpent in the garden? Most of us assume it was Satan, but maybe not. The serpent isn't named in the book of Genesis. In fact, Satan wasn't even a personal name in the Old Testament.[351]

The Hebrew term "satan," meaning "adversary" or "accuser," appears in various contexts within the Hebrew Scriptures. In the book of Job, "Satan" is portrayed as a member of the divine council (along with all the other morning stars).

Gilbert goes on to write in agreement with both Heiser and Alberino: "In Hebrew, it's not uncommon for an adjective to be converted into a noun—the term is 'substantivized.' If that's the case here, *nachash* could mean 'shining one.'"

However, here he diverges from Alberino and writes:

SERAPHIM AS EXTRATERRESTRIALS?

When the Israelites started complaining on their way out of Egypt (see Numbers 21:4–9), God sent *saraph nachash* ("fiery serpents") to bite them.

Saraph is the root word of *seraphim*, which roughly means "burning ones." But the key point of these verses in Numbers 21 is that the Hebrew words *saraph* and *nachash* are used interchangeably, meaning that rather than "fiery serpents," the actual translation should read "*saraph* serpents."[352]

Gilbert finds agreement among the translators of the Jewish Publication Society (JPS). Every version of the JPS renders Numbers 21:6 in the same manner he believes "fiery serpents" should be correctly translated:

> ...sent *seraph* serpents against the people. They bit the people and many of the Israelites died. (Numbers 21:6, The Contemporary Torah, JPS, 2006)

וַיְשַׁלַּח יְהֹוָה בָּעָם אֵת הַנְּחָשִׁים הַשְּׂרָפִים וַיְנַשְּׁ־
כוּ אֶת־הָעָם וַיָּמָת עַם־רָב מִיִּשְׂרָאֵל:

Gilbert goes on to write that, "Deuteronomy 8:15 praises Yahweh for bringing Israel through the great and terrifying wilderness, with its fiery serpents," reinforcing the interchangeability of *saraph* and *nachash*. Now, if the mental image of flaming snakes isn't weird enough, the prophet Isaiah twice referred to flying serpents (*saraph ʿuwph*, in Isaiah 14:29 and 30:6).[353]

Here too, the Jewish Publication Society agrees with him. Deuteronomy 8:15:

> ...who led you through the great and terrible wilderness with its *seraph* serpents and scorpions, a parched land with no water in it, who brought forth water for you from the flinty rock. (The Contemporary Torah, JPS, 2006)

הַמּוֹלִיכְךָ בַּמִּדְבָּר | הַגָּדֹל וְהַנּוֹרָא נָחָשׁ | שָׂרָף וְעַקְרָב וְצִמָּאוֹן אֲשֶׁר אֵין־מָיִם הַמּוֹצִיא לְךָ מַיִם מִצּוּר הַחַלָּמִישׁ:

Gilbert finishes with:

> And in his famous throne room vision, Isaiah saw: …the Lord sitting on a throne, lofty and exalted, with the train of His robe filling the temple. Seraphim were standing above Him, each having six wings: with two each covered his face, and with two each covered his feet, and with two each flew. (Isaiah 6:1–2)
>
> Again, the root word of *seraphim* is *saraph*, the same word translated "serpent" in Numbers and Deuteronomy. In fact, aside from the Isaiah 6 passage above, every single mention of seraphim in the Old Testament refers to serpentine beings!
>
> …The bottom line is this: What Adam and Eve saw in the garden wasn't a talking snake, but a nachash—a radiant, divine entity, very likely of serpentine appearance.[354]

Of course, even with the substantial arguments for the presence of a divine rebel in the Garden of Eden—not a literal talking or possessed serpent—some may point out what appears to be the obvious flaw within them all. Namely, the text calls the serpent "the shrewdest of all the creatures of the field that God had made." The text apparently classifies the "creature" as being "of the field." On its face, doesn't this point alone undo all the arguments above for anything other than an earthly creature, a talking reptile, that became a snake?

Again, not really.

In light of all the previous arguments, we see that the text is deliberately ambiguous, allegorical, and presents the serpent as probably a rebellious Seraph.

The phrase "more crafty than any beast of the field" is a comparative statement rather than one of classification. This is consistent with the fact that multiple layers of interpretation are allowed for and are common in the Hebrew Scriptures. Moreover, we've already shown that

SERAPHIM AS EXTRATERRESTRIALS?

many rabbinical sources interpret the serpent as being more than a mere "animal of the field."

The best explanation is that "creature of the field" is an explicit allusion to a rebellious, enemy entity. Why? Because, as we will see, the Hebrew Scriptures repeatedly use the term in relation to *enemies of Israel*.

For example:

Jeremiah 12:9 says:

> Is My inheritance like a speckled bird of prey to Me?
> Are the birds of prey against her on every side?
> Go, gather all the animals of the field,
> Bring them to devour!

> הַעַיִט צָבוּעַ נַחֲלָתִי לִי הַעַיִט סָבִיב עָלֶיהָ לְכוּ
> אִסְפוּ כָּל־חַיַּת הַשָּׂדֶה הֵתָיוּ לְאָכְלָה:

Here, enemy nations are described as "animals of the field" coming to attack God's people. The words in Hebrew are חַיַּת הַשָּׂדֶה—the plural of the term used in Genesis 3 for the serpent.

Again, Ezekiel 34:5–8 says:

> They scattered for lack of a shepherd, and they became food for every animal of the field and scattered.
>
> My flock strayed through all the mountains and on every high hill; My flock was scattered over all the surface of the earth, and there was no one to search or seek for them.
>
> Therefore, you shepherds, hear the word of the Lord:
>
> "As I live," declares the Lord God, "certainly, because My flock has become plunder, and My flock has become food for all the animals of the field for lack of a shepherd."

> וַתְּפוּצֶינָה מִבְּלִי רֹעֶה וַתִּהְיֶינָה לְאָכְלָה לְכָל־חַיַּת הַשָּׂדֶה וַתְּפוּצֶינָה:

> יִשְׁגּוּ צֹאנִי בְּכָל־הֶהָרִים וְעַל כָּל־גִּבְעָה רָמָה וְעַל כָּל־פְּנֵי הָאָרֶץ נָפֹצוּ צֹאנִי
> וְאֵין דּוֹרֵשׁ וְאֵין מְבַקֵּשׁ:

לָכֵן רֹעִים שִׁמְעוּ אֶת־דְּבַר יְהוָֽה׃

חַי־אָנִי נְאֻם ׀ אֲדֹנָי יֱהֹוִה אִם־לֹא יַעַן הֱיֽוֹת־צֹאנִי ׀ לָבַז וַתִּהְיֶינָה
צֹאנִי לְאׇכְלָה לְכׇל־חַיַּת הַשָּׂדֶה מֵאֵין רֹעֶה וְלֹא־דָרְשׁוּ רֹעַי
אֶת־צֹאנִי וַיִּרְעוּ הָרֹעִים אוֹתָם וְאֶת־צֹאנִי לֹא רָעֽוּ׃

Here, God criticizes the leaders of Israel, saying they have allowed His people to become "food for all the beasts of the field," with "beasts" likely referring to enemy nations. Once again, the words in Hebrew are חַיַּת הַשָּׂדֶה—the plural of the term used in Genesis 3 for the serpent.

To hammer home this point, Rabbi Dr. Gidon Rothstein, the Rosh Kollel of the Yeshiva University Community Kollel, in his commentary on Ezekiel 34, explains that the "flock" (Israel) became prey to "predatory nations" due to the failure of their leaders. This metaphorical understanding aligns with the broader prophetic theme of using "beasts" to symbolize hostile nations or external threats that prey upon Israel during times of vulnerability.[355]

Likewise, *Benson's Commentary*, *Ellicott's Commentary*, and *Matthew Poole's Commentary* all interpret the "beasts of the field" as representing Israel's enemies, emphasizing that these enemies preyed upon God's people when they were left unprotected due to the failures of their leaders.[356, 357, 358]

Then there is Hosea 2:12:

And I will destroy her vines and fig trees, Of which she said, "They are my wages for prostitution which my lovers have given me.

"And I will turn them into a forest, and the animals of the field will devour them."

וַהֲשִׁמֹּתִי גַּפְנָהּ וּתְאֵנָתָהּ אֲשֶׁר אָמְרָה אֶתְנָה הֵמָּה לִי אֲשֶׁר נָתְנוּ־לִי מְאַהֲבָי
וְשַׂמְתִּים לְיַעַר וַאֲכָלָתַם חַיַּת הַשָּׂדֶֽה׃

This is yet another place where we see "animals of the field" (חַיַּת הַשָּׂדֶה) used as a descriptor of Israel's enemies.

SERAPHIM AS EXTRATERRESTRIALS?

Thus, the crafty serpent of the field is an allegory for a bright, fiery serpentine Seraph—a rebellious enemy of God and man on a mission of deception.

As an aside: Recall that neither Eve nor Adam was frightened of the serpent, and the text never says whether this was their first, hundredth, or thousandth encounter with it! Indeed, the impression we get is that they were well acquainted with this being.

Ultimately, as we have seen, Jewish texts describe a variety of celestial beings, including Seraphim and Cherubim, each serving distinct roles and possessing unique attributes. The concept that "the Satan" could command an army comprising different angelic species isn't hard to imagine.

If a third of the stars (celestial beings) of Heaven followed Satan in a cosmic rebellion, this could possibly encompass hundreds of thousands, millions upon millions, or even billions of individuals from the various angelic species. We really have no way of knowing the numbers at this point.

However, the notion that a high-ranking Seraph could act on behalf of the satanic Cherub in the Garden of Eden is consistent with the idea of angelic intermediaries executing the will of higher-ranking beings. (And remember, just because Christian tradition holds Seraphim to be of a higher order than Cherubim, there is no scriptural support for that belief.)

In any case, an example of high-ranking fallen angels acting on the orders of higher-ranking ones might be the prince of Persia who delayed the angel sent to Daniel.[359] Surely this territorial ruler opposed God's purpose and perhaps delayed the angel sent to Daniel on direct orders from the leader of the angelic rebellion.

WITNESS TESTIMONY AND REPTILIAN ENCOUNTERS

There are countless testimonies given by individuals around the world who have encountered them—either under the circumstances of an alien abduction, chance meetings deep within the Earth, or in the context of alleged secret government operations (in cooperation with these beings).

One of the earliest, strangest reports in America was published in the *Los Angeles Times*. On January 29, 1934, the paper ran the headline "Lizard People's Catacomb City Hunted: Engineer Sinks Shaft Under Fort Moore Hill to Find Maze of Tunnels and Priceless Treasures of Legendary Inhabitants."

The report began:

> Busy Los Angeles, although little realizing it in the hustle and bustle of modern existence, stands above a lost city of catacombs filled with incalculable treasure and imperishable records of a race of humans further advanced intellectually and scientifically than even the highest type of present day peoples, in the belief of G. Warren Shufelt, geophysical mining engineer now engaged in an attempt to wrest from the lost city deep in the earth below Fort Moore Hill the secrets of the Lizard People of legendary fame in the medicine lodges of the American Indian.[360]

Calvin Dobbins picks up the narrative, along with explanation, in an article for losangeleno.com:

> According to Shufelt, he had created a machine, "Radio X-Ray," and mapped the area, which displayed amazing things.
>
> Shufelt said the X-ray showed a massive network of tunnels beneath Los Angeles covering a vast area. Supposedly, these tunnels weren't built by our ancestors but by another race called the "Lizard People." He also said that several locations in the tunnels contained treasures....
>
> Shufelt trusted his device entirely, and therefore, he wanted to continue inserting the shaft below until it reached a thousand feet. He and his aides planned to stop after that if the venture yielded no positive result. The dig didn't produce the desired outcome, so Shufelt and his aides abandoned the project by

SERAPHIM AS EXTRATERRESTRIALS?

December of that year.

Along with the story, the newspaper also printed a map created by Shufelt according to his findings with the help of the X-ray machine. Readers can understand the structure of the tunnels by looking at the image printed on page 5 of the paper.[361]

He goes on to note:

The tunnels were basically under the areas of Fort Moore Place, North Broadway, and North Hill Street. The article indicates that Shufelt and his aides believed that the Lizard People had a "Key Room" located under Broadway and 2nd Street.

The "Key Room" was supposedly a place where the ancient race made plans and stored all their treasures and important information written on gold tablets.[362]

Dobbins goes on to relate more of the story, stating that G. Warren Shufelt wasn't just another prospector chasing gold. He had this contraption he called a "radio X-ray" machine, which he claimed could detect underground tunnels and precious metals. According to him, it was picking up signs of an elaborate tunnel network right under Los Angeles.

Now, Shufelt was curious, but he wasn't exactly working with a treasure map. So, he ended up crossing paths with a Hopi Native American in Arizona. This Hopi chief shared a story that sounds straight out of a mythological archive.

According to the chief, about five thousand years ago, something catastrophic happened—a meteorite hit the area where Los Angeles now stands, causing a massive fire that burned everything down.

In response, a group he called the "Lizard People" supposedly built at least three underground cities beneath modern-day LA to protect themselves. If you believe the legend, those tunnels even stretched all the way to the coast.

The Lizard People weren't just survivors; they were described as "superior humans" who revered lizards. But there's another angle. Some say they weren't just human devotees of reptiles. They were actual reptilian beings—shape-shifters who could change their appearance at will.

So, Shufelt took this story seriously. It lined up a little too well with what he thought his machine was detecting. Whether we buy it or not, he was convinced enough to keep digging—literally and figuratively.

It's one of those tales where folklore, treasure hunting, and wild speculation converge. Maybe there's something to it, or maybe it's just a good campfire story. But for Shufelt, it was definitely worth chasing.

Moving down through history, one of the earliest abductee accounts concerning reptilian, humanoid aliens was that of Ashland, Nebraska, police officer Herbert Schirmer, who, under hypnosis, recalled being taken aboard a UFO in 1967 by humanoid beings with a slightly reptilian appearance. They wore a "winged serpent" emblem on the left side of their chests.[363, 364]

Skeptics consider his claims to be a hoax.[365]

More recent accounts, which corroborate David Icke's to a degree, include those of self-proclaimed whistleblower Phil Schneider. Although it's difficult to verify, Schneider's story is compelling. He claimed that during the construction of a deep underground military base in Dulce, New Mexico, he encountered alien entities, including reptilian aliens, and was involved in a firefight that resulted in numerous casualties.[366] His stories include descriptions of various alien species, such as Greys and Reptilians, supposedly residing in the base.

Schneider brought attention to these claims through public speeches. In a notable 1995 presentation, he detailed his experiences and injuries, including the loss of several fingers, which he attributed to the firefight mentioned above.

Schneider also spoke about alleged government secrecy and treaties with extraterrestrial beings. He claimed the US government had made agreements with aliens, allowing them to establish bases on Earth in exchange for advanced technology.

Phil's narratives often indirectly referenced reptilian aliens as part of the extraterrestrial groups involved, but their primary focus revolved around what he called Tall Grey aliens—essentially beings very much like the stereotypical, three- or four-foot-tall Greys, but much taller—and perhaps much more dangerous.

He was found—very likely murdered—in 1996.[367]

Thomas Castello is another figure often mentioned in connection with the Dulce Base. His account is similar to Phil Schneider's.[368]

Castello is purported to have been a security officer at the Dulce Base, an alleged underground facility in New Mexico. He claimed to have witnessed various extraterrestrial beings, including Greys and Reptilians, and described the base as a site for human-alien collaboration and experimentation.

His descriptions of the activities at the Dulce Base included experiments into telepathy, dreams, hypnosis, and research into human auras. He also claimed aliens had the capability of separating the "bioplasmic body" from the physical body and replacing it with an alien life force after removing the human soul.

He had this to say about certain aspects of it all:

> Some "reptoids" [Reptilians] are native to this planet. The ruling caste of "aliens" ARE reptilian.... They were an ancient race on Earth, living underground.... Reptoids rightly consider themselves "native Terrans."
>
> Perhaps they are the ones we call the Fallen Angels—maybe not.
>
> Either way, we are [considered] the "squatters" on Earth.... Since I was the Senior Security Technician at that base [Dulce], I had to communicate with them on a daily basis. If there were any problems that involved security or video cameras, I was the one they called.
>
> It was the reptilian "working caste" that usually did the physical labor in the lower levels at Dulce.[369]

However, unlike the very vocal and visible Phil Schneider, just about every claim by Costello—including his actual existence—remains unverified by any official investigative body.

Oh! And remember how the serpent in Eden was allegedly bipedal and stood at around the height of a camel? Well, according to Alex Collier, a well-known figure in the UFO and extraterrestrial research community, best known as a self-described "contactee": "The Draconians or Dracos have two main castes, the first of which…is in the 7 to 10 foot tall range."[370]

Additionally, in interviews and writings, Collier elaborates on the Draconians' belief in their "divine right" to rule the universe, tied to their self-proclaimed status as the oldest reptilian race.

We might take all that with a grain of salt since his information doesn't come from direct involvement with reptilian beings, but rather through his alleged communications with Andromedan beings.

Of course, after reading that, some folks will clutch their pearls and say it's "irresponsible" to link ancient religion with so-called alien conspiracy theories.

Really? You know what's actually irresponsible? Ignoring thousands of years of cross-cultural data, eerily consistent mythologies, and firsthand testimony—just because it makes the academic gatekeepers squirm.

That's true even if some testimonies sound like they might come from "wackos" or shady people who claim all kinds of things without any way to objectively or empirically verify a word.

Truth doesn't care about academic taboos or modern categories. If the patterns repeat, from Eden to Egypt to Aztec temples to underground military bases, then maybe we should stop worrying about what's respectable—stop the sneering—and start studying and investigating.

Maybe we should go deeper.

As stated by Dr. Michael Salla, an Australian-born scholar and author internationally recognized for his work in international politics, conflict resolution, and US foreign policy, in a paper entitled "The Dulce Report":

> In 1987 an apparent whistleblower organized the release of 30 photos, video and a set of papers to UFO researchers that were apparently physical evidence of a joint US government/

SERAPHIM AS EXTRATERRESTRIALS?

extraterrestrial base two miles beneath the Archuletta Mesa, near the town of Dulce, New Mexico.

The collection came to be called the "Dulce Papers" and provided graphic evidence of the operations of this secret underground facility....

The Dulce Papers described genetic experimentation, development of human-extraterrestrial hybrids, use of mind control through advanced computers, cold storage of humans in liquid filled vats, and even the use of human body parts as a nutritional source for extraterrestrial (ET) races.

The papers provided possible evidence that humans were used as little more than laboratory animals by ET races working directly with different US government agencies and US corporations fulfilling "black budget" military contracts in a joint base.

If the papers were genuine, experiments and projects were being conducted that involved human rights violations on a scale that exceeded even the darkest chapters of recent human history.[371]

Sounds a bit—wild...crazy...unbelievable—like, you know, nonsense. No credible scholar agrees with any of this!

But that's wrong, dead wrong. Scholars like Dr. Michael Heiser, C. S. Lewis, and even Dr. Michael Salla cracked that door wide open.

Heiser exposed the divine council hiding in plain sight. Lewis showed how myth might actually be fragmented memory. And Salla? He pulled the curtain back on the political side of the so-called extraterrestrial issue.

Different fields, same punchline: The old stories weren't fiction—they were *reporting*. The problem isn't the stories. The problem is modern minds that forget how to read them.

So, let's tie this all together before moving on to the Ishim, the Nordics, and the Tall Whites, shall we?

Seraphim, according to Christian and Jewish tradition, sit at the top of the celestial food chain. Fiery. Winged. Radiant. Intelligent. Serpentine. They're throne attendants, burning with divine fire and maybe, just maybe, a little too much pride.

Now enter the Dracos—what UFO lore calls the Reptilian overlords. What are they described as?

Fiery. Winged. Radiant. Intelligent. Serpentine. Often seven to twelve feet tall. With wings like a dragon's. Capable of shape-shifting. Interdimensional. Powerful. In charge.

Sound familiar? It should.

Whether it's David Icke's "Draco elite" or countless abductee reports describing tall, terrifying reptilian humanoids with slitted eyes and telepathic abilities, the overlap isn't just striking, it's ridiculous to ignore.

I think it's clear that I'm not saying every abductee story is gospel truth. Some accounts may be half-baked, dream-fueled, or straight-up fiction. Anecdotes aren't data—yeah, we've heard the mantra.

But here's the thing: When *hundreds,* even *tens of thousands,* of unrelated people, scattered across time, geography, and all socioeconomic and religious demographics start describing the same serpent-like overlords—we're looking at a pattern begging to be taken seriously. Yes, I know this is a drum I'm banging.

That's because there aren't enough people in the band.

This is something we should be seriously investigating, not dismissing. Even if 90 percent of these reports are noise, what about the other 10 percent? Coherent. Consistent. Creepy. And they hint at *something real.*

Same body type. Same status. Same glowing presence. Same fearsome power. Same arrogance.

I don't buy the idea that these things are tourists from the Draco constellation. That narrative smells like a cosmic psyop. A red herring. A celestial misdirection. However, I *do* think there's a very real possibility that what the UFO community calls the Dracos are in fact *fallen Seraphim.*

Simply put, the classic space-alien story leans hard on one assumption: a materialist universe. Nuts and bolts. Rockets and radar blips. But if the Seraphim are *interdimensional,* these beings aren't from *somewhere else* in the galaxy; they're from *somewhere else* in the structure of reality itself.

We're not talking about space travel; we're talking about boundary violations. Not boundary violations between planets, but between dimensions of existence—layers of reality we barely understand. They're not crossing light-years. They're crossing thresholds.

And they didn't just show up in humanity's history one day. They broke through.

> Let's get something straight: I understand that just because multiple cultures describe radiant, serpentine beings doesn't mean they're all pointing to the same entities.
>
> Critics will be quick to scream "equivocation fallacy!" and claim I'm mixing up metaphors with actual beings. Sure, snakes and dragons have been used as symbols for everything from wisdom and healing to outright evil.
>
> Big deal.
>
> This isn't about superficial symbolism or poetic metaphors. It's about recurring, specific, and consistent physical descriptions—fiery, radiant, winged, serpentine, hyperintelligent beings—showing up over and over again, across cultures and millennia not just in vague myths, but in detailed visual descriptions that echo throughout history.
>
> Critics will say I'm connecting dots that aren't there. Wrong. I'm pointing to a pattern so consistent it screams for attention.
>
> When I draw parallels between the Seraphim of Scripture and modern reports of reptilian entities, I'm not saying, "Oh, they both have scales, so they must be the same." I'm talking about direct continuity—descriptions lining up with testimonies, whether carved in stone or talked about by abductees.

Interestingly, and perhaps not coincidentally, these serpentine, reptilian beings are allegedly the puppet masters of the Greys—the beings most associated with alien abductions and that didn't even *exist* in the cultural lexicon before the mid-twentieth century.

In fact, a growing pile of testimony suggests that those cold, black-eyed little creeps take orders from *something*—and that *something* just might have scales and wings.

And do we want to talk about intent? Does kidnapping people and conducting experiments on them like they're lab mice sound like benevolence?

We'll get to that connection in a bit.

The evidence presented thus far supports the possibility that the beings known as Seraphim in biblical texts may correspond to reptilian overlords described in modern conspiracy theories and encounters. From ancient Scripture to ayahuasca visions, from prophetic literature to underground base whistleblowers, a single archetype emerges: radiant, powerful, intelligent, serpentine beings with an agenda that spans time and dimension.

By examining the Seraphim as literal, extradimensional beings rather than metaphorical constructs, we have established a foundation for understanding how these creatures may have interacted with humanity throughout history, influencing religious traditions, mythologies, and even various modern theories. These recurring descriptions—whether of beings labeled as Dracos, fiery serpents, or fallen angels—suggest the same species may have worn different cultural masks throughout human history.

So, are the Dracos real? Absolutely.

Just because the UFO community, occult, the esoteric, and the New Age crowd wrapped them in shiny cosmic packaging doesn't mean they made them up.

But are they from another star system? Not likely.

The Dracos aren't intergalactic aliens. Humanity has encountered them for thousands of years. They really have pretended to be gods. But they're from another dimension. Another realm—at least one of which is wherever God's at.

They're fallen Seraphim in disguise.

We're dealing with a war that's been going on since before Eden.

However, this analysis only covers one part of the puzzle. If the Seraphim are responsible for the Reptilian "intergalactic alien" phenomenon, what of the Nordics and Tall Whites frequently described by abductees and contactees as benevolent, human-like beings?

More importantly, I've already mentioned how reptilian Dracos are linked to the ubiquitous Greys. But is there also a connection between these and humanlike beings?

—•—•—

Before we head into the next chapter, please note:

What I am arguing isn't Gnosticism. I'm not suggesting a demiurge, a false creator, or a war between two equal gods—just in case anyone gets the wrong idea. As a messianic Jew, I fully affirm the biblical God—Yahweh, the God of Israel—as the sovereign Creator.

This view doesn't reject biblical theology, it intensifies it. It reframes the cosmic war not as metaphor, but as a real, multidimensional conflict involving actual celestial species—some loyal to God, others in rebellion.

—•—•—

To answer these questions, we must now turn our attention to another category of celestial beings: the Ishim—the manlike angels. Remember, the enemy is personal, intelligent, and ancient. Scripture gives us more clues than we've been taught to notice.

Stay tuned: After we talk about Ishim, we'll get to the Grey connection, because that's where things *really* get weird.

CHAPTER EIGHT

ISHIM
AS EXTRATERRESTRIALS

There was the simple fact that the true nature of our reality—the fact that we are not alone in the universe—was being hidden from the American people and humanity at large. Say that out loud...it's insane and wrong.
—Luis Elizondo, *Imminent: Inside the Pentagon's Hunt for UFOs*[372]

We've dug deep into the fiery, serpentine hierarchy of the Seraphim, peeled back the layers of Reptilian conspiracies, ancient myth, and modern testimony, and laid bare a chilling possibility: The Reptilian overlords, the so-called Dracos, might actually be fallen Seraphim.

But if the Dracos occupy one slot in the cosmic hierarchy, what about the rest of the cast? (Because guess what? Not every extraterrestrial encounter involves scales and wings.)

There's another category of beings we need to tackle, one that seems every bit as powerful, yet operates with an entirely different face.

Enter the Ishim (אִישִׁים).

Unlike the Seraphim, the Ishim appear human. Not just humanoid, but human, with certain individuals being almost indistinguishable. They're mentioned in various religious texts as man-like celestial beings, distinct from the fiery, serpentine species, but no less enigmatic. And the resemblance to so-called Nordic aliens and Tall Whites described in modern UFO lore? Eerie.

It's like looking in a mirror, except these guys are stunningly beautiful in almost all accounts. Physical perfection. Zero flaws. No zits, scars, or snaggle-toothed need for a trip to the dentist. Better than Fabio, his perfect flowing hair, and his disbelief that it's not butter.

Are these beings really different in purpose and agenda from the fallen Seraphim we discussed in the previous chapter? Or is it possible they're playing a coordinated game?

If the Reptilian overlords present themselves as a cosmic threat, are the Ishim-like beings presenting themselves as the solution? Good cop, bad cop. A strategic deception wherein one hand sows terror while the other offers salvation?

The possibility that these species might be working toward the same end—just with different tactics as part of an overall angelic rebellion—is a question worth asking.

The Nordic aliens, known for their tall, beautiful, humanlike appearance, often described as blond or red-haired, blue or green-eyed, and almost ethereal in their radiance, show up in testimonies across the board—especially since the 1950s. People claim these beings are benevolent, spiritual teachers—"practically angels" compared to the cold, soulless Greys and the tyrannical, scary-as-all-get-out Dracos.

(Let's be real here: If I ever came face to face with a Seraph like the ones described in Scripture, even one of the good guys still loyal to God, I'd probably react the way every prophet did: by trembling and stuttering. No bravado here. Those guys are pure terror wrapped in divine fire.)

Anyway, then there are the Tall Whites—pale, elongated, humanoid beings who show up time and again in reports of contact experiences.

From George Adamski's alleged encounters with blond, humanoid beings in the 1950s to more recent reports from military whistleblowers, the same beings keep surfacing. Whether Nordics or Tall Whites, these entities (mostly the Nordics) are portrayed as peacekeepers, guardians, or enlightened guides—offering messages of hope, enlightenment, and cosmic brotherhood.

"Yes indeed, people of Earth! Now YOU, TOO, can raise your vibration and ascend!"

But we shouldn't accept their supposed benevolence at face value. If the Ishim and the Nordics are one and the same, their nature demands scrutiny.

History is loaded with smooth-talking entities playing the "benevolent guide" card while serving their own twisted agendas. It's a classic con. From Loki and Coyote playing tricks to the serpent in Eden whispering sweet lies—it's always the same hustle. And here's the kicker: Both Jewish and Christian traditions are clear about not trusting supernatural beings just because they show up flashing a nice smile or promising enlightenment.

Paul laid it out plainly in 2 Corinthians 11:14: "No wonder, for even Satan disguises himself as an angel of light." Translation: Just because something looks divine or sounds enlightened doesn't mean it is.

Now, let's talk about the Book of Enoch. Fallen Watchers roll in claiming to be humanity's teachers, only to corrupt and poison everything with forbidden knowledge. What do you call that? Deception through guidance.

That's the same pattern we see with the Nordics.

If you think this is religious paranoia, think again. In the Middle Ages, various Christian theologians warned against the seductive promises of heretical sects claiming hidden knowledge or direct spiritual contact with angels. They noted that true angels, when appearing to mortals, weren't interested in altering doctrine or offering shortcuts to enlightenment but rather were focused on reinforcing established divine order.

Therefore, the pattern of seemingly benevolent beings offering enlightenment or new spiritual insights while subtly promoting doctrinal errors is not without precedent. It's entirely possible the Nordics, whether they are truly Ishim or something else, are presenting themselves as saviors or enlightened guides for reasons that are anything but altruistic.

So, whose banner are the Nordics operating under? Has anyone asked a representative of this species during contact whether Yeshua of Nazareth is the Son of God—you know, just to see what their reaction happens to be?

Everyone should remember what the Apostle John had to say about this: "Every spirit that does not confess Jesus is not from God; this is the spirit of the antichrist, which you have heard is coming, and now it is already in the world" (1 John 4:3).

If they act like they know who we're talking about, but their response is anything other than, "Yes, He is the Son of God," we should reject anything else that entity has to say.

"Why yes, indeed. He is an ascended master like St. Germaine. But, you know, really, you should be paying attention to and trying to attain the same status as Sanat Kumara, the Lord of the World. And, if you can't do that, you should probably aim for the level of Maitreya, the true Cosmic Christ."

Right. If you hear anything like that, you should probably do like the archangel Michael did when disputing with Satan over the body of Moses: Say, "The Lord rebuke you," then hightail it out of wherever you are—or fall on your knees and pray.

John warned about this sort of thing: 1 John 4:3:

For many deceivers have gone out into the world, those who do not acknowledge Jesus Christ as coming in the flesh. This is the deceiver and the antichrist. (2 John 1:7).

We know John wasn't just talking about unbelieving humans. The Apostle Paul backed him up in Galatians 1:8: "But even if we, or an angel from heaven, should preach to you a gospel contrary to what we have preached to you, he is to be accursed! (Anathema)."

So, experiencers should be asking themselves whether these beings are operating under the banner of God's (Yahweh's) righteousness, or are part of a larger, coordinated deception designed to manipulate human perception providing false hope and guidance? Are they pointing toward any way—other than *the* Way, the Truth, and the Life, which is Jesus Christ?

Maybe you don't care about any of that because you don't believe Jesus is the Way, either. Okay, but aren't you the least bit concerned that you're possibly getting taken for a ride by beings that—as I've mentioned in the previous few chapters—you don't know anything about?

This chapter investigates whether the Ishim—the manlike celestial beings of biblical and rabbinic tradition—are, in fact, the same entities described by UFO contactees as Nordics or Tall Whites. If they are, we need to ask the obvious follow-up question: Are they as benevolent as they appear?

We'll analyze and synthesize ancient religious descriptions of the Ishim alongside modern accounts of these humanoid entities. And we'll dig into the possibility that they are extraterrestrials, interdimensional beings, or something else entirely.

Most importantly, we're not just cataloging encounters, we're building a framework. If the Seraphim correspond to the Dracos, where do the Ishim fit in? Are they members of the same heavenly realms? Are some fallen, just as some among the Seraphim are? Or are these guys truly working in opposition to the Seraphic/Reptilian agenda?

Let's crack the whole thing wide open.

DEFINING THE ISHIM

Before we start throwing around terms like "Nordics" and "Tall Whites" and trying to draw lines between ancient texts and modern testimonies, we need to get one thing straight: What exactly are the Ishim? If we're going to make sense of any of this, we need to start with the original sources.

In Hebrew, *Ishim* (אִישִׁים) is the plural form of *Ish* (אִישׁ), which means "man."

Simple enough, right?

But when we're referring to Ishim in a theological context, we're not indicating regular human beings. We're talking about celestial beings that look enough like us—rather, since they predate us, we look enough like them—that we easily mistake them for members of our own species.

Unlike the Seraphim—again, who are depicted as fiery, serpentine entities with wings and radiant bodies—the Ishim are portrayed as almost entirely human in appearance—at least under certain circumstances. They don't strike terror into the hearts of humans as Seraphim do—at least, not by their physical appearance alone.

Where do we find these guys in Scripture? And how did later Jewish traditions expand upon their identity and purpose?

BIBLICAL SOURCES

To find out who the Ishim are, we've got to start with the foundational texts. Surprise, surprise: They show up a lot more often than most people think. (And guess what? No wings.)

Genesis 18–19: Abraham's Visitors

The first solid hint we get of Ishim-like beings occurs when Abraham is chilling near the oaks of Mamre. Suddenly, three "men" show up.

> Now the LORD appeared to Abraham by the oaks of Mamre, while he was sitting at the tent door in the heat of the day.
>
> When he raised his eyes and looked, behold, three men were standing opposite him; and when he saw *them*, he ran from the tent door to meet them and bowed down to the ground. (Genesis 18:1–2)

וַיֵּרָא אֵלָיו יְהֹוָה בְּאֵלֹנֵי מַמְרֵא וְהוּא יֹשֵׁב פֶּתַח־הָאֹהֶל כְּחֹם הַיּוֹם:

וַיִּשָּׂא עֵינָיו וַיַּרְא וְהִנֵּה שְׁלֹשָׁה אֲנָשִׁים נִצָּבִים עָלָיו וַיַּרְא וַיָּרָץ לִקְרָאתָם מִפֶּתַח הָאֹהֶל וַיִּשְׁתַּחוּ אָרְצָה:

Now pay attention.

These "men" eat, talk, and interact with Abraham like regular dudes. No flaming swords. No serpentine wings. No blinding radiance. Just three guys having a meal—except they're clearly something more than that.

The Hebrew text identifies one of them as YHVH (Yahweh)—and while major, modern Jewish interpretations, such as those from the Jews for Judaism organization, refuse to acknowledge what the Hebrew says in black and white,[373] that's not what Jewish sages such as Rashi wrote. In fact, Rashi identifies one of these "men" as God and the other two as angels. On Genesis 18:1 he wrote:

"וירא אליו AND THE LORD APPEARED UNTO HIM to visit the sick man. R. Hama the son of Hanina said: it was the third day after his circumcision and the Holy One, blessed be He, came and enquired after the state of his health. (Bava Metzia 86b)

And:

literally, יָשֵׁב WAS SITTING—The word is written ישב (without the ו) and therefore may be translated "he sat": He wished to rise, but the Holy One, blessed be He, said to him, Sit and I will stand. You shall form an example to your descendants—that I, in time to come, will stand in the assembly of the judges while they will sit, as it is said, (Psalms 82:1) "God standeth in the assembly of the judges" (Genesis Rabbah 48:7).

Further:

כחום היום IN THE HEAT OF THE DAY—The Holy One, blessed be He, brought the sun out of its sheath that he might not be troubled by travellers, and when He perceived that he was grieved that no travellers came He brought to him angels in the form of men. (Bava Metzia 86b)

In any case, two of these guys end up heading off to Sodom, while the third remains behind to speak with Abraham. Who are the two that continue their journey? We'll find out soon enough.

Genesis 19:1—Lot's Visitors

> Now the two angels came to Sodom in the evening as Lot was sitting at the gate of Sodom. When Lot saw them, he stood up to meet them and bowed down with his face to the ground.

וַיָּבֹאוּ שְׁנֵי הַמַּלְאָכִים סְדֹמָה בָּעֶרֶב וְלוֹט יֹשֵׁב בְּשַׁעַר־סְדֹם וַיַּרְא־לוֹט וַיָּקָם לִקְרָאתָם וַיִּשְׁתַּחוּ אַפַּיִם אָרְצָה:

Notice the switch in terminology. Suddenly, these "men" are called "angels." But their appearance remains human—so human, in fact, that the depraved locals of Sodom try to assault them. Even after Lot takes them into his home, they eat and talk like any other men. In fact, they have a feast!

Genesis 19:2–3:

> And he (Lot) said, "Now behold, my lords, please turn aside into your servant's house, and spend the night, and wash your feet; then you may rise early and go on your way." They said, "No, but we shall spend the night in the public square."
>
> Yet he strongly urged them, so they turned aside to him and entered his house; and he prepared a feast for them and baked unleavened bread, and they ate.

וַיֹּאמֶר הִנֶּה נָּא־אֲדֹנַי סוּרוּ נָא אֶל־בֵּית עַבְדְּכֶם וְלִינוּ וְרַחֲצוּ רַגְלֵיכֶם וְהִשְׁכַּבְתֶּם וַהֲלַכְתֶּם לְדַרְכְּכֶם וַיֹּאמְרוּ לֹּא כִּי בָרְחוֹב נָלִין:

וַיִּפְצַר־בָּם מְאֹד וַיָּסֻרוּ אֵלָיו וַיָּבֹאוּ אֶל־בֵּיתוֹ וַיַּעַשׂ לָהֶם מִשְׁתֶּה וּמַצּוֹת אָפָה וַיֹּאכֵלוּ:

Interestingly, these angels don't want to spend the night in Lot's house. But, because he insists, they politely acquiesce to his pleas. And when the time comes for divine action, they reveal their true nature. The "men" strike the mob with blindness, warn Lot of the city's impending doom, and literally drag him and his family to safety.

Again, they look like humans. They talk like humans. But they're anything but human. Later Jewish tradition would classify these types of beings as Ishim.

The Births of Samson, John the Baptist, and Jesus

The births of Samson, John the Baptist, and Jesus all involve "angels" appearing to humans in full man-like form.

Judges 13:3–5:

> Then the angel of the LORD appeared to the woman and said to her, "Behold now, you are infertile and have not given birth; but you will conceive and give birth to a son.
>
> "And now, be careful not to drink wine or strong drink, nor eat any unclean thing.
>
> "For behold, you will conceive and give birth to a son, and no razor shall come upon his head, for the boy shall be a Nazirite to God from the womb; and he will begin to save Israel from the hands of the Philistines."

וַיֵּרָא מַלְאַךְ־יְהֹוָה אֶל־הָאִשָּׁה וַיֹּאמֶר אֵלֶיהָ הִנֵּה־נָא אַתְּ־עֲקָרָה וְלֹא יָלַדְתְּ וְהָרִית וְיָלַדְתְּ בֵּן׃

וְעַתָּה הִשָּׁמְרִי נָא וְאַל־תִּשְׁתִּי יַיִן וְשֵׁכָר וְאַל־תֹּאכְלִי כָּל־טָמֵא׃

כִּי הִנָּךְ הָרָה וְיֹלַדְתְּ בֵּן וּמוֹרָה לֹא־יַעֲלֶה עַל־רֹאשׁוֹ כִּי־נְזִיר אֱלֹהִים יִהְיֶה הַנַּעַר מִן־הַבָּטֶן וְהוּא יָחֵל לְהוֹשִׁיעַ אֶת־יִשְׂרָאֵל מִיַּד פְּלִשְׁתִּים׃

This passage describes an angel appearing to Manoah's wife to announce that she, though barren, would conceive and give birth to a son—Samson. (The angel will appear later to Manoah himself as well.). This "angel" looks like a man. He speaks like a man. He even eats when Manoah offers him hospitality in a way similar to how the angels interacted with Lot.

It's worth noting that some believe this man-like being was the preincarnate Christ, not an angel, similar to the interpretation applied by Christians to one of the three "men" who visited Abraham. This is because, later, Manoah offers a sacrifice, and this "angel" vanishes into the flames—revealing that he was something far more than just a man.

The experience confuses and terrifies Manoah, who tells his wife, "We will surely die, for we have seen God." (Judges 13:15–22).

In any case, a similar situation happens with Zechariah the priest and his wife Elizabeth in the New Testament's Gospel of Luke.

> In the days of Herod, king of Judea, there was a priest named Zechariah, of the division of Abijah; and he had a wife from the daughters of Aaron, and her name was Elizabeth....
>
> Now an angel of the Lord appeared to him, standing to the right of the altar of incense.
>
> Zechariah was troubled when he saw the angel, and fear gripped him.
>
> But the angel said to him, "Do not be afraid, Zechariah, for your prayer has been heard, and your wife Elizabeth will bear you a son, and you shall name him John." (Luke 5, 11–13)

This angel then goes on to identify himself as Gabriel. Notice that, like Daniel, Zechariah is afraid of Gabriel, even though this entity looks like a man.

> The angel answered and said to him, "I am Gabriel, who stands in the presence of God, and I was sent to speak to you and to bring you this good news.
>
> "And behold, you will be silent and unable to speak until the day when these things take place, because you did not believe my words, which will be fulfilled at their proper time." (Luke 5:19–20)

An interesting fact here is that Gabriel behaves in the same strict, rigid adherence to formality and structure, in keeping with the way all of Israel was warned about regarding an angel in Exodus 23:20–21:

> Behold, I am going to send an angel before you to guard you along the way and to bring you into the place which I have prepared.

Be attentive to him and obey his voice; do not be rebellious toward him, for he will not pardon your rebellion, since My name is in him.

הִנֵּה אָנֹכִי שֹׁלֵחַ מַלְאָךְ לְפָנֶיךָ לִשְׁמָרְךָ בַּדָּרֶךְ וְלַהֲבִיאֲךָ אֶל־הַמָּקוֹם אֲשֶׁר הֲכִנֹתִי׃

הִשָּׁמֶר מִפָּנָיו וּשְׁמַע בְּקֹלוֹ אַל־תַּמֵּר בּוֹ כִּי לֹא יִשָּׂא לְפִשְׁעֲכֶם כִּי שְׁמִי בְּקִרְבּוֹ׃

This type of behavior and mentality is important, and I'll come back to it.

In any case, then Gabriel shows up in the same way to Mary, the mother of Jesus, in Luke 1:26–33:

> Now in the sixth month the angel Gabriel was sent from God to a city in Galilee named Nazareth, to a virgin betrothed to a man whose name was Joseph, of the descendants of David; and the virgin's name was Mary.
>
> And the angel said to her, "Do not be afraid, Mary, for you have found favor with God. And behold, you will conceive in your womb and give birth to a son, and you shall name Him Jesus.
>
> "He will be great and will be called the Son of the Most High; and the Lord God will give Him the throne of His father David; and He will reign over the house of Jacob forever, and His kingdom will have no end."

All this tracks with everything we've seen about the Ishim so far. They don't just appear as radiant, burning creatures. They show up as humanoid beings, just like the ones who appeared to Abraham, Lot, and Jacob.

Let's keep going.

The Glowing Man

Daniel 10:5–6:

> I raised my eyes and looked, and behold, there was a man dressed in linen, whose waist had a belt of pure gold of Uphaz.

His body also *was* like topaz, his face had the appearance of lightning, his eyes were like flaming torches, his arms and feet like the gleam of polished bronze, and the sound of his words like the sound of a multitude.

וָאֶשָּׂא אֶת־עֵינַי וָאֵרֶא וְהִנֵּה אִישׁ־אֶחָד לָבוּשׁ בַּדִּים וּמָתְנָיו חֲגֻרִים בְּכֶתֶם אוּפָז:

וּגְוִיָּתוֹ כְתַרְשִׁישׁ וּפָנָיו כְּמַרְאֵה בָרָק וְעֵינָיו כְּלַפִּידֵי אֵשׁ וּזְרֹעֹתָיו וּמַרְגְּלֹתָיו כְּעֵין נְחֹשֶׁת קָלָל וְקוֹל דְּבָרָיו כְּקוֹל הָמוֹן:

Again, this being looks like a man—dressed like a man—yet clearly, he's something far more. Despite his brilliance and power, he's still fundamentally *humanlike*.

And let's not forget about the archangel Gabriel. Here is the first time we meet him in Scripture:

While I was still speaking in prayer, the man Gabriel, whom I had seen in the vision previously, came to me in my extreme weariness about the time of the evening offering. (Daniel 9:21)

וְעוֹד אֲנִי מְדַבֵּר בַּתְּפִלָּה וְהָאִישׁ גַּבְרִיאֵל אֲשֶׁר רָאִיתִי בֶחָזוֹן בַּתְּחִלָּה מֻעָף בִּיעָף נֹגֵעַ אֵלַי כְּעֵת מִנְחַת־עָרֶב:

The Hebrew here is *ha-ish Gavriel* (הָאִישׁ גַּבְרִיאֵל)—literally, "the man Gabriel."

We need to pause here for a second and realize just how *significant* that is. Gabriel is one of the only angels—alongside Michael—explicitly named in Scripture. Yet, Gabriel consistently shows up in human form. He doesn't appear as a freaky-looking Cherub with four faces or as a radiant serpent. He appears as a *man* or *manlike,* one who seems perfectly comfortable interacting with humans.

Indeed, it's worth noting that the text in Daniel nowhere identifies Gabriel as an angel, and it doesn't use the word מַלְאָךְ or "messenger" or "angel" in connection with him even once. But Daniel's reaction is telling. He is "afraid" and falls on his face. (Afraid, just as Zechariah the priest is in the Gospel of Luke.) This reaction, therefore, suggests again that Gabriel is more than a man.

Besides that, Jewish commentators throughout the ages have consistently named Gabriel as an angel despite the absence of the term מַלְאָךְ. Let's look at some prominent examples.

Rashi said of Daniel 8:16: "and said to the angel, 'You, Gabriel.'" Here, this Jewish sage explicitly calls Gabriel an angel *mal'akh* (מלאך).

The late Rabbi Steinsaltz, a renowned Israeli Talmudic scholar, teacher, author, and spiritual leader, commented on Daniel 8:15, writing, "It was when I, Daniel, saw the vision, that I requested understanding; behold, there was a figure who had the appearance of a man standing before me, but who was actually an angel."

Before either Rashi or Rabbi Steinsaltz, however, the Book of Enoch, the New Testament, the Talmud, and the Zohar—all written primarily by Jews—specifically identify Gabriel as an angel.

What Does This Mean?

The fact that Gabriel, a (purportedly) high-ranking angel, since he "stands in the presence of God," is described as *ha-ish*—a man—has *direct implications* for understanding the Ishim. If we take the later rabbinic and mystical classifications seriously, Gabriel would likely be counted among the Ishim due to his humanlike appearance and his role as a messenger.

But there's more. Unlike the Seraphim, who are depicted as terrifying, radiant, and often reptilian in appearance, Gabriel's entire *modus operandi* is to interact with humans on their level.

RABBINIC SOURCES

When we turn to rabbinic literature, the picture of the Ishim starts to get sharper. The Talmud doesn't say much about the Ishim by name, but it often describes angels who appear as men. These beings are portrayed as messengers, helpers, guardians, and even instructors to the righteous.

For example, in Megillah 15b, the Talmud describes how three ministering angels helped Esther when she approached King Ahasuerus uninvited:

- One raised her head to highlight her beauty.
- Another endowed her with divine grace and charm.
- The third stretched out the king's scepter to ensure she was welcomed.

Kabbalistic Texts

The Zohar—the central text of Jewish mysticism—takes things further, classifying Ishim as lower-ranking angels who serve as intermediaries between the divine and humanity. While they lack the fiery, overpowering presence of Seraphim or Cherubim, their humanoid appearance makes them ideally suited to interact with humankind.

In fact, Ishim are often depicted as the most approachable of all angelic beings. They're the ones sent to deliver messages, provide assistance, or even test human faith. Unlike the terrifying Seraphim, Ishim often come across as gentle, even compassionate (in comparison to other heavenly beings).

Ishim vs. *B'nei Adam*

Finally, it's also worth noting that Rabbi Reuven HaKohen Rappaport, a rabbi and Torah scholar active in the nineteenth century in the city of Tarnopol and known for his work *Itur Sefarim* (*Ornament of Books*), "contrasts two terms for men, *ishim* and *bene adam* (עיטור ספרים)."[374] He understands *ishim* as more complementary, writing, "O men [*ishim*] I call to you—If you are good and follow the Law, you are called men [*ishim*] like the attending angels."

But, if *ishim* can mean angelic, manlike beings *or* regular human dudes, how the heck are we supposed to tell them apart? It's simple: We pay attention to the labels.

When the Bible's talking about angels, otherworldly beings, or what I'd call interdimensional entities that look like men, it'll use words like *ish* ("man") or *anashim* ("groups of men or people"). But here's the crucial thing to notice. They're never called *b'nei Adam* ("sons of Adam"). Never. That term's strictly reserved for *actual* humans—descendants of Adam. So, if we see *ishim* or *anashim*, we might be dealing with something or someone that just *looks* human.

THE NORDIC ALIENS

Now that we've laid the groundwork for understanding the Ishim, we turn our attention to alleged beings that bear an uncanny resemblance to them—*or that might actually be them*: the Nordics.

For instance, there are several noteworthy parallels between the Ishim and the beings described in modern accounts of Nordics:

- ▶ The Ishim are consistently described as having a perfect, humanlike appearance. Likewise, the Nordics are almost universally portrayed as physically flawless, with radiant skin, symmetrical features, and a generally ethereal beauty. This theme of beauty recurs in both ancient texts and modern testimonies (see Daniel 10:5–6; Matthew 28:3).[375]
- ▶ The Ishim, like many other angelic beings, can appear and disappear at will. They possess the ability to manifest visibly to humans or remain unseen. This matches reports of Nordics who seem to "appear out of nowhere" or "vanish without a trace" during contact experiences (see Genesis 18, 19; Acts 12:7, 12:10).[376]
- ▶ While less documented than their Seraphic counterparts, certain scriptures highlight angels communicating in ways beyond speech, particularly through dreams or divine insight. This aligns with reports of Nordics influencing perception, telepathic communication, or even manipulating matter in ways that defy known physics (see Genesis 31:11, Matthew 1:20).
- ▶ Both Ishim and Nordics are often portrayed as guides or messengers. In Jewish tradition, the Ishim are considered

intermediaries between God and humanity, appearing as men to deliver divine messages or provide aid. Likewise, Nordics often present themselves as spiritual teachers, offering messages of peace, enlightenment, or warnings against technological or moral decay (see Genesis 16:7–12; Daniel 9:21–23; Matthew 28:5–7).[377]

Modern Descriptions and Origin

Nordic aliens, as noted previously, are most often described as tall, beautiful, humanlike beings with strikingly Scandinavian features. They're usually reported as having long blond or reddish hair, blue or green eyes, fair skin, and perfectly symmetrical faces. While these descriptions bear a striking resemblance to the Ishim described in Jewish and Christian traditions, this comparison remains a working hypothesis rather than a definitive conclusion.

I honestly believe, however, that the similarities are way too juicy to ignore. We're talking about overlapping descriptions from ancient texts, modern-day testimonies, and some seriously compelling connections that keep popping up.

Am I claiming I've cracked the code and proven they're the same thing? Nope, not yet. But here's the point: The parallels between the Ishim and Nordics are based on a convergence of various textual descriptions, modern testimonies, and speculative correlations.

The pattern is there, which should compel us to dig deeper and see where it leads.

Now, as I've said, when it comes to sheer aesthetics, these beings are basically human perfection dialed up to eleven—at least if you go by UFO lore. They're called "Nordics" for a reason.

Why?

Because they look like the textbook definition of a tall, blond, blue-eyed Scandinavian supermodel. Think "perfected" humans straight out of some Aryan fantasy or Germanic myth. It's all about that flawless, ethereal, almost-too-good-to-be-real look.

Of course, I should mention that nowhere in the Hebrew Scriptures, the New Testament, or elsewhere do we see descriptions of the Ishim's hair or eye color. But we do get descriptions of angelic beauty.

Consider Genesis 19:5:

And they called to Lot and said to him, "Where are the men who came to you tonight? Bring them out to us that we may know them *carnally*."

וַיִּקְרְאוּ אֶל־לוֹט וַיֹּאמְרוּ לוֹ אַיֵּה הָאֲנָשִׁים אֲשֶׁר־בָּאוּ אֵלֶיךָ הַלָּיְלָה הוֹצִיאֵם אֵלֵינוּ וְנֵדְעָה אֹתָם:

Even if the men of Sodom were utterly depraved (I suppose they were since they were destroyed the next day)—does it make sense to think they would have, as a mob, demanded that Lot hand them over if they were dog ugly—heck, even if they were just so-so in the looks department—so they could be "intimate" with them? (Hey, I'm being polite.)

I don't think so.

On the other hand, if these guys were Greek Adonis types or Michaelangelo's David—it's probably more believable. Right?

However, interestingly, when it comes to Nephilim descriptions, well…we'll get to that. Let's just say that it's not beyond the pale to suggest that some, if not all, Ishim might indeed fit the description of these Nordics.

In any case, Nordics are also often described as peaceful, benevolent, and spiritually enlightened. They communicate telepathically, exhibit heightened intelligence, and project an aura of calm and compassion.

Of course, these supposed traits demand deeper scrutiny.

Hold on McFly, We're Going Back to the Fifties

Accounts since the 1950s often place the Nordic's origin within the Pleiades star cluster, hence the name "Pleiadians."[378] It's practically a brand name at this point.

Remember all those New Age channelers and UFO contactees who swear they're getting interstellar DMs from beings claiming to hail from this star cluster? Yeah, those guys. The Nordics. The tall, blond, human-looking aliens with the chiseled jawlines and friendly smiles.

These are the dudes.

Most people think the whole Nordic encounter thing kicked off in the 1950s. And, yeah, that's when the sightings blew up during America's first big UFO wave. Tons of sightings, documented like crazy with people lining up to tell their tales.

The truth is that most people have it wrong. The real deal isn't what they've been led to believe. Those '50s encounters? They're just the tip of the iceberg.

George Adamski, one of the most famous contactees of the era, said he met a blond, humanlike being named "Orthon" from Venus on November 20, 1952.[379]

Did I mention that these beings (in the 1950s, that is) first claimed to be from Venus? Early contactees also called them "Venusians" when they believed some came from Venus—that is, before our science figured out that our bright and shining celestial neighbor is a burning hot, hellhole of a blasted landscape.

In any case, according to Adamski, Orthon was deeply concerned about humanity's nuclear proliferation and sought to warn Earth's inhabitants about its destructive path. Though most skeptics dismissed Adamski's claims as fantasy, his description of a tall, blond, peaceful alien struck a chord with a segment of the public. Throughout that decade and beyond, other alleged contactees reported similar encounters with beings fitting the same description. These accounts often included messages of peace, love, and the advancement of spiritual consciousness.

Valiant Thor

This narrative, too, is about a Nordic-style alien named "Valiant Thor." Interestingly, this account, which UFO whistleblower Charles McNeal says really happened,[380] was first written about in *Stranger at the Pentagon* by Christian pastor and author Dr. Frank E. Stranges.[381]

Get ready, because I'm about to rip the lid off this Valiant Thor fairy tale. Here's the official line: According to Dr. Stranges, some "extraterrestrial human" named Valiant Thor—tall, handsome, light-haired, smooth as butter—was living at the Pentagon for three years during the Eisenhower administration. This Nordic Venusian allegedly came with an offer to help humanity eradicate disease, war, and poverty. Yep, just chilling in the heart of American military power, offering salvation on a silver platter—the whole messianic-savior routine.

All we had to do was ditch our nukes and hold hands around a campfire singing "Kumbaya." Sound familiar? It should. It's the same old script from George Adamski's *Orthon,* Admiral Byrd's Master from Hollow Earth fame, and about a thousand other New Age prophets who love to play the "benevolent alien" card.

By the way—here's a little something most people miss when they dig into the whole Adamski saga: The guy was neck deep in California's Theosophy occulture. We're talking the real-deal, mystical scene of the 1920s and 1930s. Adamski wasn't just some random dude who looked up and saw saucers, he was already marinating in a stew of half-baked mysticism and Eastern religion knockoffs.

He even cooked up his own flavor of it, dubbing it "Universal Progressive Christianity." A little Christianity here, a little Eastern spirituality there, stir it all up with some ego-driven mystic pretension, and voilà—you've got yourself a cult recipe.[382]

He got his start cozying up with Theosophy, including the I AM cult and neo-Theosophy. That's right—he was rolling with the folks who built their worldview on Helena Blavatsky's work.

If that wasn't enough, Adamski even founded his own occult group, the Royal Order of Tibet. And, get this: His buddy George Williamson, another guy who supposedly witnessed the same UFO as Adamski, was tangled up with some Theosophical gig called Soulcraft.[383]

Birds of a feather and all that.

What they really did was slap a shiny, extraterrestrial coat of paint on Blavatsky's old ideas. Theosophy 2.0. Instead of mystical "masters" in some far-off Himalayan retreat, they rebranded them as enlightened aliens cruising around the cosmos in their flying saucers.

Of course, these aliens are all about preaching Theosophy 101: endless reincarnation, discovering one's own divinity, and evolving into higher beings. The same old recycled mysticism, just with a sci-fi marketing spin.

In other words, Adamski wasn't just trying to prove aliens were real; he was peddling a *spiritual upgrade*. For the true believers, it was a lot more enticing than just watching lights in the sky.

Indeed, Adamski's coauthor, Desmond Leslie, wrote to him: "I don't know what has happened, George, but all the mediums have suddenly disposed of their Indian guides, etc, and have replaced them with space people."[384]

Anyway, back to Valiant Thor.

Here's the part where the whole thing unravels for the skeptics, the UFO buffs, the theologians, and anyone with two brain cells to rub together: This tale is riddled with enough red flags and dead giveaways to make a serial liar blush.

Is Valiant Thor an alien, an angel, or just confused? Stranges claimed Val is from Venus, where he allegedly lives underground with other humanoid beings because, you know, Venus' surface is basically a volcanic hellscape.

To be fair, a species with tech advanced enough for interstellar travel just might have tech advanced enough to have bases underground—even on an environmentally hostile world.

But I digress.

Val also drops Christian references like Skittles throughout the narrative, calling Jesus "The Master" (not the "Son of God," not the "Son of Man," just "The Master,"—like he's running a New Age yoga retreat).

Direct quote from Val: "Jesus Christ is the Alpha and Omega of your faith."

Cool sentiment, but a question comes to mind.

I mean, if Val's all down with Jesus as the "Alpha and Omega" for humanity, and Val has some kind of inside scoop that verifies that—you know, since he's got the inside scoop on making worldwide peace with no disease or poverty, too—then the next question ought to be: "Well, what is Jesus Christ to YOU, Val?"

Because, in the end, Yeshua isn't just the Alpha and Omega of the Christian faith. If the New Testament is correct, God the Father has made Him preeminent over all creation. By extension, that includes every sentient being in existence.

Anyway, while Val's supposedly from Venus, his vibe screams "angelic emissary (a dark one) with a New Age twist."

Here's a direct quote from Stranges about Valiant Thor: "Bear in mind that he is one of those beings who was directly created by the Hand of Almighty God Himself."[385]

(Never mind that no Scripture anywhere explicitly states that angelic beings of any stripe are directly created by the Hand of Almighty God Himself—at least, not in a way that explicitly outlines how their creation differs from that of humanity's.

There are simply no details either way. Some *could be interpreted* in that fashion, but that's interpretation, not something written in black and white. The truth is, we have no idea how or when God created any angelic species.)

So, is Val a celestial being slumming it in a spaceship? Or is he lying about his origins? If he's truly an angelic being sent by the Creator of the Universe, why the cover story about Venus?

We don't find within the Hebrew Scriptures OR the New Testament Gabriel or Michael claiming to be from a planet in our solar system, do we?

Here's a hint: No. We don't.

And then there's the technology:

- Zero right angles. Everything is smooth and seamless, like it was designed by Ikea on steroids.
- Lighting with no discernible source. The whole ship just glows, with no visible fixtures or light sources.
- Holographic technology and telepathic controls.

Sound familiar? Yep, abductees describing Grey aliens' ships say the same things. (We'll get to that in a bit, too.)

You'd think these two camps went to the same cosmic Home Depot.

IN THE SHADOW OF GOLIATH

Val's a Mashup, Baby

Val's not the only charming alien/spiritual guide in the game. He's basically a conglomeration of:

- Orthon, the golden-haired peace preacher who dropped in from Venus to give Adamski the same "stop blowing yourselves up" sermon.
- The Master from Admiral Byrd's Inner Earth Diary (another benevolent, human-like being warning humanity about war and nukes) mentioned him above.
- Ashtar from the Ashtar Command (the OG cosmic Jesus figure in UFO religions).
- Pretty much all other Nordic aliens (tall, blond, peaceful, and vaguely judgmental about Earth's messiness).

Apparently, the cosmic casting director has a type.

Here's Where It Gets Dicey

Let's be real. There are three possibilities here:

- Stranges made the whole thing up. If that's the case, we've got a man who is supposedly a Christian minister who lied about meeting a celestial Venusian for clout and book sales.
- Stranges was visited by an angelic being. But if Val Thor is an angel, then he's an angel lying about being from Venus, and he's dishing out a watered-down, New Agey version of Jesus. (Classic misdirection move.)
- Stranges had the story projected into his mind. Val—or whoever's pulling the strings—basically played *Inception* on Stranges to deliver this convoluted narrative.

No Matter Which Option You Pick, Here's the Result:

The Val Thor story undermines and casts shade at Christianity.
By mixing UFOs with a Christian/New Age twist and presenting

zero verifiable elements, anyone with critical thinking skills is going to look at this and think, "A Christian minister lied about all this stuff to spread a weird (and easily debunkable) version of 'the gospel' to hook people who would otherwise never give the Bible a second look."

No, the truth is at best, *Stranger at the Pentagon* is a badly written, weird sci-fi read—a knockoff of the film, *The Day the Earth Stood Still* with some overly spiritual vibes.

At worst? It's a well-orchestrated hit job by an angelic entity working through a "Christian" huckster and useful idiot to reduce the credibility of the New Testament and Christianity as a whole. Either way, Valiant Thor's Venusian act is as credible as a politician at a lie detector test.

Betty and Barney Hill Case (1961)

That's the end of the Val Thor rant. Moving on, the 1961 abduction case of Betty and Barney Hill remains one of the most famous and well-documented incidents in UFO history.[386]

While the Hills primarily reported encountering the smaller, grey-skinned entities now known as "Greys," Betty Hill later described a taller, humanlike figure observing the proceedings from the sidelines. (More on the Hills' account to follow in chapter 10.) Though this entity's appearance wasn't elaborated upon to the extent of later Nordic descriptions, it adds a compelling layer to the broader phenomenon—namely, aren't the Nordics good-guy space brothers? Yet here (and in later narratives) they seem to be just as involved with the abduction-happy Greys as the Reptilians. Makes you think, *hmmmm...*

Similarity to "The Master"

Accounts of Nordic-like beings aren't limited to contactee experiences alone. Allegedly, Admiral Richard E. Byrd, during his 1947 expedition to the Arctic, encountered a "Master" of a hidden underground city who bore striking similarities to the modern conception of Nordics.

Byrd's description of this entity depicted a tall, handsome man with blond hair who claimed to be part of an advanced, enlightened society.

It should be noted that certain books, such as *The Secret Lost Diary of Admiral Richard E. Byrd* by Timothy Green Beckley and the works of Raymond Bernard (a pseudonym for Walter Sagmeister) describe Byrd encountering a "Master" and beings referred to as the "Arianni" in a subterranean crystal city.[387]

These entities are depicted as tall, blond-haired, and speaking with a "Nordic or Germanic accent."

However, despite persistent claims to the contrary, the Byrd Polar and Climate Research Center, which holds Byrd's official archives, explicitly states there is no credible evidence of such a diary or encounters with a Hollow Earth civilization.[388]

Theoretical Origins

The mainstream UFO gospel says the Nordics hail from distant star systems—most famously, the Pleiades. And why not? The Pleiades sounds exotic, mystical, and just vague enough to work. Guys like George Adamski and Billy Meier practically built their entire careers on it.

They claim they've had sit-downs with these Pleiadians—tall, blond, spiritual Übermenschen who've apparently transcended war, poverty, and probably even traffic jams. Their mission? To guide us poor, barbaric Earthlings toward some higher state of being. Like intergalactic life coaches with better hair.

However, many scientists point out that the Pleiades is a young star cluster composed primarily of hot, massive stars with life spans too short to develop habitable planets. Thus, proponents of this theory often suggest the Pleiadians have either relocated from another system or exist in a higher-dimensional version of the Pleiades inaccessible to our current instruments. For example, according to gaia.com, Nordics are "claimed to be fourth- and fifth-density beings."[389]

What does that even mean?

A Brief Density Primer

"Density" is a term borrowed from The Law of One (Ra Material) and other New Age and esoteric beliefs.[390] Unlike "dimension," which usually refers to physical planes of existence (like height, width, and depth), "density" refers to levels of consciousness, awareness, or spiritual evolution. Think of it as a metaphysical ranking system where higher numbers mean more enlightened, spiritually advanced, or complex beings.

Here's a breakdown of the densities:

1. 1st density: Basic existence—minerals, elements, and inanimate matter. The focus is on just existing and learning through being.
2. 2nd density: Life-forms with basic awareness—plants, animals, anything with movement and growth. The goal is survival and developing a rudimentary sense of self.
3. 3rd density: That's us—humans. Self-awareness, free will, and the struggle between good and evil. This is supposedly the hardest density because it's where we make conscious moral choices.
4. 4th density: Beings who've transcended the physical/material drama of the 3rd density. They're supposedly more spiritually advanced, empathetic, and telepathic. Some say they're still partially physical, but they experience heightened emotional and spiritual awareness. They're all about *love, understanding,* and *unity.* Allegedly, many Pleiadians are 4th density.
5. 5th density: Purely spiritual or light beings. These beings focus on wisdom, learning, and understanding the true nature of reality. They're supposedly far less concerned with the material world and more about mastering consciousness and knowledge. They can manifest physically if they want, but it's more like a projection.
6. 6th density: Entities merging love and wisdom. Think of guardian-angel archetypes, guiding others while continuing their own evolution.
7. 7th density: Nearing the point of merging back into the Source or Creator. Complete unity consciousness.

8. 8th density: The return to pure, undifferentiated unity—basically, God or the Source itself.

Why do New-Age believers love this concept? Because it *sounds* deep, hierarchical, and scientific without *being* scientific. It provides a structure to the universe that blends spirituality, sci-fi, and metaphysical mumbo-jumbo into a neat little package.

So, what's the deal with 4th- and 5th-density beings?

- 4th-density beings: These are allegedly beings like the Pleiadians who have "graduated" past human petty squabbles. They're all about peace, love, unity, and other feel-good buzzwords. They still have some physicality but are mostly ethereal.
- 5th-density beings: They're even more advanced—basically energy or light beings. They've moved past emotional drama and are all about pure wisdom, spiritual insight, and guiding lower-density beings (like us) without getting their hands dirty.

Interdimensional Hypothesis

The interdimensional hypothesis offers a more sophisticated explanation for the Nordic phenomenon. Rather than existing as mere extraterrestrials from a distant planet, these beings may operate from alternate planes of reality or higher vibrational states—as Gaia.com mentioned.

According to this theory, the Nordics may exist simultaneously within our universe and in adjacent dimensions, explaining why they can seemingly appear and disappear at will or project themselves telepathically across vast distances.

Furthermore, this hypothesis aligns well with accounts of their "otherworldly" nature and profound psychic abilities.

And there —boom shakalaka boom, hey hey!

We find out these guys share the interdimensional qualities of the Reptilians…and, uh, the Ishim.

But the question remains: Are these beings truly benevolent? Or is their presentation merely a façade for something far more sinister?

Before the Pleiades and Before Venus

UFO historians note that "many of the aliens encountered in the 1950s, and ever since, are remarkably Aryan" in appearance. The term "Nordic" in ufology thus specifically denotes tall, fair, humanlike aliens.

They're sometimes even called "space Aryans" or "Aryan aliens" in pop culture discussion. Notably, George Adamski's visitors from Venus wore symbols on their clothing that drew from esoteric traditions. In fact, one of the occult symbols on Orthon's shoe was a swastika.[391]

This striking detail (whether Adamski fabricated it or not) explicitly linked the Nordic alien image with a Nazi emblem, at least in symbolism. But that's not actually strange when you know that the so-called Vril Society, named after a fictional energy in Edward Bulwer-Lytton's novel *The Coming Race* (1871)[392] and led by medium Maria Oršić in the 1920s—engaged in telepathic communication with Nordic aliens described as an advanced Aryan race allegedly from the Aldebaran star system.

As Stephen Quayle, a nationally known radio host (Survive2thrive and Coast to Coast), photographer, and author of *Empire Beneath the Ice* has noted:

> The Vril Society was founded as "The All German Society for Metaphysics" in 1921 to explore the origins of the Aryan race. It was formed by a group of female psychic mediums led by the Thule Gesellschaft medium Maria Or- sitsch (Orsic) of Zagreb, who claimed to have received communication from Aryan aliens living on Alpha Tauri, in the Aldebaran system.[393]

According to the legend, Maria Oršić and her colleagues channeled detailed technical information from these beings. At some point during these communications, Oršić presented transmissions—written in ancient Sumerian and Templar script—that contained instructions for building a flying saucer.

Gaia.com confirms the connection, writing:

> While generally seen as a benevolent species, there's a chance the Nordics influenced the Vril Society. Some factions might have deviated from the path of light, aligning with malevolent entities opposing the human race.[394]

So, before the groovy, "we're super beyond past petty squabbles and we're all about peace, love, unity, and finding your inner divinity," at least some Nordics were all down zigging to the heil with a huge dose of racial superiority, genocide, and world domination.

We've gotta ask: Were they 4th and 5th density, too?

And if the Nazi supporters were just one faction, does that faction still exist? If it does, again, how does any channeler or experiencer really know *which* Nordic faction they're communicating with? If one faction was willing to support Hitler—I mean, do you think they'd be all honorable and refuse to lie about their intentions? I don't.

You know what all this means, right?

It doesn't matter if we're looking at testimonies from the 1950s, the 1920s, or even earlier—the Nordics are always tangled up with the occult. George Adamski. George Williamson. Maria Oršić.

All of them, every time.

And that occult connection didn't stop. It's alive and kicking today. We can scroll through YouTube and find all kinds of "channeled" messages from Nordics supposedly chilling in the Pleiades.

Does that sound like some high-tech, *Star Trek*, *Star Wars*, *Stargate*, *Dr. Who*, interstellar civilization to you? Because it sure doesn't to me. It reeks of something else, something way older and way darker.

We're talking interdimensional. Fallen-angel territory.

Fallen Ishim.

Think what you want for the moment. Up next, we'll examine the testimony of abductees, whistleblowers, and researchers to see if the Nordics are as benevolent as they appear—or if their supposed goodwill is part of a deeper agenda.

The Grey Connection

As we've seen so far, the Nordics are supposed to be our space brothers—benevolent watchers ("Watchers"—did ya catch that?)—standing as cosmic lifeguards at the edge of the deep end, ready to throw us a flotation device if we start drowning in our own stupidity.

They're the shining knights of the Galactic Federation of Worlds—or Light, depending on who you ask—here to help humanity awaken to a higher consciousness and all that good jazz.[395]

But the evidence suggests something way more complicated. By "complicated," I mean potentially horrifying. Many contactees describe encounters with Greys as utterly terrifying: They report kidnappings in the dead of night, being subjected to invasive medical procedures, and being probed, prodded, and examined like lab rats. This isn't ET phoning home; it's Azael's second lieutenant's laboratory.

But here's where it gets interesting (read "suspicious," if it wasn't suspicious already).

The Greys are often reported as subservient. Workers. Foot soldiers. Biomechanical tools (nonhuman biologics, remember?) who perform grunt work while something—or someone—else calls the shots.

According to several accounts, that "someone" is often described as none other than Nordic-type aliens.

Take the infamous Travis Walton case of 1975. Walton's abduction in the Arizona woods is one of the most well-documented abduction stories in history.[396]

The twist? After being abducted by Greys, Walton later encountered tall, beautiful, humanlike beings who seemed to be running the show. Reports like these are not isolated. They pop up again and again, threading themselves through the patchwork quilt of alien-abduction lore.

Then there's the troubling narrative that Nordics are working hand-in-hand with Greys and Reptilians as part of some grand cosmic conspiracy (which, again, would fall in line with fallen angels of various interdimensional species working together). The Altairan Nordic group, for example, is allegedly part of an alliance with Greys and Reptilians known as the Ciakahrr. According to various testimonies, they are complicit in covert operations against humanity, including abductions and genetic experimentation.[397] In some reports, they're described as cold, calculating, and utterly devoid of empathy.

Whatever happened to brotherly love, man?

The Tall Whites

Who—or *what*—are the Tall Whites? And why do they matter?

Unlike the blond-haired, blue-eyed Nordics who are often framed as ethereal guides with hearts of gold, the Tall Whites come across as, well, corporate. Less benevolent space brothers, more high-strung, callous bureaucrats.

The real juice on them comes from Charles James Hall—a former US Air Force serviceman stationed at Nellis Air Force Base in Nevada during the 1960s. Hall's memoirs, the *Millennial Hospitality* series, lay out years of interactions with these aliens who supposedly operated out of a remote desert base on the Nellis ranges.[398] In *Millennial Hospitality IV: After Hours* (2007), he states that three independent witnesses came forward to confirm parts of his testimony about interactions with Tall Whites at Nellis Air Force Base.

Here's the thing—None of these so-called witnesses are named or quoted directly in the sources. Their identities? Totally undisclosed. Zero transparency. Which means their value as public corroboration is about as useful as a screen door on a submarine.

Of course, the critics love this. They scoff and say, "Oh, how convenient! No real corroboration. So, what do we have? Just one guy's wild-eyed testimony!"

However, there *is* something that smells like indirect corroboration.

Fast-forward to 2017. A US Navy pilot spills the beans about a 2004 "Tic-Tac" UFO encounter. You know, the kind that got mainstream attention: Both the *New York Times* and the *Washington Post* covered it.[399]

In December 2017, both the *Times* and the *Post* broke the story of the Pentagon's secret UFO program (Advanced Aerospace Threat Identification Program) and released declassified videos of the 2004 encounter, including the "FLIR," "GIMBAL," and "GOFAST" footage.

These videos were provided by former Pentagon official Luis Elizondo and ex Deputy Assistant Secretary of Defense Christopher Mellon.

The reports included testimony from retired Navy Commander David Fravor, who described encountering a "Tic Tac-shaped" object during a training mission off the coast of Southern California in 2004. The object was described as wingless, smooth, white, and approximately forty feet long. Both Fravor and Lieutenant Commander Alex Dietrich, who witnessed the object, emphasized its lack of wings, flight-control surfaces, and exhaust plumes. Dietrich likened it to a "large white Tic Tac breath mint."[400]

Fravor estimated the object was forty feet long, though some reports compared it to the size of his F/A-18F (fifty-six feet long). The discrepancy with Hall's alleged sixty-foot description may stem from differing eyewitness accounts or rounding.[401]

The object's maneuverability and speed were described as "well beyond the material science and capabilities" of known human technology, even in 2021.[402] The US Navy confirmed the videos as authentic in 2019, acknowledging that the phenomena remained unexplained.

In 2021, the Office of the Director of National Intelligence released a report documenting more than 144 UAP sightings since 2004, with the Tic Tac incident among the most prominent.[403] In fact, that encounter is one of the most well-documented UAP cases in modern history, supported by radar data, video evidence, and credible military testimony.[404]

Now, I'm not saying this proves Tall Whites are real. But you have to admit it's intriguing. Hall was throwing out these technical specs and descriptions *years* before the military confirmed their own encounters. And they line up almost too well.

Coincidence? Maybe. Or maybe Hall was ahead of the curve.

Not only that, but Hall has received support from Gerry Zeitlin, a researcher with the Open Seti Initiative, a life member of the Institute of Electrical and Electronic Engineers, an associate member of the Society for Scientific Exploration, and a past member of the Society for Planetary SETI Research (SPSR).

Zeitlin writes, "Hall's powerful and entirely self-consistent narrative, filled with surprising and revealing detail, is so impressive that I have chosen it as the only example of modern human-ET contact to receive major coverage in my web pages."[405]

Likewise, Dr. Michael Salla has also written positively about Hall's claims:

> Charles Hall's report (Millennial Hospitality I-III) of his encounters and deep interactions with tall humanoid beings living on the USAF Nellis Range remains without serious challenge to this day.
>
> And this is remarkable, as its implications are so radical; they reveal an entrenched presence in the American Southwest that predates the arrival of Euro-Americans in the area, and that continues with covert protection and support from the U.S. government while maintaining communications with a distant home location.[406]

So the Tall Whites, according to Hall, are seven to twelve feet in height, gaunt, and have chalky white or even translucent skin. They've got elongated faces, large (larger than a human's), blue eyes, and silver-white or silver-blond hair. They move like caffeinated greyhounds, sprinting at speeds of thirty to forty miles per hour. Some live up to seven hundred or eight hundred.

Yet for all their power and speed, Hall describes them as frail and temperamentally moody. Think: "Karen" at the homeowners' association meeting but armed with advanced alien tech. The way Hall tells it, these beings aren't here for the love of mankind. They're like temperamental landlords who barely tolerate your existence, so long as you follow *their* rules.

The Tall Whites, then, present themselves not as friendly cosmic neighbors, but as a highly territorial, exacting species willing to punish violations of their standards with lethal force. And, unlike Reptilians, Nordics, Seraphim, and Ishim, the Tall Whites have been seen with their own children. This presents a curious contradiction.

If these beings are indeed extraterrestrial—or interdimensional, as some would claim of the Nordics—then their reproductive processes are apparently similar enough to ours to involve child-rearing.

I ask you: Raising kids in a family isn't exactly the traditional picture of "angelic" activity, is it?

We're talking about supposedly extraterrestrial beings here who operate by a strict code of conduct, reproduce sexually, and guard their kids with almost rabid ferocity. That's not typical "angelic" behavior or nature—of any type (according to the party line).

There are males and females. They get jiggy with it. That's primal, mammalian, and definitely something most believe is strictly native to this material plane of existence.

Hall claims he was warned that any harm done to their children, whether intentional or accidental, would result in immediate death. No court. No jury. Just alien justice (revenge), straight and brutal.

One Tall White female, nicknamed "Teacher's Pet," supposedly held a ruthless doctrine: Any serviceman who broke protocol or upset the delicate balance of their relationship was to be killed immediately.

It's important to note that Hall's descriptions suggest a hierarchical, almost predatory, relationship with humanity. They may toss you a bone of favor now and then, but make one wrong move—especially around their kids—and it's curtains for you. Literally.

And Hall implies that people *have* died after violating their rules.

Doesn't sound like enlightened space brothers to me. It also doesn't sound like a relationship of equals.

Hall's description of the Tall Whites' relationship with humanity isn't one of mutual respect, it's one of dominance—like between a human and a beloved pet. They might be fond of us—might even care about us in their own detached, clinical way. But if we cross the line, we're toast.

It's kind of like a man who owns a dog and is very fond of the dog, but if the dog harms a child—even unintentionally—the man believes the dog has to be "put down." There's affection, but only within the rigid confines of power.

Relationship with Nordics

Unlike the Nordics—who some New Agers practically worship while channeling messages on Pleiadian veganism—the Tall Whites are grounded in the physical. Flesh and blood. Spacecraft and cold steel. And they couldn't care less about chakras or starseed awakening.

According to Hall, these beings show up in *real* spaceships, live in structured bases, and even need to suit up against the cold, like fragile old men jogging in January. No mystical dream-walking. No telepathic transmissions about cosmic oneness. Just boots on the ground and a carefully maintained distance from the hairless apes they barely tolerate. From Hall's accounts, they only interact with human military personnel out of necessity, not curiosity or goodwill. It's business.

But even if Hall insists they're not interdimensional, there's enough overlap between the Tall Whites and the Nordics to raise eyebrows. For example, some researchers speculate the Tall Whites could be a *subgroup* of Nordics—a splinter faction with their own evolutionary path or secret agenda. See, they still look "human enough" that with a little effort and disguise they can blend in with humans.

At least, the shorter, younger ones can—if barely.

But with that slight similarity in appearance—height, eye color, hair color—and yet being entirely native to this dimensional space, another possibility comes to mind: What if they're not from another star system? What if they're from right here?

We know angelic, interdimensional species descended to Earth and interbred with human women somehow, according to Genesis 6 and Enoch 1. What if the Nordics—if they're actually fallen Ishim—have done it again?

Only this time, they've perhaps done it with the permission of the US military.

Chuck Missler spoke at length about the so-called return of the Nephilim. He referenced two major passages of Scripture—one from the book of Daniel and another from the Gospel of Matthew.

Let's have a look:

Daniel 2:43:

In that you saw the iron mixed with common clay, they will combine with one another in their descendants; but they will not adhere to one another, just as iron does not combine with pottery.

(די) [וְדִי] חֲזַיְתָ פַּרְזְלָא מְעָרַב בַּחֲסַף טִינָא מִתְעָרְבִין לֶהֱוֺן בִּזְרַע אֲנָשָׁא וְלָא־לֶהֱוֺן דָּבְקִין דְּנָה עִם־דְּנָה הֵא־כְדִי פַרְזְלָא לָא מִתְעָרַב עִם־חַסְפָּא׃

I have to say that until this point, I've used the New American Standard Bible (NASB) English translation for both the Hebrew Scriptures and the New Testament. This is the first time I completely disagree with its translation.

The translation of this verse has a footnote for the portion of the verse translated as "in their descendants." That footnote reads: "Lit *the seed of men.*"

Indeed, the literal Hebrew of the verse reads "seed of men." Why the translators chose something else here, I don't know. The NASB typically does a pretty bang-up job, but here they should have left well enough alone. So, let's go with the New King James Version, which actually gets it right: Daniel 2:43:

As you saw iron mixed with ceramic clay, they will mingle with the seed of men; but they will not adhere to one another, just as iron does not mix with clay. (NKJV)

In his interpretation of Nebuchadnezzar's dream, Missler focuses on the phrase, "they shall mingle themselves with the seed of men," in the description of the iron mixed with miry clay.[407]

He suggests "they" refers to something other than the seed of men, possibly hinting at a future mingling analogous to the events of Genesis 6. As further support, he cites Matthew 24:37:

But as the days of Noah were, so also will the coming of the Son of Man be. (NKJV)

He then cites 2 Peter 2:4–5, which states that "God spared not the angels that sinned, but cast them down to Tartarus" and "spared not the old world, but saved Noah." Missler connects the sinning angels cast into Tartarus with the events of Genesis 6 and links them to the time of Noah.

Genesis 6:4 states, "There were giants on the earth in those days, and also afterward, when the sons of God came in to the daughters of men and they bore children to them."

So, there were hybrids on the Earth both before and after Noah's Flood. Some think, as Chuck Missler did, that in some way, fallen Ishim will do it again. Maybe, over the course of this last century, they *have* done it again…are continuing to do it. Right now. This very moment.

And it could be that some of the resulting hybrid offspring are these Tall Whites. They get some of the tech of their daddies while being limited to this three-dimensional reality because of their human mamas.

And that might be the point.

Maybe the Nordics are looking for a way to engineer hybrids that can blend in and really be "just human enough" to accomplish some specific end. Perhaps that's part and parcel of the Nordic's relationship with the Greys and all the abductions where they've been seen lurking in the background shadows. Maybe these Ishim aren't actually "descending to Earth" or "leaving their former estate" like their ancient brethren did.

Possibly, this time they're using Greys as their "nonhuman biologics," their material proxies in this dimensional space. In other words, the Greys are their hands and feet here. And instead of creating hybrids through sex, they're doing it through advanced science.

It's quite possible there have been bugs that have been super hard to work out of the system because the last few times they tried, the results were either colossal, monstrous, or deformed. Because even though we might outwardly look like them—*we are not them.*

We're not made of the same stuff.

There's no familial genetic line.

The only thing we have in common is the same Creator and the same stamp of heavenly royalty.

Admittedly, that's speculation. Some might even call that wild. But, hey, we're all off in Woo Woo Land right now anyway. There aren't any peer-reviewed materials to call on now, are there? (Even if there were, how fast do you want to bet the authors would be out of jobs with their tenure revoked?)

Here's just one more alternative idea regarding these Tall Whites: If they really are interstellar extraterrestrials restricted to this reality, but are *not* hybrids, then could they be the cursed people of Meroz? It's just a thought.

Honestly, they could be from some other star system altogether with zero connection to the Ishim, Meroz, or anything else we know from the Bible. The truth is, though, we don't know if these beings are figments of Charles James Hall's imagination or the real deal. But say that they are real, and they're here, somewhere in Nevada (and likely elsewhere too). We should be trying to figure out ways of verifying Hall's claims—despite obfuscation, active interference, and systematic disinformation designed to ridicule, marginalize, or outright erase credible testimonies and evidence from public discourse.

Because Dr. Salla is right.

If they've been here since before the arrival of Euro-Americans in the area—and they continue to operate on Earth with the acknowledgment and cooperation of the US government (at least in some capacity)—the American people have a right to know.

The people of Earth have a right to know.

To synthesize and wrap up what we've covered in this chapter, let me just say that the convergence of religious, historical, and modern testimonies surrounding Ishim-like beings suggests that this topic is far from mere fantasy. The parallels between ancient accounts and contemporary reports demand deeper scrutiny. If these beings are truly working within a strategic deception, then understanding their motives and methodologies is essential.

In the next chapter, we're cracking open the mystery of the Nephilim, the angelic-human hybrids everyone loves to reference but few dare to truly understand.

What if everything we think we know about them is dead wrong? What if the ancients left us breadcrumbs, and we've been too blind, lazy, or indoctrinated to see the full picture? We're about to connect the dots between ancient Hebrew texts and modern anthropological discoveries, and I'm telling you right now that I'm likely to ruffle some feathers.

Religious texts…modern reports. It's all there.

CHAPTER NINE

THE HYBRID ENIGMA

And Semjaza, who was their leader, said unto them: "I fear ye will not indeed agree to do this deed, and I alone shall have to pay the penalty of a great sin."

—1 Enoch 6:3

We've seen how deep the rabbit hole goes. We've picked apart the accounts of the Ishim, unmasking the so-called Nordics and (perhaps) the Tall Whites for what they might truly be: fallen beings cloaked in the illusion of benevolence.

We've examined the connections between modern UFO lore and ancient angelic beings, piecing together a puzzle most people don't even realize exists.

The Seraphim, the Ishim—we've looked at entities identified by religious traditions and echoed through the testimonies of abductees, whistleblowers, and conspiracy theorists alike.

But we're not finished.

What if I told you the deception we've been unraveling is rooted in an ancient incursion so catastrophic that it nearly destroyed humanity—an incursion that not only shattered divine order but sought to rewrite it from the ground up?

Genesis 6:1–2:

Now it came about, when mankind began to multiply on the face of the land, and daughters were born to them, that the sons of God saw that the daughters of mankind were beautiful; and they took wives for themselves, whomever they chose.

וַיְהִי כִּי־הֵחֵל הָאָדָם לָרֹב עַל־פְּנֵי הָאֲדָמָה וּבָנוֹת יֻלְּדוּ לָהֶם׃

וַיִּרְאוּ בְנֵי־הָאֱלֹהִים אֶת־בְּנוֹת הָאָדָם כִּי טֹבֹת הֵנָּה וַיִּקְחוּ לָהֶם נָשִׁים מִכֹּל אֲשֶׁר בָּחָרוּ׃

The Watchers.

You've heard the name before, even if you didn't realize it. Echoes of them are found not just in Jewish texts but in Christian Scripture, in some aspects of Islamic tradition, and in the myths of cultures scattered across the globe.

We had an in-depth discussion of the term "Watcher(s)" in chapter 3. The rebellion involving these beings wasn't a solitary event carried out by a small group of angels but rather a faction within a much larger and more complex insurrection.

While many are familiar with the Watchers described in the book of Daniel and in the Book of Enoch (as well as in a few others), they may not realize that this faction was most likely composed of Ishim, not Seraphim, Cherubim, or any other angelic species. They're often described as resembling mortal men more closely than any other celestial beings, which may suggest a certain compatibility or similarity in nature. Unlike the more alien forms of other angelic species, such as the Reptilians or serpentine-like Seraphim, the Ishim appear strikingly human, as we've gone over in depth. This resemblance may not be limited to physical appearance alone, but perhaps extends to certain aspects of their desires, emotions, and vulnerabilities. That's particularly true when considering some of the Jewish translations of Genesis 6:2.

For instance, the Contemporary Torah, JPS, 2006 renders the verse like this: "the [males among the] divine beings saw how pleasing the human women were and took wives from among those who delighted them." This raises the possibility of gendered beings within the category of "divine beings" (*b'nei ha-elohim,* בני האלהים).

WHY THIS WORDING?

The bracketed phrase ("the males among the") isn't there to spell things out for us; it's a loaded clue pointing to something bigger. It hints at the possibility that supernatural beings aren't all cut from the same masculine cloth.

Sure, the text doesn't flat-out mention female divine beings, but that little nod acknowledges a truth ancient Jewish thought might have danced around: Not every "divine being" was necessarily male.

And, while traditional rabbinic literature overwhelmingly describes angels as male or genderless, there are hints that female spirits or entities exist. For example, the Zohar contains discussions about female aspects of the divine (e.g., *Shekhinah*) and even female beings that are counterparts to male entities.

Of course, this opens a Pandora's box of possibilities that I frankly don't want to go into in this book. Suffice to say I think that if the angels (at least, the Ishim) were genuinely sexless or purely spiritual beings, it would be peculiar to suggest they suddenly acquired physical bodies with male genitalia after their fall—especially if that's not how God made them in the first place.

That's like suggesting: "Disobey God, head to Earth, and—*POOF!*—you've got...er, that is to say...you've been 'cursed' with...uh..."

Like the rock band Queen and lead singer Freddie Mercury belted out: "Is this a kind of magic?"[408]

No, the notion that angels are inherently sexless and there are no genders is an extrapolation, not a scriptural or rabbinic mandate. Again, that heads into a really deep rabbit hole and is tangential to the argument at hand. So, we'll breeze on by that for now.

The point is that given their humanlike nature, the Ishim would have been far more capable of interacting with humanity on a personal and intimate level. This similarity may have also made them uniquely susceptible to certain temptations other angelic species would not experience or understand.

While a human woman might be drawn to what appears to be the most beautiful man she has ever seen, she would be far less likely to be seduced by a seraphic Reptilian or otherwise nonhuman entity, regardless of its humanoid form.

Timothy Alberino agrees, stating, "It is hard to imagine a beautiful woman falling head over heels for a reptilian freak."[409]

Likewise, when L. A. Marzulli asks in reference to the Grey aliens, "Is it possible that let's say you're an Angelic entity, and your sustenance comes from the Living God, your sustenance comes from being in the presence of the Living God, so now you Rebel and you're no longer with the Living God—and you know, you're in Rebellion—is this what you look like?"[410]

I'd have to say "no" to that.

Were the Watchers Grey aliens? No, they weren't.

They were fallen. They were rebels. They were in our domain.

And, in the same way that it would be hard to imagine a beautiful human woman falling head over heels for a reptilian Seraph, it would be just as hard to imagine a beautiful woman going gaga over a bug-eyed, spindly, melon-headed alien Grey.

I said it before; I'll say it again: What people are seeing when they encounter so-called extraterrestrials (Reptilians, Nordics, Tall Whites, and Greys included) are not demons.

But I also made the distinction that fallen angels are not demons.

So, if I am saying Grey aliens are neither demons nor fallen angels (of any species)—what am I saying? Don't worry. We'll get to that.

Now, circling back to the incursion into our domain—the fallen Ishim may have been selected for this mission precisely because of their humanlike qualities, or they may have acted on their own initiative, compelled by a desire they either never sought permission to fulfill—or did seek and were denied.

If you think about it, with humanity being newly created and barely four hundred years old as a species at the time of Jared, this would make the lustful Watchers who may have been thousands upon thousands of years old akin to a creepy old uncle with unnatural desires who is ready to take advantage of his very young niece.

Or it could simply be God enacting a sort of *Star Trek*-style Prime Directive. Humanity wasn't even out of diapers, and this eons-old species wants to "go mingle?" What straight-thinking ruler would say "yes" to that?

It's no wonder God didn't, no matter what the angels' arguments for doing so might have been. They could have been enticed by the allure of human beauty, companionship, or even the desire to create something new through the mixing of their own essence with that of humanity.

Alberino thinks it's also possible that these angels were enamored with the idea of marriage and family.

He writes:

> It is interesting that the watchers saw fit to wed these women rather than simply fornicate with them. This procedure reveals that they were after more than sex.
>
> Apparently, they intended to procreate families within the covenant of marriage, almost as if they were hoping that the interspecies union might eventually be approved, or at the very least tolerated, by God.[411]

However, that's not the connotation of the Hebrew, so I'll have to respectfully disagree here.

When we read Genesis 6:2—"and they took wives for themselves, whomever they chose"—in the Hebrew, it doesn't have a romantic implication. Rather, it denotes violence. This is why I think these angels didn't even bother to ask permission, because they knew God's answer would be "no."

What does Enoch record?

> And Semjaza, who was their leader, said unto them: "I fear ye will not indeed agree to do this deed, and I alone shall have to pay the penalty of a great sin."
>
> And they all answered him and said: "Let us all swear an oath, and all bind ourselves by mutual imprecations not to abandon this plan but to do this thing."
>
> Then sware they all together and bound themselves by mutual imprecations upon it. (1 Enoch 6:3–5, R. H. Charles Translation)

It's worth mentioning that Enoch 1 is at least fifty years older than the oldest extant book of Genesis. This chronology is significant, as it indicates that Genesis may have been drawn from Enoch 1, not vice versa, or that both drew from an earlier source that has never been discovered.[412, 413, 414]

Indeed, Enoch 1 is referenced in the book of Genesis, quoted verbatim in the New Testament book of Jude, and is also referenced in 1 Peter, 2 Peter, Hebrews, and Revelation.[415]

John Strugnell, the former chief of the official Dead Sea Scrolls editorial team (deceased 2007), mentioned a well-preserved, complete, Aramaic version of Enoch 1 and the fact that it was microfilmed. He claimed to have seen the microfilm in 1990 during the Kuwait crisis but had been unable to purchase it for the editorial team.[416]

Now, let's ask: Why the oath? Why the need for mutual imprecation? They knew what they were doing was a direct violation of divine command. This was treason, pure and simple.

When we understand the overtones evident in the Hebrew, we realize their intent was never a happy family unit in the sense that humanity has ever understood "family" or the "covenant of marriage."

Of verse 2, Rashi writes, "מכל אשר בחרו OF ALL WHOM THEY CHOOSE—even if it were a married woman or a man or an animal."

Ibn Ezra likewise states, "It is possible that they took women even against their will."

And Ramban comments, "Thus Scripture tells of the violence and mentions further, *whomsoever they chose*, in order to include those who were married to others."

Yet again, Rabbi Steinsaltz says, "And they took for themselves wives, from whomever they chose, whether young or old, single or married, without consideration for laws of any kind."

In fact, regardless of how the term *b'nei Elohim* is interpreted by the rabbis, the vast consensus is that Genesis 6:2 speaks of whomever the *b'nei Elohim* are as violently taking females (sometimes males, too, and even in some cases, animals).

If that's true (I agree it is), then these angelic beings were a select group of violent sexual predators. They "took" wives from whomever they chose. This wasn't consensual.

What does that bring to mind? No asking for permission. No respect for human laws. No respect for human autonomy. No respect for human sovereignty.

"Took."

"Take."

"Taken."

"Abduction."

If the Ishim are the same as the Nordics, then the Watchers who descended to Earth and left their former estate had the same mentality as whomever is behind current alien abductions, medical and reproductive experiments, and hybridization efforts.

Recall that the connection between Nordics and Greys was discussed in the previous chapter, wherein testimony from abductees and whistleblowers consistently linked Nordics with Greys, both in collaborative operations and in acts of deception.

In other words, these beings have nothing but contempt for humanity's rights as sentient beings.

And if we believe the Nordics are fallen Ishim—the same species as the Watchers of Enoch and Genesis 6—then we understand that the origin of that contempt was the very fact that God created a new species (Adam) and gave him the same son-of-God status enjoyed by these entities.

We could say they're the equivalent of the "heavenly realm's" Ku Klux Klan, Hitler's Nazis, the Japanese under Hideki Tojo during World War II, Idi Amin in Uganda, Omar al-Bashir in Sudan, Pol Pot—the list could go on for quite some time.

These fallen angels hate humanity.

They're racists (or "species-ists"), to be more accurate. Oddly enough, while we don't know if there is any specific infighting among the Seraphim, Ishim, or other angelic species, the collective ire of all fallen species seems to be directed toward us.

The final nail in the coffin is the fact that in the Book of Enoch describes the Watchers having affection or concern for their *children*, the Nephilim, but it is notably silent about any love or emotional attachment to their *human wives*.

The text emphasizes their teaching humanity forbidden knowledge, but they don't do it out of affection. No, the Watchers' emotional investment is exclusively directed toward their *children*, not their wives. Indeed, the lack of reference to love for their human wives implies a purely exploitative relationship and a self-centered love—one that values legacy or power over genuine relational affection.

I believe the whole "teaching of forbidden knowledge" thing was a secondary goal. In case their efforts to commit genocide by breeding the original Adamic species (humans) out of existence failed, well, they'll have introduced concepts into the minds of humanity that reflect their own views more than God's.

Which, of course, brings us to their kids: the Nephilim.

THE NEPHILIM

The Nephilim were on the earth in those days, and also afterward, when the sons of God came in to the daughters of mankind, and they bore children to them. Those were the mighty men who *were* of old, men of renown. (Genesis 6:4)

הַנְּפִלִים הָיוּ בָאָרֶץ בַּיָּמִים הָהֵם וְגַם אַחֲרֵי־כֵן אֲשֶׁר יָבֹאוּ בְּנֵי הָאֱלֹהִים אֶל־בְּנוֹת הָאָדָם וְיָלְדוּ לָהֶם הֵמָּה הַגִּבֹּרִים אֲשֶׁר מֵעוֹלָם אַנְשֵׁי הַשֵּׁם: {פ}

We've been told the Nephilim were giants. And while giants are certainly part of the equation, focusing exclusively on their size is like staring at a tree and pretending we've seen the whole forest.

What if I said the term "Nephilim" refers to something much broader, far more sinister and complex than a single race of gigantic beings?

Nephilim, as evidenced by the texts, weren't merely giants. They were hybrids, new species and subspecies created through the forbidden union between celestial beings and human women.

The Hybrid Hypothesis

When we stop assuming "Nephilim" strictly means "giants," everything snaps into focus. The Nephilim included a wide array of hybrid beings resulting from angelic-human unions. The texts bear this out.

The Hebrew word *nephal* (נפל) means "to fall." The most common interpretation is that the Nephilim were "fallen ones" or beings resulting from a "fall" from purity. But the word isn't explicitly tied to size or stature. In fact, when we examine the Hebraic texts and rabbinic commentaries, we see a fractured narrative about diverse beings, not a monolithic species of giants.

Commentator Ibn Ezra, the previously-mentioned Jewish sage from Spain, stated the Nephilim were "people greater and taller than the normal people who were born to the sons of the noblemen."

He added that they were called "Nephilim" because "anyone who saw them lost heart at their huge stature."[417]

Clearly, stature was a characteristic of some Nephilim, but it wasn't the only one. The Dead Sea Scrolls contain writings of Genesis, Enoch 1, Jubilees, and the Book of Giants—all of which reference the Nephilim. Yet, the descriptions vary widely.

The apocryphal Book of Enoch expands on the Genesis account, describing the Nephilim as monstrous beings of varied nature. It is worth noting that this text is regarded as Scripture by the Ethiopian Orthodox Church (with a full copy written in Ge'ez).[418, 419, 420]

But here's the crucial point: Collectively, these texts describe not just giants, but categories and subcategories of hybrid beings.

The Divergence of Species

Jubilees 7:22 states:

And they bore children, the Naphidim, and they were all unlike and they devoured one another: and the Giants slew the Naphil, and the Naphil slew the Eljo, and the Eljo mankind, and one man another.

Here, the offspring are divided into different categories—or, perhaps, tribes (Naphidim, Giants, Naphil, Eljo)—suggesting diversity among the offspring of fallen celestial beings and human women. This isn't a single giant race but rather a taxonomy of multiple hybrid species.

Even among the giants themselves, there were tribes of differing heights. Jubilees 29:9–11 states:

But before they had called the land of Gilead the land of Raphaim, for it was the land of the Raphaim, and the Raphaim, or giants, were born there, whose length is ten, nine, eight, and seven ells, and their dwellings were from the land of the sons of Ammon to Mount Hermon, and the seats of their kingdom were Koronaem and Adra and Misur and Beon.

Further, the Zohar states that not all Nephilim were alike in appearance. It says some were "great giants," referencing Genesis 6:4's "mighty ones of old, men of renown." Then it adds that "others were not."[421]

John C. Reeves, an academic authority on ancient Jewish traditions, argues that these traditions recognized different categories of offspring from the Watcher-human unions. According to Reeves, these traditions recognized distinct categories of offspring from these unions, notably including the monstrous giants and other nefarious hybrid beings.

Indeed, he provides an extensive analysis of Watcher traditions in 1 Enoch chapters 6–7 and 2 Enoch chapter 18 in scholarly papers and lectures available through the University of North Carolina at Charlotte Judaic Studies department and related publications.

His elaboration clarifies that he sees the Watchers' hybrid progeny not as a single uniform category but as differentiated entities recognized in ancient Jewish literature and theology.[422]

A Hybrid Project Gone Awry

What emerges from all this? The term "Nephilim" refers to any hybrid species or subspecies created by the union of angel and human. Not all of them were giants. Not all of them were warriors. Some were grotesque. Others were beautiful.

Others still may have appeared almost indistinguishable from humans.

The variety of these beings isn't surprising considering the diversity within humanity itself. Why should angelic beings or the offspring of any union between angels and humans all follow a single mold?

The fixation on giants is a red herring. It's a distraction from the more profound truth that these beings—whatever their forms—represent a biological, spiritual, and existential corruption of the human species.

The emphasis on giants throughout history may be because those were the most noticeable or the most dangerous of the hybrids. But if we take the texts—Genesis, the Book of Enoch, the Book of Jubilees, Zohar, and others—at their word, the Nephilim included far more than towering behemoths.

A Question of Biological Compatibility

Let's talk genetics. Not the watered-down, family-friendly science fed to us in high school. Let's dive into the blood, bones, and molecular DNA sequences that form the blueprint of every living creature on Earth… and, if the hybridization hypothesis is true, the blueprint of something far more alien.

The Language of Life

DNA. Deoxyribonucleic acid. Four chemical bases: adenine, thymine, cytosine, and guanine arranged in pairs and wound into the double helix—the spiral staircase of life itself.[423]

It's the ultimate instruction manual. Every cell in the body reads it like a rabbi studying an ancient scroll. But it's not static; mutations, recombination, and genetic drift constantly rewrite and edit the script.

Today's scientists are steadily learning how to manipulate DNA.

Gene editing, CRISPR-Cas9, gene drives. We can alter crops, animals, even humans—but only within the boundaries of what already exists.[424]

Now, think about this: What if beings existed who mastered the very language we're only now beginning to decipher? Beings whose existence predates the Earth itself, whose knowledge of biology, genetics, and medicine has accumulated over eons? Beings who have not created themselves but have learned to understand the very fabric of creation with a precision we can scarcely imagine?

The Genesis of Hybridity

Genesis 6:1–2 states explicitly that *b'nei Elohim* (בני האלהים), divine beings, took human women and produced offspring. This isn't poetry, it's a statement of biological fact—at least, that's how the text presents it.

But how could such a union be biologically possible? Well, if these beings existed before the Earth itself, then their biological knowledge would likely be so far beyond our own they would appear Godlike. Whatever their nature, they would have bodies capable of engaging in the human reproductive process. Perhaps they knew how to adjust their physical forms to interface with human biology. Perhaps their own reproductive mechanisms were similar enough to ours to make it work without modification. Either way, the evidence is clear—the offspring were real.

What Would Be Necessary?

To produce offspring through sexual reproduction, two species must possess a degree of genetic compatibility. But "compatibility" doesn't necessarily mean "perfect compatibility."

In fact, even among species that can interbreed, the offspring may exhibit reduced fertility or carry underlying biological limitations. The result is often a creature that can live, function, and even reproduce, but often to a limited degree.

However, over successive generations, genetic weaknesses may accumulate, ultimately resulting in sterility, developmental issues, or a complete reproductive dead-end.

The same logic can be applied when considering the possibility of angel-human unions as described in ancient texts. For such reproduction to occur, several factors need to align:

1. **Genetic compatibility:** Both species require chromosomes that can successfully pair and recombine during meiosis. If angels possess a biological structure similar to that of humans—or if they have the capability to modify their own genetic code—reproduction could theoretically be possible.
2. **Reproductive mechanism alignment:** Beyond chromosomes, cellular communication, hormonal cycles, and reproductive mechanics need to match. For example, the Ishim would need gametes—sperm cells—capable of fertilizing a human egg.
3. **Intent and agency:** The ancient texts describe these beings not only taking human women but doing so deliberately, with the intention of producing offspring. This implies not just capability, but volition, suggesting they were already biologically compatible, or had the knowledge to become so.

The fact that these unions are described as being successful supports the notion of a biological framework—whether natural or technologically manipulated—that made such hybridization viable.

But it's worth reiterating: Hybrid offspring between distinct species can occur even when the resulting children possess limitations, diminished fertility, or are unable to pass their genes across multiple generations.

In short, the creation of offspring between fundamentally different beings may not have been common, easy, or sustainable, but it was biologically possible—at least under certain conditions. And that possibility has implications far deeper than biology alone.

The Central Argument

We've all heard the mainstream narrative. Homo sapiens evolved from some knuckle-dragging, thick-browed ancestor, clawing its way up the evolutionary ladder by sheer chance and mutation. It's all about "survival of the fittest," the strong devouring the weak, until suddenly we're building cathedrals, launching spacecraft, and arguing over pronouns.

But here's the thing. That story is falling apart. Slowly. Relentlessly. Like rust corroding the very foundations of a fortress built on arrogance and ignorance.

What if I said the anthropological record isn't a testament to random, unguided evolution but rather to a deliberate, catastrophic interference with the human genome by nonhuman entities?

What if the ancient texts aren't just primitive mythologies but are encoded accounts of actual events?

The ancient Hebraic and Near-Eastern narratives fit better with the observed record than the standard theory of evolution. And they do it in a way that's so blatant it's almost embarrassing that modern academia refuses to see it.

Genesis 6:1–4 outlines an event that was considered fact by the ancients: A group of nonhuman entities, the *b'nei Elohim*, descended to Earth, took human women, and produced hybrid offspring known as the Nephilim.

Every ancient culture has its own version of the story. The Sumerians spoke of the Anunnaki. The Greeks had their Titans. The Norse had their Jotunn.

Now, modern man brushes this off as fanciful mythology—except, the physical evidence doesn't lie. It just keeps piling up. There's an entire spectrum of hybrid beings that have left their genetic fingerprints across history.

The Evidence

These beings, in an act of unparalleled hubris and malevolence, devised a plan that can only be described as the first recorded attempt at interspecies genocide and ethnic cleansing.

Let that sink in for a moment.

Before the rise and fall of empires, before the etching of the first hieroglyph, these entities sought to eradicate us, hatching a sinister plot to extinguish the very flame of human consciousness from the cosmos.

However, instead of a full-on war of conquest and destruction, these entities would try to create a hybrid race (or races) with the goals of breeding the earthly imagers of God (humans) out of existence—and perhaps preventing the arrival of the Messiah, as some argue (e.g., Chuck Missler and others).

In this framework, the Nephilim narrative represents an incredible strategy by rebellious, interdimensional, higher intelligences to corrupt the human genome for nefarious purposes. From the unsanctioned comingling of angelic DNA with that of human women, the Nephilim were born. Enoch depicts them as violent beings who "devoured" humans, leading God to unleash the Great Flood to cleanse the world.

The Book of Giants further elaborates upon the story told in Genesis and Enoch 1, describing itself as "the transcription of the parables of Enoch the noted instructor" (4Q203).

According to the Book of Giants and Enoch 1, the fallen angels taught mankind forbidden knowledge like metallurgy, cosmetics, and weaponry, further contributing to the violence and chaos on Earth (1Q23).

The Book of Giants text also vividly depicts the Nephilim giants as brutal, bloodthirsty beings: "[They] slaughtered the sheep in that way.... They drank down their milky blood.... The giants ground up the bones of the beasts all together with their flesh" (4Q532).

As noted above, not only do the Hebrew Scriptures specifically name a number of giant tribes, it is also possible that not all Nephilim were giants.[425]

This finds some support within the Book of Jubilees, which states: "And they bore children, the Naphidim, and they were all unlike and they devoured one another: and the Giants slew the Naphil, and the Naphil slew the Eljo, and the Eljo mankind, and one man another" (7:22).

Also, among the giants themselves, were tribes of differing heights. Jubilees 29:9–11 states:

> But before they had called the land of Gilead the land of Raphaim, for it was the land of the Raphaim, and the Raphaim, or giants, were born there, whose length is ten, nine, eight, and

seven ells, and their dwellings were from the land of the sons of Ammon to Mount Hermon, and the seats of their kingdom were Koronaem and Adra and Misur and Beon.

Further, the Zohar states that not all Nephilim were alike in appearance. It says some were "great giants," referencing Genesis 6:4's "mighty ones of old, men of renown." But then it adds that "others were not."[426]

Finally, some scholars, like John C. Reeves, argue that ancient Jewish traditions recognized different categories of offspring from the Watcher-human unions.[427] As mind-bending as it seems, the question arises—in addition to the aforementioned giants, could the Nephilim also represent other hybrid offspring from interbreeding between humans and nonhuman entities?

Hominid Hybrids

In fact, is it possible that some, if not all, hominid species found by paleoanthropologists around the world, Neanderthals and Denisovans included, may themselves be hybrid beings?

In other words, *instead* of existing as:

- A "pre-Adamic race," as some Gap-Theory Christians believe.[428]
- "Animals created by God that lived for a period, then went extinct," as Dr. Hugh Ross' Reasons.org, teaches.[429]
- A group of humans, descended from Adam and Eve, who lived in the harsh, post-Flood world as Creationists as answersingenesis.org teaches.[430]
- A parallel evolutionary dead-end (sharing a common ancestor with homo sapiens) as proposed by the current iteration of the theory of evolution.

Couldn't modern man represent the original human, while at least some of the other hominids represent species created through an outside force tampering with the human genome?

Addressing the Gap Theory

I want to quickly take down the Gap Theory, particularly the interpretation that Neanderthals and Denisovans were pre-Adamic races existing before the biblical creation of Adam.

Neither a Christian-supported Gap Theory nor the pre-Adamic, racist theories proposed by Isaac La Peyrère in the seventeenth century fit the evidence.

Proponents of the Gap Theory (the Christian, nonracist version) argue that the apparent existence of advanced hominid species predating Adam and Eve can be explained by a period of creation and destruction occurring between Genesis 1:1 and Genesis 1:2. According to this view, Neanderthals, Denisovans, and potentially other hominid species were part of a pre-Adamic creation that was destroyed, with Adam and Eve being created afterward during a re-Creation event.

This explanation attempts to reconcile scientific findings of ancient hominid remains with a literal interpretation of Genesis.

While I believe in elements of the Gap Theory—for example, I think there is a gap in time indicated by Genesis 1:1 and Genesis 1:2—its interpretation regarding hominids, especially Neanderthal and Denisovans, suffers from several logical and evidential weaknesses:

- ▶ The Gap Theory posits that pre-Adamic races were destroyed before the creation of Adam. Yet, the evidence indicates that both Neanderthal and Denisovans coexisted during select points in history—and that both species interbred with homo sapiens.[431, 432, 433, 434] If Neanderthals and Denisovans were pre-Adamic and entirely unrelated to Adamic humanity, these facts would be unexpected and difficult to explain.
- ▶ While the Gap Theory attempts to account for the existence of hominid species, it fails to explain the specific genetic markers observed in modern humans—particularly the presence of Neanderthal nuclear DNA in European populations and the presence of Denisovan DNA in isolated, Asian human populations.

No, the existence of Neanderthal and Denisovans, in my mind, clearly took place post-Flood.

Addressing Reasons.org

It should be noted that while some humans have historically had sex with animals, at no time have these copulations produced offspring, let alone viable young capable of reproducing.

Further, if humans interbred with animals that "looked human" and their genes descended into today's human populations—with all due respect, does Reasons.org really want to argue that at least some populations carry "animal genes?"

These two points alone should put to rest the RTB (Reasons to Believe) human origins model or give them reason to reconsider and reformulate it.

Addressing Answers in Genesis

As for Neanderthals being fully human descendants of Noah with "slight genetic differences," consider that scientists have sequenced the entire Neanderthal genome and we now know some interesting things about their anatomy and social structures.[435]

For example, according to the authors of *The Neanderthals Rediscovered: How Modern Science Is Rewriting Their Story*, Neanderthals had larger braincases than modern humans, averaging 1,640 cm^3 for males and 1,460 cm^3 for females, compared to modern European males' average of 1,362 cm^3 and females' 1,201 cm^3.[436]

Further:

- ▶ Their skulls were elongated and less globular, featuring a pronounced occipital bun (a protrusion at the back of the skull). The braincase had a lower, wider, and rounder appearance, referred to as *en bombe*.
- ▶ Neanderthals had a sloping forehead, less-developed chins, and a midfacial prognathism, where the middle part of the face projected forward.

- Neanderthals had very large, broad noses.
- They had larger jaws and teeth, with a distinctive gap called the "retromolar space" behind the third molars. Their teeth showed unique morphological traits, such as thinner cuspal enamel and a higher frequency of taurodontism (enlarged pulp chambers).
- Neanderthals were more robust and stockier than modern humans, with a wider pelvis and barrel-shaped rib cages. Their average height was around five feet and five inches (5'5"). Yet, from the basic structure of the bones, we know that they were extremely strong (stronger than Homo sapiens).

Additionally, the authors state:

It has become evident that Neanderthals matured much faster than Homo sapiens. For example, a Neanderthal child from Le Moustier showed a level of maturation of a modern sixteen-year-old but has been estimated to have been only twelve years old.

The fact that Neanderthals matured at a significantly faster rate than Homo sapiens suggests something far more complex than mere evolutionary divergence.

In typical human development, extended childhood and adolescence provide ample time for brain development, social learning, and cultural transmission. This slow maturation process has long been considered a defining characteristic of humanity's evolutionary success.

However, Neanderthals exhibited a markedly different—accelerated—developmental trajectory, as evidenced by the Le Moustier child who demonstrated the physical maturity of a modern sixteen-year-old while only twelve years old. This rapid growth rate appears to be a consistent feature among various Neanderthal specimens.

If we accept the hypothesis that Neanderthals themselves were hybrids resulting from angelic-human unions, then their accelerated growth rate may be the direct consequence of their hybridized origin.

Unlike pure Homo sapiens, who exhibit a slow developmental arc, these beings may have inherited a biological template intended to produce robust adults as quickly as possible. This expedited growth could be explained as a byproduct of their unnatural genesis—the result of incompatible genetic instructions struggling to assert dominance within a single organism.

In that light, Neanderthals may not be "fully human descendants of Noah" at all but rather a now-extinct branch of *post-Edenic hybrid progeny*, whose brief and intense existence left behind an extensive biological record.

Why is this evidence of hybridization rather than a natural evolutionary or environmental adaptation?

While accelerated growth rates can and do occur within natural evolutionary processes (e.g., r-selected species prioritizing rapid reproduction and early maturity), the case of Neanderthals presents unique anomalies that don't align with standard evolutionary explanations.

Accelerated growth in natural evolutionary contexts typically correlates with environments demanding high reproductive rates to counter predation or environmental pressures. However, Neanderthals—as evidenced by their high intelligence, tool-making abilities, and complex social structures—wouldn't fit such a pattern.

Instead, their accelerated growth appears to have been paired with traits suggesting powerful physicality, increased strength, and unique cognitive architecture. Furthermore, evolutionary theory holds that adaptations generally follow incremental changes over vast periods. Therefore, the rapid emergence of distinct traits in Neanderthals—especially given their potential coexistence and interbreeding with Homo sapiens—suggests something beyond ordinary adaptation.

This same accelerated development may have directly contributed to the genetic incompatibilities observed when Neanderthals later interbred with pure Homo sapiens. Rapid growth, driven by a compromised or artificial genetic foundation, could have created developmental inconsistencies too profound for further hybridization to succeed.

Thus, the accelerated maturation of Neanderthals isn't just an odd fact, it's a crucial datapoint reinforcing the idea that these beings were hybrids, not natural evolutionary products. This aligns with the broader argument that Neanderthals were fundamentally different from pure Homo sapiens—both genetically and developmentally.

Moreover, population genetics adds another layer to this mystery.

Neanderthals and Denisovans both exhibited *extremely low genetic diversity*—with diversity levels in the Altai Neanderthal (~120,000 years ago) and Vindija Neanderthal (~50,000 years ago) being approximately 30 percent lower than that of modern humans.

While mainstream science often attributes this to population bottlenecks or geographic isolation, this explanation may fall short.

Here's why.

When we entertain the hypothesis that a species is a hybrid, low genetic diversity stops being a problem and starts looking like a clue.

Hybrid populations typically start small, are localized, and are reproductively constrained. Only a few individuals from each parent species may be genetically compatible. The hybrid offspring, in turn, as mentioned earlier, may face fertility issues or developmental inconsistencies. This would severely limit the number of viable descendants, locking in a *narrow gene pool*—a textbook setup for low genetic diversity.

So, rather than being a sign of an ancient catastrophe, the Neanderthal (and Denisovan) genetic bottlenecks might reflect a *founding hybrid event*—a limited number of viable individuals resulting from unnatural unions, isolated and cut off from wider gene flow.

This possibility rewrites the narrative.

Rather than an evolutionary offshoot, Neanderthals and Denisovans may have been *stabilized hybrid species*, frozen in time—genetically distinct yet lacking diversity due to their peculiar origins.

In my mind, the genetic evidence alone is a death blow to the theories put forward by answersingenesis.org.

Further:

▶ Neanderthals and early modern humans produced similar stone tools.

- Like humans, they ritually buried their dead.
- Like humans, they wore make-up and jewelry.
- Like humans, they made weapons.

A picture has emerged of the Neanderthals as top predators, consuming huge amounts of meat, particularly from large mammals such as woolly mammoths. They also consumed horse, red deer, reindeer and bison.[437]

There is also evidence that Neanderthals may have practiced cannibalism in some regions. (This doesn't make them unique. Obviously, pure humans have done the same.)

They weren't stupid "cavemen." They engaged in chemistry and made glue.

And interestingly—just like the Si-Te-Cah, the pale-skinned, red-haired giants from Native American legend—Neanderthals also carried genes for red hair and pale skin.

But here's the kicker: the red hair gene in Neanderthals was not the same as the one in Homo sapiens. A unique mutation in their MC1R gene, not found in modern humans, led to a similar appearance via completely different genetic pathways—pointing to a *distinct evolutionary origin.*

In other words, the red hair wasn't a result of shared ancestry—it was an entirely separate, unrelated mutation.

That shouldn't happen under standard evolutionary assumptions. But if Neanderthals were hybrids, born of angelic-human unions, then these differences make perfect sense. Rather than a coincidence or parallel evolution, the unique red-hair mutation may reflect an altered genetic template—one influenced by nonhuman DNA.

Remember: Experiencer testimony regarding Nordic aliens consistently describes beings with pale skin and red or blond hair. If some of these Nordics were indeed Ishim, and if they participated in the Watchers' rebellion, it stands to reason that red hair could be a lingering genetic signature of their tampering.

Let's recap and head deeper into the speculative zone.

Neanderthals differ from modern humans in profound ways:

- Larger braincases
- Elongated skulls with pronounced occipital buns
- Sloping foreheads and forward-projecting faces
- Faster maturation
- Incredible physical strength
- Meat-heavy diets
- Possible cannibalism

But from a "Nephilim = giants" perspective, there are two inconsistencies:

1. Neanderthals were not physically tall. Averaging about 5'5", they don't match the giant narrative.
2. Ancient Hebrew and Native American sources describe hybrid giants with six fingers and toes. Neanderthals, like us, had five.

Still, these discrepancies don't nullify the hybrid model. They suggest diversity within hybrid lineages (e.g., not all Watcher offspring had identical phenotypes).

Mitochondrial DNA and Interbreeding Limits

The genetic evidence of interbreeding between Neanderthals, Denisovans, and Homo sapiens is clear—but so is a profound anomaly: *The complete absence of Neanderthal mitochondrial DNA (mtDNA)* in modern humans.

Since mtDNA is passed only from mothers to offspring, this suggests that no Neanderthal female lineage survived in our species.

Why?

Because the mtDNA of Neanderthals may have been fundamentally incompatible with Homo sapiens biology—a genetic dead-end. And if Neanderthals themselves were hybrids, then their mitochondrial lines may have been rejected by natural selection, or too unstable to persist. This aligns with the pattern of limited hybrid fertility seen in other cross-species pairings (like mules).

From a biblical lens, it also aligns with the idea of forbidden unions resulting in fragile or corrupted lifeforms that fail to thrive in the manner intended by their makers.

Genetic Introgression: The Layered Legacy

Neanderthal and Denisovan genes didn't vanish entirely—but they remain as fragments, remnants of a failed synthesis. This is genetic introgression—where DNA from one group enters another's gene pool but is subject to filtering and selective retention.

Some Neanderthal traits (like immune-system genes, skin tone, or hair texture) were beneficial and persisted. Others—including mtDNA and perhaps neurological or reproductive elements—were purged.

If Neanderthals were themselves unnatural hybrids, this pattern makes perfect sense. Only traits compatible with pure human biology endured.

What we're seeing is more than coincidence. It's a forensic trail. These genetic patterns—low diversity, distinct mutations, selective introgression, mitochondrial incompatibility—look less like nature's slow dance and more like the aftermath of a failed genetic experiment.

Yes, this is speculative. Critics will scoff. They'll say ancient texts are no substitute for peer-reviewed science. But here's the thing: When ancient descriptions, genetic anomalies, and fossil evidence *converge*, I'd say we have a responsibility to follow the thread.

Scientists build hypotheses from fragments all the time. Why should we treat this subject any differently?

Ultimately, the convergence of ancient texts, genetic anomalies, and biological divergence suggests a coordinated genetic interference—one possibly orchestrated by nonhuman intelligences.

If Neanderthals were engineered hybrids—not evolutionary misfires—then their incompatibility with Homo sapiens isn't a mystery, it's a clue. The failed integration of Neanderthals, the selective survival of their nuclear DNA, and the total loss of their maternal lines all point to deeper forces at work. And if those same forces are still at work—perhaps behind the UFO phenomenon, abductions, and reports of genetic harvesting—then history is now.

CHAPTER TEN

UFOS AND THE GREYS

UFOs are real, burgeoning, and not going away.
—L. A. Marzulli[438]

This book is called *In the Shadow of Goliath* for a reason. Goliath wasn't just a really tall dude with a bad temper. He was a Nephilim hybrid—an echo of the Watchers' rebellion. A living testament to the corruption of the human genome, twisted and enhanced by forbidden knowledge.

His presence on the battlefield wasn't just a physical threat, it was a spiritual one. An existential one. A sign that the old corruption hadn't been wiped out; it was alive and well.

You know the story. David stepped forward with nothing but a sling, five smooth stones, and faith that made seasoned warriors look like cowards. Goliath, the hybrid monstrosity, crumbled to the dirt. But that was then.

The victory was real, but it didn't end the war. The shadow of Goliath still stretches across the world today, because here's the deal: The threat he represented didn't die with him. It evolved. It adapted. And its shadow is growing.

Everything we've covered in this book, from the Nephilim to the modern-day abduction phenomenon, points to the same overarching agenda—a relentless effort to corrupt the Adamic template, to break humanity's connection to the Creator by warping what it means to be truly human.

We're still standing in the shadow of Goliath, but the shadow has grown darker, wider, and more insidious. It's no longer just an external force to be fought on a battlefield. It's a force worming its way into the very essence of what makes us human.

If you think Goliath was terrifying, imagine a world where that corruption has been normalized. Where the hybridization agenda has advanced to the point that humanity itself is no longer recognizable.

It's happening. Right now.

And the Greys? They're just another layer of that same ancient corruption. Another tentacle of the beast that has been slithering through human history since the days of Noah.

You already know the pattern. It's always been there: The same arrogance. The same contempt for human sovereignty. The same perverse drive to twist what God created into something else.

We just covered the Nephilim. The hybrid experiment. Angelic incursion. Ishim who defied divine command and exploited humanity's newly minted genetic canvas for their own purposes. That was the past.

Or so you thought.

I made it clear in the preceding chapter that what people call Neanderthals and Denisovans (and maybe even the Paracas people of Peru; heck, perhaps even more hominins than that! Maybe the so-called Hobbits of Indonesia [*Homo floresiensis*], and more) weren't evolutionary offshoots or genetic dead-ends. They were the offspring of an ancient manipulation—one rooted in a concerted effort to corrupt the human genome, to alter the original Adamic template beyond recognition.

But what if I told you that same effort never stopped—that it evolved, adapted, and continued with a cold, relentless precision?

Because it has.

And the proof stares us in the face from every so-called abduction account, every researcher's whistleblowing testimony, every clinical hypnosis session where the veil of conscious suppression is torn away.

You've seen them before. The Grey aliens. The faceless automatons of UFO lore. The archetypal abductors described as small, spindly, hairless figures with oversized, bulbous heads and lidless, inky eyes. Not demons, not fallen angels, but something else.

Now, I believe Greys, or whatever you want to call them, are not the architects of the hybridization agenda. They're the tools—or, alternatively, the accomplices.

It's time to deconstruct the Grey phenomenon and uncover the agenda lurking behind it. Are these beings continuing the same hybridization program that began millennia ago?

Let's check it out.

WHAT'S THE PREMISE?

Are the Greys continuing the same hybridization program that began millennia ago? Let me lay it out as I see it:

Premise 1: The Watchers corrupted the human genome by breeding with human women, producing the Nephilim. This act of genetic manipulation is explicitly stated in Genesis 6 and elaborated upon in 1 Enoch.

Premise 2: Modern abduction phenomena consistently involve reports of genetic experimentation and hybridization. Victims often describe procedures aimed at extracting genetic material or implanting embryos.

Premise 3: Credible researchers such as Dr. David Jacobs and Budd Hopkins have documented numerous cases describing reproductive manipulation and hybrid children. Jacobs, in particular, has noted abductees report seeing hybrids that are both physically and behaviorally distinct from ordinary humans.[439, 440]

Premise 4: Researchers like Jacques Vallée and Dr. John Mack have argued that the hybridization phenomenon appears to be both psychological and biological, indicating a multifaceted agenda aimed at altering human perception as well as physiology.[441, 442]

Conclusion: Therefore, the genetic agenda initiated by the Watchers has likely continued through new agents, potentially including Greys. Their reported actions align with the same objectives pursued by the Watchers—corruption of the human genome and the creation of hybrids designed to further a broader, hidden agenda.

Based on the chain of logic above, I believe we can more accurately assess whether the Greys are merely tools in this ongoing agenda or autonomous agents working in tandem with other entities.

DEFINING THE GREYS

These are those scrawny suckers with large, black, emotionless, sunglasses for eyes. They have grey skin that resembles ash or rotting parchment. Described as sexless and biologically minimalistic, it's like they've been manufactured for a specific purpose.

But don't mistake their simplicity for lack of sophistication. It's entirely possible these creatures are tools—machines of some greater mind's design, or perhaps biological entities (think "replicant," ala Ridley Scott's *Blade Runner*—only, you know, uglier) streamlined through eons of manipulation and selection.

Whatever they are, they aren't what they appear to be.

Physical Characteristics

Descriptions of Greys are unnervingly consistent across the globe. Eyewitnesses recount small, slender figures, rarely exceeding four feet in height. Their skin is smooth, grey, and rubbery—lacking pigmentation or texture.

They appear sexless, devoid of any reproductive organs, hair, or other features commonly associated with living beings—with mammals, anyway. Their heads are disproportionately large compared to their bodies, with massive, almond-shaped eyes that are entirely black, reflective, and devoid of sclera or iris. These eyes are described not as windows to the soul, rather as voids—nothingness staring back. Their mouths are narrow slits, if they have mouths at all. The same goes for nostrils and ears, which are often represented as mere indentations.

Behavioral Characteristics

Greys are clinical. Cold. Detached. Witnesses often describe these entities as devoid of empathy. Their communication is predominantly telepathic—direct, emotionless, and overwhelming. In many cases, it's not communication at all, but rather a broadcast of intent, or commands masked as thoughts.

Accounts consistently describe Greys operating with a hive-mind mentality. When they act, they act as one. They show no signs of individual will, creativity, or even curiosity. Their focus is task-oriented and brutal in its precision.

As UFO researcher and hypnotist Dr. David Jacobs notes:

> They are singularly focused on their agenda. Whatever empathy or curiosity they might have once possessed is long gone—burned away by the same process that stripped them of biological and psychological individuality.[443]

ORIGINS ACCORDING TO POPULAR SOURCES

One of the most popular explanations for the origin of Greys is the Zeta Reticuli hypothesis, originating from the famed 1961 abduction case of Betty and Barney Hill, briefly mentioned earlier in the book.

Under hypnosis, Betty Hill described a star map shown to her by one of the beings. She later identified the map as resembling the Zeta Reticuli star system. While skeptics dismiss this as fantasy, the consistency of such reports across decades remains unsettling.

Yet the Zeta Reticuli hypothesis is only one thread of the larger tapestry. Others have posited that Greys aren't organic beings at all, but rather advanced biological androids—sentient but engineered.

Former Air Force employee Clifford Stone, who claims to have participated in recovery operations involving extraterrestrial beings, stated that some Greys are "manufactured entities"—biological robots designed to execute specific functions.

Even mainstream scientists who venture into the fringes of the field, like Harvard psychiatrist Dr. John E. Mack, acknowledge the disturbingly consistent reports of abductees worldwide. In his work *Abduction: Human Encounters with Aliens* (1994), Mack noted that "the consistency of these reports, regardless of cultural or geographic origin, suggests a phenomenon that transcends mere psychological projection."[444]

Testimonies Describing Greys

The Betty and Barney Hill abduction case is perhaps the most famous. During their hypnosis sessions, both Betty and Barney independently described small beings with large heads and black, emotionless eyes.

What was more chilling was their precise description of clinical procedures conducted aboard a craft—procedures aimed at extracting genetic material.[445]

Jacobs notes that many abductees describe being taken to what they perceive as medical facilities where genetic materials are harvested. Abductees often report seeing hybrid children—beings that appear partially human and partially Grey.

Budd Hopkins, in his books *Intruders* (1987) and *Witnessed* (1996), provides detailed accounts of abductees describing repeated medical experiments involving reproductive organs, egg extraction, sperm collection, and the implantation of embryos.

One prominent case, the Linda Cortile incident, involves witnesses claiming to have seen a woman levitating from her Manhattan apartment window into a hovering craft, where she later reported undergoing medical procedures involving the extraction of ova.[446]

Travis Walton's account is another noteworthy case. After being struck by a beam of light from a UFO in 1975, Walton awoke in what he described as a medical facility surrounded by small, grey-skinned beings. Their intent was ambiguous, but their clinical detachment was unmistakable.[447]

In government settings, alleged whistleblowers like Bob Lazar have reported encounters with Grey-like beings during their tenure at facilities such as Area 51, a highly classified US Air Force facility located within the Nevada Test and Training Range, about 83 miles (134 km) north-northwest of Las Vegas. Though Lazar's credibility has been questioned, his descriptions remain consistent with other accounts: small, emotionless beings engaged in activities far beyond human understanding.[448]

Testimony Shmestimony!

Critics will argue that personal testimonies from individuals like Betty and Barney Hill, Travis Walton, and countless others are unreliable by nature. They'll attribute these accounts to psychological explanations such as sleep paralysis, false memory syndrome, or outright fabrication. But those objections fall apart under closer scrutiny.

Consistency Across Cultures and Decades

Over the last several decades, reports of encounters with Greys have poured in from every corner of the globe. Despite cultural, linguistic, and geographic differences, these descriptions are strikingly consistent.

Witnesses—often with no prior knowledge of the phenomenon—describe the same physical traits, behaviors, and procedures. This kind of consistency is not what we'd expect from hallucinations or fabricated tales. It points to a shared, objective experience.

Physical Evidence

Beyond anecdotal testimony, there's hard evidence. Abductees frequently report physical manifestations: scars, burns, implants—injuries and anomalies verified by medical professionals offering no conventional explanation.

Dr. Roger Leir, for instance, a podiatric surgeon specializing in the removal of alleged alien implants, documented over a dozen cases in which foreign objects were extracted from patients' bodies. In each case, there were no visible entry wounds, and the objects showed no signs of bodily rejection.[449]

That's not something we can chalk up to suggestion or delusion.

Psychological Profiling

The argument that the individuals providing these testimonies are simply mentally unstable doesn't hold up, either. Clinical evaluations of abductees repeatedly demonstrate that most are psychologically stable, coherent, and articulate.

They don't fit the profile of individuals prone to hallucinations or psychosis. Researchers like Dr. John Mack have extensively documented this, showing that many abductees experience genuine trauma consistent with real—not imagined—events.[450]

Look, the pattern couldn't be more obvious.

We've got consistent testimonies stacking up over decades, from all over the world. Different cultures, different languages, same descriptions. Greys. Same physical traits, same bizarre procedures. It's like they're all reading from the same script—except nobody handed them one.

Then there's physical evidence like the earlier-mentioned scars, burns, implants, et cetera, documented by real doctors who have verified that there were no entry wounds and no signs of rejection. Yet, critics want to pretend it's all in their heads? Yeah, right.

And what about the psychological evaluations? These aren't deranged lunatics spewing nonsense. Clinical evaluations prove it: They're mentally stable.

But the "experts" keep parroting the same tired lines: Sleep paralysis. Hallucinations. Fabrication. They sound like broken records, clinging to theories that died years ago.

Here's the uncomfortable truth: The data is there. It's been there. And the longer we pretend it isn't, the more credibility we lose.

Connections to Nordic and Reptilian Entities

I don't believe the Greys are the ones in charge. Most in the UFO community don't think they are, either. They're just foot soldiers. The programmed grunts. Disposable. Interchangeable.

I think we're talking about a hierarchy, and the Greys occupy one of—if not "the"—lowest rung. While Reptilians and Nordics appear to occupy higher rungs of the hierarchy—often described as issuing commands or providing oversight—the Greys serve as functionaries.

Whether they are biological constructs, clones, or engineered beings programmed for specific tasks, their position is consistent with a "drone" or "worker ant" role. They're puppets. Biological tools designed for a singular purpose: Serve and obey. They operate under a command structure, and that command structure leads right back to the Nordics and Reptilians.

Mechanisms of Control

While the evidence suggests a hierarchical structure in which Greys operate under the command of higher entities such as Reptilians, Nordics, and perhaps even fallen angelic beings, the exact nature of this control remains unclear. However, based on available testimony and research, several possibilities emerge:

- ▶ If the Greys are indeed biological constructs or engineered beings, it's plausible that they've been genetically programmed to obey higher entities without question. This would align with their behavior as functionaries rather than autonomous agents.
- ▶ Reports of telepathic communication between Greys and abductees suggest the Greys may themselves be subject to psychic control exerted by higher beings. Reptilians and Nordics, if they're of greater authority, may influence Greys through advanced psychic or technological means.
- ▶ It's also possible that Greys operate under technological directives—akin to drones or remotely controlled devices. Advanced technology designed by fallen angelic beings or higher entities could be directing their activities.

While it isn't yet possible to determine which, if any, of these methods are definitive, what remains clear is the Greys aren't calling the shots. Not even close.

Abductee accounts consistently describe the Greys operating under the direction of taller, more authoritative beings—whether Nordics, Reptilians, or something else entirely. In fact, Clifford Stone, the former US Army sergeant who claimed to have participated in extraterrestrial recovery operations, stated, "The Greys are like drones. Their autonomy is limited. They act under instruction, not independent will."[451]

Connection to the Fallen Ishim

Now, I'm just speculating, but what if the Greys are remnants of the original Watcher incursion? Genetic or biological constructs left behind by the Ishim, programmed to carry out tasks long after their creators were removed from the picture?

Some researchers suggest the Greys' sterile, emotionless nature is a result of eons of refinement and degradation—a biological machine—a "nonhuman biologic."

They were tools then. They're tools now. It's the same pattern: corruption of the Adamic template. Modification. Hybridization.

With that in mind, stick with me, because there are some interesting hypotheticals to consider.

The Greys as Watcher Technology

If the Greys were created by the Ishim during their incursion, then their origin lies in a pre-Flood or early post-Flood genetic manipulation project. The Watchers (Ishim) would have had advanced knowledge and capabilities—likely rooted in biological engineering, possibly genetic manipulation, or artificial life creation.

Implication:

- The Greys were designed with a purpose. If the Ishim created them, their design was intentional and tailored to perform specific functions.
- They may possess characteristics suited for surveillance, genetic experimentation, communication, or manipulation of human populations.
- Their lack of individuality and emotional expression suggests a deliberate attempt to remove traits deemed unnecessary or detrimental for their intended tasks.

The Greys as Abandoned or Autonomous Constructs

If the Ishim were removed, destroyed, or otherwise incapacitated (as suggested by the scriptural and apocryphal accounts of divine judgment), then the Greys may have been left to operate autonomously or according to preprogrammed directives.

Implication:

- They could be operating under residual programming, continuing tasks originally set forth by the Ishim—such as monitoring human genetics, gathering information, or continuing the hybridization project.
- The Greys' lack of emotional depth and robotic demeanor would make sense if they are fulfilling old directives without adaptation or moral considerations.
- If the Ishim are their creators, and their creators are gone, the Greys might not even understand the original purpose of their existence. They may simply be executing directives encoded in them long ago.
- If the Ishim intended the Greys to carry out genetic modification or monitoring, then their actions during modern abduction scenarios may reflect a continuation of this program.
- They might be trying to achieve a predetermined genetic state or experimenting with new combinations, seeking to perfect or adapt the hybridization process.

Evolution of Purpose

If the Greys were once under direct command of the Ishim but now operate independently, it's possible their purpose has evolved or degenerated over time.

Implication:

- Without their creators' oversight, the Greys might be caught in a recursive loop—carrying out directives without adaptation or understanding.
- Alternatively, they may have evolved their own hierarchy or control structure to compensate for the absence of the Ishim.

- If Greys are programmed for a task-centric existence, any deviation from that task would suggest either a breakdown in their programming or an adaptation to changing circumstances.

Potential Risks to Humanity

If the Greys are continuing a Watcher-originated hybridization program, then their purpose is likely antithetical to human sovereignty and the preservation of the original Adamic template.

Implication:

- If the Greys are actively engaging in genetic manipulation, the implication is that their actions are deliberate, systematic, and guided by a higher purpose—whether known to them or not.
- The apparent lack of empathy or individuality in the Greys suggests they may not value human life or agency, making their actions inherently dangerous.
- If their programming is fundamentally antagonistic to humanity's genetic integrity, then their presence represents a direct and ongoing threat.

Two Other Hypotheses for the Origin of Greys

So—you think the Greys are from Zeta Reticuli?

Here's the deal. We already mentioned Betty and Barney Hill. They're not the only ones with well-known testimonies regarding these guys.

Bob Lazar. You know, the guy who dropped the mother of all UFO bombshells in 1989. Says he was working at S-4 (that's the basement to Area 51's basement), reverse-engineering flying saucers built by, wait for it—Greys. Supposedly from Zeta Reticuli.

Then there's Marjorie Fish. A schoolteacher-turned-stargazer who analyzed a star map Betty Hill scribbled down under hypnosis and went, "Yep. That's Zeta Reticuli alright."

How?

She built a 3D model of local space using beads and fishing line. Pretty analog, but whatever, it got the UFO crowd buzzing.

But there are some problems with this hypothesis even if the Greys are real aliens and not biological robots or tools of some interdimensional power.

- Zeta Reticuli is a binary star system, and while it is similar to our sun, the region surrounding it hasn't shown signs of habitable planets. Without evidence of habitable planets, it's speculative to assume intelligent life originates there.
- If Greys were truly conducting long-term observation missions from a star system as relatively close as Zeta Reticuli, one would expect some observable signatures (communication signals, propulsion trails, et cetera.). Yet, astronomers haven't detected any signs of intelligent activity from that region.
- If Greys are indeed extraterrestrial and come from a completely different evolutionary history, it is unlikely their biology would be compatible with ours for meaningful genetic experimentation—which would mean that if they are conducting genetic experimentation, it would likely be on behalf of another species. So, again, who's off in the shadows?

Biological Androids, Clones, or Nonhuman Biologics

The term "nonhuman biologics" wasn't coined by conspiracy theorists. It was used by government whistleblowers like David Grusch, a former US intelligence officer who disclosed details of classified recovery operations involving nonhuman biological remains.

According to Grusch's testimony, these entities are not human and not traditionally biological in the way we understand life. They are something else.[452]

If we're dealing with nonhuman biologics, then we're talking about beings that mimic life—down to the cellular level—but are fundamentally alien. Not just in origin, in essence. Think of them as constructs—biological machines made to appear alive. To pass as life. To interact with us. But there's nothing human about them.

The agenda isn't just experimentation. It's integration. A steady, calculated effort to rewrite the human blueprint. To seed hybrids. To spread their corrupted essence throughout humanity.

If you think that sounds like hyperbole, consider how many testimonies involve reproductive procedures. How many abductions revolve around extracting ova, sperm, or implanting embryos?

However, to be honest—the same issues arise here.

Regardless of point of origin—whether they're part of an actual alien species or replicant-style biological robots—their physical nature and the type of activities they're associated with suggest they are operating in our dimensional space under the control of—or in alliance with—a power greater than themselves.

Greys as Proxies

Here's another hypothesis. The original rebellion was smashed but not obliterated. The generals, the real architects of the corruption, were never physically present. They didn't descend. They didn't take wives. They didn't get their hands dirty.

They deployed the Watchers as expendable assets—knowing full well they would fall. When they did, God made an example of them.

After the fall of the Watchers, God set something in motion. A force of restraint to prevent the same catastrophic incursion from repeating. Sure, we know the Nephilim appeared again after Noah's Flood. But the second time around it seemed much more limited in scope. Maybe there's a reason for that.

As Paul wrote:

> And you know what restrains him now, so that he will be revealed in his time. For the mystery of lawlessness is already at work; only he who now restrains will do so until he is removed. (2 Thessalonians 2:6–7)

So, if the generals were never chained, what's stopping them now?

I propose that the rebel forces—the real architects of corruption—are now operating under restraint. Whatever or whoever this restraining force is (probably unfallen angelic beings perhaps under the command of Michael—and ultimately, God), it is preventing them from deploying the same brute-force strategies employed by the Watchers.

But constraints aren't the same as defeat. That's where the Greys come in.

Greys as Scouts

Think about it. When we need to gather intelligence, we don't send our elite. We send scouts. Probes. Tools designed to sneak in, gather data, and perform tasks beneath the enemy's direct attention.

That's the Greys: genetic scouts deployed to infiltrate, abduct, harvest, and experiment.

The crucial point, however, is that they're not operating on their own. They're the shank slipped under the prison door.

Why?

Because the Seraphim, Ishim, and other angelic rebels are restrained from physically descending to Earth like the Watchers did. They can't pull the same stunt twice without triggering divine wrath.

So, they improvise and operate by proxy. Greys do the dirty work—gather DNA, probe genetics, conduct brutal experiments—while their creators keep their hands clean.

Literally.

The fallen angels can turn around and say, "But I wasn't there!"—and they'd be right. Physically, they weren't there.

It's a calculated exploitation of the rules.

Angelic Behavior and The Fairy Connection

Speaking of rules, let's revisit something important. Something I hinted at earlier.

Exodus 23:20–21:

Behold, I am going to send an angel before you to guard you along the way and to bring you into the place which I have prepared. Be attentive to him and obey his voice; do not be rebellious toward him, for he will not pardon your rebellion, since My name is in him.

הִנֵּה אָנֹכִי שֹׁלֵחַ מַלְאָךְ לְפָנֶיךָ לִשְׁמָרְךָ בַּדָּרֶךְ וְלַהֲבִיאֲךָ אֶל־הַמָּקוֹם אֲשֶׁר הֲכִנֹתִי:

הִשָּׁמֶר מִפָּנָיו וּשְׁמַע בְּקֹלוֹ אַל־תַּמֵּר בּוֹ כִּי לֹא יִשָּׂא לְפִשְׁעֲכֶם כִּי שְׁמִי בְּקִרְבּוֹ:

Angels enforce rules with brutal efficiency. Remember Gabriel? He punished John the Baptist's father just for not believing him. Angelic justice is harsh, immediate, and inflexible.

But that's not unique. It's the same kind of merciless literalism found in old tales of fairies.

Consider:

- **Angels and fairies are bound by rules.** Angels operate under divine law, and fairies follow their own supernatural customs. But both are rigid about their codes. Break the rules and you're punished. Period.
- **Language and precise formulations matter.** Angels in Hekhalot literature respond only to exact words and names. Fairies exploit linguistic ambiguity, twisting spoken agreements to their advantage. The devil is in the details—literally.
- **Both lack human empathy.** Their literalism isn't just cruelty, it's a fundamental difference in how they perceive reality. Angels enforce divine commands; fairies follow their own bizarre rules. Humans? Just pieces on the board.

Look at the folklore:

- Fairies are notorious for punishing the slightest deviation from agreements. Misspeak or fail to uphold your end of the bargain, and they pounce.

- Fairies exploit ambiguities. Offer them "anything they desire" and they'll interpret your words in the most literal, devastating way possible.
- The Seelie and Unseelie courts? Strict social codes and rituals. Break them and you're dead meat—or worse.

So what's the point?

I think the tales of fairies are distorted echoes of encounters with fallen angels. And here's the bigger point: At least parts of the angelic world, and at least some species, operate under strict, unyielding rules. And these rules? They know how to exploit them.

If the fallen ones tell Michael or whoever is holding them back, "We didn't do what the Watchers did," then the enforcers—angels or otherwise—have no grounds to retaliate because, technically, they haven't broken the rule. They're exploiting a legalistic loophole, using proxy forces like the Greys to do their dirty work without exactly violating the terms of their restraint.

It's not just plausible. It's exactly the kind of hyper-literal mentality and gamesmanship we see throughout Scripture, folklore, and even modern UFO lore.

UFOS—PHYSICAL CRAFT OR INTERDIMENSIONAL TECHNOLOGY?

David Grusch has thrown a grenade into the "official narrative" and walked away like a man with nothing left to lose. As a former US intelligence officer and Air Force veteran, he isn't your average whistleblower.

His disclosures about classified recovery operations involving what he calls "nonhuman biologics" and advanced craft aren't wild claims; they're accusations against the entire government structure for hiding a truth that redefines everything.

Back in 2023, Grusch, a former senior intelligence officer with the National Geospatial-Intelligence Agency, delivered a statement before the House Oversight Subcommittee on National Security that hit like a sledgehammer.[453]

No fluff. No ambiguous political maneuvering.

Just a blunt, straight-to-the-point declaration:

The US government possesses unidentified anomalous phenomena (UAPs).

They're not just rumors, not hypothetical occurrences. Not some sketchy lights seen in the middle of nowhere by conspiracy theorists hiding in tinfoil hats. Grusch made his assertion based on testimony gathered from "over 40 witnesses over four years."[454]

He explicitly stated he "knows the exact locations" of these UAPs and provided that information to the Inspector General and intelligence committees.

If you think the guy's just some crackpot attention-seeker, you might want to reevaluate. His background is formidable.

He spent fourteen years in the US Air Force and National Geospatial-Intelligence Agency, including time spent at the National Reconnaissance Office (NRO) handling top-tier intelligence duties. The man's career was built on credibility.

And when it comes to whistleblowing, he's gone through the right channels—filing a PPD-19 urgent concern complaint with the Intelligence Community Inspector General. This isn't a bitter ex-employee throwing around baseless accusations. It's someone with direct connections to the intelligence community who is willing to risk his reputation and career to get the truth out.

Speaking of that risk, Grusch openly admitted during the hearing that he's faced "brutal" and "very unfortunate" retaliation for stepping forward. This goes far beyond routine red tape or the occasional sarcastic remark from colleagues; the guy's talking about professional and personal damage—serious, deliberate attempts to silence him. He wouldn't give the full details in the public setting, citing an ongoing whistleblower-reprisal investigation.

The real gut-punch came when Tim Burchett—one of the few Congress members treating this issue with any real urgency—asked Grusch point-blank if he had personal knowledge of people being harmed or injured in efforts to cover up or conceal extraterrestrial technology. Grusch's answer?

"Yes. Personally."455

Now, he wouldn't spill details about anyone being murdered, but he did say he's directed individuals with that knowledge to the "appropriate authorities." And considering that the whole point of these hearings is to get the truth out there, you can bet that information isn't going to stay under wraps forever.

Here's the million-dollar question: Are these UFOs physical craft? Or are they something else—some kind of interdimensional technology our twenty-first-century brains can't quite process?

Grusch's testimony suggests physicality. Physical craft recovered, reverse-engineered, and studied by secret programs operating beyond the scope of congressional oversight. Programs Grusch says he was actively blocked from accessing despite his high-level security clearance.

But what Grusch left unsaid is just as tantalizing. He didn't speculate on the origin of these craft. He didn't make any wild claims about them being alien, interdimensional, or anything else. He stuck to the facts as he knew them, based on the testimony of credible witnesses who had firsthand knowledge.

The takeaway? Something tangible is being hidden.

Whether it's extraterrestrial, interdimensional, or something else entirely, Grusch's revelations should be a wake-up call for anyone still clinging to the idea that UAPs are nothing more than fanciful hallucinations. Whatever these things are, they're real.

And if Grusch is right, the government's been sitting on that truth for decades.

Luis Elizondo's Testimony

As a former counterintelligence agent, Elizondo led the Advanced Aerospace Threat Identification Program (AATIP) after being recruited into the Advanced Aerospace Weapons System Application Program (AAWSAP) under the Defense Intelligence Agency.

In his book, *Imminent: Inside the Pentagon's Hunt for UFOs*, Elizondo notes the existence of UAP is not speculative. From his perspective, the question is not if UAPs are real but rather what they are and why they're operating with apparent impunity in controlled airspace.

He maintains these craft exhibit technological capabilities that defy conventional understanding of physics. They can accelerate and maneuver at extreme speeds, transition seamlessly between air, water, and space, and do so without producing sonic booms or detectable propulsion systems.

For example, he writes:

> They were dropping vertically from extreme altitudes at fantastic speeds to around 20,000 feet, hovering briefly, then instantaneously accelerating, sometimes to extreme speeds.
>
> After several days of observation, two US Navy F/A-18s from the Nimitz managed to intercept one of these strange craft at close quarters in conditions of perfect visibility.
>
> For Navy Commander Dave Fravor, the 48-feet-long, wingless white craft he observed from the cockpit of his F/A-18 was so radical in behavior and appearance, so vastly more capable than any known aircraft, it seemed clear to this high-ranking officer and his fellow pilots that it was...not from this world.[456]

Listen, after reading that, if you're still clinging to the old, comfortable narrative that UFOs are just misidentified planes, weather balloons, or some shiny new toy cooked up by the Chinese or Russians, you're in for a rude awakening because Luis Elizondo isn't some basement-dwelling conspiracy theorist scribbling wild theories on his walls. He says these crafts are playing by their own rulebook and using technology that makes our most advanced aircraft look like Fisher-Price toys.

According to his research, these things have been buzzing around our airspace since at least World War II. No nation has caught one. No nation has controlled one. They're untouchable, operating like they own the sky.

But wait, it gets better. Elizondo's claims aren't just rooted in blurry photos or vague testimonies. The guy's handled alleged alien implants ripped straight from human bodies. We're talking about microchip-looking things encased in some bizarre, semitranslucent tissue that seems to have its own metabolism. Yet, when tests are run on these implants, all the researchers find is the patient's DNA. No circuitry, no wires, nothing that screams "man-made."[457]

He's blunt about it: It's a potential national security nightmare that, at worst, is an existential threat.

Elizondo's book doesn't mince words. He's not asking us to believe; he's saying the conversation has already shifted. It's no longer about whether these things are real. It's about figuring out what they are, what they want, and why they're here.

Then There's Ryan Graves

Ryan Graves is not some conspiracy theorist sitting in his mom's basement watching grainy YouTube videos and ranting about flying saucers. He's a former F-18 pilot with over a decade of service in the US Navy, including two deployments during Operation Enduring Freedom and Operation Inherent Resolve. And he's not out there merely flapping his gums for attention.

Graves founded Americans for Safe Aerospace, a nonprofit organization with nearly five thousand members designed to support, research, and educate the public about UAPs. He's also the chair of the UAP Integration & Outreach Committee for the American Institute of Aeronautics and Astronautics, heading up a volunteer team of almost eighty PhDs and aerospace engineers.

In other words, he's legit.

What Graves is saying is simple and sobering: UAPs are real, they're showing up routinely in our airspace, and the government knows more about them than they're letting on.[458]

And the scary part? Graves says the government has been keeping crucial information classified and sweeping incidents under the rug for years.

During a public hearing before the House Oversight Subcommittee on National Security, the Border, and Foreign Affairs, Graves laid it all out. According to him, pilots are encountering these things so often they've become part of *daily briefings*.

He describes UAPs as physical objects that can be tracked on multiple sensor systems—not just radar, but infrared sensors, too. In other words, this isn't spiritual mumbo-jumbo. These aren't demons freewheeling through the atmosphere…but they are doing things that shouldn't be possible.

Think objects accelerating at Mach 1, holding their position in hurricane-force winds and operating for extended periods without any visible propulsion system. No wings, no engines, no control surfaces.

Just—there.

We're not talking about rogue balloons or a misidentified drone. Graves reported an incident in which two F/A-18 jets nearly collided with a dark gray cube inside of a clear sphere—hanging motionless in the sky right at the entry point of a designated training area off the coast of Virginia Beach.

The jets had to take evasive action to avoid a midair collision. His squadron submitted a safety report. The response? Crickets.

The encounters Graves describes don't sound like anything in the conventional inventory of human technology. In fact, when Rear Admiral Tim Gallaudet, former head of NOAA and an oceanographer for the Navy, received a classified email about UAP encounters in 2015, he couldn't believe the nonchalance from his superiors.[459]

The email, with a subject line, "Urgent safety of flight issue," included the now-famous GO-FAST UAP video recorded by a Navy F/A-18. It specifically highlighted the risk of near-midair collisions in the area where Graves had encountered these objects.[460]

The next day, the email was wiped from Gallaudet's system, and it was never brought up again. His conclusion? It was probably removed because of a classified special-access program. Translation: Someone upstairs decided this wasn't for public consumption.

According to Graves, aircrews along the East Coast continue to encounter advanced UAPs nearly a decade later, and their identities remain unknown. He believes the government's obsession with secrecy—classifying every UAP video since 2021 as "Secret" or higher—is only making things worse. Not only does it keep important data out of the hands of scientists who could analyze it, but it also feeds the kind of wild speculation the government claims it wants to avoid.

Now, here's where Graves' testimony gets even more interesting.

UAP sightings from military personnel and commercial pilots are both part of what he's addressing. These are trained observers—many of them military veterans—reporting UAPs at altitudes as high as forty thousand feet. They're seeing more than lights in the sky. We're talking about objects performing maneuvers like right-hand turns, retrograde orbits, or sharp "j-hooks" at speeds and altitudes that leave any conventional aircraft in the dust.

And it's happening all over the place. Graves mentions recurring reports north of Hawaii and over the North Atlantic. If these objects are foreign drones as some skeptics suggest, that's a pretty big deal.

If they're something else? Well, that's a much *bigger* deal.

Graves doesn't claim to have all the answers. But he's crystal clear about one thing: Whatever these objects are, they are a *threat to aviation safety* and a national security issue. If these encounters represent technology far beyond our own, the implications are staggering.

The technology he describes makes our most advanced fighter jets look like tricycles chasing Ferraris.

The whole discussion boils down to one basic question: Are we dealing with physical craft built by some advanced civilization? Or are these things interdimensional—existing outside our standard model of reality?

Graves doesn't try to settle that question. He simply wants the evidence to be studied openly, and without the suffocating grip of government secrecy.

WHAT'S THE ENDGAME?

You want to know what's really going on, right? The endgame. The truth nobody wants to face head-on.

I believe there's one overarching theory, really—and it all has to do with deception. It's all part of one big, tangled web—some strands cut, others fraying at the edges. But on the whole, it's remarkable that there is what amounts to a broad consensus.

Let's break it down.

Christianity's View

I'm painting with a huge brush here. I am not trying to speak for all Christians everywhere. I'm simply relating what I've seen and what I think seems apparent.

With that said, we've got Christians on one side, treating "disclosure" like it's a theological apocalypse. Christians who dive into the UFO phenomenon aren't messing around. They're not starry-eyed New Agers whispering about peace treaties with Pleiadians. They're calling this what they think it is: spiritual warfare.

To many, it's all demonic. According to them, the entire UFO phenomenon is a satanic plot designed to yank people away from God through deception.

Gary Bates, a well-known Christian apologist, argues that UFOs display supernatural abilities that defy any conventional technology—instant acceleration, dematerialization, the whole package. He and others argue that what we're seeing are not aliens but fallen angels with a PR facelift. After all, "Satan himself masquerades as an angel of light" (2 Corinthians 11:14). Reports of abduction experiences stopping cold when abductees invoke the name of Jesus only feed the narrative.[461]

The real fear for Christians is the eschatological deception. They see this lining up with end-times prophecy like clockwork. Revelation 12:12 says Satan goes all-out with his deceptions because he knows his time is running out.

To Christians like Jason Jimenez, the UFO phenomenon is just one more tentacle of a satanic plot to seduce humankind into forgetting about God and embracing a false messiah.[462]

L. A. Marzulli appears to agree and has a catchphrase on his YouTube show, which I partially quoted at the very beginning of this chapter:

"UFOs are real, burgeoning, and not going away. This is the coming great deception. However, when we go up they come down. When we go up they show up."[463]

He believes whatever it is that's restraining the fallen angels from showing up en masse in a way that may appear to be an interstellar, alien task force ala *V*, the 1980s miniseries[464] (not the remake; it simply wasn't as good as the original) will be taken out of the way when the Church is raptured and believers are caught up to Heaven. Marzulli considers this a mercy to prevent followers of Jesus Christ from experiencing the horrific Tribulation spoken about in the books of Daniel and Revelation (see Daniel 9:24–27; Revelation 6–19).

In any case, many Christians believe when the "alien space brothers" show up, world leaders and the mass media will say something along the lines of, "Here's your savior from the stars." And millions will eat it up.

Why?

First, consider the words of President Ronald Reagan. In an address to the Forty-second Session of the United Nations General Assembly in New York on September 21, 1987, he said:

> In our obsession with antagonisms of the moment, we often forget how much unites all the members of humanity. Perhaps we need some outside, universal threat to make us recognize this common bond.
>
> I occasionally think how quickly our differences worldwide would vanish if we were facing an alien threat from outside this world.[465]

The public has been primed for almost a hundred years for some type of official disclosure moment with statements like his made by various world leaders.

Second, if the government suddenly announces, "We've made contact," it's going to make the Bible look like old-world mythology to millions of people. A religious relic surpassed by enlightened cosmic neighbors.

As Gary Bates, the CEO of Creation Ministries International (CMI), puts it, "Any validation of alien life would challenge the core tenets of salvation and creation."[466, 467]

You already know how I feel about that. I think the basic premise in Bates' statement is total hogwash. But in a way, he's not far wrong. Many don't think critically at all.

"Give me my beer, my pizza, and my Xbox, and don't talk to me about anything that actually matters! Shush now. I'm shooting zombies."

Others do think, but they're believers in what they've been taught—and they put their trust in what others teach rather than searching the Scriptures for themselves.

It makes me think of something from the book of Acts:

Now these people were more noble-minded than those in Thessalonica, for they received the word with great eagerness, examining the Scriptures daily to see whether these things were so. (Acts 17:11)

Paul and Silas rolled into Berea after getting chased out of Thessalonica by an angry mob. They were preaching the gospel, the same message they were taking everywhere. But Berea? Different vibe entirely.

See, most places Paul went, he was met with two things: curiosity or outrage. People either loved him or wanted to stone him. Nothing in between. But the Bereans had something going for them that most folks didn't.

Paul himself called them "more noble."

Why?

It's simple: They didn't just nod along like hypnotized sheep. They didn't take Paul's word as gospel just because he was a charismatic, well-traveled, intellectual heavyweight. They didn't reject him outright, either, just because his message sounded foreign or threatening to their traditions.

Instead, they did something rare: They checked his work.

Paul would preach, laying out his case that Jesus was the Messiah who had been promised throughout the Hebrew Scriptures. But instead of knee-jerk reactions—either hostile or fawning—the Bereans took the most respectable route possible. They listened with open minds, sure. But they didn't leave their brains at the door. They went home, pulled out their scrolls, and searched the Scriptures daily.

They did it every day. That's consistency. That's diligence. They weren't content to take Paul's word for it. They wanted to see if the man's claims held up against the only real measuring stick that mattered to them—God's Word.

And Paul? He wasn't offended by their skepticism. He praised them for it. In his eyes, this wasn't an insult. It was the highest compliment you could pay a teacher: Do your own homework. Verify the truth.

Why does this matter? Because the Bereans weren't just more noble than the Thessalonians. They were more noble than most people today, who either swallow what they're told like it's sugar-coated medicine or spit it out like poison without a second thought. Hardly anyone tests what they hear. Few have the guts or discipline to dig for the truth themselves.

Honestly, that's one of the biggest themes of this entire book. I believe it's a lesson every serious truth-seeker—of any faith or no faith at all—should take to heart.

Now, going back to the overall scenario most Christians believe is going to happen vis-a-vis "the alien agenda," I tend to agree. I don't believe in any way that the existence of interstellar aliens challenges the core tenets of Yeshua's mission or what He did to reconcile humanity (and all of creation) to the Father.

But I do believe a deception is coming. It may have something to do with interstellar extraterrestrials, or the scenario may end up being a mishmash of what Christians think and what non-Christian UFO believers and whistleblowers believe. It may have elements that reflect both positions. I'll explain the logic of that in a moment.

The UFO Community's Perspective

Many of the hardcore UFO researchers are talking about deception, too. Only they aren't pointing at Satan; they're pointing at the government, shadowy cabals, and possibly even the entities themselves.

Hey, I'm right there with them in some respects. I totally don't get why there seems to be this false dichotomy: It's either Satan or the government or the aliens themselves.

Why can't all three work together?

Who says they don't?

Honestly, if we accept that some species of interstellar aliens may be interdimensional—advanced—nonhuman intelligences who just so happen to match both angelic and alien descriptions—*and* we believe they've had interactions with world governments already, what's the problem?

Anyway, I absolutely believe governments have kept a lot of information from the general public. I don't think whistleblowers with serious credentials are going around lying about it as part of some new disinformation campaign. I mean, we already talked about David Grusch, Luis Elizondo, and Ryan Graves. There are others. Lots of others.

The consensus is that the truth is locked up behind so many layers of security clearance that even Congress can't get near it.

In any case, the scenario as put forth by secular sorts like Dr. Steven Greer detail a psychological chess game with the public's mind as the board.

Let's start with the basics. You've probably heard the old line about the powers that be staging some kind of "black-flag operation." Something like a fake alien invasion. The idea is simple: Create a big, scary enemy out of thin air. I mean literally. UFOs buzzing across the sky, alien "craft" crashing into populated areas, panicked witnesses, headlines screaming about extraterrestrial threats.

What's the goal? Fear. Control. And, most importantly, justification. Justification for militarization, surveillance, and stripping away our freedom under the pretense of "protection." A well-oiled propaganda machine cranking out phony encounters, all designed to keep the public jumpy, paranoid, and looking to Big Brother for security.

Dr. Greer—the guy who's been blowing the whistle on all this for years—says it's not just about faking alien attacks. It's about faking alien abductions, too. Not by little green men, but by good ol' human operatives. Think alphabet agencies. Think rogue factions with cutting-edge technology meant to simulate alien encounters.

Why would they do that? Easy. To discredit real contact experiences. To make anyone who says they've seen or communicated with actual extraterrestrials sound like a tinfoil-hat-wearing loon. And if they can't outright silence whistleblowers?

Discredit them. Launch smear campaigns. Release media hit pieces. It's all about controlling the narrative.

But, according to Greer, this cover-up is about more than just power. It's about keeping humanity dumbed down and afraid. Because—and here's the shocker—he insists that most extraterrestrial civilizations out there are benevolent.

They're not here to conquer or enslave; quite the opposite. They're here to help us break free from our own shackles—technological, spiritual, psychological, you name it.

Greer's out there pushing what he calls "C5 Contact Protocols" (C5: "close encounters of the fifth kind"). According to him, these protocols are a structured framework for initiating peaceful, bilateral communication with extraterrestrial intelligence (ETI) through conscious intent, meditation, and technology.[468]

But when we boil it down, all the protocols amount to is teaching people how to "channel" and make contact with entities. You know, the same way mediums and New Age channelers get down and boogie with the Pleiadians and a host of other beings of "light."

Of course, according to Greer and those who follow him, Hollywood's been in on this, too, if you believe the narrative. Think about it. Almost every blockbuster about aliens has them blowing up landmarks, harvesting human brains, or whatever other nightmare fuel the scriptwriters dream up.

Independence Day. War of the Worlds. The Fourth Kind. These films and others are all about reinforcing one message: aliens = threat. According to Greer, covert groups have been feeding this garbage to Hollywood for decades, because if the public's primed to expect hostile aliens, then when the time comes to stage their big, fake invasion, everyone's already mentally programmed to accept whatever "solution" they roll out.

As I said before, I get it. There are elements of truth here—the same as I think there are elements of truth in the Christian narrative.

Something's up. Something's gonna go down.

When? What's the timing?

I think it's probably sooner than most believe.

The Common Ground

It doesn't matter if you think the culprits are fallen angels or interstellar tricksters. The core suspicion is the same: We are being lied to. Either by the entities, the governments supposedly covering them up, or both.

The Outliers

There are only a few outliers in terms of theories—and, honestly, they're pretty unbelievable.

For example, the late Dr. John Mack—a Harvard psychiatrist and abduction researcher—proposed that nonhuman intelligences (NHIs) operate outside conventional physics, interacting with humans to catalyze spiritual or evolutionary growth. He saw abductions as part of a broader cosmic plan to awaken humanity to ecological or existential crises.[469, 470]

In other words, he saw alien abductions—people being taken against their will—and having sexual experiments performed on their bodies—non-consensually—as a good thing.

His excuse? These beings might be preparing a "cosmic insurance policy" to preserve life if humans fail to address ecological crises.

Sorry, I'm not buying it. Whatever happened to "rape is rape?" Because that's what's essentially happening—even if the "experiment" isn't getting down and jiggy. If someone's body is violated in any way, sexually or not, it's an offense against their person.

The reasons are beside the point. You can't justify it by pointing to altruism.

Then there's Joe Jordan, who believes "alien abductions" are interdimensional spiritual attacks by deceptive entities masquerading as extraterrestrials. The documentary *Alien Intrusion: Unmasking a Deception* (2018), which Jordan contributed to, explores this theory by arguing that "aliens" may be demonic spirits using extraterrestrial guise as a deception.

Thus, for him, this isn't something that's physically happening to the abductee.[471]

I think you know where I stand on this issue by now, but just in case you don't, I'll be blunt: I believe the abductees. They really have been abducted—usually by the alien Greys. This is something physical.

After the experience, again, many are left with skin lesions and marks, burns, and radiation-like effects, scars from implants or procedures, reproductive system injuries, and more.[472]

I mean, we have the testimony of people like Luis Elizondo, who talked about alien implants ripped straight from human bodies. That sounds pretty physical to me—not so spiritual.

L. A. Marzulli also covered this phenomenon in his documentary *Watcher* series in which he featured Dr. Roger Leir, a surgeon known for removing alleged alien implants from seventeen patients. It includes physical evidence of these implants and electron microscope analyses to examine their composition.[473]

In any case, Joe Jordan believes there are cases where invoking Jesus' name halted abduction experiences, suggesting the phenomenon is rooted in the supernatural rather than physical beings. However, Timothy Alberino has shown rather conclusively this simply isn't true—at least in most cases.

He writes:

> The popular claim that alien abductions can be interrupted by invoking the name of Jesus is patently false. Abduction accounts are filled with instances in which sincere Christians vigorously rebuke their abductors to no avail (the author has personally interviewed believers who have testified to this fact).
>
> Being abducted by gray aliens is, to some extent, no different than being abducted by human traffickers.[474]

Now, I am not attacking Joe Jordan here or Creation.com. I simply don't agree with the suppositions these individuals or organizations put forth at all. Nevertheless, they seem to be the dominant conclusions in many Christian circles, and I think that's too bad.

I think the mindset is too narrow and it needs to change, post-haste.

WHAT'S WRONG WITH THE PICTURE?

Before I lay out exactly what I see wrong here, I want to be transparent and say many of the arguments and perspectives I present below are heavily influenced by the work of Timothy Alberino.

While I've built upon his foundational insights, my intention is to expand and explore areas he hasn't fully addressed, particularly in how the abduction phenomenon integrates into the broader narrative of deception.

So, the problem with each of the theories presented above is that none of them seem to take the abduction phenomenon into account.

Okay, deception is coming. Okay, there might be a fake alien invasion—or maybe a real one conducted by fallen angels.

We're gonna install the Antichrist.

Got it.

But how and where does the abduction phenomenon fit in? What does that have to do with the overall narrative of deception? How does it tie back to Genesis 6? Enoch 1?

Because if you look at the dominant "alien agenda" narratives put forth by Christians and secular folks alike, this aspect seems glaringly absent.

I've quoted Alberino a lot in this book, frankly because I think he's more on the money than just about anyone else I've ever read on this topic. While I disagree with him on a few points, largely, I believe he has a deeper understanding than most Christians.

According to him, the endgame or ultimate agenda of the alien Greys and the broader angelic rebellion is a coordinated effort to usurp the dominion of humanity over Earth and ultimately replace it with a new, posthuman species that aligns with the agenda of the fallen entities.

In his book, he frames this as a deliberate, multifaceted operation involving genetic manipulation, technological corruption, and ideological deception. I believe the conclusions Alberino comes to are within the realm of possibility. Honestly, I think they're more likely than some of the other popular claims being made right now.

In other words, the whole alien agenda—abductions, genetic experiments, hybridization—isn't a random side plot. It's the central thread woven through the entire narrative of deception—the same agenda that started with the Watchers in Genesis 6 and that's elaborated on in Enoch 1.

Here's where I want to dig deeper.

Alberino's analysis is thorough, and while he delves into the abduction phenomenon, and he rightly sees it as a part of the overall, nefarious agenda of fallen beings, I don't think he pays enough attention to psychological manipulation.

Think about it. The same way the Watchers of Genesis 6 descended and corrupted humanity's genetic makeup, these modern entities—alien Greys or otherwise—are corrupting not just the biological framework of mankind, but also our mental and spiritual bearing.

Abductees aren't just being physically experimented on. What if they're being programmed? Reports of abductees often describe altered states of consciousness, telepathic messages, and manipulative dreamlike encounters.

What if these methods are deliberate? What if the point isn't just to alter genetics, but to modify belief systems, allegiances, and perceptions of reality itself? What if part of it is about creating potential sleeper agents, people who will be aligned with the "alien agenda" at the right time, ready to help push the masses into the arms of an "alien savior?" Or ready to push friends, family, neighbors, et cetera. into a new system where they either upgrade or kiss their ability to buy and sell goodbye?

After all, these abductees are also mentally pressured to "hug" and accept hybrid children, according to reports.[475]

Alberino's overarching argument is that these beings are attempting to create a posthuman species aligned with their agenda. Fair enough. But what if this process has two dimensions? What if one side is physical transformation, while the other is ideological corruption, achieved through psychological manipulation?

Don't get me wrong. I'm not saying abductees are now the bad guys. I believe they are victims. But I also see a danger that I haven't heard many talk about.

Let's rewind.

Genesis 6 describes the Watchers descending, cohabiting with human women, and producing offspring. Enoch 1 spells out that their corruption was more than just moral, it was biological.

This wasn't mere instruction in forbidden things—it was open sabotage. It was a direct assault on God's design. Polluting it. Diluting it. *Breeding out* the image of God in humanity.

And they excelled at controlling human perception. They were revered as gods, worshiped, and manipulated entire cultures. Fast forward to today, and the so-called aliens are doing the exact same thing.

Alberino's correct when he talks about the alien Greys and the broader angelic rebellion working toward a unified objective: hijacking humanity's God-given dominion over Earth and replacing us with something…less.[476]

A posthuman species that's compatible with the agenda of these fallen entities. And all the genetic manipulation and abduction phenomena? It's all part of that same old operation.

But it's not just about changing what we are. It's about changing how we think. How we believe. How we perceive our own identity and purpose.

Even if angels, fallen or otherwise, are considered "sons of God" and Adam is considered a "son of God," it doesn't necessarily follow that blending the two creates something with that same status. We're not the same beings, and we weren't created for the same purposes. Jamming those two blueprints together doesn't produce something that necessarily inherits the birthright. If we cross a lion and a tiger, we get a liger. Cool, but it's also sterile—a dead end.

And if we manage to create a hybrid being—whether it's from angelic DNA, alien DNA, or some new transhumanist concoction—it won't be human in the sense God intended. It won't be angelic, either. It's something less. Something fundamentally flawed.

That's true even if that hybrid being has Marvel Comics superpowers.

That's the goal, you see: to turn humanity into something it was never meant to be.

Alberino nailed it. He understands this is all about destroying our place in God's kingdom by altering our very nature. We're not simply talking about making people "better," we're talking about making people *other*.[477]

If we're no longer truly human—if we've corrupted the essence of what it means to bear the image of God—we forfeit our birthright.

That's where the deception leads. This goes far beyond installing a charismatic leader with supernatural powers. It's about selling the lie that we can "evolve" beyond our humanity by integrating the DNA of angels, aliens, or whatever other entities are posing as superior beings.

The same way Esau gave up his birthright for a bowl of stew, humanity is being offered something flashy, superficial—enhanced intelligence, perfect health, maybe even a few centuries of life extension. But compare that to the real birthright: eternal life with the Creator of the universe, a Body that outclasses anything transhumanism could cook up. It's not even close.

The ancient pagans called it the Golden Age.

The late Tom Horn quoted the Cumaean Sibyl in his book *Apollyon Rising 2012: The Final Mystery of the Great Seal Revealed*.[478] In the book, he argues that the mottoes *Annuit Coeptis* ("He approves [our] undertakings") and *Novus Ordo Seclorum* ("New Order of the Ages") found on the Great Seal of the United States derive from the Cumaean Sibyl's prophecy about Apollo's reign.

He posits that the "He" in *Annuit Coeptis* refers to Jupiter/Zeus, Apollo's father, and that the prophecy aligns with a hidden narrative of a coming "counter-Jesus" figure.

The Cumaean Sibyl, a prophetess of Apollo, is central to Virgil's *Eclogue IV*, which describes a divine child ushering in a new era:

> Now the last age by Cumae's Sibyl sung
>
> Has come and gone, and the majestic roll

> Of circling centuries begins anew:
> Justice returns, returns old Saturn's reign,
> With a new breed of men sent down from heaven.
> Only do thou, at the boy's birth in whom
> The iron shall cease, the golden race arise,
> Befriend him, chaste Lucina; 'tis thine own
>
> Apollo reigns.[479]

The Sybils prophesied about a time when gods would walk among men and a new race would be born. Sound familiar? It's a thread running through human history. And if we're talking about Apollo—the favorite son of the old gods—it's possible Antichrist himself could be a new hybrid being, engineered to fit the bill of a resurrected god-king.

But even if he's not, the overarching plan remains the same: Convince humans to "upgrade" themselves without God. Break away from the divine blueprint. Corrupt the seed once and for all.

This is where Alberino's assessment is spot-on. This time, the fallen entities are doing more than handing out forbidden knowledge. They're offering forbidden transformation. They're luring humanity into rejecting their birthright for something as worthless as a bowl of stew. It's the oldest trick in the book, and it may be about to play out on the grandest scale imaginable.

If this deception is about corrupting the image of God in humanity, then salvation is about restoring it. If the enemy's agenda is to manipulate, hybridize, and obscure the truth, then Yeshua's mission is to make the truth known and restore what's been broken.

The corruption of humanity's genetic and spiritual essence is a violation of everything God intended. It's an attempt to sever the link between humanity and the Creator, replacing it with something counterfeit.

That's where the truth of Yeshua cuts through the lie. Where deception seeks to pervert and destroy, He seeks to redeem and restore. He is the image of the invisible God, the only perfect representation of what humanity was meant to be. Through Him, we have a way back—a restoration of our original purpose, identity, and relationship with the Creator.

WINDING DOWN

I believe we're on the fast track to the end of the age. Take a look at the news, and even without the almost-daily UFO sightings around the world, there's all kinds of freakishness going on.

There are earthquakes in diverse places. Wars. Rumors of wars. Famines. New diseases and old diseases popping up. All of it scares the living daylights out of people, with their hearts failing them for fear, and for looking after those things coming on the Earth.

And the hearts of everyone we meet are cold and wicked. People all over the place are calling evil good, and good evil. They're calling darkness light, and light darkness. Bitter is sweet and sweet is bitter.

Who even needs an alien agenda? Aren't we lost enough already?

I'd say "yes" to that, but something has to come along to push us, as a species, over the edge. I don't think AI or a host of other new technologies, despite the risks they pose to personal privacy or the current financial system worldwide, is enough to thrust humanity into the terrible times spoken of in the books of Daniel and Revelation.

I believe something cataclysmic is on its way, something that will shatter the reality we all live in. It will be so horrific that most people are going to scream for someone to save them—and they're not going to care much who that someone is. They'll be willing to give up their freedoms and more, and when that time comes, someone will step into the breach.

The new golden age Apollo will hold out his hand and make what sounds like a godfather offer—one we won't be allowed to refuse—if we want to keep on keeping on as global citizens.

Either Disclosure, a fake alien invasion, or even an armada showing up in orbit with a "we come in peace" mantra might be a part of all that. Remember, we might get some type of upgrade as an incentive.

Think of that!

But as for me and my house, we will serve the Lord. We will not bow the knee to any but the God of Israel and His chosen Messiah.

◆—◆—◆

Listen, I've wandered through a huge maze of competing voices—ancient texts, modern mystics, scientists, and self-styled spiritual gurus—seeking truth. But none of them offered what I found in Yeshua: not just knowledge, but *life*.

I've read countless books, absorbed the wisdom of philosophers, analyzed the theories of researchers, and meditated on the insights of mystics. All offered something—a fragment, a glimpse, a moment of clarity. But none of them provided the whole truth.

I was chasing shadows, trying to put together a puzzle with half the pieces missing. It wasn't until I turned to Yeshua that the puzzle began to take shape. He was the missing piece. The cornerstone I'd been searching for all along.

The world offers an endless array of distractions, philosophies, and doctrines, all promising enlightenment or salvation. But they're just distortions of the ultimate truth that only Yeshua embodies. He is the Source, the Key, the Only Way Back to the Creator.

It's my hope and prayer that if you aren't a follower of Yeshua (Jesus) the Messiah you will come to know Him…and follow Him.

There are many voices in the world today.

There have been other voices throughout the ages, and they're getting louder, more brazen, and more insistent that we listen to anyone—as long as we aren't paying attention to Jesus.

Listen to Buddha! Listen to the Vedic Rishis! Listen to Deepak Chopra, Eckhart Tolle, Abraham-Hicks, Neville Goddard, Robert Monroe, Teal Swan, Ashtar, the Pleiadians, Amorah Quan Yin, Bashar, the Arcturians, Saint Germain, or Thoth.

Listen to Rambam, the Rebbe, the Baal Shem Tov.

Anybody but Jesus!

But what did God say?

Let me tell you a quick story.

This isn't your average stroll up a mountain. It's Jesus, leading His inner circle—Peter, James, and John—up to a secluded, high place up on Mount Hermon. Yeah, the same place the Watchers descended.

Why did He lead them up there?

Because He's about to blow their minds, and God's going to shove it in the faces of the fallen.

Suddenly, *boom*: Jesus *transfigures* right in front of them. His face starts shining like the sun, His clothes flash white like pure light. No cheap parlor tricks or Egyptian sorcery here. He pulled back the curtain on His divinity for a few seconds to give them a glimpse of who He really is.

He's the Son of God—fully human—and He's showing everyone what Adam was meant to be.

Then, to turn the intensity dial all the way up, Moses and Elijah show up out of nowhere and start having a chat with Jesus. Yeah, *that* Moses and Elijah. Not exactly small-time names if you know your Hebrew Scriptures.

This moment is loaded with symbolism—Moshe (Moses) represents the Torah, Eliyahu (Elijah) represents the Prophets, and Yeshua stands there as the fulfillment of everything they ever pointed to.

Peter, overwhelmed and probably babbling from shock, decides to play event-planner: "Lord, this is incredible! Let's set up three tabernacles—one for You, one for Moses, and one for Elijah."

His heart's in the right place, but he's missing the point. He's trying to commemorate the moment instead of understanding it.

Again, what did God say?

This is My beloved Son, with whom I am well pleased; listen to Him! (Matthew 17:5)

I did.

But I listened to a lot of others before him. And I explored pretty much all the voices I mentioned above. There is no life in any of them.

We won't ever be able to raise our vibration enough to ascend to where we really want to be. No matter how many mantras we chant and no matter how much we visualize—we won't be able to manifest everlasting life.

Neville Goddard is dead.

Even after I began listening to Yeshua, I didn't follow Him right away. It took me a long time of mulling ideas over and arguing with others. There are a lot—a lot—of debates that are intellectually difficult to overcome.

Within Judaism there are objections that seem almost insurmountable, that make it seem impossible that Yeshua could be who He says He is.

But the truth is the truth.

And, as Yeshua Himself stated:

Ask, and it will be given to you; seek, and you will find; knock, and it will be opened to you. For everyone who asks receives, and the one who seeks finds, and to the one who knocks it will be opened. (Matthew 7:7–8)

I asked for the truth. It was a hard road for me, but I kept seeking. Yeshua led me to Himself. And, in the end, I am His.

You don't have to believe me; that's okay.

The deception is real, but so is the truth. It's not an ideology or an institution, it's a Person. Yeshua the Messiah. The One who can restore the image of God within you.

All the stuff I've talked about in this book—the theories, the conspiracies, all the old texts, the stuff that might sound like mumbo-jumbo—might be overwhelming. It's easy to get lost, to doubt, to feel like nothing makes sense.

But the reality is, the truth has been right in front of us all along.

The God of Israel, my God, and the Father of Yeshua is not a God of confusion. His light pierces the darkness. His love disarms the fear. And when you come to know Him and continue to seek Him, deception loses its power.

If you're a truth-seeker, seek it with all your heart. If you've never sought the truth before, start now.

We hear New Agers on YouTube all the time telling viewers that they're divine: "You've got the truth within. You don't need anything more. You're enough."

The truth is, no you're not. By yourself, you never will be.

But Yeshua is.

> I hope you find out before it's too late
>
> That there's really nobody else
> You know it's breaking His heart the longer you wait
> 'Cause you've only been lying to yourself
> 'Cause no one believes a thing you say
> Not even you
> You know you're gonna find out that He's the way
> No matter which way you choose
>
> But I pray you find out by His love for you.[480]

It's time to make a choice. The world will keep pushing you toward a thousand different answers, but there's only one truth that can restore, redeem, and save.

If you've read this far, thank you. I've laid out everything I know, everything I believe, because I care about the truth—and about you. Whatever deception clouds your vision, I pray you find the One who tears the veil away.

—Will Blesch

P.S.

I realize most of what I've written applies to people who believe in "something." I haven't said much to those of you who may not believe in anything or for whom physical evidence is the only thing you *do* believe in.

Some of you may not believe Yeshua was a real person. Some, particularly some Jewish readers, might believe the entire New Testament was an intentional effort to subvert the Jewish faith by operatives of Rome.

All of those objections have solid answers that allow those willing to study to overcome them.

I will end (really, this time) with a quote from Puddleglum, an honest Marshwiggle—one of my all-time favorite characters in C. S. Lewis' *The Chronicles of Narnia*:

> Suppose we have only dreamed, or made up, all those things—trees and grass and sun and moon and stars and Aslan himself. Suppose we have. Then all I can say is that, in that case, the made-up things seem a good deal more important than the real ones.
>
> Suppose this black pit of a kingdom of yours is the only world. Well, it strikes me as a pretty poor one. And that's a funny thing, when you come to think of it.
>
> We're just babies making up a game, if you're right. But four babies playing a game can make a play-world which licks your real world hollow.
>
> That's why I'm going to stand by the play-world. I'm on Aslan's side even if there isn't any Aslan to lead it. I'm going to live as like a Narnian as I can even if there isn't any Narnia.[481]

I'm on the God of Israel's side even if there isn't any God, and I'm going to live as like a loyal subject of His kingdom as I can, even if there isn't any kingdom.

ENDNOTES

1. Theresa Bane, *Encyclopedia of Giants and Humanoids in Myth, Legend, and Folklore* (Jefferson, NC: McFarland & Co., 2016), 1.
2. Bereishit Rabbah 26:7, quoted in Midrash Rabbah, trans. H. Freedman and Maurice Simon (London: Soncino Press, 1939), accessed April 4, 2025, https://www.sefaria.org/Bereishit_Rabbah.26.7.
3. Adrienne Mayor, *Fossil Legends of the First Americans* (Princeton: Princeton University Press, 2005), 51–53.
4. Sarah Winnemucca Hopkins, *Life Among the Piutes: Their Wrongs and Claims* (Boston: Cupples, Upham & Co., 1883), 73–75.
5. Miranda Green, *Celtic Myths* (Austin: University of Texas Press, 1994), 28–32.
6. W. B. Yeats, ed., *Irish Fairy and Folk Tales* (London: Walter Scott, 1888), 120–123.
7. Jeffrey Gantz, trans., *The Mabinogion* (London: Penguin, 1976), 191–194.
8. Robin McKie, "Piltdown Man: British Archaeology's Greatest Hoax," *The Guardian*, February 5, 2012, https://www.theguardian.com/science/2012/feb/05/piltdown-man-archaeologys-greatest-hoax.
9. Richard L. Thornton, "Fort Loudoun and George Washington," Access Genealogy, accessed April 4, 2025, https://www.accessgenealogy.com/native/fort-loudoun-and-george-washington.htm.
10. Richard L. Thornton, email correspondence with author, February 2025.
11. Rod Meldrum, "Giants Discovered by George Washington," Book of Mormon Evidence, accessed April 4, 2025, https://bookofmormonevidence.org/giants-discovered-by-george-washington/.
12. French & Indian War Foundation, email correspondence with author, February 2025.
13. "The Discovery of Troy: Myth Turned Reality." *The Archaeologist*, February 13, 2025. https://www.thearchaeologist.org/blog/the-discovery-of-troy-myth-turned-reality.
14. "The Rediscovery of the Hittites." *Hethitologie-Portal Mainz*, University of Würzburg, accessed April 4, 2025. https://www.hethport.uni-wuerzburg.de/HPM/hpm-en.php?p=anfhet-en.
15. Alwin Kloekhorst, "Personal Names from Kaniš: The Oldest Indo-European Linguistic Material," *Academia.edu*, accessed April 4, 2025, https://www.academia.edu/9794131/Personal_names_from_Kani%C5%A1_the_oldest_Indo_European_linguistic_material.

ENDNOTES

16   Roy P. Basler, ed., *The Collected Works of Abraham Lincoln*, Volume 2 (New Brunswick, NJ: Rutgers University Press, 1953), 10.
17   "Is This the Ancestor of the American Race?," *New York Journal*, June 10, 1890.
18   "Giants' Skeletons Found," *New York Times*, February 11, 1902.
19   "Scientists Still Baffled from Giant Human Skeletons Up to 10 Feet Tall," *New York Post*, January 4, 2024.
20   Graham Hancock, *Fingerprints of the Gods* (New York: Crown, 1995), xv.
21   David D. Gilmore, *Monsters: Evil Beings, Mythical Beasts, and All Manner of Imaginary Terrors* (Philadelphia: University of Pennsylvania Press, 2009), 5–6.
22   "Elongated Skulls Found in Peru," NDTV, accessed April 4, 2025, https://www.ndtv.com/world-news/elongated-skulls-found-in-peru-ancient-giants-crossed-oceans-1234567.
23   John Verano, "Cranial Deformation in South America," *American Journal of Physical Anthropology* 130, no. 2 (2006): 241–248.
24   Mark Laplume, personal interview with author, January 2025.
25   Ibid.
26   Brien Foerster, *The Enigma of Cranial Deformation: Elongated Skulls of the Ancients* (Paracas History Press, 2013), 55–60.
27   Jonathan L. Rees, "Genetics of Hair and Skin Color," *Annual Review of Genetics* (December 2003): 67–90. https://doi.org/10.1146/annurev.genet.37.110801.143233.
28   L. A. Marzulli, *On the Trail of the Nephilim, Volume 1* (CreateSpace Independent Publishing Platform, 2016).
29   L. A. Marzulli, *On the Trail of the Nephilim, Volume 2: New Archaeological Research* (Spiral of Life, 2014).
30   Carl Jung, *Aion: Researches into the Phenomenology of the Self*, trans. R. F. C. Hull (Princeton, NJ: Princeton University Press, 1959), 16.
31   Timothy Alberino, *Birthright: The Coming Posthuman Apocalypse and the Usurpation of Adam's Dominion on Planet Earth* (Crane, MO: Defender, 2020), 29.
32   Ibid.
33   Ibid.
34   Erik Lacitis, "'Flying Saucers' Became a Thing 70 Years Ago Saturday with Sighting near Mount Rainier," *Seattle Times*, June 22, 2017, https://www.seattletimes.com/seattle-news/northwest/flying-saucers-became-a-thing-70-years-ago-saturday-with-sighting-near-mount-rainier/.
35   *The Day the Earth Stood Still*. Directed by Robert Wise. Produced by Julian Blaustein. 20th Century Fox, 1951.
36   Jacques Vallée, *Passport to Magonia: From Folklore to Flying Saucers* (Chicago: Henry Regnery Co., 1969).
37   Jacques F. Vallée, "Five Arguments Against the Extraterrestrial Origin of Unidentified Flying Objects," *Journal of Scientific Exploration* 4, no. 1 (1990): 105–117.
38   Jacques Vallée, The Invisible College: What a Group of Scientists Has Discovered About UFO Influences on the Human Race (New York: E. P. Dutton, 1975).
39   Jacques Vallée, *Messengers of Deception: UFO Contacts and Cults* (Berkeley, CA: And/Or Press, 1979).
40   Jacques Vallée, *Forbidden Science: Journals, 1957–1969* (Berkeley, CA: North Atlantic Books, 1992)

ENDNOTES

41 Mark O'Connell, *The Close Encounters Man: How One Man Made the World Believe in UFOs* (New York: Dey Street Books, 2017).
42 John A. Keel, *The Mothman Prophecies* (New York: Signet, 1976).
43 John A. Keel, *The Eighth Tower: The Cosmic Puzzle of UFOs* (New York: Saturday Review Press, 1975).
44 Pliny the Elder. *Naturalis Historia*. Rome, AD 77–79.
45 Julius Obsequens, *Liber Prodigiorum* (Rome, fourth or fifth century AD).
46 Sophie Page, "Astrology, Ritual, and Revolution in the Later Middle Ages: The Otia Imperialia of Gervase of Tilbury," *Journal of Medieval History* 45, no. 3 (2019): 345–361.
47 David J. Halperin, *The Merkabah in Rabbinic Literature*, American Oriental Series, vol. 62 (New Haven, CT: American Oriental Society, 1980). Published in American Oriental Society (Vol. 100, No. 2), this peer-reviewed study analyzes early Jewish mystical texts, such as the Hekhalot literature, which describe visions of divine chariots (Merkavah) resembling otherworldly vehicles. These accounts are rooted in Ezekiel 1:4–28 and later Kabbalistic interpretations.
48 David Grusch, testimony before the House Oversight Committee, July 26, 2023, *Congressional Record*, accessed April 4, 2025.
49 CBS News, "Former Military Official Says U.S. Has Recovered Non-human 'Biologics'," CBS News, July 26, 2023, https://www.cbsnews.com/news/david-grusch-ufo-hearing-non-human-biologics-recovered-crash-sites/.
50 Tim Gallaudet, public statements, July 2023.
51 Karl Nell, public statements, July 2023.
52 Thomas Kuhn, *The Structure of Scientific Revolutions*, 3rd ed. (Chicago: University of Chicago Press, 1996).
53 Brian Sharpless, *Sleep Paralysis: Historical, Psychological, and Medical Perspectives* (New York: Oxford University Press, 2015), 49–52.
54 Susan Blackmore, "Alien Abduction: The Inside Story," *New Scientist* 159, no. 2146 (1998): 28–31.
55 Enrico Fermi, quoted in Edward Teller, *Memoirs: A Twentieth-Century Journey in Science and Politics* (Cambridge, MA: Perseus, 2001), 141.
56 Stephen Webb, *If the Universe Is Teeming with Aliens... Where Is Everybody?: Fifty Solutions to the Fermi Paradox and the Problem of Extraterrestrial Life* (New York: Springer, 2002).
57 John Boli, *Globalization: A Very Short Introduction* (New York: Oxford University Press, 2012), 35–39.
58 Erich von Däniken, *Chariots of the Gods? Unsolved Mysteries of the Past*, trans. Michael Heron (New York: G. P. Putnam's Sons, 1968).
59 Zecharia Sitchin, *The Earth Chronicles Series* (New York: HarperCollins, Avon Books, and William Morrow, 1976–2007).
60 George Orwell, *1984* (New York: Harcourt, Brace, 1949).
61 Petra, "Pied Piper," Beat the System, Star Song, 1984, accessed April 4, 2025, https://www.lyrics.camp/petra/pied-piper.html.
62 The Dead Sea Scrolls." Imj.Org.Il, The Israel Museum, Jerusalem, www.imj.org.il/en/wings/shrine-book/dead-sea-scrolls. Accessed May 27, 2024.
63 Richard N Ostling, "Religion: Secrets of the Dead Sea Scrolls." *Time*, August 14, 1989, time.com/archive/6703199/religion-secrets-of-the-dead-sea-scrolls/.

ENDNOTES

64. "Israel Fires Controversial Editor of Dead Sea Scrolls," *Los Angeles Times*, January 1, 1991, www.latimes.com/archives/la-xpm-1991-01-01-mn-7436-story.html.)
65. Marcel Griaule and Germaine Dieterlen, *Un système soudanais de Sirius, Journal de la Société des Africanistes* 20, no. 2 (1950): 273–294.
66. The Apkallu were seven sages in Mesopotamian mythology sent by the god Enki (Ea) to teach humanity wisdom, civilization, and science. They were described as half human, half fish, emerging from the waters to impart knowledge. This lines up perfectly with the Dogon's Nommo, who were amphibious, fishlike beings that descended from the sky to bring wisdom.
67. Sarah Taitz, "Five Things to Know About NSA Mass Surveillance and the Coming Fight in Congress," American Civil Liberties Union, April 11, 2023, https://www.aclu.org/news/national-security/five-things-to-know-about-nsa-mass-surveillance-and-the-coming-fight-in-congress.
68. Guardian US Interactive Team and Ewen MacAskill, "NSA Files Decoded: Edward Snowden's Surveillance Revelations Explained," *The Guardian*, November 1, 2013, https://www.theguardian.com/world/interactive/2013/nov/01/snowden-nsa-files-surveillance-revelations-decoded.
69. "French Church Abuse: 216,000 Children Were Victims of Clergy—Inquiry," BBC News, October 5, 2021, https://www.bbc.com/news/world-europe-58801183.
70. Cary Stacy Smith, "Roman Catholic Priests Scandal," EBSCO Research Starters, 2022, https://www.ebsco.com/research-starters/history/roman-catholic-priests-scandal.
71. Katherine Fung, "What Is MKULTRA? CIA Secret 'Mind Control' Program Records Unsealed," *Newsweek*, January 12, 2024, https://www.newsweek.com/mkultra-cia-secret-mind-control-program-records-unsealed-2005560.
72. Alonso Martínez, "70 Years of MKUltra, the CIA 'Mind-Control' Program That Inspired 'Stranger Things'," *El País*, April 13, 2023, https://english.elpais.com/usa/2023-04-13/70-years-of-mkultra-the-cia-mind-control-program-that-inspired-stranger-things.html.
73. "Potential New Human Species May Redraw the Family Tree." Natural History Museum, www.nhm.ac.uk/discover/news/2021/november/potential-new-human-species-may-redraw-family-tree.html. Accessed May 27, 2024.
74. "Interspecies Competition Led to Even More Forms of Ancient Human—Defying Evolutionary Trends in Vertebrates." University of Cambridge, April 17, 2024.
75. Graham Hancock, *Fingerprints of the Gods*. (MJF Books, 2011).
76. "Antikythera Mechanism." *Encyclopædia Britannica*, March 29, 2024, www.britannica.com/topic/Antikythera-mechanism.
77. "Graham Hancock on the Antikythera Mechanism | Joe Rogan." YouTube, April 23, 2019, www.youtube.com/watch?v=hkL5Wkj1gYk&t=16s.
78. D. E. Von Handorf, *The Baghdad Battery—Myth or Reality?*, www.nmfrc.org/pdf/psf2002/050284.pdf. Accessed May 27, 2024.
79. Andrew Collins, *From the Ashes of Angels: The Forbidden Legacy of a Fallen Race*. Inner Traditions, 2007.
80. Anonymous. *The Epic of Gilgamesh*. Translated by Andrew George. (New York: Penguin Classics, 2003).
81. William Ryan and Walter Pitman, *Noah's Flood: The New Scientific Discoveries About the Event That Changed History* (New York: Simon & Schuster, 1998). Their book

ENDNOTES

proposes that a catastrophic flood around 5600 BCE, caused by Mediterranean waters breaching the Bosporus and flooding the Black Sea basin, may have inspired Mesopotamian and biblical flood myths.

82 Valentina Yanko-Hombach, et al., "Controversy Over the Great Flood Hypotheses in the Black Sea in Light of Geological, Paleontological, and Archaeological Evidence," *Quaternary International* 167–168 (2007): 91–113, https://doi.org/10.1016/j.quaint.2006.08.004.

83 R. B. Firestone, et al., "Evidence for an Extraterrestrial Impact 12,900 Years Ago That Contributed to the Megafaunal Extinctions and the Younger Dryas Cooling," *Proceedings of the National Academy of Sciences* 104, no. 41 (2007): 16016–16021, https://doi.org/10.1073/pnas.0706977104. This work argues that a comet impact ~12,800 years ago (Younger Dryas period) caused abrupt climate change, sea-level rise, and catastrophic flooding, which may have been preserved in oral traditions.

84 Ibid.

85 Graham Hancock, *Magicians of the Gods: The Forgotten Wisdom of Earth's Lost Civilization* (New York: Thomas Dunne, 2015).

86 Bruce Bjornstad, "Washington's Surreal Channeled Scablands: An 'Outrageous Hypothesis'," Scenic Washington State, accessed April 4, 2025, https://www.scenicwa.com/story/ice-age-floods-in-washington-state.

87 Riley Black, "Devastating Ice Age Floods That Occurred in the Pacific Northwest Fascinate Scientists," *Smithsonian Magazine*, April 19, 2022, https://www.smithsonianmag.com/science-nature/devastating-ice-age-floods-that-occurred-in-the-pacific-northwest-fascinate-scientists-180979749/.

88 Ibid.

89 Charles H. Hapgood, *Earth's Shifting Crust: A Key to Some Basic Problems of Earth Science* (New York: Pantheon, 1958).

90 Ibid.

91 Elisabetta Canetta, "Physics and Beyond: 'God Does Not Play Dice'—What Did Einstein Mean?" *St Mary's University News*, October 2014, https://www.stmarys.ac.uk/news/2014/physics-and-beyond-god-does-not-play-dice-what-did-einstein-mean.

92 Hancock, *Fingerprints of the Gods*: The Evidence of Earth's Lost Civilization (New York: Crown, 1995).

93 Barry J. Marshall and J. Robin Warren, "Unidentified Curved Bacilli in the Stomach of Patients with Gastritis and Peptic Ulceration," *The Lancet* 323, no. 8390 (1984): 1311–1315, https://doi.org/10.1016/S0140-6736(84)91816-6.

94 Alfred Wegener, *Die Entstehung der Kontinente, Geologische Rundschau* 3, no. 4 (1912): 276–292, https://doi.org/10.1007/BF02202896.

95 Stanley B. Prusiner, "Novel Proteinaceous Infectious Particles Cause Scrapie," *Science* 216, no. 4542 (1982): 136–144, https://doi.org/10.1126/science.6801762.

96 J. Jeyan, Muruga Lal, et al., "Comparative Study of Ancient Indian Vimanas and Modern Spacecraft a Conceptual Approach." JETIR, www.jetir.org/view?paper=JETIR2103351. Accessed June 2, 2024.

97 "Vimanas: The Mystical Flying Machines of Ancient Indian Lore." *The Archaeologist*, August 27, 2023, www.thearchaeologist.org/blog/vimanas-the-mystical-flying-machines-of-ancient-indian-lore.

ENDNOTES

98 Manatha Nath Dutt (translator), Ramayana, (Calcutta: Elysium Press, 1892 and New York, 1910).

99 Encyclopædia Britannica (n.d.), "*Popol Vuh*," https://www.britannica.com/topic/Popol-Vuh.

100 Office of the Director of National Intelligence, "Preliminary Assessment: Unidentified Aerial Phenomena," June 25, 2021, https://www.dni.gov/files/ODNI/documents/assessments/Prelimary-Assessment-UAP-20210625.pdf.

101 Helene Cooper, Ralph Blumenthal, and Leslie Kean, "'Wow, What Is That?' Navy Pilots Report Unexplained Flying Objects," *New York Times*, May 26, 2019, https://www.nytimes.com/2019/05/26/us/politics/ufo-sightings-navy-pilots.html.

102 U.S. House of Representatives, Committee on Oversight and Accountability, "Unidentified Anomalous Phenomena: Implications on National Security, Public Safety, and Government Transparency," July 26, 2023, https://oversight.house.gov/hearing/unidentified-anomalous-phenomena-implications-on-national-security-public-safety-and-government-transparency/.

103 Anna Hopkins, "Former US Defense Official: We Know UFOs Are Real—Here's Why That's Concerning," Fox News, May 29, 2019, https://www.foxnews.com/science/christopher-mellon-official-ufo-sightings-real.

104 Helene Cooper, Ralph Blumenthal, and Leslie Kean, "Glowing Auras and 'Black Money': The Pentagon's Mysterious U.F.O. Program," *New York Times*, December 16, 2017, https://www.nytimes.com/2017/12/16/us/politics/pentagon-program-ufo-harry-reid.html.

105 Micah Hanks, "Imminent: Former Counterintelligence Agent's New Memoir Reveals an Insider's Look at UFOs," *The Debrief*, August 22, 2024, https://thedebrief.org/imminent-former-counterintelligence-agents-new-memoir-reveals-an-insiders-look-at-ufos/.

106 Joseph Campbell, et al. *The Power of Myth*. (Turtleback Books, 2012).

107 Michael S. Heiser, *The Unseen Realm: Recovering the Supernatural Worldview of the Bible*. (Lexham Press, 2019).

108 Helen Morales, *Classical Mythology: A Very Short Introduction*. (Oxford University Press, 2007).

109 Neil deGrasse Tyson, *Astrophysics for People in a Hurry* (W. W. Norton & Co., 2017).

110 Mark R. Whittington, opinion contributor. "Finding a Dyson Sphere Could Be Our First Contact with Alien Life," The Hill, May 31, 2024, thehill.com/opinion/technology/4696800-finding-a-dyson-sphere-could-be-our-first-contact-with-alien-life/.

111 M. Suazo, et al. "Project Hephaistos—II. Dyson Sphere Candidates from Gaia DR3, 2MASS, and Wise," *OUP Academic* (Oxford University Press, May 6, 2024. academic.oup.com/mnras/article/531/1/695/7665761?

112 Gabriella Contardo and David W. Hogg, "A Data-Driven Search for Mid-Infrared Excesses among Five Million Main-Sequence FGK Stars." arXiv.Org, March 27, 2024, arxiv.org/abs/2403.18941.

113 Richard E. Green, et al., "A Draft Sequence of the Neandertal Genome." *Science* (New York), US National Library of Medicine, May 7, 2010, www.ncbi.nlm.nih.gov/pmc/articles/PMC5100745/.

114 D. Reich; R. E. Green; M. Kircher; J. Krause; N. Patterson; E. Y. Durand; B. Viola; A. W. Briggs; U. Stenzel; P. L. Johnson; T. Maricic; J. M. Good; T. Marques-Bonet;

ENDNOTES

C. Alkan; Q. Fu; S. Mallick; H. Li; M. Meyer; E. E. Eichler; M. Stoneking; M. Richards; S. Talamo; M. V. Shunkov; A. P. Derevianko; J. J. Hublin; J. Kelso; Sl. "Genetic History of an Archaic Hominin Group from Denisova Cave in Siberia." *Nature*, US National Library of Medicine, pubmed.ncbi.nlm.nih.gov/21179161/. Accessed June 4, 2024.

115 Aaron Pfennig, et al., "Evolutionary Genetics and Admixture in African Populations." *Genome Biology and Evolution*, US National Library of Medicine, April 6, 2023, www.ncbi.nlm.nih.gov/pmc/articles/PMC10118306/.

116 "The Search for Extraterrestrial Life: Recent Developments," *SpringerLink*, Springer Netherlands, link.springer.com/book/10.1007/978-94-009-5462-5. Accessed June 4, 2024.

117 Arnold Hanslmeier, *Astrobiology the Search for Life in the Universe*. (Place of publication: Bentham Science Publishers, 2013).

118 Alberino, *Birthright: The Coming Posthuman Apocalypse*.

119 Lewis Page, "'Something May Come through' Dimensional 'Doors' at LHC," The Register®—Biting the Hand That Feeds IT, November 6, 2009, www.theregister.com/2009/11/06/lhc_dimensional_portals/.

120 John 20:26–29: "After eight days His disciples were again inside, and Thomas with them. Jesus came, the doors having been shut, and stood in their midst and said, 'Peace be with you.' Then He said to Thomas, 'Reach here with your finger, and see My hands; and reach here your hand and put it into My side; and do not be unbelieving, but believing.' Thomas answered and said to Him, 'My Lord and my God!' Jesus said to him, 'Because you have seen Me, have you believed? Blessed are they who did not see, and yet believed.'"

121 Mika Ahuvia's translation of "*Shalom Aleichem*," following Israel Davidson's notes: "of the King of Kings" could also be translated "from the King of Kings," emphasizing that the angels are sent from God. Davidson attributes this piyyut to the Kabbalists (*Thesaurus of Mediaeval Hebrew Poetry* 3:1268, p. 465). Brettler observes that the verbs come, bless, and go relate to the order of these verbs in Deuteronomy 28:6 (*My People's Prayer Book*), 68.

122 Moses Maimonides, *Guide for the Perplexed*. Translated by Shlomo Pines. (Chicago: University of Chicago Press, 1963).

123 Serge-Thomas Bonino, "Angels in Christian Theology," *St Andrews Encyclopaedia of Theology*, 2024, https://www.saet.ac.uk/Christianity/AngelsinChristianTheology.

124 Ibid.

125 Ibid.

126 Baruch S. Davidson, "What Are Angels?" Chabad.org, accessed April 4, 2025, https://www.chabad.org/library/article_cdo/aid/692875/jewish/What-Are-Angels.htm.

127 Moses Maimonides,. *The Guide for the Perplexed*. Translated from the original Arabic text by M. Friedländer. Second Edition, Revised Throughout. (London: Routledge & Kegan Paul Ltd., 1904). Accessed April 4, 2025. https://www.ccel.org/ccel/maimonides/guide.vi.vii.html.

128 Rabbi Karyn D. Kedar, *Angel Spotting*, ReformJudaism.org, October 2021, https://reformjudaism.org/learning/torah-study/torah-commentary/angel-spotting.

129 Fr. Hugh Barbour, O. Praem., "What Do Catholics Believe About Angels?" *Catholic Answers Focus*, April 13, 2020, https://www.catholic.com/audio/caf/what-do-catholics-believe-about-angels.

ENDNOTES

130 Ibid.
131 Solène Tadié, "Renowned Angel Expert Explains Amazing Facts Every Catholic Should Know About Angels," *EWTN Global Catholic Television Network*, September 30, 2020, https://ewtn.co.uk/article-renowned-angel-expert-explains-amazing-facts-every-catholic-should-know-about-angels/.
132 Saint John the Evangelist Orthodox Church, "The Orthodox Church's Teachings on Angels," August 22, 2023, https://www.saintjohnchurch.org/the-orthodox-churchs-teachings-on-angels/.
133 Thomas Hopko, "Angels and Evil Spirits," *The Orthodox Faith*, Orthodox Church in America, https://www.oca.org/orthodoxy/the-orthodox-faith/doctrine-scripture/the-symbol-of-faith/angels-and-evil-spirits.
134 Ibid.
135 Moran Mor Ignatius Zakka I Iwas, "The Angels," *Syriac Orthodox Church of Antioch*, May 4, 2010, https://syrianorthodoxchurch.org/2010/05/the-angels/.
136 Paul J. Barth, "Four Reasons Angels Do Not Have Bodies," *Purely Presbyterian*, July 15, 2024, https://purelypresbyterian.com/2024/07/15/four-reasons-angels-do-not-have-bodies/.
137 Alexandra Walsham, "Invisible Helpers: Angelic Intervention in Post-Reformation England," *Past & Present* 208, no. 1 (August 2010): 77–130, https://doi.org/10.1093/pastj/gtq002.
138 Ibid.
139 Hebrews 1:14: "Are they not all ministering spirits, sent out to render service for the sake of those who will inherit salvation?"
140 National Association of Christian Ministers, "Doctrine of Angels," NACM Manual to Ministry. Accessed April 4, 2025, https://ministry-tools.nacministers.org/docs/doctrine/angelology/.
141 Peter G. Lake, "Angels in the Anglican Tradition (1547–1662)" (PhD diss., King's College London, 1982), https://kclpure.kcl.ac.uk/portal/files/2931155/407628.pdf.
142 Alexandra Walsham, "Invisible Helpers: Angelic Intervention in Post-Reformation England," Past & Present 208, no. 1 (August 2010): 77–130, https://doi.org/10.1093/pastj/gtq002.
143 First Baptist Church of Troy, "Angelology," First Baptist Church of Troy, accessed April 4, 2025, https://fbctroy.org/about/our-beliefs/angelology/.
144 Patheos, "Methodist: Ultimate Reality and Divine Beings," Patheos, accessed April 4, 2025, https://www.patheos.com/library/methodist/beliefs/ultimate-reality-and-divine-beings.
145 *It's a Wonderful Life*. Directed by Frank Capra. Performed by James Stewart, Donna Reed, Lionel Barrymore, Thomas Mitchell, and Henry Travers. RKO Radio Pictures, 1946.
146 Genesis 3:24: "So He drove the man out; and at the east of the garden of Eden He stationed the cherubim and the flaming sword which turned every direction to guard the way to the tree of life."
147 Psalm 82: 1: "God takes His stand in His own congregation; He judges in the midst of the rulers."

   Psalm 82:8: "Arise, O God, judge the earth! For it is You who possesses all the nations."

ENDNOTES

148 1 Kings 22:19–22: "Micaiah said, 'Therefore, hear the word of the Lord. I saw the Lord sitting on His throne, and all the host of heaven standing by Him on His right and on His left.' The Lord said, "Who will entice Ahab to go up and fall at Ramoth-gilead?" And one said this while another said that. Then a spirit came forward and stood before the Lord and said, "I will entice him." The Lord said to him, "How?" And he said, "I will go out and be a deceiving spirit in the mouth of all his prophets." Then He said, "You are to entice him and also prevail. Go and do so."

149 Job 1:6–7: "Now there was a day when the sons of God came to present themselves before the Lord, and Satan also came among them. The Lord said to Satan, 'From where do you come?' Then Satan answered the Lord and said, 'From roaming about on the earth and walking around on it'."

150 Daniel 10:1: "In the third year of Cyrus king of Persia a message was revealed to Daniel, who was named Belteshazzar; and the message was true and one of great conflict, but he understood the message and had an understanding of the vision."

Daniel 10:13: "But the prince of the kingdom of Persia was withstanding me for twenty-one days; then behold, Michael, one of the chief princes, came to help me, for I had been left there with the kings of Persia."

Daniel 10:21: "However, I will tell you what is inscribed in the writing of truth. Yet there is no one who stands firmly with me against these forces except Michael your prince."

151 Revelation 12:7–9: "And there was war in heaven, Michael and his angels waging war with the dragon. The dragon and his angels waged war, and they were not strong enough, and there was no longer a place found for them in heaven. And the great dragon was thrown down, the serpent of old who is called the devil and Satan, who deceives the whole world; he was thrown down to the earth, and his angels were thrown down with him."

152 Luke 1:19: "The angel answered and said to him, 'I am Gabriel, who stands in the presence of God, and I have been sent to speak to you and to bring you this good news'."

Luke 1:26–27: "Now in the sixth month the angel Gabriel was sent from God to a city in Galilee called Nazareth, to a virgin engaged to a man whose name was Joseph, of the descendants of David; and the virgin's name was Mary."

153 Genesis 6:1–4: "Now it came about, when men began to multiply on the face of the land, and daughters were born to them, that the sons of God saw that the daughters of men were beautiful; and they took wives for themselves, whomever they chose. Then the Lord said, 'My Spirit shall not strive with man forever, because he also is flesh; nevertheless his days shall be one hundred and twenty years.' The Nephilim were on the earth in those days, and also afterward, when the sons of God came in to the daughters of men, and they bore children to them. Those were the mighty men who were of old, men of renown."

154 Revelation 12:7–9: "And there was war in heaven, Michael and his angels waging war with the dragon. The dragon and his angels waged war, and they were not strong enough, and there was no longer a place found for them in heaven. And the great dragon was thrown down, the serpent of old who is called the devil and Satan, who deceives the whole world; he was thrown down to the earth, and his angels were thrown down with him."

ENDNOTES

155 The Koren Jerusalem Bible. (Jerusalem: Koren Publishers, 2009). Genesis 6:2.
156 *The Torah: Translation and Commentary.* (Brooklyn, NY: Metsudah, 2009). Genesis 6:2.
157 Jewish Publication Society. *The Holy Scriptures According to the Masoretic Text.* (Philadelphia: The Jewish Publication Society of America, 1917). Genesis 6:2.
158 The Living Bible: Paraphrased. (Wheaton, IL: Tyndale House Publishers, 1971). Genesis 6:2.
159 Charles Kahane. *The Torah: A Modern Commentary.* (New York: Hebrew Publishing Co., 1963). Genesis 6:2.
160 Lancelot C. L. Brenton, *The Septuagint Version of the Old Testament, with an English Translation.* (London: Samuel Bagster & Sons, 1851). Genesis 6:2.
161 Ibid.
162 Tractate Kallah Rabbati 3:9, Yoma 67b:7, Bava Batra 15b:12, Bava Batra 16a:3, Midrash Tanchuma, Balak 2:1, Midrash Tanchuma Buber, Appendix to Chukat 1:1, Pirkei DeRabbi Eliezer 7:6, Targum Jonathan on Genesis 6:4, Sifrei Devarim 306:37 on Job 1:6.
163 Rashi on Genesis 6:2, Rashi on Genesis 6:4, Rashi on Job 1:6, Minchat Shai on Genesis 6:2.
164 Reshit Chokhmah, the Zohar.
165 Rabbi Steinsaltz commentary on Job 1:6, 2:1.
166 Jewish English Torah, opensiddur.org, Digitization: Sefaria.org, License: CC-BY-SA.
167 Modernized Tanakh—Based on JPS 1917, Edited by Adam Cohn, modernizedtanakh.blogspot.com, Digitization: Sefaria.org, License: CC-BY.
168 Job 38:7." Ibn Ezra commentary, *Sefaria*, www.sefaria.org/Job.38.7?lang=bi&with=Ibn+Ezra&lang2=en. Accessed June 11, 2024.
169 Alberino, *Birthright*.
170 Ibid.
171 The Lamp and The Dawn, biblehub.com/sermons/auth/thomson/the_lamp_and_the_dawn.htm. Accessed May 30, 2024.
172 Jamieson, Fausset & Brown. "Commentary on Revelation 2 by Jamieson, Fausset & Brown." Blue Letter Bible, Blue Letter Bible, February 19, 1970, www.blueletterbible.org/Comm/jfb/Rev/Rev_002.cfm.
173 "Revelation 2—the Expositor's Greek Testament - Bible Commentaries." StudyLight.Org, www.studylight.org/commentaries/eng/egt/revelation-2.html. Accessed 30 May 2024.
174 Revelation 2 Pulpit Commentary, biblehub.com/commentaries/pulpit/revelation/2.htm. Accessed May 30, 2024.
175 "Revelation 22:16—Bible Verse Meaning and Commentary." Bible Study Tools, www.biblestudytools.com/commentaries/gills-exposition-of-the-bible/revelation-22-16.html. Accessed May 30, 2024.
176 Alberino, *Birthright*.
177 Ψαλμὸς 8—Psalms—the Septuagint: LXX." Ψαλμὸς 8—Psalms—The Septuagint: LXX, www.septuagint.bible/-/psalmos-8. Accessed May 30, 2024.
178 "The Greek Old Testament (Septuagint)." 1 [For the End, Concerning the Wine-Presses, a Psalm of David.] 2 O Lord, Our L... PSALMS / ΨΑΛΜΟΙ8 - Bilingual Septuagint, www.ellopos.net/elpenor/greek-texts/septuagint/chapter.asp?book=24&page=8. Accessed May 30, 2024.

ENDNOTES

179 Saul Sadka, "The Lubavitcher Rebbe as a God." *Haaretz.com*, February 10, 2007, www.haaretz.com/2007-02-11/ty-article/the-lubavitcher-rebbe-as-a-god/0000017f-dc1a-df9c-a17f-fe1aa9c40000.

180 "The Rebbe Is God Says Chabad Messianic Jew | News in Judaism." YouTube, June 30, 2023, www.youtube.com/watch?v=CRdzSl-M9JQ.

181 David Berger, *The Rebbe, the Messiah, and the Scandal of Orthodox Indifference*. (Oxford University Press, 2021).

182 Michael S. Heiser, *The Unseen Realm: Recovering the Supernatural Worldview of the Bible*. (Bellingham, WA: Lexham Press, 2015.)

183 John H. Walton, *The Lost World of Genesis One: Ancient Cosmology and the Origins Debate*. (Downers Grove, IL: IVP Academic, 2009).

184 Aryeh Kaplan, *The Living Nach: Early Prophets* (Brooklyn, NY: Moznaim Publishing, 1994), Kaplan's commentary often links Ezekiel's angelology (e.g., the *Chayot* and *Ophanim* in Ezekiel 1) to Daniel's "Watchers" (*Irin* in Aramaic) and "Holy Ones" (*Qaddishin*) in Daniel 4:14, emphasizing a structured celestial hierarchy rooted in Jewish mystical tradition.)

185 Michael S. Heiser and Gordon Greenhill, *The Unseen Realm: Recovering the Supernatural Worldview of the Bible* (Bellingham, WA: Lexham Press, 2024)..

186 Ibid.

187 Ibid.

188 Abraham Ibn Ezra, *Commentary on Psalms 82:1*. In *The Book of Psalms with Ibn Ezra's Commentary*. Sefaria, accessed April 4, 2025. https://www.sefaria.org/Psalms.82.1?lang=bi&with=Ibn%20Ezra&lang2=en.

189 Heiser, *Unseen Realm*.

190 "And Melchizedek king of Salem brought out bread and wine; now he was a priest of God Most High. He blessed him and said, 'Blessed be Abram of God Most High, Possessor of heaven and earth; And blessed be God Most High, Who has delivered your enemies into your hand.' He gave him a tenth of all" (Genesis 14:18–20).

191 "The Lord says to my Lord: 'Sit at My right hand Until I make Your enemies a footstool for Your feet.' The Lord will stretch forth Your strong scepter from Zion, saying, 'Rule in the midst of Your enemies'" (Psalm 110:1–2).

192 Chuck Missler reiterated this principle throughout his teachings, including *Learn the Bible in 24 Hours* (Koinonia House). While the exact phrase appears in multiple formats, it reflects a consistent hermeneutic theme in his work: Biblical anomalies point to profound truths.

193 Heiser, *Unseen Realm*.

194 "For if God did not spare angels when they sinned, but cast them into hell and committed them to pits of darkness, reserved for judgment" (2 Peter 2:4).

195 "And angels who did not keep their own domain, but abandoned their proper abode, He has kept in eternal bonds under darkness for the judgment of the great day" (Jude 1:6).

196 R. H. Charles, trans. *The Book of Enoch*. (Oxford: Clarendon Press, 1912). Accessed April 4, 2025. https://www.ccel.org/c/charles/otpseudepig/enoch/ENOCH_1.HTM.

197 R. H. Charles, trans. *The Book of Jubilees*, or *The Little Genesis* (London: Adam and Charles Black, 1902).

ENDNOTES

198 Geza Vermes, *The Complete Dead Sea Scrolls in English* (London: Penguin Books, 1997).

199 "Therefore the woman ought to have a symbol of authority on her head, because of the angels" (1 Corinthians 11:10).

200 Tertullian, *On the Veiling of Virgins*. Trans. S. Thelwall. In *Ante-Nicene Fathers*, Vol. 4, edited by Alexander Roberts and James Donaldson, 27–38. (Edinburgh: T & T Clark, 1885).

201 "And angels who did not keep their own domain, but abandoned their proper abode, He has kept in eternal bonds under darkness for the judgment of the great day" (Jude 1:6).

202 "But Michael the archangel, when he disputed with the devil and argued about the body of Moses, did not dare pronounce against him a railing judgment, but said, 'The Lord rebuke you!'" (Jude 1:9).

203 R. H. Charles, trans. *The Assumption of Moses*. In *The Apocrypha and Pseudepigrapha of the Old Testament*, Vol. 2, edited by R. H. Charles, 407–424. (Oxford: Clarendon Press, 1913).

204 Matt Slick, "Did Paul Quote Pagan Philosophers?" *Christian Apologetics & Research Ministry*, June 10, 2016. Accessed April 4, 2025. https://carm.org/defending-the-faith/did-paul-quote-pagan-philosophers/.

205 Chaim Vital, *Sha'ar HaGilgulim (Gate of Reincarnations)*. Trans. Yitzhak Bar Chaim. (Jerusalem: Yeshivat HaMekubalim, 1999).

206 Raziel HaMalakh, *efer Raziel HaMalakh (The Book of Raziel)*. Trans. Steve Savedow. (York Beach, ME: Weiser Books, 2000).

207 Peter Schäfer, *The Origins of Jewish Mysticism* (Tübingen: Mohr Siebeck, 2009).

208 "And behold, an angel of the Lord suddenly appeared and a light shone in the cell; and he struck Peter's side and woke him up, saying, 'Get up quickly.' And his chains fell off his hands" (Acts 12:7).

209 "He took curds and milk and the calf which he had prepared, and placed it before them; and he was standing by them under the tree as they ate" (Genesis 18:8).

210 "But the prince of the kingdom of Persia was withstanding me for twenty-one days; then behold, Michael, one of the chief princes, came to help me, for I had been left there with the kings of Persia" (Daniel 10:13).

"Then he said, 'Do you understand why I came to you? But I shall now return to fight against the prince of Persia; so I am going forth, and behold, the prince of Greece is about to come'" (Daniel 10:20).

211 "The stars fought from heaven, From their courses they fought against Sisera" (Judges 5:20).

212 "And his tail swept away a third of the stars of heaven and threw them to the earth. And the dragon stood before the woman who was about to give birth, so that when she gave birth he might devour her child" (Revelation 12:4).

213 Chuck Missler, *Esther Series*. Koinonia House. Accessed April 4, 2025. https://www.youtube.com/playlist?list=PLwUkm-o4yd-_eupY6DiP1N-xwm_X-8TGx.

214 Glen A. Larson, creator. *Battlestar Galactica*. Performed by Lorne Greene, Richard Hatch, Dirk Benedict, and Jane Seymour. (Universal Television, 1978–1979).

215 Michael S. Heiser, "Heiser's Laws for Bible Study." Dr. Michael Heiser's Blog, July 16, 2011. Accessed April 4, 2025. https://drmsh.com/heisers-laws-for-bible-study/.

216 Heiser, *Unseen Realm*.

ENDNOTES

217 Alberino, *Birthright*.
218 Heiser, *Unseen Realm*.
219 Alberino, *Birthright*.
220 "the son of Enosh, the son of Seth, the son of Adam, the son of God" (Luke 3:38).
221 בן מימון. משנה תורה (י״ד חזקה) לרבנו משה בן מימון
 Bet ha-Hotsa'at ha-'Ivri, היברו פובלישינג קומפני, 1967.
222 "Halakhah, Mishneh Torah." Sefaria, www.sefaria.org/texts/Halakhah/Mishneh%20 Torah. Accessed June 18, 2024.
223 "The Celestial Hierarchy" by Pseudo-Dionysius the Areopagite.
224 "The appearance of the wheels and their workmanship was like sparkling beryl, and all four of them had the same form, their appearance and workmanship being as if one wheel were within another" (Ezekiel 1:16).
225 Greg Mottola, director. *Paul*. Written by Simon Pegg and Nick Frost. Performed by Simon Pegg, Nick Frost, Seth Rogen, Jason Bateman, and Kristen Wiig. (Universal Pictures, 2011).
226 Alberino, *Birthright*.
227 Haemunot Vehadeot, Sefaria, www.sefaria.org/HaEmunot_veHaDeot. Accessed June 18, 2024.
228 Leon Roth, *The Guide for the Perplexed by Moses Maimonides* (Hutchinson's University Library, 1948).
229 Gavin Michal, "Maimonides Calls the Belief in Angels an 'Evil and Blind Foolishness'," Kotzk Blog, March 25, 2023. Accessed April 4, 2025. https://www.kotzkblog.com/2023/03/423-maimonides-calls-belief-in-angels.html.
230 Maimonides' own writings: In the "Guide for the Perplexed" (Moreh Nevukhim), Maimonides frequently cites and relies upon the teachings of Aristotle and other Greek philosophers. For example: "The greatest philosopher, our teacher, has stated..." (referring to Aristotle) - Guide 2:22, "This is the word of the prophets and also the word of the philosophers who came later..." (linking Jewish prophecy to Greek philosophy) - Guide 2:37, Shmuel Ibn Tibbon's introduction to his Hebrew translation of the Guide notes Maimonides' reliance on Aristotelian thought., Joseph Ibn Aknin, a Jewish poet, praised Maimonides as "the analytic philosopher who knows Aristotle completely." Rabbi Hasdai Crescas in "Or Hashem" claimed Maimonides "absorbed their (Greek philosophers') views excessively." Rabbi Yosef Shalom del Medigo in "Novelot Homadot" stated Maimonides was "captivated by the exterior beauty of Greek philosophy." "Maimonides drew from the rich tradition of Aristotelianism." Isadore Twersky, *Introduction to the Code of Maimonides: (Mishneh Torah)* (Yale University Press, 2010). "He (Maimonides) was an avid student of Greek philosophy, especially Aristotle." Kenneth Seeskin, *Jewish Philosophy in a Secular Age* (State University of New York Press, 1990).
231 Isadore Twersky, *Rabad of Posquières: A Twelfth-Century Talmudist* (Varda Books, 2001). *The Rivash: Responsa* edited and translated by Eliezer David Jaffe, The writings of Nachmanides, including his critiques of Maimonides' philosophy and legal interpretations found in his commentaries and disputations.
232 Nachmanides (Ramban) on Genesis 18:1: In his commentary on this verse, Nachmanides directly addresses Maimonides' view that angels cannot have physical bodies and therefore

ENDNOTES

must be understood figuratively or as prophetic visions. Nachmanides argues against Maimonides' interpretation and asserts that the Torah clearly depicts angels as taking on physical bodies to interact with humans in the real world. Further, "Ramban ends by throwing down the gauntlet and declaring Maimonides' position to be out of bounds no matter how it is read: 'Such words contradict scripture. It is forbidden to listen to them, all the more to believe them!'" "Torah Narratives with Angels Never Actually Happened: Heretical or Sublime?" TheTorah.Com, www.thetorah.com/article/torah-narratives-with-angels-never-actually-happened-heretical-or-sublime. Accessed June 18, 2024.

233 "Emden questioned the *Guide for the Perplexed*, which he found to contain heretical tendencies; he did not believe that Maimonides was its author." *Jacob Emden*, www.jewishvirtuallibrary.org/jacob-emden. Accessed June 18, 2024.

234 Thomas Aquinas was significantly influenced by Maimonides' philosophical approach. Aquinas adopted a similar stance in interpreting biblical descriptions of God and angels. He argued that human language is inadequate to fully describe divine realities, and thus, many biblical descriptions should be understood metaphorically. *Maimonides and Aquinas on Divine Attributes the Importance...*, epublications.marquette.edu/cgi/viewcontent.cgi?article=1786&context=phil_fac. Accessed June 18, 2024.

235 "Question 1. the Nature and Extent of Sacred Doctrine." *Summa Theologiae: The Nature and Extent of Sacred Doctrine (Prima Pars, Q. 1)*, www.newadvent.org/summa/1001.htm. Accessed June 18, 2024.

236 Matthew Walsh, "Angels Associated with Israel in the Dead Sea Scrolls," MacSphere, January 1, 1970, macsphere.mcmaster.ca/handle/11375/19901.

237 Michael R. Jost, "The Liturgical Communion of the Yaḥad with the Angels." Brill, July 20, 2021, brill.com/view/journals/dsd/29/1/article-p52_3.xml?language=en.

238 Chagigah 13b: The Talmud describes the Seraphim as having six wings, aligning with the description in Isaiah 6:2. "Each one had six wings: with two he covered his face, with two he covered his feet, and with two he flew" (Chagigah 13b). Bava Metzia 86b: This passage discusses the three angels who visited Abraham, each with a specific mission. "Michael came to bring the tidings to Sarah [of Isaac's birth]; Raphael, to heal Abraham; and Gabriel, to overturn Sodom" (Bava Metzia 86b), Sanhedrin 95b: The Talmud describes the appearance of angels in human form, as seen in the story of the three angels who visited Abraham. "Michael, Gabriel, and Raphael appeared to Abraham in the form of men."

239 Rashi's commentary on Cherubim is particularly notable in his interpretation of Genesis 3:24, where Cherubim are described as guarding the entrance to the Garden of Eden with a flaming sword. Rashi interprets these as "angels of destruction" (מלאכי חבלה) who prevent Adam and Eve from re-entering the Garden of Eden. This interpretation aligns with a more literal understanding of Cherubim as powerful, fearsome beings tasked with divine protection and enforcement. (Rashi on Genesis 3:24), "with two he would cover his feet for modesty, so as not to bare his entire body before his Creator. And in Tanhuma (Emor 8), I saw that the feet were covered because they are like the sole of the foot of a calf, in order not to remind Israel of the sin of the golden calf" (Rashi on Isaiah 6:2).

240 Mika Ahuvia, *On My Right Michael, on My Left Gabriel: Angels in Ancient Jewish Culture* (University of California Press, 2021).

ENDNOTES

241 C. S. Lewis, "Religion and Rocketry," *The World's Last Night and Other Essays* (New York: Harcourt, Brace and Co., 1960).

242 Tony Ganzer, "Why Catholics Should Think about 'Aliens'." Faith Full Catholic Podcast, December 26, 2022. Accessed April 4, 2025. https://www.faithfullpod.com/why-catholics-should-think-about-aliens/.

243 Paul Thigpen, "Aliens and the Catholic Church," *Catholic Answers Magazine*, December 4, 2024. Accessed April 4, 2025. https://www.catholic.com/magazine/online-edition/aliens-and-the-catholic-church.

244 "Race," *Encyclopaedia Britannica*. Accessed April 4, 2025. https://www.britannica.com/topic/race-human.

245 Mary Fairchild, "How Many Religions Are There in the World?" Learn Religions, June 13, 2024. Accessed April 4, 2025. https://www.learnreligions.com/how-many-religions-are-there-in-the-world-5114658.

246 Jonathan Merritt, "What C. S. Lewis Thought About Space Exploration and Aliens," Religion News Service, November 25, 2014. Accessed April 4, 2025. https://religionnews.com/2014/11/25/c-s-lewis-thought-space-exploration-aliens/.

247 Larry Norman, "UFO." Track 3 on In Another Land. (Solid Rock Records, 1976). Accessed April 4, 2025. https://larrynorman.bandcamp.com/track/ufo-9.

248 Tzvi. "UFOs and Jews Living on a Different Planet." Aish.Com, May 23,2021, aish.com/ufos-and-jews-living-on-a-different-planet/.

249 Answers in Genesis. "About Answers in Genesis." Accessed April 4, 2025. https://answersingenesis.org/about/.

250 "Alien Life." Answers in Genesis. Accessed June 13, 2024. answersingenesis.org/astronomy/alien-life/.

251 Rabbi Braham David, "A Jewish Take on the Search for Extraterrestrial Life." *Sinai and Synapses*, November 26, 2024. Accessed April 4, 2025. https://sinaiandsynapses.org/content/a-jewish-take-on-the-search-for-extraterrestrial-life/.

252 Ibid.

253 1 Enoch 6–8 (angels rebel against God by lusting after human women and teaching forbidden knowledge), Jubilees 5:6 (the angels who sinned with human women are described as having "transgressed the commandment of the Lord"), Genesis 6:2, Mo'ed Katan 28a (the Angel of Death is portrayed as having a degree of discretion in carrying out its duties), Devarim Rabbah 3:12 (the fallen angel Samael, identified with Satan and the Angel of Death, exhibits the ability to act independently attempting to hinder Moses), Chagigah 16a. (There is a debate between Rabbi Yehoshua ben Levi and Elijah the Prophet regarding whether angels have free will. Rabbi Yehoshua ben Levi argues that angels do not have free will, while Elijah asserts that they do). The Zohar on Genesis (Here, Samael is associated with the serpent in the Garden of Eden. In this interpretation, Samael's role in tempting Adam and Eve to eat the forbidden fruit is seen as a manifestation of his independent agency), Rashi on Genesis 6:2 (Ramban argues that the fallen angels described in the Book of Enoch did possess free will and chose to sin by lusting after human women, writing "Another explanation of בני האלהים is that these were princely angels who came as messengers from God: they, too, intermingled with them (the daughters of men)."

254 "For Christ also died for sins once for all, the just for the unjust, so that He might bring us to God, having been put to death in the flesh, but made alive in the spirit;

ENDNOTES

in which also He went and made proclamation to the spirits now in prison, who once were disobedient, when the patience of God kept waiting in the days of Noah, during the construction of the ark, in which a few, that is, eight persons, were brought safely through the water" (1 Peter 3:18–20).

255 "Chuck Missler - 1 Peter (Session 4) Chapter 3." YouTube, March 15, 2023, www.youtube.com/watch?v=2QFAYXEPBOo.

256 The notes on 1 Peter 3:19 in the classic Scofield Study Bible teach that the "spirits in prison" refer to fallen angels. Many reprinted editions contain these notes. The Spirit Filled Life Bible (Thomas Nelson Publishers): The study notes on 1 Peter 3:19 in this Bible also interpret the "spirits" as fallen angels imprisoned after the days of Noah. Dialogue with Trypho (circa AD 155–167). An early church father, Justin taught that the "spirits in prison" were the fallen angels who sinned in Genesis 6. A Treatise on the Soul (circa AD 210). Tertullian, another early father, echoed the view that 1 Peter refers to Christ preaching to imprisoned fallen angels. Commentaries from a dispensationalist perspective like the Bible Knowledge Commentary (Walvoord/Zuck) have promoted this angelic interpretation.

257 Clement of Alexandria (circa AD150–215 AD): In his work "The Stromata," Clement suggests that Christ's preaching in Hades gave all souls, including angels, the opportunity for repentance and salvation. Origen (circa AD 184–253), in his work, "Contra Celsum," argued that the redemptive work of Christ extended to all rational beings, including demons and fallen angels. Gregory of Nyssa (circa AD 335–395), in his catechetical orations, speculated that fallen angels may have a path of repentance through Christ.

258 Thomas Talbott, *The Inescapable Love of God*. (Cascade Books, 2014).

259 "And the devil who deceived them was thrown into the lake of fire and brimstone, where the beast and the false prophet are also; and they will be tormented day and night forever and ever" (Revelation 20:10).

260 " 'Curse Meroz,' said the angel of the Lord, 'Utterly curse its inhabitants; Because they did not come to the help of the Lord, To the help of the Lord against the warriors," (Judges 5:23).

261 Alberino, *Birthright*.

262 "Is There Life on Other Planets? The Jewish View on Ufos, Aliens and Extraterrestrial Intelligence—Questions & Answers," www.chabad.org/library/article_cdo/aid/3012/jewish/Is-There-Life-on-Other-Planets.htm. Accessed June 13, 2024.

263 Babylonian Talmud, Shevuot 36a; Moed Katan 16a. See also Rashi on Judges 5:23.

264 Aryeh Kaplan, *The Living Nach: Early Prophets*. (Brooklyn, NY: Moznaim, 1994).

265 Rabbi Benjamin Blech, "Judaism and Life on Other Planets." Aish, February 23, 2017. Accessed April 4, 2025. https://aish.com/judaism-and-life-on-other-planets/.

266 Hasdai Crescas, *Ohr Hashem (The Light of the Lord)*. Trans. Harry A. Wolfson (Cambridge, MA: Harvard University Press, 1929).

267 Alberino, *Birthright*.

268 "Rashi on Judges 5:23." *Tanakh: The Holy Scriptures*. Sefaria. Accessed April 4, 2025. https://www.sefaria.org/Judges.5.23?lang=bi&with=Rashi&lang2=en.

269 Central Intelligence Agency, "Flying Saucers UFO Reports." CIA FOIA Electronic Reading Room. Accessed April 4, 2025. https://www.cia.gov/readingroom/document/cia-rdp81r00560r000100010002-9.

ENDNOTES

270 Henry George Liddell; Robert Scott, *A Greek-English Lexicon at the Perseus Project*.
271 A. P. Hatzes, et al., "Long-lived, Long-period Radial Velocity Variations in Aldebaran: A Planetary Companion and Stellar Activity." *Astronomy & Astrophysics*. May 15, 2015. 580.
272 Vril Aldebaran, *1917 Extraterrestrials Messages to Maria Orsic and the Birth of the First German-Made UFO*.
273 Axel Stoll, *Hochtechnologie im Dritten Reich* (*High Tech in the Third Reich*) (in German). (Rottenburg: Kopp Verlag, 2004). p. 111ff. ISBN 978-3930219858.)
274 P. Cori, *The Sirian Revelations: Galactic Prophecies for the Awakening Human*. (North Atlantic Books, 2007).
275 B. Meier, *The Pleiadian Mission: A Time of Awareness*. (Wild Flower Press, 2004).
276 H. P. Blavatsky, *The Secret Doctrine* (The Theosophical Publishing House, 1888).)
277 R. Bauval and G. Hancock, *The Message of the Sphinx: A Quest for the Hidden Legacy of Mankind* (Crown Publishing, 1996).
278 *The Biggest Secret*, 1999.
279 *Discussions in Egyptology*, volume 13, and *The Orion Mystery*, 1994.
280 Jeanette Kazmierczak, "NASA's TESS Discovers Planetary System's Second Earth-Size World." NASA, January 10, 2023. Accessed April 4, 2025. https://www.nasa.gov/universe/nasas-tess-discovers-planetary-systems-second-earth-size-world/.
281 "NASA Telescope Reveals Largest Batch of Earth-Size, Habitable-Zone Planets Around Single Star," NASA, February 22, 2017. Accessed April 4, 2025. https://www.nasa.gov/news-release/nasa-telescope-reveals-largest-batch-of-earth-size-habitable-zone-planets-around-single-star/.
282 Charles McNeal, "@truthtold24." X (formerly Twitter). Accessed April 4, 2025. https://x.com/truthtold24.
283 Douglas Charles, "Alleged Air Force Whistleblower Claims Aliens Are About To Reveal Themselves," BroBible, October 1, 2024. Accessed April 4, 2025. https://brobible.com/culture/article/air-force-whistleblower-aliens-reveal-themselves/.
284 Ibid.
285 Charles Benjamin McNeal, Acclimate The Public NOW. Accessed April 4, 2025. https://www.acclimatenow.com/.
286 Emily Walla, "Powerful Particles and Tugging Tides May Affect Extraterrestrial Life," *University of Arizona News*, April 16, 2019. Accessed April 4, 2025. https://news.arizona.edu/news/powerful-particles-and-tugging-tides-may-affect-extraterrestrial-life.
287 Jacques F. Vallée, *Dimensions: A Casebook of Alien Contact* (Chicago: Contemporary Books, 1988).
288 See Isaiah 14:12–15; Ezekiel 28:12–17; Luke 10:18; and Revelation 12:7–9. See also Augustine of Hippo, *The City of God* (Book XII, Ch. 9), Thomas Aquinas, *Summa Theologica* (I, Q. 63, Art. 3), and Catechism of the Catholic Church (CCC 391–395)).
289 See 1 Enoch 15:8–12, Jubilees 10:1–14, Philo of Alexandria (*On the Giants*, 6–8), Justin Martyr—*Second Apology* (5), Babylonian Talmud—Berakhot 6a, The Midrash—Bereshit Rabbah 7:5, Augustine of Hippo—*City of God* (Book XV, Ch. 23), The Vilna Gaon on Sifra DeTzniuta, Dr. Michael S. Heiser—*The Unseen Realm* (2015), The Jewish Encyclopedia, 1906.
290 https://www.sefaria.org/I_Samuel.16.14?lang=bi&with=Steinsaltz&lang2=en.

ENDNOTES

291 "1 Samuel 28:12—Verse-by-Verse Bible Commentary," StudyLight.org. Accessed April 4, 2025. https://www.studylight.org/commentary/1-samuel/28-12.html.
292 John Wesley, *Wesley's Notes on the Bible*. Accessed April 4, 2025. https://www.studylight.org/commentaries/wen.html.
293 Ibid.
294 Matthew Henry, "1 Samuel 28." *Matthew Henry Commentary on the Whole Bible (Complete)*. Accessed April 4, 2025. https://www.biblestudytools.com/commentaries/matthew-henry-complete/1-samuel/28.html.
295 Sjirk Bajema, "1 Samuel 28—The Devilish Vice Becomes the Lord's Device." *Christian Library*, 2001. Accessed April 4, 2025.
296 John E. Mack, *Abduction: Human Encounters with Aliens* (New York: Scribner's, 1994).
297 David M. Jacobs, *Walking Among Us: The Alien Plan to Control Humanity* (San Francisco: Disinformation Books, 2015).
298 *The Waterboy*, Tom Shadyac, director. Performed by Adam Sandler, Kathy Bates, Henry Winkler, and Fairuza Balk (Touchstone Pictures, 1998).
299 Lewis, *Religion and Rocketry*.
300 Vallée, *Messengers of Deception*.
301 Graham Hancock, *Supernatural: Meetings with the Ancient Teachers of Mankind* (London: Century, 2005), p.264.
302 Kenneth Johnson, creator, *V*. Performed by Marc Singer, Faye Grant, Jane Badler, and Michael Ironside. (NBC, 1983–1985).
303 "Channeling the 9th Dimensional Pleiadian Collective—Interview with Extra-Dimensionals." YouTube, November 11, 2023, www.youtube.com/watch?v=xS-UKlpguQk.
304 "A Conversation with a Real Alien—Lacerta Files Part 1," YouTube video, 1:02:45. Accessed April 4, 2025. https://www.youtube.com/watch?v=QYn84QTOGEw.
305 "L1 ~ Liquid Light Frequency Infusion Meditation ~ Raise Your Vibration - Sirian Starseed," YouTube, February 1, 2024, www.youtube.com/watch?v=RDx3qGPZqng&list=PLgpqdaSnWe6jdBh6-CXDOM_OHEgUjmlTX.
306 May Energy Activation // Channeled Message from the Arcturian Council." YouTube, May 12, 2024, www.youtube.com/watch?v=XDbG6omhMFc.
307 "Channeling & Healing from Solomon, a White Dragon from Orion." YouTube, December 18, 2019, www.youtube.com/watch?v=41nPXlbcw7Y.
308 "Lightworker Gateway: Channeled Messages from Zeta Reticuli and Crystal Grid." YouTube, September 29, 2023.
309 Diane Stein, *Essential Reiki: A Complete Guide to an Ancient Healing Art* (Crossing Press, 2000).
310 "International Association of Reiki Professionals IARP," Reiki, www.iarpreiki.org/. Accessed June 14, 2024.
311 www.reiki.org/. Accessed June 14, 2024.
312 Ibid.
313 William Rand, "What Is Holy Fire® Reiki?" Reiki, March 7, 2019, www.reiki.org/what-holy-fire-reiki.
314 "Channeled Angelic Reiki/W Light Language." *YouTube*, YouTube, 27 May 2022, www.youtube.com/watch?v=yLYZAXDw7aQ.

ENDNOTES

315 "Reiki to Receive Archangel Michael's Blessings Guidance & Protection." YouTube, August 27, 2017. www.youtube.com/watch?v=jZwsOiLyUv0.
316 "Reiki with the Energy of the Pleiades." YouTube, December 23 2019. www.youtube.com/watch?v=fLURZswriq4.
317 "Aphrodite Empowerment with High Heart Activation." YouTube, June 24 2018. www.youtube.com/watch?v=4AC0GQJDN9Y.
318 "Simple powerfu• Reiki with Ascended Masters." YouTube, July 10, 2021, www.youtube.com/watch?v=D-QOCwemHmo.
319 "Ce5 et Contact and Consciousness Conference," drstevengreer.ticketspice.com/ce5-et-contact-and-consciousness-conference. Accessed June 14, 2024.
320 Alberino, *Birthright*.
321 "'Star Trek v: The Final Frontier' Quotes." *Star Trek V: The Final Frontier* Quotes, Movie Quotes—Movie Quotes.Com.
322 *Star Trek V: The Final Frontier*. Star Trek V: The Final Frontier Quotes, www.quotes.net/movies/star_trek_v:_the_final_frontier_10890. Accessed 14 June 2024.
323 John Daniel Davidson, *Pagan America: The Decline of Christianity and the Dark Age to Come* (Regnery Publishing, 2024).
324 Jacques F. Vallée, *Dimensions: A Casebook of Alien Contact* (Chicago: Contemporary Books, 1988).
325 David Icke, *The Biggest Secret* (Lexington Volunteer Recording Unit, 2001).
326 Ibid.
327 Graham Hancock, *Supernatural: Meetings with the Ancient Teachers of Mankind* (London: Century, 2005).
328 Giorgio Samorini, *Animals and Psychedelics: The Natural World and the Instinct to Alter Consciousness*. trans. Tami Calliope (Rochester, VT: Park Street Press, 2002).
329 Michael J Winkelman, *Shamanism: A Biopsychosocial Paradigm of Consciousness and Healing*. 2nd ed. (Santa Barbara, CA: Praeger, 2010).
330 Richard J. Castillo," Culture, Trance, and the Mind-Brain," *Anthropology of Consciousness* 6, no. 1 (1995): 17–34. https://doi.org/10.1525/ac.1995.6.1.17.
331 "You shall not allow a sorceress to live" (Exodus 22:18).
332 Rick Strassman, *DMT: The Spirit Molecule: A Doctor's Revolutionary Research into the Biology of Near-Death and Mystical Experiences* (Rochester, VT: Park Street Press, 2001).
333 Karla Turner, *Taken: Inside the Alien-Human Abduction Agenda* (Kelt Works, 1994).
334 C. S. Lewis, *God in the Dock: Essays on Theology and Ethics*, Ed. Walter Hooper (Eerdmans Publishing Co., 1970). Specifically, see the essay "Myth Became Fact."
335 Helena Petrovna Blavatsky, *The Secret Doctrine: The Synthesis of Science, Religion, and Philosophy*. (1888) Vol. 2, pp. 195–351.
336 "…and said to Him, 'If You are the Son of God, throw Yourself down; for it is written, 'He will give His angels orders concerning You'; And 'On their hands they will lift You up, So that You do not strike Your foot against a stone'" (Matthew 4:6).
337 "For such men are false apostles, deceitful workers, disguising themselves as apostles of Christ. No wonder, for even Satan disguises himself as an angel of light. Therefore it is not surprising if his servants also disguise themselves as servants of righteousness, whose end will be according to their deeds" (2 Corinthians 11:13–15).
338 Charles Q Choi, "Did Another Advanced Species Exist on Earth Before Humans?"

ENDNOTES

     NBC News, April 30, 2018. Accessed April 4, 2025. https://www.nbcnews.com/mach/science/did-another-advanced-species-exist-earth-humans-ncna869856.

339 Karl Shuker, "A Bipedal Snake in the Garden of Eden? What Did the Pre-Cursed Serpent Look Like?" ShukerNature (blog), March 9, 2011. Accessed April 4, 2025. https://karlshuker.blogspot.com/2011/03/bipedal-snake-in-garden-of-eden-what.html.

340 Heiser, *Unseen Realm*.

341 Ibid.

342 Ibid.

343 Ibid.

344 Alberino, *Birthright*.

345 Heiser, *Unseen Realm*.

346 Ibid.

347 Dovid Rosenfeld, "What Was the Serpent?" Aish.com, March 9, 2011. Accessed April 4, 2025. https://aish.com/what-was-the-serpent/.

348 *Pirkei de-Rabbi Eliezer*, Trans. Gerald Friedlander (London: Kegan Paul, Trench, Trübner & Co., 1916).

349 Zohar, Bereshit A, verses 437–457. Accessed April 4, 2025. https://www.zohar.com/zohar/Bereshit%20A/verses/437-457.

350 Alberino, *Birthright*.

351 Derek P. Gilbert, *The Great Inception: Satan's Psyops from Eden to Armageddon*. (Crane, MO: Defender, 2017).

352 Ibid.

353 Ibid.

354 Ibid.

355 Gidon Rothstein, 'Ezekiel—Chapter 34." OU Torah, n.d. Accessed April 4, 2025. https://outorah.org/p/3714/.

356 Joseph Benson, "Commentary on Ezekiel 34." In *Benson's Commentary of the Old and New Testaments*. 1857. Accessed April 4, 2025. https://www.studylight.org/commentaries/eng/rbc/ezekiel-34.html.

357 Charles J. Ellicott, "Ezekiel 34." In *Ellicott's Commentary for English Readers*. Accessed April 4, 2025. https://www.kingjamesbibleonline.org/Ezekiel-34_Commentary-Ellicott/.

358 Matthew Poole, "Commentary on Ezekiel 34." In *Matthew Poole's Commentary on the Holy Bible*. Accessed April 4, 2025. https://biblehub.com/commentaries/poole/ezekiel/34.htm.

359 "Then he said to me, 'Do not be afraid, Daniel, for from the first day that you set your heart on understanding this and on humbling yourself before your God, your words were heard, and I have come in response to your words. But the prince of the kingdom of Persia was withstanding me for twenty-one days; then behold, Michael, one of the chief princes, came to help me, for I had been left there with the kings of Persia'" (Daniel 10:12–13).

360 Jean Bosquet, "Lizard People's Catacomb City Hunted," *Los Angeles Times*, January 29, 1934. Accessed April 4, 2025. https://documents.latimes.com/jan-29-1934-lizard-people/.

361 Calvin Dobbins, "The Lizard People of Los Angeles Real or Fantasy?" *Los Angeleno*, April 30, 2020. Accessed April 4, 2025. https://losangeleno.com/strange-days/lizard-people/.

ENDNOTES

362 Ibid.
363 Nikhil Pandey, "Archaeologists Investigate Claims of Giant Skeletons in Nevada Caves of Us." NDTV.Com, March 30, 2024. www.ndtv.com/science/archaeologists-investigate-claims-of-giant-skeletons-in-nevada-caves-of-us-5338671.
364 (PDF) "The Story of Elongated Skulls and the Denied History of Ancient People: An Interview with Mark Laplume, www.researchgate.net/publication/270395024_The_Story_Of_Elongated_Skulls_And_The_Denied_History_Of_Ancient_People_An_Interview_With_Mark_Laplume. Accessed May 26, 2024.
365 Ibid.
366 Joanie Faletto, "Allegedly, There Is a Secret Underground Alien Base in Dulce, New Mexico." Discovery, August 1, 2019. Accessed April 4, 2025. https://www.discovery.com/exploration/Secret-Underground-Alien-Base-Dulce-New-Mexico.
367 The Underground—Director's Cut, 2021. Accessed April 4, 2025. https://www.imdb.com/video/vi3840655641/.
368 "Dulce Base—Part One | Mystery Beneath the Mesa," YouTube video, 2:06:00.. Accessed April 5, 2025. https://www.youtube.com/watch?v=lgPAnDmo8ak.
369 Branton, "The Dulce Book—Chapter 11: The Dulce Wars," *Biblioteca Pleyades*. Accessed April 5, 2025. https://www.bibliotecapleyades.net/branton/esp_dulcebook11.htm.
370 Alex Collier, "Galactic History According to Alex Collier and the Andromedans." AlexCollier.org. Accessed April 5, 2025. https://www.alexcollier.org/alex-collier-galactic-history-according-to-alex-collier-and-the-andromedans/.
371 Michael E. Salla, "The Dulce Report: Investigating Alleged Human Rights Abuses at a Joint US Government-Extraterrestrial Base at Dulce, New Mexico," Exopolitics.org. September 25, 2003. Accessed April 5, 2025. https://www.slideshare.net/slideshow/the-dulce-report/7092616.
372 Luis Elizondo, *Imminent: Inside the Pentagon's Hunt for UFOs* (New York: William Morrow, 2024).
373 "Abraham's Three Visitors," Jews for Judaism, n.d. Accessed April 5, 2025. https://jewsforjudaism.org/knowledge/articles/abrahams-three-visitors.
374 עיטור ספרים, Rabbi Reuven HaKohen Rappaport, pp. 47–48.
375 Christine Aprile, "Nordic Aliens: What Are These Extraterrestrial Beings?" Gaia, August 6, 2024. Accessed April 5, 2025. https://www.gaia.com/article/nordic-aliens.
376 Elaine Westfield, "Nordic Aliens: The Truth About These Cosmic Visitors" (Hangar 1 Publishing, n.d.) Accessed April 5, 2025. https://hangar1publishing.com/blogs/ufos-uaps-and-aliens/nordic-aliens.
377 "Nordic Aliens: Pleiadians, Myths, and Cosmic Wisdom," Thalira, December 16, 2024. Accessed April 5, 2025. https://thalira.com/blogs/esoteric-blog/nordic-aliens.
378 Debbora Battaglia,. *E.T. Culture: Anthropology in Outerspaces* (Duke University Press). pp. 52–. ISBN 0-8223-8701-8. (January 9, 2006).
379 Westfield, "Nordic Aliens."
380 @truthtold24. *X* (formerly Twitter). Accessed April 5, 2025. https://x.com/truthtold24/status/1827234516127121576.:contentReference{index=1.
381 Frank E. Stranges, *Stranger at the Pentagon* (Van Nuys, CA: IEC, Inc., Book Division, 1967).

ENDNOTES

382 "Profiles in Pseudoscience: George Adamski," University of Texas at Austin, Physics Department. Accessed April 5, 2025. https://web2.ph.utexas.edu/~coker2/index.files/adamski.htm.

383 Chris Root, "The Man Who Met a Venusian (Allegedly)." Denver Public Library, August 30, 2022. Accessed April 5, 2025. https://history.denverlibrary.org/news/western-history/man-who-met-venusian-allegedly.

384 Jules Evans, "The Dark Historical Roots of 'Starseeds,'" *Medium*, April 29, 2022. Accessed April 5, 2025. https://julesevans.medium.com/the-weird-history-of-starseeds-7df5127be9c3. Quoted in Flying Saucers Farewell, p. 61.

385 Stranges, *Stranger at the Pentagon*, p. 80.

386 University of New Hampshire Library, "Betty and Barney Hill Papers, 1961–2006." University of New Hampshire Library. Accessed April 5, 2025. https://library.unh.edu/find/archives/collections/betty-barney-hill-papers-1961-2006.

387 Timothy Green Beckley, comp. *The Secret Lost Diary of Admiral Richard E. Byrd and The Phantom of the Poles* (Clarksburg, WV: Inner Light—Global Communications, 2012).

388 Raimund E. Goerler, ed. *To the Pole: The Diary and Notebook of Richard E. Byrd, 1925–1927* (Columbus: Ohio State University Press, 1998).

389 Christine Aprile, "Nordic Aliens: What We Know About These Extraterrestrials." Gaia, August 6, 2024. Accessed April 5, 2025. https://www.gaia.com/article/nordic-aliens.

390 "The Law of One Densities," Law of One, n.d. Accessed April 5, 2025. https://www.lawofone.info/c/Densities.

391 Jules Evans, "The Dark Historical Roots of 'Starseeds,'" Medium, April 29, 2022. Accessed April 5, 2025. https://julesevans.medium.com/the-weird-history-of-starseeds-7df5127be9c3.

392 Edward Bulwer-Lytton, *The Coming Race* (Edinburgh: William Blackwood and Sons, 1871).

393 Stephen Quayle, *Empire Beneath the Ice: How the Nazis Won World War II* (Bozeman, MT: End Time Thunder Publishers, 2015).

394 Aprile, "Nordic Aliens."

395 Elena Danaan, "QA Live—Nov 17 2020—Nordic Aliens: Who Are They?" Cosmic Library, November 17, 2020. Accessed April 5, 2025. https://www.cosmic-library.de/danaan/transcripts/danaan-2020-11-17.htm.

396 Howard Callahan, "The Travis Walton Abduction: America's Most Compelling UFO Case," Hangar 1 Publishing, March 2025. Accessed April 5, 2025. https://hangar1publishing.com/blogs/ufos-uaps-and-aliens/travis-walton-abduction.

397 Danaan, "QA Live - Nov 17 2020 - Nordic aliens."

398 Charles James Hall, *Millennial Hospitality* series (Bloomington, IN: AuthorHouse, 2002–2012).

399 Eli Rosenberg, "Former Navy Pilot Describes UFO Encounter Studied by Secret Pentagon Program." *Washington Post*, December 18, 2017. Accessed April 5, 2025. https://www.washingtonpost.com/news/checkpoint/wp/2017/12/18/former-navy-pilot-describes-encounter-with-ufo-studied-by-secret-pentagon-program/.

400 Pavithra George, " 'Normalizing' UFOs—Retired U.S. Navy Pilot Recalls Tic Tac Encounter." Reuters, June 25, 2021. Accessed April 5, 2025. https://www.reuters.com

ENDNOTES

/lifestyle/science/normalizing-ufos-retired-us-navy-pilot-recalls-tic-tac-encounter-2021-06-25/.
401 Ibid.
402 Aliza Chasan, "The Story Behind the 'Tic Tac' UFO Sighting by Navy Pilots in 2004." *CBS News*, July 26, 2023. Accessed April 5, 2025. https://www.cbsnews.com/news/tic-tac-ufo-sighting-uap-video-dave-fravor-alex-dietrich-navy-fighter-pilots-house-testimony/.
403 Ibid.
404 Ibid.
405 "Millennial Hospitality IV: After Hours by Charles James Hall," Amazon, accessed April 5, 2025. https://www.amazon.com/Millennial-Hospitality-IV-After-Hours/dp/1434342670.
406 Ibid.
407 "Chuck Missler Return of the Nephilim Part 2." YouTube video, 1:29:54. Posted by Theoria Logos, approximately 4.3 years ago. Accessed April 5, 2025. https://www.youtube.com/watch?v=ERx-sP-Aezk.
408 Queen, "It's a Kind of Magic," Track 1 on *A Kind of Magic* (EMI Records, 1986).
409 Alberino, *Birthright*.
410 L. A. Marzulli, "Skinny Bob the Grey! Is It Fake?" YouTube video, 10:15. Posted by L. A. Marzulli, March 3, 2023. Accessed April 5, 2025. https://www.youtube.com/watch?v=6Cqm652wpZg.
411 Alberino, *Birthright*.
412 James VanderKam and Peter Flint, *The Meaning of the Dead Sea Scrolls: Their Significance for Understanding the Bible, Judaism, Jesus, and Christianity* (HarperOne, 2014).
413 James H. Charlesworth, *The Old Testament Pseudepigrapha*. Vol. 2, *Expansions of the "Old Testament" and Legends, Wisdom and Philosophical Literature, Prayers, Psalms, and Odes, Fragments of Lost Judeo-Hellenistic Works* (Doubleday, 1985).
414 *1 (Ethiopie Apocalypse of) Enoch*, www.ma.huji.ac.il/~kazhdan/Shneider/EarlyMyst2010/1Enoch.from.OTP.pdf. Accessed June 11, 2024.
415 Genesis 5:18–24; Genesis 6:1–4; Hebrews 11:5; 1 Peter 3:19–20; 2 Peter 2:4–5; Jude 1:14–15; quotes from the Book of Enoch verbatim, Revelation 2:14, Revelation 2:20.
416 Hershel Shanks, "An Interview with John Strugnell." The BAS Library, library.biblicalarchaeology.org/article/an-interview-with-john-strugnell/. Accessed June 11, 2024.
417 Ibn Ezra on Genesis 6:4.
418 Hedley Frederick Davis Sparkes, *The Apocryphal Old Testament*, Ed. by H. F. D. Sparks (Oxford University Press, 1995).
419 The Book of Enoch, trans. R. H. Charles (Neeland Media LLC, 2018).
420 Michael Owen Wise, et al. *The Dead Sea Scrolls: A New Translation* (HarperSanFrancisco, 2005).
421 Zohar, Bereishit 58a.
422 John C. Reeves, *Jewish Lore in Manichaean Cosmogony* (Hebrew Union College Press, 2016). Also, readers can find a ton of Reeves' writings here: https://uncc.academia.edu/JohnCReeves.
423 Bruce Alberts, Alexander Johnson, Julian Lewis, Martin Raff, Keith Roberts, and Peter Walter, "The Structure and Function of DNA." In *Molecular Biology of the Cell*,

ENDNOTES

4th ed. (New York: Garland Science, 2002). Accessed April 5, 2025. https://www.ncbi.nlm.nih.gov/books/NBK26821/.

424 Misganaw Asmamaw and Belay Zawdie, "Mechanism and Applications of CRISPR/Cas-9-Mediated Genome Editing." Biologics: Targets & Therapy 15 (August 21, 2021): 353–361. https://doi.org/10.2147/BTT.S326422.

425 Anakim (Numbers 13:33, Deuteronomy 1:28, 9:2), Rephaim (Genesis 14:5, Deuteronomy 2:11, 2:20, 3:11, 3:13, Joshua 12:4, 13:12, 15:8, 17:15, 18:16), Emim (Genesis 14:5, Deuteronomy 2:10-11), Zamzummim (Deuteronomy 2:20), Avvim (Deuteronomy 2:23).

426 Zohar, Bereishit 58a.

427 John C. Reeves, *Jewish Lore in Manichaean Cosmogony* (Hebrew Union College Press, 2016).

428 "What Is the Gap Theory? (The Ruin and Reconstruction Theory?)." Blue Letter Bible, www.blueletterbible.org/faq/don_stewart/don_stewart_654.cfm. Accessed 13 June 2024.

429 Fazale "Fuz" Rana, "Neanderthal Gene Deserts Provide Oasis for RTB's Creation Model." Reasons to Believe, November 28, 2023, reasons.org/explore/blogs/the-cells-design/neanderthal-gene-deserts-provide-oasis-for-rtbs-creation-model.

430 "Neanderthal." Answers in Genesis, answersingenesis.org/human-evolution/neanderthal/. Accessed 13 June 2024.

431 Richard E. Green, et al. "A Draft Sequence of the Neandertal Genome." *Science* (New York, NY), US National Library of Medicine, May 7, 2010, www.ncbi.nlm.nih.gov/pmc/articles/PMC5100745/.

432 M. Kuhlwilm; I. Gronau; J. J. Hubisz; C. de Filippo; J. Prado-Martinez; M. Kircher; Q. Fu ; H. A. Burbano; C. Lalueza-Fox; M. de la Rasilla; A. Rosas; P. Rudan; D. Brajkovic; Z. Kucan ; I. Gušic; T. Marques-Bonet; A. M. Andrés; B. Viola; S, Pääbo; M. Meyer; A. Siepel; S. Castellano; "Ancient Gene Flow from Early Modern Humans into Eastern Neanderthals." *Nature*, U.S. National Library of Medicine, pubmed.ncbi.nlm.nih.gov/26886800/. Accessed June 11, 2024.

433 David Reich, et al. "Genetic History of an Archaic Hominin Group from Denisova Cave in Siberia." *Nature News*, Nature Publishing Group, December 22, 2010, www.nature.com/articles/nature09710.

434 Sriram Sankararaman, et al. "The Genomic Landscape of Neanderthal Ancestry in Present-Day Humans." *Nature News*, Nature Publishing Group, January 29, 2014, www.nature.com/articles/nature12961.

435 Kay Prüfer, Fernando Racimo, Nick Patterson, Flora Jay, Sriram Sankararaman, Susanna Sawyer, Anja Heinze, et al., "The Complete Genome Sequence of a Neanderthal from the Altai Mountains," *Nature* 505, no. 7481 (January 2, 2014): 43–49. https://doi.org/10.1038/nature12886.

436 Dimitra Papagianni and Michael Ari Morse, *The Neanderthals Rediscovered: How Modern Science Is Rewriting Their Story* (Thames & Hudson, 2017).

437 Papagianni, Dimitra, and Michael Ari Morse, *The Neanderthals Rediscovered: How Modern Science Is Rewriting Their Story* (Thames & Hudson, 2017).

438 Marzulli, "Skinny Bob the Grey!"

439 David M. Jacobs, *The Threat: The Secret Agenda—What the Aliens Really Want and How They Plan to Get It* (New York: Simon & Schuster, 1998).

ENDNOTES

440 Budd Hopkins, *Intruders: The Incredible Visitations at Copley Woods* (New York: Ballantine Books, 1987).
441 Jacques Vallée, *Messengers of Deception: UFO Contacts and Cults* (Berkeley, CA: And/Or Press, 1979).
442 Mack, *Abduction*.
443 Jacobs, *The Threat*.
444 Mack, *Abduction*.
445 John G. Fuller, "Interrupted Journey: Two Lost Hours Aboard a Flying Saucer" (1966).
446 Budd Hopkins, Witnessed: The True Story of the Brooklyn Bridge UFO Abductions (New York: Pocket Books, 1996).
447 Travis Walton, *The Walton Experience* (New York: Berkley Publishing Group, 1978).
448 Bob Lazar, *Dreamland: An Autobiography*. Foreword by George Knapp. (Amherst, WI: Interstellar, 2019). https://www.simonandschuster.com/books/Dreamland/Bob-Lazar/9780578437057.
449 Roger K. Leir, *The Aliens and the Scalpel: Scientific Proof of Extraterrestrial Implants in Humans* (Columbus, NC: Granite Publishing, 1999). ISBN 9781893183018.
450 Mack, *Abduction*.
451 Clifford Stone, *Eyes Only: The Story of Clifford Stone and UFO Crash Retrievals*. Foreword by Robert Salas. Introduction by Paola Leopizzi Harris (North Charleston, SC: CreateSpace Independent Publishing Platform, 2011). ISBN 9781467958677.
452 David Grusch, testimony before the House Oversight Committee, July 26, 2023, *Congressional Record*, accessed April 4, 2025.
453 Ibid.
454 Ibid.
455 Ibid.
456 Luis Elizondo, *Imminent: Inside the Pentagon's Hunt for UFOs* (New York: William Morrow, 2024).
457 Ibid.
458 Ryan Graves, "Testimony before the House Oversight Subcommittee on National Security, the Border, and Foreign Affairs," House Committee on Oversight and Accountability, July 2023. https://oversight.house.gov/wp-content/uploads/2023/07/Ryan-HOC-Testimony.pdf.
459 Ibid.
460 Ibid.
461 Dean Smith, "A Christian Response to UFOs." OpentheWord.org, June 8, 2023. https://opentheword.org/2023/06/08/a-christian-response-to-ufos/.
462 Ibid.
463 Marzulli, "Skinny Bob."
464 *V*. Directed by Kenneth Johnson. Aired May 1–2, 1983, NBC.
465 Ronald Reagan, "Address to the 42d Session of the United Nations General Assembly in New York, New York." Ronald Reagan Presidential Library & Museum, September 21, 1987. https://www.reaganlibrary.gov/archives/speech/address-42d-session-united-nations-general-assembly-new-york-new-york.
466 Theresa Tan, "Aliens: Real or Fake? An Interview with Gary Bates." *City News*, May 30, 2018. https://www.citynews.sg/2018/05/30/aliens-real-fake-interview-dr-gary-bates/.

ENDNOTES

467 Creation.com., n.d. *Creation Talk*. Series. Accessed April 5, 2025. https://creation.com/th/series/creation-talk?page=96&episodes=1&sort=published_on&episodes_limit=250.
468 Steven. Greer, n.d. *Expedition—CE5* Introduction, "Core Principles." Accessed April 5, 2025. https://drstevengreer.com/expedition-guidelines-copy/.
469 John Mack, n.d. *Interview with John Mack*. NOVA Online. Accessed April 5, 2025. https://www.pbs.org/wgbh/nova/aliens/johnmack.html.
470 Jill Neimark, "The Harvard Professor & the UFOs." *Psychology Today*, March 1, 1994. https://www.psychologytoday.com/us/articles/199403/the-harvard-professor-the-ufos.
471 *Alien Intrusion: Unmasking a Deception*. Directed by Gary Bates. Performed by John Schneider. (Creation Ministries International, 2018). DVD.
472 Giulio Perrotta, "Clinical Evidence in the Phenomenon of Alien Abduction." *Annals of Psychiatry and Treatment* 5, no. 1 (December 21, 2021): 107–115. https://www.neuroscigroup.us/articles/APT-5-137.php.
473 L. A. Marzulli, 2020. *Watchers 1—UFOs are Real*. Directed by Richard Shaw. UFO-TV. Amazon Prime Video. https://www.primevideo.com/detail/Watchers-1---UFOs-are-Real/0QG3W5HSIKSJOF3LFXPXUR9XZB.
474 Alberino, *Birthright*.
475 Jacobs, *The Threat*.
476 Ibid.
477 Ibid.
478 Thomas Horn, *Apollyon Rising 2012: The Lost Symbol Found and the Final Mystery of the Great Seal Revealed* (Crane, MO: Defender, 2009).
479 Virgil. *Eclogue IV*. 40 BC.. Accessed April 5, 2025. https://allpoetry.com/Eclogue-IV.
480 Keith Green, "Altar Call." *The Ministry Years, Volume Two (1980–1982)*. (Sparrow Records, 1988.
481 C. S. Lewis and Pauline Baynes. *The Silver Chair* (Macmillan, 1953). Chapter 12, "The Queen of Underland."

www.ingramcontent.com/pod-product-compliance
Ingram Content Group UK Ltd.
Pitfield, Milton Keynes, MK11 3LW, UK
UKHW040238250426
12048UKWH00043B/1575